Lecture Notes in Artificial Intelligence   8306

Subseries of Lecture Notes in Computer Science

LNAI Series Editors

Randy Goebel
University of Alberta, Edmonton, Canada
Yuzuru Tanaka
Hokkaido University, Sapporo, Japan
Wolfgang Wahlster
DFKI and Saarland University, Saarbrücken, Germany

LNAI Founding Series Editor

Joerg Siekmann
DFKI and Saarland University, Saarbrücken, Germany

Elizabeth Black   Sanjay Modgil   Nir Oren (Eds.)

Theory and Applications of Formal Argumentation

Second International Workshop, TAFA 2013
Beijing, China, August 3-5, 2013
Revised Selected Papers

 Springer

Volume Editors

Elizabeth Black
Sanjay Modgil
King's College London
Department of Informatics
Strand, London, WC2R 2LS, UK
E-mail: {elizabeth.black, sanjay.modgil}@kcl.ac.uk

Nir Oren
University of Aberdeen
Department of Computing Science
Aberdeen, AB24 3UE, UK
E-mail: n.oren@abdn.ac.uk

ISSN 0302-9743   e-ISSN 1611-3349
ISBN 978-3-642-54372-2   e-ISBN 978-3-642-54373-9
DOI 10.1007/978-3-642-54373-9
Springer Heidelberg New York Dordrecht London

Library of Congress Control Number: 2014931379

© Springer-Verlag Berlin Heidelberg 2014
This work is subject to copyright. All rights are reserved by the Publisher, whether the whole or part of
the material is concerned, specifically the rights of translation, reprinting, reuse of illustrations, recitation,
broadcasting, reproduction on microfilms or in any other physical way, and transmission or information
storage and retrieval, electronic adaptation, computer software, or by similar or dissimilar methodology
now known or hereafter developed. Exempted from this legal reservation are brief excerpts in connection
with reviews or scholarly analysis or material supplied specifically for the purpose of being entered and
executed on a computer system, for exclusive use by the purchaser of the work. Duplication of this publication
or parts thereof is permitted only under the provisions of the Copyright Law of the Publisher's location,
in its current version, and permission for use must always be obtained from Springer. Permissions for use
may be obtained through RightsLink at the Copyright Clearance Center. Violations are liable to prosecution
under the respective Copyright Law.
The use of general descriptive names, registered names, trademarks, service marks, etc. in this publication
does not imply, even in the absence of a specific statement, that such names are exempt from the relevant
protective laws and regulations and therefore free for general use.
While the advice and information in this book are believed to be true and accurate at the date of publication,
neither the authors nor the editors nor the publisher can accept any legal responsibility for any errors or
omissions that may be made. The publisher makes no warranty, express or implied, with respect to the
material contained herein.

Typesetting: Camera-ready by author, data conversion by Scientific Publishing Services, Chennai, India

Printed on acid-free paper

Springer is part of Springer Science+Business Media (www.springer.com)

Preface

Recent years have witnessed a rapid growth of interest in formal models of argumentation and their application in diverse sub-fields and domains of application of AI, including reasoning in the presence of inconsistency, non-monotonic reasoning, decision making, inter-agent communication, the Semantic Web, grid applications, ontologies, recommender systems, machine learning, neural networks, trust computing, normative systems, social choice theory, judgment aggregation and game theory, and law and medicine. Argumentation thus shows great promise as a theoretically grounded tool for a wide range of applications.

The Second International Workshop on the Theory and Applications of Formal Argumentation (TAFA 2013) aimed to promote further investigations into the use of formal argumentation and links with other fields of AI. Co-located with the International Joint Conference on Artificial Intelligence (IJCAI 2013) in Beijing, China, TAFA 2013 built on the success of TAFA 2011 with a range of strong papers submitted by authors from Europe, Japan, and China. The workshop received 22 submissions, of which 15 were accepted for presentation. The workshop was attended by over 20 participants, and the presentations spawned many lively and thought-provoking discussions.

Argumentation theory centers around the idea that arguments authored by human users or constituted as premises entailing some conclusion in a given logic can be organized into directed graphs such that the directed links between arguments represent relations of attack and support etc. Such graphs can also be annotated with additional information to capture, for example, argument strength, preferences, or degrees of belief, and can be processed so as to evaluate the winning arguments. The following proceedings include papers identifying how properties of these graphs can impact on the computational complexity of evaluating the winning arguments, as well as specific computational techniques for evaluating graphs. A distinguishing feature of a number of the workshop papers is the development of formal models based on empirical observations of human dialogue and debate; for example, in social networks in which humans exchange and vote on opinions and assess the extent to which any given opinion is a valid counter to (attack on) another. New insights into how computational models can inform and indeed enhance the rationality of discourse and debate among humans are also presented. A key feature of argumentation is its wide range of applicability in sub-areas of AI, and a number of papers report on advances in these areas. For example, preliminary work on correspondences between argumentative and decision theoretic principles are introduced, and research on the use of argumentation to resolve conflicts among conflicting norms is included.

Other papers report on the use of arguments to augment and improve the performance of learning algorithms, and on the evaluation and categorization of arguments exchanged in dialogues observed between human experts.

The editors would like to thank the members of the Program Committee and the additional reviewers for their efforts in reviewing submissions to TAFA 2013.

December 2013   Elizabeth Black
                                                                 Sanjay Modgil
                                                                    Nir Oren

Organization

TAFA 2013 took place at the Tsinghua University, Beijing, China, during August 3–4, 2013, as a workshop at IJCAI 2013, the 23rd International Joint Conference on Artificial Intelligence.

Workshop Chairs

Elizabeth Black   King's College London, UK
Sanjay Modgil   King's College London, UK
Nir Oren   University of Aberdeen, UK

Program Committee

Leila Amgoud   IRIT, Toulouse, France
Katie Atkinson   University of Liverpool, UK
Pietro Baroni   University of Brescia, Italy
Floris Bex   University of Dundee, UK
Elizabeth Black   King's College London, UK
Elise Bonzon   Université Paris Descartes, France
Richard Booth   University of Luxembourg, Luxembourg
Gerhard Brewka   Leipzig University, Germany
Katarzyna Budzynska   Polish Academy of Sciences, Poland,
     and University of Dundee, UK
Martin Caminada   University of Aberdeen, UK
Federico Cerutti   University of Aberdeen, UK
Carlos Chesñevar   Universidad Nacional del Sur, Argentina
Madalina Croitoru   Université Montpellier 2, France
Sylvie Doutre   Université Toulouse 1 Capitole, France
Massimiliano Giacomin   University of Brescia, Italy
Tom Gordon   Fraunhofer FOKUS, Germany
Anthony Hunter   University College London, UK
Souhila Kaci   Université Montpellier 2, France
Antonis Kakas   University of Cyprus, Cyprus
Nicolas Maudet   Université Paris 6, France
Peter McBurney   King's College London, UK
Sanjay Modgil   King's College London, UK
Pavlos Moraitis   Paris Descartes University, France
Nir Oren   University of Aberdeen, UK
Simon Parsons   City University of Liverpool, UK

Henry Prakken	University of Utrecht and University of Groningen, The Netherlands
Chris Reed	University of Dundee, UK
Tjitze Rienstra	University of Luxembourg, Luxembourg
Chiaki Sakama	Wakayama University, Japan
Guillermo Ricardo Simari	Universidad Nacional del Sur, Argentina
Yuqing Tang	Carnegie Mellon University, USA
Francesca Toni	Imperial College London, UK
Leon Van Der Torre	University of Luxembourg, Luxembourg
Srdjan Vesic	Université d'Artois, France
Serena Villata	Inria Sophia Antipolis, France
Toshiko Wakaki	Shibaura Institute of Technology, Japan
Simon Wells	Aberdeen University, UK
Stefan Woltran	Vienna University of Technology, Austria
Adam Wyner	University of Aberdeen, UK

Additional Reviewers

Ringo Baumann	Leipzig University, Germany
Wolfgang Dvorak	University of Vienna, Austria
Xiuyi Fan	Imperial College London, UK
Maria Vanina Martinez	University of Oxford, UK
Claudia Schulz	Imperial College London, UK

Table of Contents

Revisiting Abstract Argumentation Frameworks

Sanjay Modgil

Department of Informatics, King's College London
sanjay.modgil@kcl.ac.uk

Abstract. This paper argues that many extensions of Dung's framework incorporating relations additional to binary attacks, are best viewed as abstractions of human rather than computational models of reasoning and debate. The paper then discusses how these additional relations may be reified into object level knowledge, thus enabling reconstruction of the extended framework as a Dung framework, and providing rational guidance for further reasoning and debate.

1 Introduction

In Dung's seminal theory of abstract argumentation [9], Dung frameworks (*DF*s) are directed graphs in which the arguments (nodes) are related to other arguments by binary attack relations (arcs). A 'calculus of opposition' is then applied to a framework to determine sets of justified arguments (extensions). Dung was explicit in considering the arguments and conflict based attacks as being defined, or 'instantiated', by sets of formulae (theories) in some formal logic, so that the claims of justified arguments then identify the inferences that follow from the instantiating theories. In this way, the inference relations of existing non-monotonic logics have been given argumentation based characterisations [5,9].

Dung's abstract theory was subsequently extended in a number of directions. For example, some works formalise collective attacks from *sets* of arguments [13]. [11] included arguments that attack attacks, while [2] then generalised this idea to recursive attacks on attacks. Other works augmented *DF*s with *support* relations between arguments (e.g.,[1,14]). While some of the aforementioned works explicitly considered logical instantiations of their frameworks (e.g., [11]), many did not. This paper reviews the aforementioned extended frameworks, and then: 1) argues that they should more properly be studied as networks relating locutions as they are used in everyday reasoning and debate; 2) proposes a methodology for reconstructing these networks as Dung frameworks so as to facilitate rational reasoning and debate, and; 3) suggests ways to address the challenges that arise when obtaining these reconstructions.

The paper is organised as follows. Section 2 reviews Dung's theory of argumentation and the *ASPIC*⁺model of arguments and attacks [12,16]. The latter is reviewed as reference to the internal structure of arguments will prove crucial in developing the above mentioned argument and methodology, and *ASPIC*⁺describes a *general* account of the structure of arguments that has been shown to capture many existing approaches to argumentation. Sections 3.1 and 3.2 then review the above mentioned extensions, and argue that the additional abstract relations that many of these frameworks introduce

E. Black, S. Modgil, and N. Oren (Eds.): TAFA 2013, LNAI 8306, pp. 1–15, 2014.
© Springer-Verlag Berlin Heidelberg 2014

are not warranted by logical instantiations. This is because they either fail to meaningfully abstract from underlying logical concepts, or because the interpretation of these additional relations suggest that the logical information that gives rise to them can be used to reconstruct Dung frameworks, without need for recourse to the additional relations. This critique then leads to the development of two lines of argument explored in Sections 3.3 and 3.4:

1. Firstly, if the underlying logical instantiations of extended frameworks give rise to Dung frameworks that preserve the intended meaning of the additional abstract relations, then acceptability semantics defined for the extended frameworks should yield justified arguments that correspond to the justified arguments yielded by the reconstructed Dung frameworks. I show that in some cases these correspondences fail.
2. Secondly, extended frameworks should more properly be motivated as networks that relate locutions as they are used and related in everyday reasoning and debate.

These two lines of argument then lead to Section 4s proposal that these networks be mapped to a computational model of structured arguments - the $ASPIC^+$ model - and subsequently reconstructed as Dung frameworks in which the evaluated status of arguments provides feedback to users. In generating these reconstructions, one needs to 'reifiy' the abstract relations into the object level knowledge that these relations implicitly encode. However, multiple such reifications, and thus multiple reconstructed Dung frameworks, are possible. I therefore conclude by suggesting how reasoning and dialogue can be guided in order to resolve uncertainties as to what are the intended reifications. Users can be prompted to reveal the implicit knowledge encoded in the relations they assert as holding, and in so doing both enable reconstruction of Dung frameworks, and render such knowledge explicit and available for use in further reasoning and debate.

2 Background

2.1 Dung's Theory of Argumentation

A Dung argumentation framework (DF) is a pair $(\mathcal{A}, \mathcal{R})$, where $\mathcal{R} \subseteq \mathcal{A} \times \mathcal{A}$ is an attack relation on the arguments $\mathcal{A}$. Then:

Definition 1. $S \subseteq \mathcal{A}$ *is conflict free iff no two arguments in S attack each other. For any $S \subseteq \mathcal{A}$, X is acceptable w.r.t. S iff for every Y that attacks X, there is a $Z \in S$ that attacks Y (in which case Z is said to defend or 'reinstate' X). Then for any conflict free $S \subseteq \mathcal{A}$, S is :*

- *an* admissible *extension if every argument in S is acceptable w.r.t. S;*
- *a* complete *extension if it is admissible and every argument acceptable w.r.t. S is in S;*
- *a* preferred *extension if it is a maximal under set inclusion complete extension;*
- *the* grounded *extension if it is the minimal under set inclusion complete extension;*

– a stable *extension if it is preferred. and every argument not in S is attacked by an argument in S.*

The justified arguments of $(\mathcal{A}, \mathcal{R})$ under semantics $T \in \{preferred, grounded, stable\}$ are those arguments in every T extension.

2.2 Arguments and Attacks in the $ASPIC^+$ Framework

The remainder of this paper assumes arguments are structured as in the $ASPIC^+$ framework [12,16]; i.e., as trees whose leaf nodes are premises in a given knowledge base, and whose non-leaf nodes N are either defeasible or strict inference rules of the form $\phi_1, \ldots, \phi_{n-1} \Rightarrow \phi_n$, respectively $\phi_1, \ldots, \phi_{n-1} \to \phi_n$, where for $i = 1 \ldots n - 1$, N has a child node N_i that is either a premise ϕ_i, or a strict or defeasible rule with conclusion ϕ_i. Note that a premise (node) is itself an argument.

A' is then a *sub-argument* of A if A' is a sub-tree of A (including the case that A' is a leaf node (premise)). Note that A is a sub-argument of itself, whereas *proper sub-arguments* of A are sub-arguments of A excluding A itself. For simplicity I will in the remainder of this section only consider arguments with defeasible rules. Figure 1 shows four arguments B, C, D and E. Note the argument B with sub-arguments $B, B1, B2$, and $B3$.

The claim of an argument A, denoted $\mathtt{Claim}(A)$, is ϕ if A's root node is a rule with consequent ϕ, or A is a single node (premise) ϕ. We also say that A forward-extends B on ϕ, equivalently B backward extends A on ϕ, if B is a proper sub-argument of A, and $\mathtt{Claim}(B)$ is ϕ. Finally, $\mathtt{Concs}(A)$ denotes the claims of all sub-arguments of A. For example, in Figure 1, $\mathtt{Concs}(B) = \{f, b, w, q\}$.

Definition 2. *A attacks B on ϕ, if $\mathtt{Claim}(A)$ is the negation of some ϕ such that:*

- $\phi \in \mathtt{Concs}(B)$ *(i.e., ϕ is a premise or consequent of a defeasible rule in B), or:*
- ϕ *is a name (a constant in the object level language) assigned to a defeasible inference rule in B (A is then said to 'undercut' B).*

Figure 1 shows examples of attacks, from E, C and D, to B. Note that [12,16] prohibits attacks an any ϕ that is the conclusion of a strict inference rule, since as first shown in [7], this leads to violation of rationality postulates for argumentation.

The generality of $ASPIC^+$ accounts for this paper's assumption that arguments and attacks conform to the $ASPIC^+$ model. Note that one is free to choose the strict and defeasible inference rules, and the object level language in which wff ϕ are expressed. For example defeasible rules may be domain specific inference rules such as $bird(X) \Rightarrow fly(X)$ (akin to Reiter's default rules) so that given the premise $bird(tweety)$ an argument with root node $bird(tweety) \Rightarrow fly(tweety)$ claims $fly(tweety)$. On the other hand, such rules may be domain independent. For example *defeasible modus ponens*: $\phi, \phi \rightsquigarrow \psi \Rightarrow \psi$ ($\rightsquigarrow$ being the defeasible implication connective in the object level language). Then, given premises $bird(tweety)$, $bird(X) \rightsquigarrow fly(X)$, we have an argument claiming $fly(tweety)$, with root node: '$bird(tweety), bird(tweety) \rightsquigarrow fly(tweety) \Rightarrow fly(tweety)$'.

Note that [12,16] also generalise the notion of negation allowing one to specify that a wff is a contrary of another wff ($\neg$ is then a special case, i.e., ϕ is a contrary of ψ

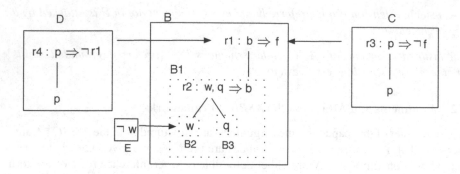

Fig. 1. Propositions b, f, w, q, p respectively denote that Tweety is a *bird*, *f*lies, has *w*ings, *q*uacks, and is a *p*enguin. $r_i, i = 1 \ldots 4$, are propositions naming rules

whenever ψ is of the form $\neg \phi$ or ϕ is of the form $\neg \psi$). It is this notion of contrary that [12,16] refer to when defining attacks. [12,16] then show that many logical instantiations of Dung frameworks and other general structured approaches to argumentation can be formalised as instances of the $ASPIC^+$ framework, in the sense that the arguments and attacks they define are special cases of $ASPIC^+$ arguments and attacks. For example, classical logic instantiations of Dung frameworks, where premises may be taken from a knowledge base of classical wff, and arguments are constructed using only strict classical inference rules (e.g., modus ponens etc).

3 Abstract Argumentation Frameworks: Acceptability Semantics and Instantiations

This section reviews examples of abstract argumentation frameworks (AAFs) that extend DFs with support and variants of binary attack relations. I will assume that, as in the case of DFs, these AAFs are instantiated by underlying logical theories. I then argue that in cases where abstract level relations are meaningful abstractions of underlying logical relations, one can reconstruct DFs from the underlying theories. I then conclude that : 1) the reconstructions shed light on how evaluation of the justified arguments in the AAFs may need to be modified; 2) AAFs should more properly be viewed as modelling human reasoning and debate, rather than as abstractions of underlying theories in some formal logic.

3.1 Support Relations

I begin by considering frameworks with support relations. In particular, [1]'s bipolar argumentation framework (BAF) is of the form $(\mathcal{A}, \mathcal{R}_{att}, \mathcal{R}_{supp})$, where $\mathcal{R}_{supp}$ is a support relation and $\mathcal{R}_{att}$ an attack relation ([1] call $\mathcal{R}_{att}$ a 'defeat relation',). The question arises as to what these support relations abstract from, in the sense that if A attacks B on ϕ, then the attack abstracts from the object level logical relationship of negation relating Claim(A) and ϕ ? [1] explicitly answer this question for specific kinds of arguments of the form (H, h) where H is a set of consistent classical wff (premises) that minimally (under set inclusion) classically entail h. Then (H, h) supports (H', h') if $h \in H'$ or $h = h'$. Generalising this notion to $ASPIC^+$ arguments:

A supports B on ϕ if $\text{Claim}(A) = \phi$, $\phi \in \text{Concs}(B)$.   **S1**

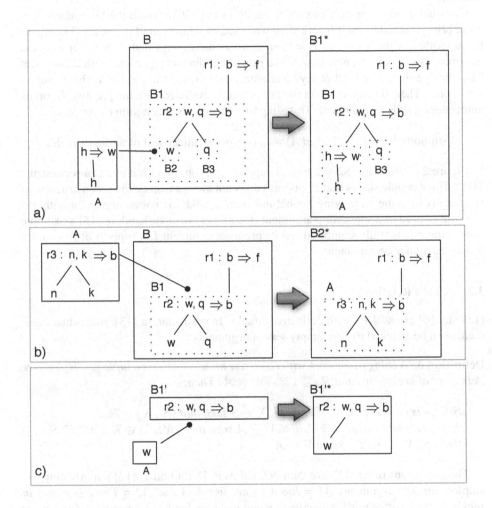

Fig. 2. Support relations are represented as lines with swollen ends. Note that n, k, h respectively denote that Tweety builds *n*ests, has a bea*k*, and is fea*th*ered.

Figures 2-a) and 2-b) show $ASPIC^+$arguments A supporting B on w and b respectively. That **S1** is the intended interpretation of support is further testified to by the motivating example dialogues in [1], e.g., in Example 6 in [1], $F =$ '*I* concerns a problem of public health, so *I* is important information' supports $A =$ '*I* is important information, so we must publish it'. However, this interpretation of support then implies that if X supports Y on ϕ, then X backward extends Y on ϕ to define another argument Y^*. This is illustrated in Figures 2-a) and 2-b) : A backwards extends B on w and b respectively, so that one can 'reconstruct' arguments $B1^*$ and $B2^*$. In other words, given the same logical information, one can instantiate a DF consisting only of arguments and binary attacks.

Consider another example of support relations in [15], in which the 'argument' $X =$ "The bridge should be built where slow water exists without mud (i.e.at x,y)" is said to be supported by the argument $B =$ "Our historic survey says that slow water exists at coordinates x,y". Firstly, note that X is a rule rather than an argument, with consequent "The bridge should be built at x,y" and antecedent "slow water exists without mud at x,y" holds. Then B supports X in the sense that X extended with the premise B, on its antecedent, yields an argument. This suggest a second distinct notion of support :

A supports B on ϕ if $\texttt{Claim}(A) = \phi$, ϕ is in the antecedent of a rule in B. **S2**

Figure 2 c) illustrates S2-support: A supports $B1'$ on w, so that one can reconstruct $B1'^*$. The example shows that s2-support does not always licence the reconstruction of arguments from the underlying logical information; $B1'^*$ is not an argument, rather it is a rule in need of a supporting argument (for q). On the other hand, in [15]'s example above, the rule is 'fully supported' on its premise; argument B's support of X enables reconstruction of an argument.

3.2   Attack Relations

[13] and [4] extend DFs with collective attacks. In particular, in [13], individual arguments can be attacked by non-empty sets of arguments:

Definition 3. *A Dung framework with collective attacks (AF_c) is a tuple $(\mathcal{A}, \mathcal{R}_c)$ where $\mathcal{A}$ is a set of arguments, and $\mathcal{R}_c \subseteq (2^{\mathcal{A}} \setminus \emptyset) \times \mathcal{A}$. Then:*

- *$S \subseteq \mathcal{A}$ is conflict free iff $\neg \exists S' \subseteq S, X \in S$ such that $(S', X) \in \mathcal{R}_c$.*
- *X is acceptable w.r.t. $S \subseteq \mathcal{A}$ iff $\forall \mathcal{A}' \subseteq \mathcal{A}$ such that $(\mathcal{A}', X) \in \mathcal{R}_c$, $\exists S' \subseteq S$ such that $(S', Y) \in \mathcal{R}_c$ for some $Y \in \mathcal{A}'$.*

The extensions of an AF_c are then defined as in Definition 1. [13]'s motivating example considers arguments $A1 = $ *Joe does not like Jack* and $A2 = $ *There is a nail in Jack's antique coffee table* collectively attacking $B = $ *Joe has no arms, so Joe cannot use a hammer, so Joe did not strike a nail into Jack's antique coffee table*. Quoting from [13], $A1$ and $A2$ "jointly provide a case for the conclusion that Joe has a struck a nail into Jack's antique coffee table". This implies that the collective attack is an abstraction of a rule relating the claims of $A1$ and $A2$ to the negation of the claim of B. This suggests we can reconstruct a DF, given that $A1$ and $A2$ can be extended with a rule *'If Joe does not like Jack* and *there is a nail in Jack's antique coffee table* then *Joe has a struck a nail into Jack's antique coffee table'* to define an argument A that directly attacks B on its conclusion. In general:

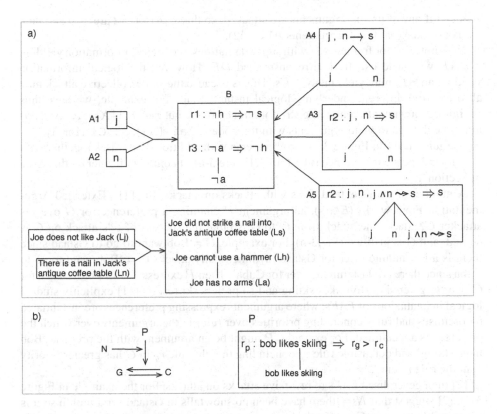

Fig. 3. a) Natural language representation of locutions Lj, Ln, La, Lh, Ls involved in a collective attack are shown, with the corresponding logical formulation of the collective attack from $\{A1, A2\}$ to B, and reconstructed arguments $A3, A4$ and $A5$ based on the collective attack. b) shows a preference attack on an attack (P), and a recursive attack on an attack (N).

Definition 4. *Let* $X_1, \ldots, X_n$ *collectively attack* Y *on* ϕ ($\phi \in$ Concs(Y) *or* ϕ *names a defeasible inference rule in* Y). *Then:*

$recon_c(\{X_1, \ldots, X_n\}, \phi)$ *is the argument* X, *whose root node is the defeasible rule* Claim$(X_1), \ldots,$ Claim$(X_n) \Rightarrow \neg\phi$, *backward extended by arguments* $X_1, \ldots, X_n$, *such that* X *attacks* Y *on* ϕ.

Figure 3-a) illustrates, showing how $A3 = recon_c(\{A1, A2\}, \neg s)$ is backward extended by $A1$ and $A2$. $A3$ then attacks B on $\neg s$.

While [13] acknowledge that collectively attacking arguments can be extended to single arguments which then attack their target, they maintain that collective attacks are still warranted by logical instantiations, since, referring to the example in Figure 3-a), it may be that $A1$ or $A2$ are attacked, but $A3$ is not attacked. But a structured account of argumentation shows this cannot be the case. Recalling Definition 2, an argument is attacked if any of its sub-arguments are attacked, so that if $A1$ or $A2$ are attacked then $A3$ is attacked (on its sub-arguments $A1$ or $A2$).

Now note that for frameworks with support relations, the logical information yielding a BAF will yield exactly one reconstructed DF. However, the logical information yielding an AF_c may yield many DFs. This is because the same collective attack may abstract from different underlying logical instantiations. For example, we have thus far ignored arguments containing strict inference rules, but $recon_c(\{X_1, \ldots, X_n\}, \phi)$ might be defined to yield arguments with top nodes $\texttt{Claim}(X_1), \ldots, \texttt{Claim}(X_n) \rightarrow \neg\phi$ (argument $A4$ in Figure 3-a)) or arguments with additional premises together with domain independent inference rules ($A5$ in Figure 3-a)). I comment further on this issue in Section 4.

A number of works extend DFs with attacks on attacks. In [11]'s Extended Argumentation Frameworks (EAFs), an argument P claiming a preference for G over its attacker C, attacks the attack from C to G, so that the success of C's attack on G is denied, and G is justified (Fig.3-b). For example, $G =$'Bob want to go to Gstaad since there is a last minute offer for Gstaad' symmetrically attacks $C = $ 'Bob want to go to Cuba since there is a last minute offer for Cuba'. Then P expresses Bob's preference for G over C given that Bob likes skiing and so prefers ski resorts.[11] explicitly studied logical instantiations of EAFs, where arguments expressing preferences are instantiated by premises and rules concluding priorities over rules in the arguments over which the preferences are claimed. For example, P might be an argument with the premise 'Bob likes skiing' and defeasible rule r_p concluding that the rule r_g in G has greater priority than the rule r_c in C.

[2] then generalised EAFs to recursive attacks on attacks. For the example in Figure 3-b), [2] suggest that $N = $ 'there have been no snowfalls in Gstaad for a month so it is not possible to ski in Gstaad' attacks the preference attack from P. However, what is not apparent is what kind of logical instantiation would yield such a recursive attack, since (unlike P) N is supposedly claiming a preference for an *attack* $C \rightarrow G$ over the *argument* P. Indeed, it might seem more intuitive to consider N as claiming $\neg r_p$, so undercutting P on its rule, since not being able to ski in Gstaad denies the defeasible inference step from Bob likes skiing, to a preference for (the rule in) G over (the rule in) C. Finally, note that while recursive attacks do not seem well motivated when considering logical instantiations, I will in Section 3.4 suggest an alternative motivation.

3.3   Acceptability Semantics for Abstract Argumentation Frameworks

The previous section's discussion suggests that if AAFs such as bipolar frameworks (BAFs) and frameworks with collective attacks (AF_cs) can be reconstructed as Dung frameworks, then one would expect a correspondence between the status of arguments in the AAFs and their status in the reconstructed DFs.

Firstly, let us examine how arguments are evaluated in [1]'s BAFs. If A supports B, and B symmetrically attacks C, then the preferred extensions defined in [1] are $\{A, B\}$ and $\{C\}$, since [1] suggest that since A supports B and B attacks C then there is a supported attack from A to C, and so $\{A, C\}$ is not conflict free. Suppose now we have the $ASPIC^+$ arguments[1] $A = [p; p \Rightarrow q]$, $B = [q; q \Rightarrow t]$, $C = [\neg t]$, where A supports B on the premise q. Then we can reconstruct the additional argument B^* $=[p; p \Rightarrow q; q \Rightarrow t]$ which also symmetrically attacks C. The preferred extensions of the reconstructed DF are $\{A, B, B^*\}$ and $\{C, A\}$ (ignoring arguments $[p]$ and $[q]$ which make no difference to the analysis). Thus the expected correspondence does not hold, since A is justified in in the reconstructed DF, but A is not justified in the original BAF. The discrepancy arises because it seems that in the abstract BAF, A is assumed to support B on its claim, in which case a correspondence would then hold, since in the reconstructed DF, A would symmetrically attack C. This illustrates that further consideration needs to be given to the evaluation of arguments in a BAF, and that such evaluation needs to account for the structure of arguments and targets of support relations (ie., the sub-arguments that are supported).

Consider now DFs reconstructed from AF_cs. Once again there may be a discrepancy between the justified arguments of the AF_c and its reconstructed DF. Recall that any given AF_c may yield more than one reconstruction, as a collective attack may be an abstraction of a number of different logical instantiations. In Fig.3, $\{A1, A2\}$ asymmetrically attacks B, and since no arguments attack $A1$ or $A2$ then B is not in an admissible extension of the AF_c. But if we reconstruct with the argument $A3$, then since $A3$ and B have contradictory claims obtained by application of defeasible rules, they symmetrically attack (by Definition 2), and so B can defend itself and is in an admissible extension. Furthermore, since B attacks $A3$, then in the corresponding AF_c, one would expect that B attacks $\{A1, A2\}$, but attacks on sets of arguments are not allowed in [13]. If instead we assume the reconstructed argument $A4$ then we would then have that $A4$ asymmetrically attacks B (recall from Section 2.2 that attacks cannot target the conclusions of strict rules), and so the desired correspondence would obtain.

To conclude, I have argued that acceptability semantics for AAFs need to account for the structure of arguments, such that a correspondence obtains with the acceptability semantics of the associated reconstructed DFs.

3.4 Abstract Locution Networks

In Sections 3.1 and 3.2, I argued that relations additional to binary attacks are not well motivated under the assumption that AAFs are instantiated by logical theories, in the sense that the same logical information gives rise to DFs. In what follows I argue that they are more properly motivated under the assumption that they are required to model the way humans reason and debate.

As stated in Section 1, non-monotonic inference relations can be characterised in terms of the claims of justified arguments, whose evaluation is based on the fundamental principle of reinstatement (Definition 1). It is the simplicity and familiarity of these principles in everyday reasoning and dialogue that partly accounts for the continuing impact of Dung's theory, and its envisaged role as a uniform bridging formalism for integrating computational and humans modes of reasoning and dialogue in the presence of uncertainty and conflict [18]: computational reasoning processes can be informed by

---

[1] Henceforth $ASPIC^+$ arguments may be represented as square brackets enclosing premises and rules separated by semi-colons.

argumentation-based characterisations of human reasoning and dialogue, and human reasoning and dialogue can be informed by argumentation-based characterisations of computational reasoning. To facilitate this bridging role requires development of argumentation models that account for human reasoning and dialogue as conducted in practice. This suggests a more constructive reformulation of the critique that AAFs do not adequately motivate abstract concepts and relations additional to binary attacks, in terms of formal logical instantiations. Rather, AAFs should be studied under the assumption that they are motivated by requirements for modelling relations between locutions as used in every day reasoning and debate. This is of course implied by the works reviewed in this paper, in which motivating and illustrative examples are primarily taken from every-day dialogue and reasoning. [15]'s example in Section 3.1 illustrates the use of support to account for locutions that do not always consist of fully formed arguments, but may instead be rules, so that arguments are implicitly constructed piecemeal by possibly different interlocutors supplying different elements of an argument. More generally, humans often make statements in support of other statements, as witnessed by numerous natural language examples in [1,14,15] and other works utilising support. Furthermore, [13] explicitly motivate collective attacks for modelling human dialogue, giving examples of locutions submitted by different interlocutors, that combine to define collective attacks. However, I suggest that this motivation for AAFs is under-appreciated by the research community, and will in what follows suggest further implied research directions.

To begin with, I propose that AAFs should be viewed as special cases of *Abstract Locution Networks* (ALNs), in which the nodes are locutions related by binary attacks, support relations, collective attacks, attacks on attacks, recursive attacks e.t.c. Note that abstract dialectical frameworks (ADFs) [6] might be considered as a candidate formalism for such networks, but the technical machinery associated with ADFs suggests that they are unsuitable candidates for modelling reasoning and dialogue as conducted in practice[2].

In order to now motivate future research directions, consider a software tool for single users or users engaged in dialogue, that enables: 1) entry of locutions that can in turn be linked to other locutions so as to structure rules and arguments; 2) linking of individual locutions, rules and arguments to denote relationships of support and various kinds of attack.

4   From Abstract Locution Networks to Computational Knowledge

The above described 'ALN tool' would contribute to the plethora of existing argument visualisation and mapping tools [10]. A key research goal is to then map the arguments diagrammed in these tools to computational models of argument, so that they can can be evaluated under Dung's various semantics [3], and thus inform reasoning and debate by: ensuring that the assessment of arguments is formally and rationally grounded; enabling

---

[2] Also note that Section 3.3's argument that acceptability semantics for AAFs needs to account for the structure of arguments, also applies to the acceptability semantics defined for ADFs that consider relations between unstructured nodes.

humans to track the status of arguments so that they can be guided in which arguments to respond to.

Assume an ALN tool and a mapping of the contained linked locutions to $ASPIC^+$ premises, rules and arguments[3]. The key point to note is that unlike the previous section's AAFs, that are assumed to be instantiated by formal logical theories, the diagrammed ALNs are authored by humans, and the goal is to map these to computational knowledge[4] so that one can instantiate a Dung framework in order to provide dialectical feedback to users. The challenge is to then account for the fact that ALNs do not consist exclusively of arguments related by binary attacks.

Section 3 suggests a methodology for addressing this challenge. To illustrate, consider the natural language diagramming of the collective attack in Figure 3, mapped to the $ASPIC^+$ arguments $A1, A2, B$ and their constituent premises and rules. In order to then reconstruct a DF based on this computational knowledge, a choice has to made as to how to *reify*[5] the collective attack so as to yield the additional computational knowledge – either $j, n \rightarrow s$ or $j, n \Rightarrow s$ or $j \wedge n \rightsquigarrow s$ - that would then be used to construct either of the arguments $A3, A4$ and $A5$ respectively. As discussed in Section 3.3, the choice of reification and thus additional constructed arguments, will affect the evaluated status of arguments in the reconstructed DF. In other words, given the diagramming of the collective attack, there remains some uncertainty as to how to reify this attack. Indeed, such uncertainty is likely to be the norm, given that not all relevant information is explicitly articulated in everyday reasoning and dialogue; much is left implicit. In this example, not only is the additional rule needed to reconstruct the argument not rendered explicit in the locutions related by the attack, *but also the target of the attack is implicit*. How is one to disambiguate whether the locutions Lj and Ln collectively attack on La. Lh or Ls ? (although it is assumed that the attack is on Ls; hence the assumed reifications of rules concluding s). How then is one to resolve such uncertainties, so that one can deterministically reconstruct a DF in order to provide dialectical feedback ?

This issue also arises when considering binary support and attack relations, given the commonplace use of *enthymemes* (arguments in which information is omitted) in everyday discourse. For example, consider the following dialogue:

> Paul argues that "Tony Blair is no longer a public figure, the information about his affair is not in the public interest, and the information is private, so the information should not be published" (X). Trevor counter-argues with "but Blair is UN envoy for the Middle East" (Y).

Y is just such an enthymeme. The very fact that Y is moved as an attack on X, but the attack is not explicitly targeted, is indicative of an incomplete rule of the form

---

[3] Such mappings are described in [3], via intermediate translation to the Argumentation Interchange Format [8].

[4] Recall that we are not committing to a particular computational model of argument, but any of the broad range of models shown to be instances of $ASPIC^+$.

[5] Note that in the previous section we referred to abstract relations such as attack, collective attacks and supports as 'abstractions' of underlying logical relations. However, given an ALN with diagrammed abstract relations, the task is to now reify these to yield computational knowledge.

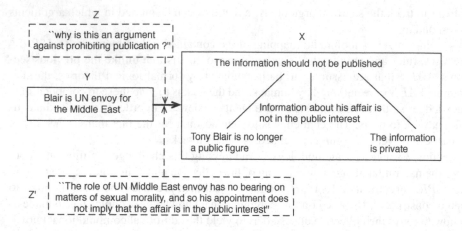

Fig. 4. An attack by an enthymeme Y on X

'if someone is a UN envoy for the Middle East then (s)he is ...', where the missing information is some claim negating an element in X. We thus need to reify a *binary attack* to obtain a rule that can be used together with the premise *Blair is UN envoy for the Middle East* to yield an argument Y^* that attacks X. But then should the reified rule be $mi \Rightarrow pf$ or $mi \Rightarrow pi$ or $mi \Rightarrow \neg pr$ or $mi \Rightarrow \neg pub$, or $mi \Rightarrow \neg r_1$, where $mi = Blair\ is\ UN\ Middle\ East\ Envoy$, pf, pi, pr and pub respectively denote *Blair is a public figure*, *the information is in the public interest*, *the information is private*, and *the information should be published*, and r_1 names the defeasible rule in the computational representation of X ?

Notice that the same issue arises with support relations. Suppose Paul supports his argument X with B = "Blair holds no public office". Once again, we see a requirement for reifying the support relation, to obtain a rule that would then augment the premise (enthymeme) B, so yielding an argument B^* claiming $\neg pf$ or $\neg pi$ or pr or $\neg pub$ that would then s1-support X on one of its conclusions.

To summarise, in order to reconstruct a DF on the basis of locutions related in an ALN, and thus provide dialectical feedback to users, one needs to resolve uncertainties as to how the abstract relations relating locutions are reified. One way to resolve such uncertainties is through the prompting of further dialogue moves, such that responses to these moves furnish the required information to decide upon a reification. For example, suppose the dialogue above now continues as follows:

> Paul then counters by asking "why is this an argument against prohibiting pub-
> lication ?" (Z). Trevor responds with "because his appointment as UN Middle
> East envoy implies that the information about his affair is in the public interest"
> (V)

Hence, the uncertainty is resolved in favour of the reification of the attack being $mi \Rightarrow pi$. Thus, we see a form of dialectical feedback whereby further dialogical moves are prompted, resulting in rendering explicit, knowledge (V) implicitly encoded in the attack, so that this knowledge is available for use in further reasoning and debate, and can be used to reconstruct the DF to provide evaluative feedback.

I conclude by noting that attacks as conceived in Dung's theory play two roles. That Y attacks X is an abstraction of the declarative incompatibility of Y's claim and some element in X, as well as an abstract characterisation of the dialectical, procedural use of Y as a counter-argument to X. Definition 1's notion of a conflict free set accounts for the declarative denotation, whereas the notion of acceptability of arguments accounts for the dialectical denotation. Preference attacks in EAFs invalidate the dialectical use of attacks. However, one cannot question, in a formal logical context, the declarative basis of an attack from Y to X on ϕ, since to do so would be to question the fundamental logical principle that a formula (i.e., $\text{Claim}(Y)$) and its negation (i.e., ϕ) are in conflict.

However, since attacks and support relations in ALNs may implicitly encode object level knowledge, this suggests one can attack the declarative rationale for an attack (and indeed support) relation. This also suggests a motivation for [2]'s recursive attacks, which in Section 3.2 were claimed to be not well motivated by logical instantiations. Such 'rationale attacks' can shift the burden of proof to the proposer of the attack to furnish the declarative rationale for the attack, e.g., Paul submits the rationale attack Z on the attack from Y to X, and Trevor then fulfils his burden of proof by providing the rationale V. Of course, Paul may (perhaps mistakenly) assume from the outset the intended rationale for the attack from Y to X, and submit an alternative rationale attack Z' on $Y \rightarrow X$: Z' = "The role of UN Middle East envoy has no bearing on matters of sexual morality, and so his appointment does not imply that the affair is in the public interest".

5 Conclusions

This paper has argued that various extensions of Dung's abstract framework should be studied under the assumption that they model human reasoning and debate, and should therefore account for the fact that locutions do not consist of fully formed arguments that can be related by binary attacks, but rather as statements, rules and incomplete arguments organised into networks in which they are related to each other in more complex ways. I then proposed reconstruction of these networks as Dung frameworks in order that reasoning and debate can be informed by rational models of argument. Such reconstruction requires reification of these relations to the object level knowledge they implicitly encode. Given that locutions often consist of incomplete arguments (enthymemes) I illustrated requirements for reification of binary attacks in addition to other relations that augment these attacks in extended frameworks. For any given relation, many such reifications are possible, with the choice of reification impacting on the evaluation of arguments in the reconstructed Dung framework that it defines. I then suggested that resolution of these choices should prompt dialogical moves that elicit replies confirming the intended reification, thus resolving the choice of reconstructed framework, and making available implicit knowledge for use in further reasoning and debate.

This paper lays foundations for a programme of research. The first task, currently underway, is to formalise reconstruction of networks of locutions as Dung frameworks consisting of $ASPIC^+$ arguments and attacks, building on the methodology suggested in this paper. This would involve broadening the range of networks considered in this paper, to include (for example) networks in which arguments or statements are asserted as being for, or against a claim. That the latter reconstructions are possible is attested to by a recent translation of the Carneades model of argumentation to $ASPIC^+$[19] (Carneades models arguments for and against claims). In this paper I have also suggested how recursive attacks on attacks, and indeed attacks on supports, can intuitively be motivated in the context of everyday reasoning and debate. The second task is to then augment existing models of dialogue so that the required reconstruction of underlying Dung frameworks prompts the submission of dialogue moves for eliciting implicit knowledge. Note also, that the focus in this paper has been on 'assertive' [17] locutions that commit speakers to the truth of expressed propositions. However, as illustrated by Section 4's dialogue in which Paul issues a 'why' locution, other types of locution will need to be considered. In this case the relationship with Trevor's locution can still be interpreted as an attack, but other types of locution and dialogues in the Walton and Krabbe typology [20], will warrant a broader range of relations considered in this paper, with different interpretations that may or may not admit reification to object level knowledge. Finally, these two tasks would contribute to the long term aim of linking tools for mapping reasoning and debate to computational models of argument and dialogue, so that the latter can rationally guide the former.

Acknowledgements. I would like to thank the anonymous reviewers for their helpful comments.

References

1. Amgoud, L., Cayrol, C., Lagasquie-Schiex, M., Livet, P.: On bipolarity in argumentation frameworks. International Journal of Intelligent Systems 23(10), 1062–1093 (2008)
2. Baroni, P., Cerutti, F., Giacomin, M., Guida, G.: Afra: Argumentation framework with recursive attacks. International Journal of Approximate Reasoning 52(1), 19–37 (2011)
3. Bex, F., Modgil, S., Prakken, H., Reed, C.: On logical specifications of the argument interchange format. Journal of Logic and Computation (2012), doi:10.1093/logcom/exs033
4. Bochman, A.: Collective argumentation and disjunctive programming. Journal of Logic and Computation 13(3), 405–428 (2003)
5. Bondarenko, A., Dung, P.M., Kowalski, R.A., Toni, F.: An abstract, argumentation-theoretic approach to default reasoning. Artificial Intelligence 93, 63–101 (1997)
6. Brewka, G., Woltran, S.: Abstract dialectical frameworks. In: Principles of Knowledge Representation and Reasoning (KR 2010), pp. 102–111 (2010)
7. Caminada, M., Amgoud, L.: On the evaluation of argumentation formalisms. Artificial Intelligence 171(5-6), 286–310 (2007)
8. Chesnevar, C., McGinnis, J., Modgil, S., Rahwan, I., Reed, C., Simari, G., South, M., Vreeswijk, G., Willmott, S.: Towards an argument interchange format. The Knowledge Engineering Review 21(4), 293–316 (2006)
9. Dung, P.M.: On the acceptability of arguments and its fundamental role in nonmonotonic reasoning, logic programming and n-person games. Artificial Intelligence 77(2), 321–358 (1995)
10. Kirschner, P.A., Buckingham Shum, S.J., Carr, C.S. (eds.): Visualizing Argumentation: Software Tools for Collaborative and Educational Sense-Making. Springer, London (2003)

11. Modgil, S.: Reasoning about preferences in argumentation frameworks. Artificial Intelligence 173(9-10), 901–934 (2009)
12. Modgil, S., Prakken, H.: A general account of argumentation with preferences. Artificial Intelligence 195, 361–397 (2013)
13. Nielsen, S.H., Parsons, S.: A generalization of dung's abstract framework for argumentation: Arguing with sets of attacking arguments. In: Maudet, N., Parsons, S., Rahwan, I. (eds.) ArgMAS 2006. LNCS (LNAI), vol. 4766, pp. 54–73. Springer, Heidelberg (2007)
14. Oren, N., Norman, T.J.: Semantics for evidence-based argumentation. In: Computational Models of Argument: Proceedings of COMMA 2008, pp. 276–284 (2008)
15. Oren, N., Norman, T.J., Preece, A.: Evidential reasoning in bipolar argumentation frameworks. In: Proceedings of the Fourth International Workshop on Argumentation in Multi-Agent Systems (2007)
16. Prakken, H.: An abstract framework for argumentation with structured arguments. Argument and Computation 1(2), 93–124 (2010)
17. Searle, J.R.: A taxonomy of illocutionary acts. In: Gunderson, K. (ed.) Language, Mind, and Knowledge (Minnesota Studies in the Philosophy of Science VII), pp. 344–369. University of Minisota Press (1975)
18. Modgil, S., Toni, F., et al.: The added value of argumentation. In: Ossowski, S. (ed.) Agreement Technologies, ch. 21, pp. 357–403. Springer (2013)
19. van Gijzel, B., Prakken, H.: Relating Carneades with abstract argumentation via the ASPIC+ framework for structured argumentation. Argument and Computation 1, 21–47 (2012)
20. Walton, D.N., Krabbe, E.C.W.: Commitment in Dialogue: Basic Concepts of Interpersonal Reasoning. SUNY Series in Logic and Language. State University of New York Press, Albany (1995)

Extending Social Abstract Argumentation
with Votes on Attacks

Sinan Eğilmez[1], João Martins[1,2], and João Leite[1]

[1] CENTRIA and Departamento de Informática, FCT, Universidade Nova de Lisboa
s.egilmez@campus.fct.unl.pt, jleite@fct.unl.pt
[2] Computer Science Department, Carnegie Mellon University, Pittsburgh PA
jmartins@cs.cmu.edu

Abstract. Social abstract argumentation laid theoretical foundations
for future online debating systems with formal backbones and semantics. The advantage of these envisioned new systems is their capability
of formally justifying the social outcomes of their debates. Many recent extensions proposed for argumentation in general have addressed
the issue that not all attacks between arguments are equal, especially in
the eyes of the crowd. This work generalises social abstract argumentation to incorporate voting on attacks, inducing a social notion of attack
strengths.

1 Introduction

The Web 2.0 proved extremely successful and its use has become second nature
to most of the Internet population. With social networks now widely adopted
and their users beating the one billion mark in 2013, the initial boom is over. As
social networks become established, the patterns of these new social interactions
slowly emerge. It is becoming apparent that many people are growing unsatisfied
with the depth (or lack thereof) of interactions on social websites. A growing
percentage of users are giving up on the Web 2.0 entirely for lack of intellectually
stimulating discussions to which it is possible to attribute some sort of outcome.

This has given rise to websites that revolve around more meaningful interactions, and some of them purport to be a platform for serious debate.[1] Typically,
these online debating systems (ODS) try to engage users with different degrees of
desired involvement. On the one hand, experts and strongly opinionated people
can propose their own debates, arguments, and go head to head against oppo-
nents. On the other hand, less involved users can simply share their opinion by
means of simple voting mechanisms.

Despite their merits, these websites have several characteristics that limit
their adoption in a wide Social Web scale, namely: 1) only two antagonistic
users can engage in a debate, others can only vote for the winning side, but not
on arguments themselves; 2) the debate structure is very rigid, with a pre-fixed
number of rounds and very strict debate rules not known by most; 3) there are

---

[1] The websites debategraph.org, idebate.org, debate.org are a few examples.

E. Black, S. Modgil, and N. Oren (Eds.): TAFA 2013, LNAI 8306, pp. 16–31, 2014.
© Springer-Verlag Berlin Heidelberg 2014

no facilities to reuse arguments and debates, although recent initiatives can help overcome this [6]; and 4) they stop short of reasoning with the debate data and votes/opinions, yielding very simplistic and naïve outcomes.

1.1   The Envisioned Online Debating System

Argumentation theory grounds debates in solid logical foundations and has in fact been shown to be applicable in a multitude of real-life situations [18]. *Social Abstract Argumentation* [16] in particular provided the theoretical foundations on which to build an ODS that gives deeper meaning to online debates, in a more robust, flexible, pervasive and interesting fashion than those currently available. In fact, it has already been used and extended in a prototype business directory allowing users to formally discuss and rank businesses [9], giving customers better control over who they hire.

Social Abstract Argumentation addresses many issues important to ODSs. It does away with the two-sides, one-winner approach typical of current systems. Instead, any user can propose any argument at any time. This yields a much more flexible debate structure, making it easier for users to get engaged and participate. The system also reasons and provides outcomes at the argument level at which users are now allowed to vote. The finer granularity makes outcomes more interesting, detailed and insightful.

When engaging in a debate, users always propose arguments for specific purposes, like making a claim central to the issue being discussed, or defeating arguments supporting an opposing claim. Thus, the envisioned ODS can allow users to formally describe an abstract argument, capable of attacking other arguments, simultaneously with its natural language (or image, video, link, etc.) representation. Therefore, the formal specification of arguments and attacks becomes a natural by-product of the users' intent when proposing new arguments. To make this process as painless and easy as possible, and enable more people to participate, no particularly deep knowledge (such as logics) can be required.

It is natural that a new argument might attack a previously proposed argument - indeed, that was likely the object of its creation. However, it is also possible that an older argument attacks the new argument as well. Therefore, the ODS should allow users to add this new attack relation formally to the system.

Those users who do not wish to engage in proposing arguments or attacks, for whatever reason, should also be accommodated in the system through a less complex participation scheme. Thus, in the ODS, users may simply read the arguments in natural language (or image, video, link, etc.) and formally state whether they agree with them. This induces a voting mechanism similar to what is found in current ODSs. There are alternatives, such as having argument's social trustworthiness be based on people's opinion's of who proposed it. Voting on arguments was chosen over these alternatives since it is the closest to current ODSs, and thus offers the path of least resistance. It is the role of the ODS to continuously provide an up to date view of the outcome of the debate e.g. by assigning value to each argument that somehow represents its social strength, taking the structure of the argumentation framework (arguments and attacks) and the votes into account. A nice GUI e.g. depicting arguments with a size and/or color proportional to these values would make the debate easier to follow, bringing forward relevant (socially) winning arguments, while downgrading unsound, unfounded (even troll) arguments. So that users may understand and follow a debate, small changes in the underlying argumentation framework and its social feedback (i.e. votes) should result in small changes to the formal outcome of the debate. If a single new vote entirely changes the outcome of a debate, users cannot gauge its evolution and trends, and are likely to lose interest.

Any debating system as the one envisioned must also ensure that a few crucial properties are satisfied. ODSs without the following properties are highly unlikely to be seriously adopted by online communities.

- There should always be at least one solution to a debate. The users must get *some* outcome for their effort. If the system is incapable of providing solutions to every debate, then there is too much risk involved in using it.
- There should always be at most one solution to a debate. Logicians and mathematicians find it perfectly natural for there to be multiple, or even infinite, solutions to a given problem. However, in a social context as far-reaching as the Internet, it is disingenuous to assume that the general user-base, which likely covers a large portion of the educational spectrum, shares these views with the same ease. It is very hard for someone who has invested personal effort into a debate to accept that all arguments are in fact true (in a multitude of models)!
- Argument outcomes should thus be represented very flexibly. In particular, to accurately represent the opinions of thousands of voting users, arguments should be valuated using degrees of acceptability, or gradual acceptability. Two-valued or three-valued semantics risk grossly underrepresenting much of the userbase.
- Formal arguments and attacks must be easy to specify. For example, assuming knowledge of first-order logic for specifying structured arguments [13] would alienate many potential users when the present goal is to include as many as possible. Moreover, simpler frameworks turn implementing and deploying such a system in different contexts (web forums, blogs, social networks, etc) much easier.

The above properties have been studied in the context of Social Abstract Argumentation, which uses abstract arguments in the sense of Dung [7], but has argument outcomes take values in the $[0,1] \subseteq \mathbb{R}$ interval. A "well-behaved" family of semantics is known to guarantee the existence of outcomes, whereas uniqueness of outcomes has been proven for specific semantics.

1.2   Contribution

Despite the interesting properties of social abstract argumentation, it is apparent that not all attacks bear the same weight. Some attacks might have an obvious logical foundation (e.g. undercuts or rebuts), thus gaining trust from the more perceptive users. Other attacks might be less obvious or downright senseless, especially in open online contexts, making users doubt or wish to discard them.

Thus, extending the ability to vote to attacks, already suggested in [16,18], becomes eminently desirable. Not only does voting on attacks more accurately represent a crowd's opinion in a variety of situations, but it also allows the ODS to self-regulate by letting troll-attacks be "downvoted" to irrelevance. Following this view, recent formalisms have incorporated the notion of attack weights [11,8].

In this work, social abstract argumentation is extended with votes on attacks, and the properties that hold in social argumentation investigated.

This paper is organised as follows. Sect. 2 develops the extension to social abstract argumentation and studies concrete semantics. Sect. 3 provides a concrete example highlighting the role of votes on attacks. Sect. 4 covers related work, and Sect. 5 concludes.

2   Extended Social Argumentation Frameworks

This section will present ESAFs as an extension of social argumentation frameworks [16] by adding votes to attacks, besides arguments. We refer to these votes as the *social support* of the respective argument or attack.

Extended social argumentation frameworks, which build on social argumentation frameworks from [16], have an added parameter for votes on attacks; votes on arguments were already a feature of SAFs.

Definition 1 (Extended social argumentation frameworks). *An extended social argumentation framework is a 4-tuple* $F = \langle \mathcal{A}, \mathcal{R}, V_{\mathcal{A}}, V_{\mathcal{R}} \rangle$, *where*

- $\mathcal{A}$ *is the set of arguments,*
- $\mathcal{R} \subseteq \mathcal{A} \times \mathcal{A}$ *is a binary attack relation between arguments,*
- $V_{\mathcal{A}} : \mathcal{A} \to \mathbb{N} \times \mathbb{N}$ *stores the crowd's pro and con votes for each argument.*
- $V_{\mathcal{R}} : \mathcal{R} \to \mathbb{N} \times \mathbb{N}$ *stores the crowd's pro and con votes for each attack.*

Notation 1 *Let* $\mathcal{R}^-(a) \triangleq \{a_i \in \mathcal{A} : (a_i, a) \in \mathcal{R}\}$ *be the set of direct attackers of an argument* $a \in \mathcal{A}$. *Let also* $V_{\mathcal{A}}^+(a) \triangleq x$ *and* $V_{\mathcal{A}}^-(a) \triangleq y$ *whenever* $V_{\mathcal{A}}(a) = (x, y)$. *Votes on attacks are handled similarly with* $V_{\mathcal{R}}$.

Following the approach of [16], semantic frameworks are used to aggregate operators representing the several parametrisable components of a semantics:

- An operation to obtain the combined strength of an argument's attackers. This value should be computed by aggregating together their individual strengths into a single, stronger value.
- An operation to restrict an argument's attack strength by the respective attack's social support. In an attack, the attacker can never be stronger than its social support, nor stronger than the attack's own social support.
- An operation to restrict an argument's social support by the value of its aggregated attackers. Notice that it would be socially unacceptable for an argument's final value to be above what was originally its social support.

- An operation that computes a limiting factor from a given attack strength. This limiting factor can then be used to restrict an argument's original strength with the above operator.
- Computing social support values from pro/con votes cast by the community.

All the parametrisable components of a semantics, matching the operations mentioned above, are captured in the following definition.

Definition 2 (Semantic Framework). *A semantic framework is a 6-tuple* $\langle L, \curlywedge_{\mathcal{A}}, \curlywedge_{\mathcal{R}}, \curlyvee, \neg, \tau \rangle$ *where:*

- *L is a totally ordered set with top and bottom elements $\top$, $\bot$, containing all possible valuations of an argument.*
- *$\curlywedge_{\mathcal{A}}, \curlywedge_{\mathcal{R}} : L \times L \to L$, are two binary algebraic operations used to restrict strengths to given values.*
- *$\curlyvee : L \times L \to L$, is a binary algebraic operation on argument valuations used to combine or aggregate valuations and strengths.*
- *$\neg : L \to L$ is a unary algebraic operation for computing a restricting value corresponding to a given valuation or strength.*
- *$\tau : \mathbb{N} \times \mathbb{N} \to L$ is a function that aggregates positive and negative votes into a social support value.*

Notation 2 *As a useful shortcut, let $\tau(a) \triangleq \tau(V_{\mathcal{A}}^{+}(a), V_{\mathcal{A}}^{-}(a))$ and $\tau((a_1, a_2)) \triangleq \tau(V_{\mathcal{R}}^{+}((a_1, a_2)), V_{\mathcal{R}}^{-}((a_1, a_2)))$. Let $R = \{x_1, x_2, ..., x_n\}$ be a multiset of elements of L. Then, with a small abuse of notation:*

$$\biggdownarrow_{x \in R} x \triangleq (((x_1 \curlyvee x_2) \curlyvee ...) \curlyvee x_n)$$

Notice also that the valuation set L of arguments is parametrisable. L could be $[0, 1] \subseteq \mathbb{R}$, but it could also be any finite, countable or uncountable set of values such as booleans, colours, textures, or any other set that is deemed appropriate for users of the final application, so long as it is totally ordered.

The heart of the semantics is in the definition of a model, which combines the operators of a semantic framework $\mathcal{S}$ into a system of equations, one for each argument, that must be satisfied.

Definition 3 (Model). *Let $F = \langle \mathcal{A}, \mathcal{R}, V_{\mathcal{A}}, V_{\mathcal{R}} \rangle$ be a social argumentation framework, $\mathcal{S} = \langle L, \curlywedge_{\mathcal{A}}, \curlywedge_{\mathcal{R}}, \curlyvee, \neg, \tau \rangle$ be a semantic framework. A $\mathcal{S}$-model of F is a total mapping $M : \mathcal{A} \to L$ such that for all $a \in \mathcal{A}$,*

$$M(a) = \tau(a) \curlywedge_{\mathcal{A}} \neg \bigveee_{a_i \in \mathcal{R}^{\cdot}(a)} (\tau((a_i, a)) \curlywedge_{\mathcal{R}} M(a_i))$$

The value assigned to an argument a by model M, or $M(a)$ is called the *valuation* of a under model M.

A model M is a solution to the equation system with one equation of the form in Definition 3 for each argument. An alternative interpretation is that models are fixpoints of the assignments induced by the equations.

We now analyse the equation to facilitate its understanding.

If an argument a_1 attacks another argument a_2, then the strength of the attack is the valuation of the attacking argument a_1 reduced by the social support of the attack: no argument's attack is stronger than either its own valuation or the social support of the attack itself. We use $\curlywedge_{\mathcal{R}}$ to restrict these values.

$$\tau\left((a_1, a_2)\right) \curlywedge_{\mathcal{R}} M\left(a_1\right)$$

Since an argument may have multiple attackers, all of their attack strengths must be aggregated to form a stronger combined attack value, using operator $\curlyvee$.

$$\curlyvee_{a_i \in \mathcal{R}^-(a)} \left(\tau\left((a_i, a)\right) \curlywedge_{\mathcal{R}} M\left(a_i\right)\right)$$

The above equation results in a combined attack strength that must be turned into a restricting value using the $\neg$ operator.

$$\neg \curlyvee_{a_i \in \mathcal{R}^-(a)} \left(\tau\left((a_i, a)\right) \curlywedge_{\mathcal{R}} M\left(a_i\right)\right)$$

In a social context where the crowd has given its opinion of an argument a, it is clear that a's valuation should never turn out higher than a's social support $\tau(a)$. Thus, an argument's valuation is given by restricting $\tau(a)$ with the value of the aggregated attack using the final operator $\curlywedge_{\mathcal{A}}$.

$$\tau(a) \curlywedge_{\mathcal{A}} \neg \curlyvee_{a_i \in \mathcal{R}^-(a)} \left(\tau\left((a_i, a)\right) \curlywedge_{\mathcal{R}} M\left(a_i\right)\right)$$

2.1 Specific Semantics

Fully specifying semantics means that any derivable properties are likely to apply only to that particular case. For that reason, this section starts by restricting a semantic framework in limited, sensible, even intuitively desirable ways, and investigating what derives therefrom. The following definition formalises well-behavedness in a social context.

Definition 4 (Well-behaved semantic frameworks). *A semantic framework* $S = \langle L, \curlywedge_{\mathcal{A}}, \curlywedge_{\mathcal{R}}, \curlyvee, \neg, \tau \rangle$ *is well-behaved if*

- $\neg$ *is antimonotonic, continuous,* $\neg\bot = \top$, $\neg\top = \bot$ *and* $\neg\neg a = a$;
- $\curlywedge_{\mathcal{A}}, \curlywedge_{\mathcal{R}}$ *are continuous, commutative, associative, monotonic w.r.t. both arguments and* $\top$ *is their identity element,*
- $\curlyvee$ *is continuous, commutative, associative, monotonic w.r.t. both arguments and* $\bot$ *is its identity element;*

Some important notions guided Definition 4. Continuity of operators guarantees small changes in the social inputs result in small changes in the models. Were this not the case, outcomes of debates would be very unstable, hard to follow and more easily exploited by trolls. The remaining algebraic properties simply state that the order in which arguments are attacked makes no difference; that an argument's valuation is proportional to its crowd support; that aggregated attacks are proportional to the attacking arguments; and so forth.

From these simple restrictions it is already possible to derive some important results regarding existence of models under well-behaved semantics.

Theorem 3 (Existence of Models). *Let $F = \langle \mathcal{A}, \mathcal{R}, V_{\mathcal{A}}, V_{\mathcal{R}} \rangle$ be an extended social argumentation framework and $\mathcal{S} = \langle L, \curlywedge_{\mathcal{A}}, \curlywedge_{\mathcal{R}}, \Upsilon, \neg, \tau \rangle$ a well behaved semantics. Then F has at least one $\mathcal{S}$-model.*

Consider now the following concrete semantics, suitable for studying specific behaviours and for implementation. It is a generalisation of its social abstract argumentation counterpart [16].

Definition 5 (Product semantics). *Let $\mathcal{S}_\epsilon^{\cdot} = \langle [0,1], \curlywedge^{\cdot}, \curlywedge^{\cdot}, \Upsilon^{\cdot}, \neg, \tau_\epsilon \rangle$ be a semantic framework, $x, y \in [0,1]$ and*

- $x \curlywedge^{\cdot} y = x \cdot y$, *i.e. the product T-norm.*
- $x \Upsilon^{\cdot} y = 1 - (1-x) \cdot (1-y)$, *i.e. the T-conorm dual to the product T-norm.*
- $\neg x = 1 - x$
- $\tau_\epsilon(a) = \frac{V^+(a)}{V^+(a) + V^-(a) + \epsilon}$, *with $\epsilon > 0$, and similarly for attacks*

The τ_ϵ function used to compute the social support deserves special mention. It is a minor variation of a simple percentage. The reason for this modification will become apparent after the following example.

Example 1. Imagine a symmetric situation where two mutually attacking arguments, a and b have only received positive votes, as have their attacks. Figure 1 represents such a scenario, with the annotations indicating the social support of arguments and attacks, using τ_0.

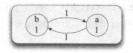

Fig. 1. Symmetric situation with mutually attacking arguments

Considering semantics $\mathcal{S}_0^{\cdot}$, it is easy to derive that the valuations of a and b are given by $M(a) = 1 - M(b)$ and $M(b) = 1 - M(a)$. Therefore, the system of equations that results from using $\tau_0(a) = \frac{V^+(a)}{V^+(a) + V^-(a)}$ is linearly dependent and results in infinitely many models with $M(a) + M(b) = 1$.

It turns out multiple models only arise in the extremely symmetrical situations depicted in Figure 1, with only positive votes. Similar odd-length cycles have a unique model. Furthermore, a single negative vote on any argument or attack is enough to break linear dependence and making uniqueness hold again.

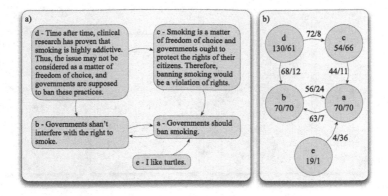

Fig. 2. Social Argumentation Framework: a) arguments and attacks; b) votes

This led to the introduction of the arbitrarily small $\epsilon > 0$ in Definition 5, making scenarios such as those of Figure 1 have unique models. The resulting single model has the property that $M(a) = M(b)$, which preserves the argumentation framework's symmetry in the outcome as well.

The situation when $\epsilon = 0$ can still be made sense of by taking the limit of ϵ as it goes to 0. In fact, $\lim_{\epsilon \to 0} M(a) = \lim_{\epsilon \to 0} M(b) = 0.5$, which is the model that best preserves the symmetry of the framework, as do the models when $\epsilon > 0$.

The product semantics is a well-behaved semantics, which means that the existence of a model is guaranteed as per Theorem 3. The following result provides some clarification in regards to the uniqueness of models.

Theorem 4 (Uniqueness of Models). *Let F be an ESAF such that $|\mathcal{R}^-(a)| \cdot V_\mathcal{A}(a) < 1$, for every $a \in \mathcal{A}$. Then, F has one and only one model under $\mathcal{S}_\epsilon^{\cdot}$.*

Additionally, we expect the result will hold for $\epsilon > 0$, without the $|\mathcal{R}^-(a)| \cdot V_\mathcal{A}(a) < 1$ condition, though this has not been proven yet.

3   Example

Consider a social interaction inspired by [21] where several participants, while arguing about the role of the government in what banning smoking is concerned, set forth the arguments and attack relations depicted in Fig. 2 a).

Despite the fact that these arguments are structurally different: a and b are unsupported claims, c and d contain multiple premises and a conclusion, while e, despite being rather consensual (who doesn't like turtles?), seems to be totally out of context and can hardly be seen as an attack on a (here, the attack by e on a is meant to represent a troll attack). Our goal is to show that ESAFs' level of abstraction allows meaningful arguments to be construed out of most participations – in fact, with suitable GUIs, arguments could even be built from videos, pictures, links, etc. – while the participation through voting will help deal

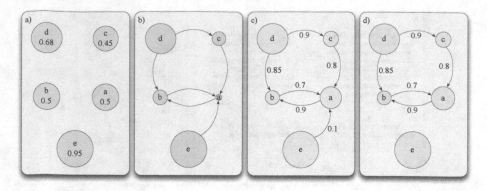

Fig. 3. Model of the Social Abstract Argumentation Framework considering: a) social support only; b) attacks but not their strength; c) attack strength; d) attack strength, without the attack from e to a

with mitigating the disturbing effect of unsound arguments and poorly specified (troll) attacks.

After a while, the arguments and attacks garner the pro/con votes depicted in Fig. 2 b). Arguments a and b obtain the same direct social support as expressed by the 70 *pro* and *con* votes. Meanwhile, a's attack on b is deemed stronger than its counterpart, judging from their votes. One might speculate that this is a consequence of a delivering a more direct message. Whereas argument c does not get much love from the crowd (a vote ratio of 54/66), its attack on a is still supported by the community (44/11). Perhaps initially there was a better sentiment towards c but the introduction of d, which amassed a decent amount of support itself (130/61), turned the odds against c. Both of d's attacks on b and c materialise to be strong enough, the former being slightly weaker (72/8 versus 68/12). Lastly, argument e received just a mere number of votes, most being positive (19/1). However, there seems to have been a significant effort from the users on discrediting the attack on a by e (4/36). Note that e is a perfectly legitimate argument. Indeed the crowd endorses the fondness for turtles – it's the attack, not the argument, that is not logically well-founded.

With the abstract argumentation framework and the votes on arguments and attacks in hand, we can turn our attention to the valuation of the arguments.

If we consider the social support of each argument, i.e. its value considering only the votes it obtained while ignoring attack relations, we obtain the following values:[2] $\tau_0(a) = 0.50$, $\tau_0(b) = 0.50$, $\tau_0(c) = 0.45$, $\tau_0(d) = 0.68$ and $\tau_0(e) = 0.95$, as depicted in Fig. 3 a) (where the size of each node is proportional to its value).

The original Social Abstract Argumentation semantics [16], which considers attacks between arguments but not the votes on attacks, assigns the following values to arguments: $M(a) = 0,02$, $M(b) = 0,16$, $M(c) = 0,14$, $M(d) = 0,68$ and $M(e) = 0,95$, as depicted in Fig. 3 b). As expected, d and e retain their initial social support values, since they are not attacked, while the remaining

---

[2] We will consider the Product Semantics as in Def.5, with $\epsilon = 0$.

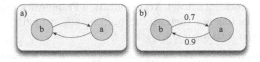

Fig. 4. a) symmetric attacks without attack strength; b) symmetric attacks with attack strength

arguments see a decrease in their social support value. Argument a decreases the most while b and c maintain a reasonable fraction of their initial strength. Since two of a's attackers – b and c – are attacked by d, which is a non-attacked argument with strong social support, their value is weakened, so their effect on a is lessened. Thus, we can conclude that the main cause for the downfall in a's value is e's attack.

We can now turn our attention to the model proposed in this paper, which also takes votes on attacks into consideration, and assigns the following values to arguments: $M(a) = 0,35$, $M(b) = 0,14$, $M(c) = 0,17$, $M(d) = 0,68$ and $M(e) = 0,95$, as depicted in Fig. 3 c). The value assigned to a by the model increases from 0.02 to the more plausible level of 0.34, mostly due to e's weakened capability to attack a. Indeed, the crowd's overwhelming con votes on the (troll) attack of e on a essentially neutralised it. To confirm, we compare it with the model obtained if the attack from e to a was simply removed, depicted in Fig. 3 d), whose valuations of $M(a) = 0,39$, $M(b) = 0,14$, $M(c) = 0,17$ and $M(d) = 0,68$ are very similar to those obtained in the presence of the very weakened attack from e to a, which allows us to conclude for the success of ESAF's in discounting attacks that are socially deemed unsound, such as troll attacks. Since the weights of the remaining attacks are relatively high and also close to each other at the same time, their impact is somewhat minimal.

For convenience, all values regarding the figures are listed in Table 1.

One last remark worth noting is that the inclusion of votes on attacks enables the model to break stand-stills when attacks are not equally strong. Figure 4 a) and b) show how two arguments enjoying the same direct social support, arguments a and b in our example, become distinguishable once the weights of attacks are taken into account.

4   Related Work

4.1   Gabbay's Equational Approach to Argumentation

Here we compare with [10,11], and how some of their proposed semantics can be captured by ESAFs. Gabbay's equational approach to argumentation [10] is a very general formalism that deserves its differences to ESAFs highlighted.

It uses a fixed domain of $[0,1]$, unlike a generic L. For every argument a, whose attackers are $x_1, ..., x_n$, the semantics and models are given by $\mathbf{h}_a$:

$$\mathbf{f}(a) = \mathbf{h}_a\left(\mathbf{f}(x_1), ..., \mathbf{f}(x_n)\right)$$

Table 1. Model of the Social Abstract Argumentation Framework considering: a) social support only; b) attacks but not their strength; c) attack strength; d) attack strength, without the attack from e to a

Argument	Fig. a	Fig. b	Fig. c	Fig. d
a	0.50	0.02	0.35	0.39
b	0,50	0,16	0,14	0.14
c	0,45	0,14	0,17	0.17
d	0,68	0,68	0,68	0.68
e	0,95	0,95	0,95	0.95

The intuition is that a's model depends on the models of its attackers $x_1 \ldots x_n$ according to formula $\mathbf{h}_a$, entirely like ESAFs, implying models are fixpoints.

Because different $\mathbf{h}_a$ can be used for each argument, the equational approach can be seen as more general than ESAFs (cf. Definition 3). It is nonetheless interesting to note that all proposed semantics use the same formula for all arguments, except for the *suspect semantics* whose desired meaning is unclear.

The complete generality of the equational approach is appealing because any formula can be written, so presumably any other formalism is capturable by it. Ultimately, however, this generality results in very few derivable properties. In fact, [10] focuses mostly on studying specific semantics and possible extensions to those semantics rather than on properties of the general system.

The comparison that follows will focus on subsequent work [11] which is of a more social nature than [10]. It allows initial weights on attacks, which fill the same role as social support in ESAFs.

The semantics proposed therein make use of $V_0(a)$ as the initial value for arguments and of $\xi(a_1, a_2)$ for attacks. They are called inverse semantics and maximum semantics, defined below:

$$\mathbf{f}_{inv}(a) = V_0(a) \cdot \prod_{a_i \in \mathcal{R}^-(a)} (1 - \xi(a_i, a) \mathbf{f}_{inv}(a_i))$$

$$\mathbf{f}_{max}(a) = V_0(a) - \max_{a_i \in \mathcal{R}^-(a)} \{\xi(a_i, a) \mathbf{f}_{max}(a_i)\}$$

These semantics can be captured in ESAFs, as the following results show.

Proposition 1. *Eq_{inv} can be represented using ESAFs when initial values are rational.*

Proof. First, it will be necessary to show that the initial values $V_0(a), V_{\mathcal{R}}(a_1, a_2) \in \mathbb{Q}$ can be represented as votes. The following lemma shows that they can.

Lemma 1. *Let $x \in \mathbb{Q}$ such that $0 \leq x \leq 1$. Then there is $y, z \in \mathbb{N}$ such that $x = \frac{y}{y+z}$ and $\frac{y}{y+z}$ is irreducible.*

Proof. From $x \in \mathbb{Q}$ it follows that there is an irreducible fraction $x = \frac{a}{b}$. From $0 \leq x \leq 1$ it follows that $a \leq b$. Then, let $y = a$ and $z = b - a \Leftrightarrow z + a = b \Leftrightarrow y + z = b$.

Back to the proposition. Consider the product semantics defined above as $\mathcal{S}_\epsilon = \langle [0,1], \curlywedge^\cdot, \curlywedge^\cdot, \curlyvee^\cdot, \neg, \tau \rangle$. Then, since $V_0(a), V_\mathcal{R}(a_1, a_2) \in \mathbb{Q}$, by the lemma, there are $V_\mathcal{A}^+(a), V_\mathcal{A}^-(a), V_\mathcal{R}^+(a_1, a_2), V_\mathcal{R}^-(a_1, a_2) \in \mathbb{N}$ such that $\tau(a) = V_0(a)$ and $\tau(a_1, a_2) = V_\mathcal{R}(a_1, a_2)$.

T-norms and their dual T-conorms are distributive, and the generalised de Morgan laws apply. This justifies the first step in the following derivation.

$$
\begin{aligned}
M(a) &= \tau(a) \curlywedge^\cdot \neg \bigcurlyvee_{a_i \in \mathcal{R}^-(a)}^\cdot (\tau(a_i, a) \curlywedge^\cdot M(a_i)) \\
&= \tau(a) \curlywedge^\cdot \bigcurlywedge_{a_i \in \mathcal{R}^-(a)}^\cdot (\neg (\tau(a_i, a) \curlywedge^\cdot M(a_i))) \\
&= V_0(a) \cdot \prod_{a_i \in \mathcal{R}^-(a)} (1 - \xi(a_i, a) \cdot M(a_i)) = \boldsymbol{f}_{inv}(a)
\end{aligned}
$$

While it was not necessary for Eq_{inv}, two different $\curlywedge$ operators are needed to subsume Eq_{max}, since it uses both subtraction and multiplication as restrictive operations.

Proposition 2. *Eq_{max} can be represented using ESAFs when initial values are rational.*

Proof. Let $\mathcal{S}^{max} = \langle L, \curlywedge_\mathcal{A}, \curlywedge_\mathcal{R}, \curlyvee, \neg, \tau \rangle$ such that: $L = [0,1]$; $V_\mathcal{A}(a)$ and $V_\mathcal{R}(a_1, a_2)$ are handled as in Proposition 1; $l_1 \curlywedge_\mathcal{A} l_2 = l_1 - l_2$, arithmetic subtraction; $l_1 \curlywedge_\mathcal{R} l_2 = l_1 \cdot l_2$, arithmetic multiplication; $l_1 \curlyvee l_2 = \max\{l_1, l_2\}$, maximum aggregation operation; and $\neg l_1 = l_1$.

Notice that $\mathcal{S}^{max}$ is not a well-behaved framework since $\curlywedge_\mathcal{A}$, or subtraction, is not commutative. The de Morgan laws also do not apply.

$$
\begin{aligned}
M(a) &= \tau(a) \curlywedge_\mathcal{A} \neg \bigcurlyvee_{a_i \in \mathcal{R}^-(a)} (\tau(u_i, a) \curlywedge_\mathcal{R} M(a_i)) \\
&= V_0(a) \curlywedge_\mathcal{A} \neg \bigcurlyvee_{a_i \in \mathcal{R}^-(a)} (\xi(a_i, a) \curlywedge_\mathcal{R} M(a_i)) \\
&= V_0(a) - \bigcurlyvee_{a_i \in \mathcal{R}^-(a)} (\xi(a_i, a) \cdot M(a_i)) \\
&= V_0(a) - \max_{a_i \in \mathcal{R}^-(a)} \{\xi(a_i, a) M(a_i)\} = \boldsymbol{f}_{max}(a)
\end{aligned}
$$

These propositions serve as evidence that several semantics can be captured using ESAFs. Some accommodate the notion of well-behaved semantics naturally, but others do not. This could stem from how closely related with multi-valuedness the semantics are. For example, $\boldsymbol{f}_{max}$ is very two-valued at its core. It actually coincides with stable extensions [7] when $V_0(a) = 1$ for all $a \in \mathcal{A}$, $\xi(a_1, a_2) = 1$ for all $(a_1, a_2) \in \mathcal{R}$, and an argument is taken to be accepted when $\boldsymbol{f}_{max}(a) = 1$. In fact, it follows that $\boldsymbol{f}_{max}(a) \in \{0, 1\}$! The product semantics is more tightly connected with the valuations being $[0,1] \subseteq \mathbb{R}$, and that appears to be part of the reason for its well-behavedness.

4.2   Graduality in Argument Valuations

Other proposals have broached the subject of graduality, or multi-valuedness, in argumentation, which is so important in large-scale online debates. Graduality in argumentation was studied in [5], proposing $\mathbb{R}$ as the domain of argument valuations, and aggregation and reduction operators applied in an explicit equational way, not unlike the present work. However, no social context is assumed, and so all attacks and arguments are perfectly sound by default. Their initial values, or social support, are 1, not a function of a crowd's opinion.

As seen in Section 4.1, [10] uses a very flexible equational method with argument valuations over $[0, 1]$. In [11], that approach, extended with voting, is applied to the context of merging several agents' different perceptions of a single debate into a unified framework with a social outcome. Each agent votes positively on arguments and attacks it agrees with locally, and votes negatively on those that he doesn't agree with. This can be seen as a restricted use of the voting mechanism of ESAFs.

4.3   Social Contexts in Argumentation

Whereas ESAFs incorporate the social aspect of argumentation using voting, alternative proposals explicitly model properties of the social context in which debates are carried out.

In [20], arguments have values (e.g. free-market, human rights, family), and a specific audience will order values according to personal preferences. By incorporating a probabilistic model of the audience's preferences, [20] estimates the probability that each argument will convince the audience of a certain proposition. The arguments more likely to convince the audience can be chosen first.

Along a similar line, arguments can be related to topics on which certain people are experts [15]. This allows votes on attacks to have different weights depending on the expertise of the voter in the related topics. Furthermore, if a debate is controversial, i.e. with a fickle outcome balancing on a knife's edge, [15] draws some preliminary considerations on computing the best expert to call forward to propose the next argument, hopefully settling the debate.

4.4   Applications of Argumentation to the Web 2.0

Some recent applications have focused on applying argumentation theory to Twitter as a source of abundant social information in the form of concise comments. These systems are very close to the intended application of SAFs [16] and ESAFs. In fact, using the notion of arguments and attacks, it is possible to automatically mine Twitter for arguments and attacks between them [14]. These result in argument trees such as those found in classical dialogue-based argumentation.

A different approach, more reliant on users, is to allow them to annotate their tweets with agreement or disagreement towards a particular subject [12]. The new annotations are used to create arguments and attacks. Given a stream given by a hashtag, it is thus possible to induce an argumentation framework that represents the ongoing discussion, and obtain formal outcomes. This functionality has been implemented and tested.

The above implementations are showing how argumentation theory can be applied to the Web 2.0, although they currently do not feature crowd voting.

5   Conclusions

In closing, the work on *Extended Social Argumentation Frameworks* takes another step towards capturing the essence of social debates. It builds on the theoretical foundations laid by [16] that provided debates with formal and justifiable outcomes. In this work the social notion of attack strengths has been introduced via incorporating votes on attacks. A new family of semantics is introduced for the new framework and illustrated by the means of an example. Certain semantics suggested in [10,11] are proven to be special cases of ESAF.

The originality of the proposed framework lies in its practicality and generality. The semantics for ESAFs can be tailored in different ways to meet the needs and expectations of varied applications and user groups. Whereas we focused more on gradual valuations, in a scenario where a clear decision is to be taken, it might make more sense to use a semantics with a family of operators that results in a classical in/out approach as in Dung-like argumentation frameworks.

Furthermore the framework can be extended in multiple ways.

Some authors have advocated the addition of a support relation between arguments (e.g. [1,3]). Whereas there has been a debate regarding the adequacy of such relation – some argue that since arguments are accepted by default, any support should take the form of an attack on its attackers – its incorporation into ESAF's might prove beneficial, and certainly worth future investigation.

Allowing votes on attacks resembles the abstract resolution semantics in [2]. Even though it's not exactly how we envision our system, it might be an interesting idea to explore a possible extension by admitting arguments with internal structure, taking into careful consideration the observation that properties of abstract resolution semantics are not always preserved by instantiations [19], which could result in the loss the list of desired properties of our framework.

The work in [4] allows the automatic detection and generation of the abstract arguments from natural language. Such a framework can be utilized hand in hand with ESAFs to capture the semantics of unstructured social debate platforms.

Another possible extension is to consider attacks on the attack relations themselves. Prior work on this topic such as [17] builds on [7] by following the generic accepted/defeated approach regarding the arguments. In this regard ESAFs can improve the novelty of the work by the flexible evaluation mechanism.

Finally, it should be noted that the work on ESAFs will proceed in near future via articulating the capabilities of the framework proposed in this paper in capturing the semantics of other existing approaches in the field.

Acknowledgments. We would like to thank the anonymous reviewers for their insightful comments and suggestions. J. Leite was partially supported by FCT project ERRO – PTDC/EIA-CCO/121823/2010.

References

1. Amgoud, L., et al.: On bipolarity in argumentation frameworks. Int. J. Intell. Syst. 23(10), 1062–1093 (2008)
2. Baroni, P., Giacomin, M.: On principle-based evaluation of extension-based argumentation semantics. Artif. Intell. 171(10-15), 675–700 (2007)
3. Boella, G., et al.: Support in abstract argumentation. In: Procs. of COMMA 2010. FAIA, vol. 216. IOS Press (2010)
4. Cabrio, E., Villata, S.: Natural language arguments: A combined approach. In: Procs. of ECAI 2012. FAIA, vol. 242. IOS Press (2012)
5. Cayrol, C., Lagasquie-Schiex, M.C.: Graduality in argumentation. J. Artif. Intell. Res. 23, 245–297 (2005)
6. Chesñevar, C., et al.: Towards an argument interchange format. Knowledge Eng. Review 21(4), 293–316 (2006)
7. Dung, P.M.: On the acceptability of arguments and its fundamental role in non-monotonic reasoning, logic programming and n-person games. Artif. Intell. 77(2), 321–358 (1995)
8. Dunne, P., et al.: Weighted argument systems: Basic definitions, algorithms, and complexity results. Artif. Intell. 175(2), 457–486 (2011)
9. Evripidou, V., Toni, F.: Argumentation and voting for an intelligent user empowering business directory on the web. In: Krötzsch, M., Straccia, U. (eds.) RR 2012. LNCS, vol. 7497, pp. 209–212. Springer, Heidelberg (2012)
10. Gabbay, D.M.: Equational approach to argumentation networks. Argument & Computation 3(2-3), 87–142 (2012)
11. Gabbay, D., Rodrigues, O.: A numerical approach to the merging of argumentation networks. In: Fisher, M., van der Torre, L., Dastani, M., Governatori, G. (eds.) CLIMA XIII 2012. LNCS (LNAI), vol. 7486, pp. 195–212. Springer, Heidelberg (2012)
12. Gabbriellini, S., Torroni, P.: Large scale agreements via microdebates. In: Procs. of AT 2012. CEUR Workshop Proceedings, vol. 918 (2012)
13. García, A., Dix, J., Simari, G.: Argument-based logic programming. In: Rahwan, I., Simari, G.R. (eds.) Argumentation in Artificial Intelligence, pp. 153–171. Springer (2009)
14. Grosse, K., Chesñevar, C.I., Maguitman, A.G.: An argument-based approach to mining opinions from Twitter. In: Procs. of AT 2012. CEUR Workshop Proceedings, vol. 918 (2012)
15. Kontarinis, D., et al.: Picking the right expert to make a debate uncontroversial. In: Procs. of COMMA 2012. FAIA, vol. 245. IOS Press (2012)
16. Leite, J., Martins, J.: Social abstract argumentation. In: Procs. of IJCAI 2011. IJCAI/AAAI (2011)
17. Modgil, S.: Reasoning about preferences in argumentation frameworks. Artif. Intell. 173(9-10), 901–934 (2009)
18. Modgil, S., et al.: The added value of argumentation. In: Ossowski, S. (ed.) Agreement Technologies. Law, Governance and Tech. Series, vol. 8, pp. 357–403. Springer (2013)

19. Modgil, S., Prakken, H.: Resolutions in structured argumentation. In: Procs. of COMMA 2012. FAIA, vol. 245, IOS Press (2012)
20. Oren, N., Atkinson, K., Li, H.: Group persuasion through uncertain audience modelling. In: Procs. of COMMA 2012. FAIA, vol. 245. IOS Press (2012)
21. Walton, D.: Argumentation theory: A very short introduction. In: Rahwan, I., Simari, G.R. (eds.) Argumentation in Artificial Intelligence, pp. 1–22. Springer (2009)

A Normal Form for Argumentation Frameworks

Cosmina Croitoru[1] and Timo Kötzing[2]

[1] MPI, Saarbrücken, Germany
[2] Universität Jena, Jena, Germany

Abstract. We study formal argumentation frameworks as introduced by Dung (1995). We show that any such argumentation framework can be syntactically augmented into a normal form (having a simplified attack relation), preserving the semantic properties of original arguments.

An argumentation framework is in *normal form* if no argument attacks a conflicting pair of arguments. An *augmentation* of an argumentation framework is obtained by adding new arguments and changing the attack relation such that the acceptability status of original arguments is maintained in the new framework. Furthermore, we define join-normal semantics leading to augmentations of the joined argumentation frameworks. Also, a rewriting technique which transforms in cubic time a given argumentation framework into a normal form is devised.

1 Introduction

Abstract argumentation frameworks, introduced by Dung [11], constitute a common mechanism for studying reasoning in defeasible domains and for relating different non-monotonic formalisms. General network reasoning models investigating the informal logic structure of many social and economic problems instantiate Dung's argumentation frameworks, and therefore can be implemented based on an unifying principle.

This graph-theoretic model of argumentation frameworks focuses on the manner in which a specified set A of abstract arguments interact via an attack (defeat) binary relation D on A. If $(a,b) \in D$ (argument a *attacks* argument b) we have a conflict. A *conflict-free* set of arguments is a set $T \subseteq A$ such that there are no $a, b \in T$ with $(a,b) \in D$. An *admissible* set of arguments is a conflict-free set $T \subseteq A$ such that the arguments in T defend themselves "collectively" against any attack: for each $(a,b) \in D$ with $b \in T$, there is $c \in T$ such that $(c,a) \in D$.

In this model, the main aim of argumentation is deciding the status of arguments. The acceptability of an argument a is defined based on its membership in an admissible set of arguments satisfying certain properties (formalizing different intuitions about which arguments to accept on the basis of the given framework) called *semantics*. The attack graph is given in advance – abstracting on the underlying logic and structure of arguments, as well on the reason and nature of the attacks – and provides a defeasible-based conceptualization of commonsense reasoning.

It is well-known that the syntactical structure of argumentation frameworks directly influences the output [11, 12, 1], and the complexity of algorithms for deciding acceptability questions [13]. In [21], a four-layers succession for any AI-argumentation process was proposed. First we have the *logical layer* in which arguments are defined.

E. Black, S. Modgil, and N. Oren (Eds.): TAFA 2013, LNAI 8306, pp. 32–45, 2014.
© Springer-Verlag Berlin Heidelberg 2014

Second, in the *dialectical layer*, the attacks are defined. Next, in the *procedural layer*, are defined rules that control the way arguments are introduced and challenged. Last layer, the *heuristics layer*, contains the remaining parts of the process, including methods for deciding the justification status of arguments.

In this paper, keeping the abstract character of arguments and attacks, we are interested in understanding the syntactical properties of argumentation frameworks related to the *procedural layer*. We prove in a formal way that a discipline policy can be adopted in forming of an argumentation framework, without changing the semantic properties. It follows from our result that if the output of a dispute is obtained using an extension based reasoning engine, then it will be not influenced if we impose the following rule: any new argument added by an agent attacks no existing pair of conflicting arguments and, at the same time, at most one argument from any existing pair of conflicting argument can attack the new argument.

We formalize this by considering σ-extensions (for σ a classical semantics), and introducing the notion of σ-*augmentation of an argumentation framework AF*. An argumentation framework AF' is a σ-*augmentation* of AF if it contains all arguments of AF, and the attacks of AF' are such that, for any set S of arguments of AF, S is contained in a σ-extension of AF if and only if S is contained in a σ-extension of AF'. We show that for suitable *join-normal* semantics the join of two argumentation frameworks gives rise to a common σ-augmentation of the joined argumentation frameworks. In the main result of this paper, we prove that *for any argumentation framework AF there is a σ-augmentation AF' in normal form*, where σ is any Dung's classical semantics. An argumentation framework is in normal form if the set of arguments attacked by any argument contains no two attacking arguments. We prove that an argumentation framework is in normal form if and only if it can be constructed by adding its arguments one after one (the order does not matter), such that each new argument cannot attack two attacking arguments already added, and cannot be attacked by a pair of two attacking arguments already added.

The remainder of this paper is organized as follows. In Section 2, we discuss basic notions of Dung's theory of argumentation. In Section 3, σ-*augmentations of argumentation frameworks* are introduced and their basic properties are studied. In Section 4, we show that each argumentation framework admits an *admissible* augmentation in *normal form* (which can be constructed in cubic time). Finally, Section 5 concludes the paper and discusses future work.

2   Dung's Theory of Argumentation

In this section we present the basic concepts used for defining classical semantics in abstract argumentation frameworks introduced by Dung in 1995, [11]. All notions and results, if not otherwise cited, are from this paper (even some of them are not literally the same). We consider U a fixed countable *universe* of arguments.

Definition 1. An *Argumentation Framework* is a digraph $AF = (A, D)$, where $A \subset U$ is finite and nonempty, the vertices in A are called *arguments*, and if $(a, b) \in D$ is a directed edge, then *argument a defeats (attacks) argument b*. A, the argument set of

AF, is referred as $Arg(AF)$ and its attack set D is referred as $Def(AF)$. The set of all argumentation frameworks (over U) is denoted by $\mathbb{AF}$.

Two argumentation frameworks AF_1 and AF_2 are *isomorphic* (denoted $AF_1 \cong AF_2$) if there is a bijection $h : Arg(AF_1) \rightarrow Arg(AF_2)$ such that $(a,b) \in Def(AF_1)$ if and only if $(h(a),h(b)) \in Def(AF_2)$. h is called an *argumentation framework isomorphism*, and it is emphasized by the notation $AF_1 \cong_h AF_2$. If $S \subseteq Arg(AF_1)$ and h is an isomorphism between AF_1 and AF_2, then $h(S) \subseteq Arg(AF_2)$ is $h(S) = \{h(a)|a \in Arg(AF_1)\}$. Similarly, if $M \subseteq 2^{Arg(AF_1)}$, then $h(M) \subseteq 2^{Arg(AF_2)}$ is $h(M) = \{h(S)|S \in M\}$.

The extension-based acceptability semantics is a central notion in Dung's argumentation framework, which we define as follows (see also [2]).

Definition 2. An *extension-based acceptability semantics* is a function σ that assigns to every argumentation framework $AF \in \mathbb{AF}$ a set $\sigma(AF) \subseteq 2^{Arg(AF)}$, such that for every two argumentation frameworks $AF_1, AF_2 \in \mathbb{AF}$, if h is an isomorphism between AF_1 and AF_2 ($AF_1 \cong_h AF_2$) then $\sigma(AF_2) = h(\sigma(AF_1))$. A member $E \in \sigma(AF)$ is called a σ-extension in AF.

If a semantics σ satisfies the condition $|\sigma(AF)| = 1$ for any argumentation framework AF, then σ is said to belong to the *unique-status approach*, otherwise to the *multiple-status approach* [22].

The main conditions on the acceptability status of an argument with respect to a given semantics are defined as follows.

Definition 3. Let $AF = (A,D)$ be an argumentation framework, $a \in A$ be an argument and σ be a semantics.

a is σ-*credulously accepted* if and only if $a \in \bigcup_{S \in \sigma(AF)} S$.
a is σ-*sceptically accepted* if and only if $a \in \bigcap_{S \in \sigma(AF)} S$.

Let $AF = (A,D)$ be an argumentation framework. For each $a \in A$ we denote $a^+ = \{b \in A| (a,b) \in D\}$ the set of all arguments *attacked* by a, and $a^- = \{b \in A| (b,a) \in D\}$ the set of all arguments *attacking* a. These notations can be extended to sets of arguments. The set of all arguments *attacked by* (the arguments in) $S \subseteq A$ is $S^+ = \bigcup_{a \in S} a^+$, and the set of all arguments *attacking* (the arguments in) S is $S^- = \bigcup_{a \in S} a^-$. We also have $\emptyset^+ = \emptyset^- = \emptyset$. The set S of arguments *defends* an argument $a \in A$ if $a^- \subseteq S^+$ (i.e. any a's attacker is attacked by an argument in S). The set of *all arguments defended by* a set S of arguments is denoted by $F(S)$.

If $\mathbb{M}_{AF}$ is a non-empty set of sets of arguments in AF, then $\mathbf{max}(\mathbb{M}_{AF})$ denotes the set of maximal (w.r.t. inclusion) members of $\mathbb{M}_{AF}$ and $\mathbf{min}(\mathbb{M}_{AF})$ denotes the set of its minimal (w.r.t. inclusion) members.

We now define the main admissibility extension-based acceptability semantics.

Definition 4. Let $AF = (A,D)$ be an argumentation framework.

- A *conflict-free set* in AF is a set $S \subseteq A$ with property $S \cap S^+ = \emptyset$ (i.e. there are no attacking arguments in S). We will denote $\mathbf{cf}(AF) = \{S \subseteq A|S \text{ is conflict-free set }\}$.
- An *admissible set* in AF is a set $S \in \mathbf{cf}(AF)$ with property $S^- \subseteq S^+$ (i.e. defends its elements). We will denote $\mathbf{adm}(AF) = \{S \subseteq A|S \text{ is admissible set }\}$.

- A *complete extension* in AF is a set $S \in \mathbf{cf}(AF)$ with property $S = F(S)$. We will denote $\mathbf{comp}(AF) = \{S \subseteq A | S$ is complete extension $\}$.
- A *preferred extension* in AF is a set $S \in \mathbf{max}(\mathbf{comp}(AF))$. We will denote $\mathbf{pref}(AF) :=$ $\mathbf{max}(\mathbf{comp}(AF))$.
- A *grounded extension* in AF is a set $S \in \mathbf{min}(\mathbf{comp}(AF))$. We will denote $\mathbf{gr}(AF) :=$ $\mathbf{min}(\mathbf{comp}(AF))$.
- A *stable extension* in AF is a set $S \in \mathbf{cf}(AF)$ with the property $S^+ = A - S$. We will denote $\mathbf{stb}(AF) = \{S \subseteq A | S$ is stable extension $\}$.

Note that $\emptyset \in \mathbf{adm}(AF)$ for any AF (hence $\mathbf{adm}(AF) \neq \emptyset$) and if $a \in A$ is a self-attacking argument (i.e. $(a,a) \in D$), then a is not contained in an admissible set. It is not difficult to see that any admissible set is contained in a preferred extension, which exists in any AF; the preferred extension is unique if AF has no directed cycle of even length [4, 1].

The grounded extension exists and it is unique in any argumentation framework. It can be constructed by considering all non-attacked arguments, deleting these arguments and those attacked by them from the digraph, and repeating these two steps for the digraph obtained until no node remains.

An equivalent way to express Dung's extension-based semantics is using argument labellings as proposed by Caminada [7] (originally introduced in [18]). The idea underlying the labellings-based approach is to assign to each argument a label from the set $\{I,O,U\}$. The label I (i.e. In) means the argument is accepted, the label O (i.e. Out) means the argument is rejected, and the label U (i.e. Undecided) means one abstains from an opinion on whether the argument is accepted or rejected.

Definition 5. *[7]* Let $AF = (A,D)$ be an argumentation framework. A *complete labelling* of AF is a function $Lab : A \to \{I,O,U\}$ such that $\forall a \in A$:
- $Lab(a) = I$ if and only if $a^- \subseteq Lab^{-1}(O)$,
- $Lab(a) = O$ if and only if $a^- \cap Lab^{-1}(I) \neq \emptyset$,
- $Lab(a) = U$ if and only if $a^- \cap Lab^{-1}(I) = \emptyset$ and $a^- \cap Lab^{-1}(U) \neq \emptyset$.

A *grounded labelling* of AF is a complete labelling Lab such that there is no complete labelling Lab_1 with $Lab_1^{-1}(I) \subset Lab^{-1}(I)$. A *preferred labelling* of AF is a complete labelling Lab such that there is no complete labelling Lab_1 with $Lab^{-1}(I) \subset Lab_1^{-1}(I)$. A *stable labelling* of AF is a complete labelling Lab such that $Lab^{-1}(U) = \emptyset$.

In [7] it was proved that, for any argumentation framework $AF = (A,D)$ and any semantics $\sigma \in \{\mathbf{comp},\mathbf{gr},\mathbf{pref},\mathbf{stb}\}$, a set $S \subseteq A$ satisfies $S \in \sigma(AF)$ if and only if there is a σ-labelling Lab of AF such that $S = Lab^{-1}(I)$. We close this introductory section by noting that the above construction of the grounded extension can be related in a nice way to complete labellings, which explains their close relationship with the so called P,N,D-partitions from combinatorial game theory ([16]). More precisely, it is not difficult to prove the following observation, which gives an intrinsic characterization of complete labellings which are grounded labellings.

Observation 6. *Let $AF = (A,D)$ be an argumentation framework. A complete labelling Lab of AF is a grounded labelling if and only if there is a linear order $<$ on $Lab^{-1}(I)$ such that the following condition holds:*
if $a \in Lab^{-1}(I)$ and $b \in a^-$ then there is $a' \in Lab^{-1}(I) \cap b^-$ such that $a' < a$.

3 The σ-Augmentations

We introduce the following binary relation between argumentation frameworks.

Definition 7. Let $AF, AF' \in \mathbb{AF}$ and σ be a semantics.
We say that AF' is a σ-*augmentation* of AF, denoted $AF \sqsubseteq_\sigma AF'$, if

- $Arg(AF) \subseteq Arg(AF')$,
- for any $S \in \sigma(AF)$ there is $S' \in \sigma(AF')$ s.t. $S \subseteq S'$, and
- for any $S' \in \sigma(AF')$ there is $S \in \sigma(AF)$ s.t. $S' \cap Arg(AF) \subseteq S$.

The binary relation $\sqsubseteq_\sigma$ between argumentation frameworks is a preorder: clearly $\sqsubseteq_\sigma$ is reflexive, and it is transitive as the following proposition shows.

Proposition 8. *If* $AF \sqsubseteq_\sigma AF'$ *and* $AF' \sqsubseteq_\sigma AF''$, *then* $AF \sqsubseteq_\sigma AF''$.

Proof. Clearly, $Arg(AF) \subseteq Arg(AF'')$.
Let $S \in \sigma(AF)$. Since $AF \sqsubseteq_\sigma AF'$, there is $S' \in \sigma(AF')$ such that $S \subseteq S'$, and since $AF' \sqsubseteq_\sigma AF''$, there is $S'' \in \sigma(AF'')$ such that $S' \subseteq S''$. Hence for any $S \in \sigma(AF)$ there exists $S'' \in \sigma(AF'')$ such that $S \subseteq S''$.
Let $S'' \in \sigma(AF'')$. Since $AF' \sqsubseteq_\sigma AF''$, there is $S' \in \sigma(AF')$ such that $S'' \cap Arg(AF') \subseteq S'$. Since $AF \sqsubseteq_\sigma AF'$, there is $S \in \sigma(AF)$ such that $S' \cap Arg(AF) \subseteq S$. Since $Arg(AF) \subseteq Arg(AF')$ it follows that $S'' \cap Arg(AF) \subseteq S'' \cap Arg(AF') \subseteq S'$, hence $S'' \cap Arg(AF) \subseteq S' \cap Arg(AF) \subseteq S$.   □

It follows that we define $AF \equiv_\sigma AF'$ if and only if $AF \sqsubseteq_\sigma AF'$ and $AF' \sqsubseteq_\sigma AF$ then, we obtain an equivalent relation on $\mathbb{AF}$. Two $\equiv_\sigma$-equivalent argumentation frameworks have the same set of arguments, but they are not isomorphic in general. For example, $AF = (\{a,b\}, \{(a,a),(a,b)\})$ and $AF' = (\{a,b\}, \{(a,a),(b,b)\})$ are $\equiv_{\mathbf{adm}}$ (since $\mathbf{adm}(AF) = \{\emptyset\} = \mathbf{adm}(AF')$), but, clearly, they are not isomorphic.

It is not necessary that the attack set of the σ-augmentation is a a superset of the attack set of the initial argumentation framework, as the following example shows.

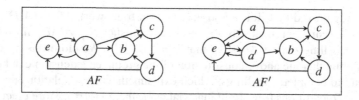

Fig. 1. AF' is an admissible augmentation of AF

Example 9. Let us consider the two argumentation frameworks in the Figure 1. We have $A' = A \cup \{a'\}$ and $D' = (D - \{(a,b)\}) \cup \{(e,a'),(a',e),(a',b)\}$, hence $D \nsubseteq D'$. However, $AF \sqsubseteq_{\mathbf{adm}} AF'$. Indeed, the admissible sets in AF are $\emptyset$, $\{a\}$, and $\{a,d\}$ (no conflict-free set containing b defends the attack (d,b), no conflict-free set containing

c defends the attack (b,c)), which remain admissible sets in AF'. The admissible sets in AF' are $\emptyset$, $\{a\}$, $\{a'\}$, $\{a,a'\}$, $\{a,d\}$, $\{a',d\}$, and $\{a,a',d\}$ (the "new" conflict-free sets $\{a,b\}$ and $\{a',c\}$ can not be extended to admissible sets in AF' due to the attacks (a',b), respectively (a,c)), and their intersections with A are contained in admissible sets of AF.

The next proposition follows easily from the definition.

Proposition 10.

(i) *If $\sigma(AF) = \emptyset$, then we have $AF \sqsubseteq_\sigma AF'$ if and only if $Arg(AF) \subseteq Arg(AF')$ and $\sigma(AF') = \emptyset$.*

(ii) *If $\sigma(AF) = \{\emptyset\}$, then we have $AF \sqsubseteq_\sigma AF'$ if and only if $Arg(AF) \subseteq Arg(AF')$, $\sigma(AF') \neq \emptyset$, and $S' \cap Arg(AF) = \emptyset$ for all $S' \in \sigma(AF')$.*

It is easy to prove that the σ-credulous acceptability of an argument in a given AF is not changed in a σ-augmentation AF' of AF. More precisely, the following proposition holds.

Proposition 11. *If $AF \sqsubseteq_\sigma AF'$ and $a \in Arg(AF)$ then a is σ-credulously accepted in AF if and only if a is σ-credulously accepted in AF'.*

Proof. If there is $S \in \sigma(AF)$ such that $a \in S$, then since $AF \sqsubseteq_\sigma AF'$ it follows that there is $S' \in \sigma(AF')$ such that $S \subseteq S'$, hence there is $S' \in \sigma(AF')$ such that $a \in S'$, that is a is σ-credulously accepted in AF'. Conversely, if there is $S' \in \sigma(AF')$ such that $a \in S'$, then since $AF \sqsubseteq_\sigma AF'$ and $a \in Arg(AF)$, it follows that there is $S \in \sigma(AF)$ such that $S' \cap Arg(AF) \subseteq S$, hence there is $S \in \sigma(AF)$ such that $a \in S$, that is a is σ-credulously accepted in AF. □

The converse of Proposition 11 does not hold. Indeed, if $AF = (\{a,b\}, \{(a,b),(b,a)\})$, $AF' = (\{a,b,a',b'\}, \{(a,a'),(a',b),(b,b'),(b',a)\})$, and $\sigma = \mathbf{adm}$, then a and b are $\mathbf{adm}$-credulously accepted in AF and AF'. However, $AF \not\sqsubseteq_{\mathbf{adm}} AF'$, since the admissible set $\{a,b\}$ in AF' is not contained in an admissible set in AF.

If σ is an admissibility-based semantics, the σ-sceptical acceptance is not preserved in general by the σ-augmentations. Indeed, let the argument a be σ-sceptically accepted in the argumentation framework AF, for $\sigma \in \{\mathbf{comp, pref, gr, stb}\}$. Let AF' be the argumentation framework obtained from AF by adding a new copy a' of a, each attack (a,x) or (x,a) giving rise to a new attack (a',x) or (x,a'), and adding the attacks (a,a') and (a',a). It is not difficult to see that $\sigma(AF') = \sigma(AF) \cup \{S - \{a\} \cup \{a'\} | S \in \sigma(AF), a \in S\}$. It follows that $AF \sqsubseteq_\sigma AF'$ but a is not σ-sceptically accepted in the argumentation framework AF'.

A simple way of constructing σ-augmentations is given by the join of two argumentation frameworks.

Definition 12. Let AF_1 and AF_2 be disjoint argumentation frameworks, that is $Arg(AF_1) \cap Arg(AF_2) = \emptyset$.

- The *disjoint union* of AF_1 and AF_2 is the argumentation framework $AF' = AF_1 \uplus AF_2$, where $Arg(AF') = Arg(AF_1) \cup Arg(AF_2)$ and $Def(AF') = Def(AF_1) \cup Def(AF_2)$.
- The *sum* of AF_1 and AF_2 is the argumentation framework $AF'' = AF_1 + AF_2$, where $Arg(AF'') = Arg(AF_1) \cup Arg(AF_2)$ and $Def(AF'') = Def(AF_1) \cup Def(AF_2) \cup \{(a_1, a_2), (a_2, a_1) | a_i \in Arg(AF_i), i = 1, 2\}$.
- If σ is a semantics then it is *join-normal* if $\sigma(AF_1 \uplus AF_2) = \{S \cup S' | S \in \sigma(AF_1), S' \in \sigma(AF_2)\}$ and $\sigma(AF_1 + AF_2) = \sigma(AF_1) \cup \sigma(AF_2)$.

If $\sigma \in \{\textbf{adm, comp, pref, gr, stb}\}$ then σ is join-normal. Indeed, S is a conflict-free set in $AF_1 \uplus AF_2$ if and only if $S_i = S \cap Arg(AF_i)$ is a conflict-free set in AF_i ($i \in \{1, 2\}$). Also, $S^+ = S_1^+ \uplus S_2^+$. Similarly, S is a conflict-free set in $AF_1 + AF_2$ if and only if $S \in \textbf{cf}(AF_1)$ or $S \in \textbf{cf}(AF_2)$. If $S \in \textbf{cf}(AF_1)$ then $S^+ = Arg(AF_2) \cup S^+ \cap Arg(AF_1)$ and if $S \in \textbf{cf}(AF_2)$ then $S^+ = Arg(AF_1) \cup S^+ \cap Arg(AF_2)$.
The next proposition follows easily from the definition above.

Proposition 13. *Let AF_1 and AF_2 be disjoint argumentation frameworks, and σ a join-normal semantics. Then $AF_1, AF_2 \sqsubseteq_\sigma AF_1 \uplus AF_2$, and $AF_1, AF_2 \sqsubseteq_\sigma AF_1 + AF_2$.*

We close this section by noting that σ-augmentations can be defined equivalently, for $\sigma \in \{\textbf{adm, comp, pref, gr, stb}\}$, using Caminada's labellings. More precisely, the following proposition is easy to prove from Caminada's characterizations ([7]) of σ-extensions, where the extension of a labelling from a subset to a larger set is the usual function extension.

Proposition 14. *Let $\sigma \in \{\textbf{adm, comp, pref, gr, stb}\}$. AF' is a σ-augmentation of the argumentation framework AF if and only if i) $Arg(AF) \subseteq Arg(AF')$, ii) any σ-labelling of AF can be extended to a σ-labelling of AF', and iii) the restriction of any σ-labelling of AF' to $Arg(AF)$ can be extended to a σ-labelling of AF.*

4 Normal Forms

In this section we confine ourselves only to $\sigma = \textbf{adm}$ and we refer to an **adm**-augmentation as an admissible augmentation. The results obtained for admissible augmentations can be easily adapted for σ-augmentations, where $\sigma \in \{\textbf{comp, pref, gr, stb}\}$.

An admissible augmentation can be viewed as adding "auxiliary" arguments in order to simplify the combinatorial structure of the given argumentation framework and, at the same time, maintaining all the credulous acceptability conclusions (see Proposition 11). We consider this simplified structure a *normal form* as follows.

Definition 15. An argumentation framework $AF = (A, D)$ is in *normal form* if for each $a \in A$ there are no $b, c \in a^+$ such that $b \neq c$ and $(b, c) \in D$. A set $S \subseteq A$ with the property, that $(a, b) \notin D$ for $a, b \in S$ and $a \neq b$, is referred as *d-conflict-free*.

Some properties of an argumentation framework in normal form are given in the next proposition. Note that the part ii) of this proposition shows that an argumentation framework is in normal form if and only if it can be constructed by adding its arguments one after one (the order does not matter), such that each new argument cannot attack two attacking arguments already added, and cannot be attacked by a pair of two attacking arguments already added.

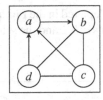

Fig. 2. An induced K_4 in AF

Algorithm 1. ELIM1$(AF; a, b, c)$

Input $AF = (A, D)$ *an argumentation framework,* $a, b, c \in A$ *with* $(a, b), (a, c), (b, c) \in D$;
Output $AF' = (A', D')$;
    add to A two new arguments a_1, a_2 giving A';
    put in D' all attacks in D;
    delete from D' the attack (a, b);
    add to D' the attacks $(a, a_1), (a_1, a_2), (a_2, b)$;
Return AF'

Proposition 16.

(i) *Let* $AF = (A, D)$ *be an argumentation framework in normal form. Then for each* $a \in A$ *the set* a^- *is d-conflict-free. Moreover, in any set of four arguments of* AF *there are two non-attacking arguments.*

(ii) *An argumentation framework* $AF = (A, D)$ *is in normal form if and only if for any ordering* $A = \{a_1, a_2, \ldots, a_n\}$, *the sets* $\bar{a}_i^- = a_i^- \cap \{a_1, \ldots, a_{i-1}\}$ *and* $\bar{a}_i^+ = a_i^+ \cap \{a_1, \ldots, a_{i-1}\}$ *are d-conflict-free, for all* $i \in \{2, \ldots, n\}$.

Proof (i) Suppose that there is $a_0 \in A$ such that a_0^- is not a d-conflict-free set, that is, there are $b, c \in a_0^-$ such that $b \neq c$ and $(b, c) \in D$. But then, $a_0, c \in b^+$ and $(c, a_0) \in D$, that is the set b^+ is not d-conflict free, a contradiction.
If there are four pairwise attacking arguments $\{a, b, c, d\} \subseteq A$, then the underlying undirected graph of AF contains a complete graph K_4 as an induced subgraph, with nodes a, b, c, d and the edge $\{a, b\}$ generated by the attack $(a, b) \in D$ (see Figure 2 below). Since a^+ in AF is d-conflict-free, we are forced to have $(c, a) \in D$ and $(d, a) \in D$; but then, a^- contains c and d, and since $(c, d) \in D$ or $(d, c) \in D$, a^- is not d-conflict-free, a contradiction.

(ii) Clearly, if AF is in normal form, then for any ordering $A = \{a_1, a_2, \ldots, a_n\}$, and any $i \in \{2, \ldots, n\}$, a_i^+ and a_i^- are d-conflict-free sets, therefore their subsets $\bar{a}_i^+$ and $\bar{a}_i^-$ are d-conflict-free. Conversely, let $AF = (A, D)$ satisfying the property stated. If AF is not in normal form, there are $a, b, c \in A$ such that $(a, b), (a, c), (b, c) \in A$. Any ordering of A with $a_1 := a, a_2 := b, a_3 := c$ has $\bar{a}_3^- = \{a, b\}$ which is not d-conflict-free, a contradiction. □

The next algorithm eliminates an attack between arguments attacked by the same argument in a given argumentation framework.

The effect of $ELIM1(AF;a,b,c)$ is depicted in the Figure 3. The squiggly arrows signify sets of all attacks, between arguments a,b,c and the sets of arguments in the rectangular boxes.

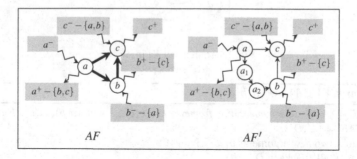

Fig. 3. Elimination of a bad triangle

Proposition 17. *The argumentation framework $AF' = (A', D')$, returned by $ELIM1(AF; a, b, c)$, is an admissible augmentation of AF.*

Proof. Let $S \subseteq A$ be an admissible set in AF. We prove that $S' \subseteq A'$ is an admissible set in AF', where:

$$S' = \begin{cases} S \cup \{a_2\} & \text{if } a \in S, \\ S \cup \{a_1\} & \text{if } a \notin S, b \in S, \\ S & \text{if } a \notin S, b \notin S. \end{cases}$$

If $S \subseteq A$ is an admissible set containing a in AF, then $S' = S \cup \{a_2\}$ is a conflict-free set in AF'. Indeed, no attack between the arguments in A is added by the algorithm ELIM1, hence S is conflict free in AF'. The only attacks containing a_2 are (a_1, a_2) and (a_2, b). But $a_1 \notin S$ (because $a_1 \notin A$), and $b \notin S$ (because $a \in S$, $(a, b) \in D$, and S is conflict-free set in AF). It follows that $S \cup \{a_2\}$ is a conflict-free set in AF'. The attack (a_1, a_2) against $S \cup \{a_2\}$ is defeated by (a, a_1), since $a \in S$. Any attack (x, y) with $x \in A - S$ and $y \in S$ is defeated by an attack (z, x) with $z \in S$, since S is admissible set in AF. It follows that $S \cup \{a_2\}$ is a conflict-free set in AF' which defends itself against any attack in AF', that is, $S \cup \{a_2\}$ is an admissible set in AF'.

If S is an admissible set in AF such that $a \notin S$ but $b \in S$, then adding a_1 to S we obtain a conflict-free set in AF' (since $a \notin S$ and $a_2 \notin S$, the only attacks involving a_1 – (a, a_1) and (a_1, a_2) – are not between arguments from $S \cup \{a_1\}$). The attack (a_2, b) on $S \cup \{a_1\}$ is defeated by (a_1, a_2). The attack (a, a_1) must be defeated by some argument $x \in a^- \cap S$, because in AF the attack (a, b) must be defeated. Any attack (x, y) with $x \in A - S$ and $y \in S$ is defeated by an attack (z, x) with $z \in S$, since S is admissible set in AF. It follows that $S \cup \{a_1\}$ is admissible set in AF'.

If S is an admissible set in AF not containing a and b, then S remains conflict-free since no attacks between arguments in A are added. Also all attacks from an arguments in S remain in AF', and no new attack against S is introduced. It follows that S continues to defend itself against any attack in AF', hence S is admissible set in AF'.

On the other hand, let $S' \subseteq A'$ be an admissible set in AF'. We prove that $S = S' \cap A$ is an admissible set in AF.

If S' is an admissible set containing a_2 in AF', then $a_1, b \notin S'$ (since S' is conflict-free and $(a_1, a_2), (a_2, b) \in D'$). Since $(a_1, a_2) \in D'$ and S' is admissible, it follows that a_1 must be attacked by S' in AF'. The only attack on a_1 in AF' is (a, a_1). Hence $a \in S'$. $S' - \{a_2\}$ is conflict free in AF, because $b \notin S'$. Any attack (x, y) with $x \in A - S$ and $y \in S$ is defeated by an attack (z, x) with $z \in S$, since S' is admissible set in AF'. It follows that $S' - \{a_2\} = S' \cap A$ is admissible set in AF.

If S' is admissible set containing a_1 in AF', a similar proof shows that $S' - \{a_1\} = S' \cap A$ is an admissible set in AF.

If S' is an admissible set in AF' such that $a_1, a_2 \notin S'$, we can suppose that $b \notin S'$. Otherwise, if $b \in S'$ then the attack (a_2, b) can not be defeated by S', since the only attack on a_2 in AF' is (a_1, a_2). Since the only additional attack involving at least one argument in S' can be (a, b), it follows that S' is a conflict-free set in AF and also defends itself against any attack in AF (because it was an admissible set in AF'). □

Proposition 18. *The argumentation framework $AF' = (A', D')$ given by ELIM1 $(AF; a, b, c)$ satisfies $AF \sqsubseteq_\sigma AF'$ for $\sigma \in \{comp, pref, gr, stb\}$.*

Proof. For $\sigma \in \{\textbf{comp, pref}\}$ the proof follows from Proposition 17. Indeed, if $S \in \sigma(AF)$ then S is an admissible set in AF and, by Proposition 17, can be extended to an admissible set in AF'. Since any admissible set can be extended to a complete or preferred extension, it follows that there is $S' \in \sigma(AF')$ such that $S \subseteq S'$. Conversely, if $S' \in \sigma(AF')$ then S' is an admissible set in AF' and, by Proposition 17, $S' \cap A$ can be extended to an admissible set in AF. Since any admissible set can be extended to a complete or prefered extension, it follows that there is $S \in \sigma(AF)$ such that $S' \cap A \subseteq S$.

For $\sigma = \textbf{stb}$ it is not difficult to verify that if $S \in \textbf{stb}(AF)$ then $S' \in \textbf{stb}(AF')$, where

$$S' = \begin{cases} S \cup \{a_2\} & \text{if } a \in S, \\ S \cup \{a_1\} & \text{if } a \notin S \end{cases}$$

and, if $S' \in \textbf{stb}(AF')$ then $S \in \textbf{stb}(AF)$, where

$$S = \begin{cases} S' - \{a_2\} & \text{if } a \in S', \\ S' - \{a_1\} & \text{if } a \notin S'. \end{cases}$$

For $\sigma = \textbf{gr}$, we use Proposition 14 and Observation 6. Clearly, if each $x \in Arg(AF)$ satisfies $x^- \neq \emptyset$, then the same property holds in AF' and $\textbf{gr}(AF) = \textbf{gr}(AF') = \{\emptyset\}$. Suppose that $\textbf{gr}(AF) = \{S\}$, $S \neq \emptyset$ and let Lab a $\textbf{gr}$-labelling of AF such that $S = Lab^{-1}(I)$. If $a \in S$, then we extend Lab to AF' by taking $Lab(a_1) = O, Lab(a_2) = I$, and the linear ordering of $Lab^{-1}(I)$ in AF' is obtained by considering a_2 the successor of a. It is not difficult to see that we obtain a $\textbf{gr}$-labelling of AF'. If $a \notin S$, and $Lab(a) = O$ then a $\textbf{gr}$-labelling of AF' is obtained by taking $Lab(a_1) = I$ and the linear ordering of $Lab^{-1}(I)$ in AF' is obtained by considering a_1 the successor of an attacker of a labeled

1. If $a \notin S$, and $Lab(a) = U$ then *Lab* remains a **gr**-labelling of AF'. A similar analysis can be used to show that the restriction to AF of a **gr**-labelling of AF' gives rise to a **gr**-labelling of AF.   □

By iterating the algorithm ELIM1, we obtain:

Algorithm 2. ELIMALL(AF)

$AF' := AF$;
foreach $a,b,c \in Arg(AF)s.t.(a,b),(a,c),(b,c) \in Def(AF)$ **do**
    $AF' := $ ELIM1$(AF';a,b,c)$
end
Return AF'

Proposition 19. *For any argumentation framework $AF = (A,D)$ there is an admissible augmentation $AF' = (A',D')$ in normal form. Furthermore, AF' can be constructed from AF in $O(|A|^3)$ time.*

Proof. Using Propositions 8 and 17, the above iteration of the algorithm ELIM1 returns an admissible augmentation AF' of the given AF. The for condition assures that AF', the returned argumentation framework, is in normal form. It remains to prove that the algorithm finishes.
We call a triangle $\{a,b,c\} \subseteq A'$ with $(a,b),(a,c),(b,c) \in D'$, a *bad triangle*. Clearly, the algorithm finishes when there is no bad triangle in the current argumentation framework.
In each for-iteration the total number of bad triangles of the current argumentation framework AF' decreases by 1. Indeed, the algorithm ELIM1$(AF';a,b,c)$ destroys a bad triangle and creates no new bad triangle, since the two new arguments a_1 and a_2 are not contained in a triangle in the new argumentation framework. Since the number of bad triangles in AF it at most $\binom{|A|}{3}$, and the running time of ELIM1$(AF';a,b,c)$ is $O(1)$, the final argumentation framework AF' is obtained in $O(|A|^3)$ time.   □

Summarizing the results obtained in this section, using Propositions 16ii), 18 and 19, we have the following theorem.

Theorem 20. *Any argumentation framework $AF = (A,D)$ has an admissible augmentation $AF' = (A',D')$ which can be formed by adding the arguments one after one such that each argument attacks a d-conflict-free set of its predecessors and is attacked by a d-conflict-free set of its predecessors. Furthermore AF' is also a σ-augmentation of AF for any Dung's classical semantics σ.*

The Figure 4 below suggests the way ín which the argumentation framework AF' from the above theorem is formed. Any new argument a_{new} added by an agent in a round cannot attack an existing pair of conflicting arguments, that is a_{new} attacks only a coherent set of existing arguments. The agent knows that, if she wants, in a later round can use a surrogate of a_{new} to attack other arguments which in the actual round are in conflict with those selected to be attacked. In the same time, from the set of existing arguments only a coherent set can attack the new argument. The other attacks will be simulated in future rounds by using again special surrogate arguments. In this way, a more logical scene of dispute can be devised, which is however (polynomially) longer as one in which our discipline policy is not followed.

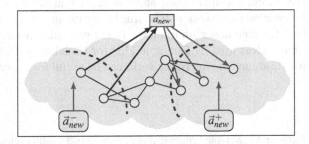

Fig. 4. Discipline policy in forming an *AF*

5 Discussion

In this paper we analyzed the syntactical structure of argumentation frameworks using σ-*augmentations* of argumentation frameworks. The use of σ-augmentations of argumentation frameworks for simplifying their syntactical structure is new with respect to the existing literature. Instead of studying the problem of how an argumentation framework may change if new arguments and/or attack relations are added (deleted) as usual in dynamic argumentation field [10, 5, 3], we are interested in transformations of argumentation frameworks with the property that the basic outcome – Dung's extensions – is not essentially changed. However, the results obtained in Proposition 13 for the particular case of join-normal semantics were already established in the above papers. Our results complements those in [15, 14], where the goal is to transform a given argumentation framework into a new one such that the σ-extensions of the original framework are in a certain correspondence with the σ'-extensions of the modified framework. Also, our method of obtaining the normal form is similar to rewriting techniques studied in other non-monotonic formalisms, as in [6].

Our discipline policy in the construction of argumentation framework can be useful for designing models of on-line social debates or legal disputes. However, it cannot be applied to argumentation formalisms that use defeasible argument schemes in combination with logic, i.e. deductive argumentation frameworks. In these frameworks the internal structure of the arguments generates and explains the nature of the attacks [8, 19]. If the existence of an attack (a, b) is solely determined by the information carried by the arguments a and b, we cannot forbid it. Our result could be an explanation of the difficulties encountered in instantiating (structured) logical argumentation graphs, where the attack relation depends solely on pairs of arguments and uses no other information about the set of arguments this pair belongs in (see [9, 17, 20]).

For future work, we intend to relate our result on the existence of the admissible augmentation normal form for an arbitrary argumentation framework to argument game based proof theories. An interesting research question(suggested by a referee) would be to study a converse of our augmentation relation which can be called *contraction*. More precisely, we intend to study the following problem: given an argumentation framework $AF = (A,D)$, a semantics σ, and $A_1 \subset A$, find $D_1 \subseteq A_1 \times A_1$ such that $AF_1 = (A_1,D_1)$ satisfies $AF_1 \sqsubseteq_\sigma AF$.

Also, we believe that our attempt to study and eventually simplify the structure of the attacks in an argumentation framework will be fruitful for the future algorithmic developments. Since bipartite argumentation frameworks are particular instances of normal forms, the algorithmic ideas used by Dunne in [13] for credulously acceptance of an argument in a bipartite argumentation frameworks can be useful for the general case.

References

[1] Baroni, P., Giacomin, M.: Solving semantic problems with odd-length cycles in argumentation. In: Nielsen, T.D., Zhang, N.L. (eds.) ECSQARU 2003. LNCS (LNAI), vol. 2711, pp. 440–451. Springer, Heidelberg (2003)

[2] Baroni, P., Giacomin, M.: On principle-based evaluation of extension-based argumentation semantics. Artificial Intelligence 171, 675–700 (2007)

[3] Baumann, R., Brewka, G.: Expanding argumentation frameworks: Enforcing and monotonicity results. In: Proc. of COMMA 2010, pp. 75–86 (2010)

[4] Bench-Capon, T.: Persuasion in practical argument using value-based argumentation frameworks. Journal of Logic and Computation 13, 429–448 (2003)

[5] Boella, G., Kaci, S., van der Torre, L.: Dynamics in argumentation with single extensions: Attack refinement and the grounded extension (Extended version). In: McBurney, P., Rahwan, I., Parsons, S., Maudet, N. (eds.) ArgMAS 2009. LNCS (LNAI), vol. 6057, pp. 150–159. Springer, Heidelberg (2010)

[6] Brass, S., Dix, J.: Characterizations of the disjunctive stable semantics by partial evaluation. Journal of Logic Programming 32, 207–228 (1997)

[7] Caminada, M.: On the issue of reinstatement in argumentation. In: Fisher, M., van der Hoek, W., Konev, B., Lisitsa, A. (eds.) JELIA 2006. LNCS (LNAI), vol. 4160, pp. 111–123. Springer, Heidelberg (2006)

[8] Caminada, M., Amgoud, L.: On the evaluation of argumentation formalisms. Artificial Intelligence 171, 286–310 (2007)

[9] Caminada, M., Wu, Y.: On the limitations of abstract argumentation. In: BNAIC, pp. 59–66 (2011)

[10] Cayrol, C., de Dupin Saint-Cyr, F., Lagasquie-Schiex, M.C.: Change in abstract argumentation frameworks: Adding an argument. Journal of Artificial Intelligence 38, 49–84 (2010)

[11] Dung, P.M.: On the acceptability of arguments and its fundamental role in nonmonotonic reasoning, logic programming and n-person games. Artificial Intelligence 77, 321–357 (1995)

[12] Dunne, P., Bench-Capon, T.: Coherence in finite argument systems. Artificial Intelligence 141, 187–203 (2002)

[13] Dunne, P.E.: Computational properties of argument systems satisfying graph-theoretic constraints. Artificial Intelligence 171, 701–729 (2007)

[14] Dvořák, W., Spanring, C.: Comparing the expressiveness of argumentation semantics. In: Proc. of COMMA 2006, pp. 261–272 (2012)

[15] Dvorák, W., Woltran, S.: On the intertranslatability of argumentation semantics. Artificial Intelligence 41, 445–475 (2011)
[16] Fraenkel, A.: Combinatorial game theory foundations applied to digraph kernels. The Electronic Journal of Combinatorics 4, 100–117 (1997)
[17] Hunter, A., Gorogiannis, N.: Instantiating abstract argumentation with classical logic arguments: Postulates and properties. Artificial Intelligence 175, 1479–1497 (2011)
[18] Pollock, J.L.: Cognitive Carpentry. A Blueprint for How to Build a Person. MIT Press, Cambridge (1995)
[19] Prakken, H.: An abstract framework for argumentation with structured arguments. Argumentation and Computation 1, 93–124 (2010)
[20] Prakken, H.: Some reflections on two current trends in formal argumentation. In: Artikis, A., Craven, R., Kesim Çiçekli, N., Sadighi, B., Stathis, K. (eds.) Sergot Festschrift 2012. LNCS (LNAI), vol. 7360, pp. 249–272. Springer, Heidelberg (2012)
[21] Prakken, H., Sartor, G.: A dialectical model of assessing conflicting arguments in legal reasoning. Artificial Intelligence and Law 4, 331–368 (1996)
[22] Prakken, H., Vreeswijk, G.: Logics for defeasible argumentation. In: Handbook of Philosophical Logic, 2nd edn., vol. 4, pp. 218–319. Kluwer (2002)

Graph-Based Dispute Derivations
in Assumption-Based Argumentation

Robert Craven[1], Francesca Toni[1], and Matthew Williams[2]

[1] Department of Computing / [2] Faculty of Medicine,
Imperial College London
{robert.craven,ft}@imperial.ac.uk, mhw@doctors.org.uk

Abstract. Arguments in structured argumentation are usually defined as trees. This introduces both conceptual redundancy and inefficiency in standard methods of implementation. We introduce *rule-minimal arguments* and *argument graphs* to solve these problems, studying their use in assumption-based argumentation (ABA), a well-known form of structured argumentation. In particular, we define a new notion of *graph-based dispute derivations* for determining acceptability of claims under the grounded semantics in ABA, study formal properties and present an experimental evaluation thereof.

1 Introduction

Assumption-Based Argumentation (ABA) [1,2,3,4,5] is a well-known framework for structured argumentation where, in contrast to abstract argumentation [6], arguments and attacks are not primitives but are derived from the rules of a given deductive system, assumptions and contraries. ABA has been applied in several settings (e.g. to support medical decision-making [7] and e-procurement [8]). ABA's applicability relies on the existence of computational mechanisms, based on various kinds of *dispute derivations* [2,3,5] that are formally proven to be correct procedures for conducting structured argumentation under various semantics. For example, [3] proposes *GB-dispute derivations* (GB-DDs in short) for determining whether sentences can be justified by *grounded* sets of arguments and assumptions.

Dispute derivations rely upon the computation of arguments that can be understood as trees [4], in a way similar to other frameworks for structured argumentation (e.g. [9,10,11,12]). This introduces both conceptual redundancy and inefficiency in standard methods of implementation, in that within an argument different rules for deriving the same conclusion may be used, potentially introducing unnecessarily points of attack and requiring additional defence efforts.

In this paper, we give a novel computational mechanism for ABA, in the form of *graph-Based GB-dispute Derivations* (gGB-DDs in short), and prove that they are correct under the *grounded* semantics for argumentation, in the same way that GB-DDs are. However, gGB-DDs avoid the conceptual redundancy and inefficiency of arguments as trees, by computing *rule-minimal arguments*,

E. Black, S. Modgil, and N. Oren (Eds.): TAFA 2013, LNAI 8306, pp. 46–62, 2014.
© Springer-Verlag Berlin Heidelberg 2014

corresponding to *argument graphs*, and making sure that only *parsimonious sets of arguments* from the grounded set are generated in support of sentences whose acceptability is being ascertained. In addition to using *argument graphs*, gGB-DDs also incorporate a loop-checking mechanism, inspired by that proposed by [13] for abstract argumentation [6].

In addition to studying theoretical properties of correctness of gGB-DDs, we also perform an empirical evaluation thereof, by comparing it with an implementation of standard GB-DDs. We perform two groups of experiments. The first uses randomly generated frameworks and randomly selected sentences from them, and the second uses a real-life example of the formalization within ABA of treatment recommendations for breast cancer. Both sets of experiments show promise both in terms of completion time for (successful) derivations as well as termination of (unsuccessful) derivations.

2   Background

ABA frameworks [4] are tuples $(\mathcal{L}, \mathcal{R}, \mathcal{A}, ^-)$:

- $(\mathcal{L}, \mathcal{R})$ is a deductive system, with $\mathcal{L}$ a set of *sentences* and $\mathcal{R}$ a set of *(inference) rules*, in this paper of the form $s_0 \leftarrow s_1, \ldots, s_n$, for $n \geqslant 0$ and $s_0, s_1, \ldots, s_n \in \mathcal{L}$;
- $\mathcal{A} \subseteq \mathcal{L}$ is a non-empty set, called the *assumptions*;
- $^-$ is a total mapping from $\mathcal{A}$ to $\mathcal{L}$; $\bar{a}$ is the *contrary* of a.

In the remainder of the paper, we take as given an ABA framework $(\mathcal{L}, \mathcal{R}, \mathcal{A}, ^-)$.

In ABA, arguments are proofs using rules and ultimately dependent on assumptions [4]:

- a *proof for $s \in \mathcal{L}$ supported by $S \subseteq \mathcal{L}$* is a (finite) tree with nodes labelled by sentences in $\mathcal{L}$ or $\top$, where the root is labelled by s and:
  - for all non-leaf nodes N (labelled by s_0), there is some rule $s_0 \leftarrow s_1, \ldots, s_n \in \mathcal{R}$ s.t. either (i) $n = 0$ and the child of N is labelled by $\top$ or (ii) $n > 0$ and N has n children, labelled by $s_1, \ldots, s_n$ respectively; and
  - S is the set of all sentences in $\mathcal{L}$ labelling the leaves;
- an *argument for $s \in \mathcal{L}$ supported by* a set of assumptions $A \subseteq \mathcal{A}$ is a proof for s supported by A.

For an argument a for s supported by A, $claim(\mathsf{a}) = s$ (s is the claim of a) and $support(\mathsf{a}) = A$

In ABA, an argument b *attacks* an argument a iff there is some $a \in support(\mathsf{a})$ s.t. $\bar{a} = s$, where $s = claim(\mathsf{b})$; a set of arguments B attacks a set of arguments A iff some $\mathsf{b} \in \mathsf{B}$ attacks some $\mathsf{a} \in \mathsf{A}$.

There are parallel, equivalent notions for sets of assumptions rather than arguments [3,14]. *A set of assumptions B attacks a set of assumptions A* iff there is some an argument for $\bar{a}$ supported by some $B' \subseteq B$, for some $a \in A$. Then *a set of assumptions* is deemed:

- *admissible* iff it does not attack itself and attacks every set of assumptions attacking it;
- *complete* iff it is admissible and contains all assumptions it can defend (by attacking all attacks against them);
- *grounded* iff it is minimally (w.r.t. $\subseteq$) complete.

A *sentence* $s \in \mathcal{L}$ is *admissible/complete/grounded* (optionally, *w.r.t.* $A \subseteq \mathcal{A}$) iff there are (i) (respectively) a set of assumptions $A \subseteq \mathcal{A}$ s.t. A is admissible or $A \subseteq A' \subseteq \mathcal{A}$ for some complete/grounded A' and (ii) an argument a s.t. *claim*(a) $= s$ and *support*(a) $\subseteq A$.

Several algorithms for determining acceptability of sentences in ABA have been proposed (e.g. see [2,3]). Here, we focus on GB-dispute derivations [3] (GB-DDs in short). Given a *selection function* (taking a multi-set and returning an element occurring in it) a *GB-DD* of a *defence set* $\Delta \subseteq \mathcal{A}$ for a sentence $s \in \mathcal{L}$ is a finite sequence of tuples[1] $\langle \mathcal{P}_0, \mathcal{O}_0, D_0, C_0 \rangle, \dots, \langle \mathcal{P}_n, \mathcal{O}_n, D_n, C_n \rangle$ where:

$$\mathcal{P}_0 = \{s\}, \ D_0 = \mathcal{A} \cap \{s\}, \ \mathcal{O}_0 = C_0 = \{\}$$
$$\mathcal{P}_n = \mathcal{O}_n = \{\}, \ \Delta = D_n$$

and for every i s.t. $0 \leqslant i < n$, only one σ in $\mathcal{P}_i$ or one S in $\mathcal{O}_i$ is selected, and:

1. If $\sigma \in \mathcal{P}_i$ is selected then
    (i) if $\sigma \in \mathcal{A}$, then
    $$\mathcal{P}_{i+1} = \mathcal{P}_i - \{\sigma\} \qquad \mathcal{O}_{i+1} = \mathcal{O}_i \cup \{\{\overline{\sigma}\}\}$$
    (ii) if $\sigma \notin \mathcal{A}$, then there exists some inference rule $\sigma \leftarrow R \in \mathcal{R}$ s.t. $C_i \cap R = \{\}$ and
    $$\mathcal{P}_{i+1} = (\mathcal{P}_i - \{\sigma\}) \cup R \qquad D_{i+1} = D_i \cup (\mathcal{A} \cap R)$$

2. If S is selected in $\mathcal{O}_i$ and σ is selected in S then
    (i) if $\sigma \in \mathcal{A}$, then
        (a) either σ is ignored, i.e.
        $$\mathcal{O}_{i+1} = (\mathcal{O}_i - \{S\}) \cup \{S - \{\sigma\}\}$$
        (b) or $\sigma \notin D_i$ and
        $$\mathcal{O}_{i+1} = \mathcal{O}_i - \{S\} \qquad \mathcal{P}_{i+1} = \mathcal{P}_i \cup \{\overline{\sigma}\}$$
        $$D_{i+1} = D_i \cup (\{\overline{\sigma}\} \cap \mathcal{A}) \qquad C_{i+1} = C_i \cup \{\sigma\}$$
    (ii) if $\sigma \notin \mathcal{A}$, then
    $$\mathcal{O}_{i+1} = (\mathcal{O}_i - \{S\}) \cup \{(S - \{\sigma\}) \cup R \mid \sigma \leftarrow R \in \mathcal{R}\}$$

Intuitively, GB-DDs can be seen as games between two (fictitious) players: a *proponent* ($\mathcal{P}_i$) and an *opponent* ($\mathcal{O}_i$), the former accumulating its *supporting/defending assumptions* (D_i), the latter being defeated on a number of *culprit assumptions* (C_i). Theorem 4.2 in [3] proves that GB-DDs are sound: if there is a GB-DD of Δ for s then s is grounded and Δ is admissible and contained in the grounded set of assumptions.

---

[1] This definition is adapted from [3] but adopting the convention, when defining changes in tuples, that omitted elements are unchanged. We will do the same for gGB-DDs in section 4.

3   Rule-Minimal Arguments

The notion of argument in ABA enforces a form of relevance (of the support to the claim), afforded by the notion of tree. However, this notion allows redundancies in arguments, in the sense illustrated by the following example. (Note that in depicting arguments as trees and (later) graphs, we follow the convention of letting nodes labelled by the heads of rules appear *above* nodes labelled by the sentences in the rules' bodies; this allows us to omit direction arrows on arcs.)

Example 1. Consider the ABA framework with $\mathcal{R} = \{p \leftarrow b; \quad p \leftarrow q, a; \quad q \leftarrow p\}; \mathcal{A} = \{a, b\};$ $\bar{a} = x, \bar{b} = y.$ Shown are arguments a_1 (left) and a_2 (right) for p, supported by $\{a, b\}$ and $\{b\}$ respectively. Argument a_1 is (redundantly) using two different rules to prove the two occurrences of p. ⌋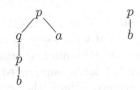

It is clear that such a situation is toxic, in that p has been proved in a certain way, which depends on p itself (which is then proved in a different way). A less toxic sort of case, but still involving redundancy, would be if some sentence s were proved in two different ways in an argument, but without there being one of those proofs depending on the other (so there would be no directed path from the two nodes labelled by s). Formally, these toxic forms of argument are charactered as follows.

Definition 1. *An argument* a *is* circular *if it contains a directed path from a node N labelled by some $s \in \mathcal{L}$ to another node N' labelled by s. An argument* a *is* flabby *if there are different nodes N, N', with the same labels, such that the children of N are labelled by different members of $\mathcal{L} \cup \{\top\}$ from those labelling the children of N'.* ⌋

It is easy to show that an argument may be flabby without being circular, but that where an argument is circular, it is necessarily flabby (see below-left). Note, though, not all nodes N, N' by which the argument counts as circular need determine the argument as flabby (see the nodes labelled p, below-right).

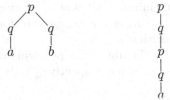

We take the view that both the 'toxic' case of circularity, and the 'merely redundant' case of flabbiness, are undesirable. Accordingly, we define a restricted notion of argument, enforcing that, for every sentence in an argument, the same rules are used to justify the sentence at all its occurrences. Given that circularity of a implies flabbiness, the definition just marks out the non-flabby arguments. Formally:

Definition 2. *An argument* a *is* rule-minimal *iff for any two nodes* N, N' *in* a *labelled by the same* $s \in \mathcal{L}$ *the children of* N *and* N' *are labelled by the same elements of* $\mathcal{L} \cup \{\top\}$.

Clearly, an argument a is rule-minimal iff it is neither circular nor flabby.

In example 1, a_2 is rule-minimal whereas a_1 is not. Note that there are infinitely many arguments for p in this example; a_2 is the only rule-minimal one.

Rule-minimal arguments may still contain redundancies in their support, as illustrated by the following example.

Example 2. Consider the ABA framework in example 1 but with $q \leftarrow p$ in $\mathcal{R}$ replaced by $q \leftarrow b$. Shown are rule-minimal arguments a_1 (left) and a_2 (right) for p, supported by $\{a, b\}$ and $\{b\}$ respectively. Here, the support of a_1 is non-minimal, as $support(a_1) \subset support(a_2)$.

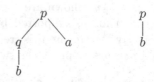

Definition 3. *An argument* a *is* support-minimal *iff there is no* a' *such that* $claim(a')=claim(a)$ *and* $support(a') \subset support(a)$.

Example 2 shows that rule-minimal arguments may not be support-minimal. The following example shows that support-minimal arguments may not be rule-minimal.

Example 3. Consider the ABA framework with $\mathcal{R} = \{p \leftarrow p; p \leftarrow a\}; \mathcal{A} = \{a\}; \bar{a} = x$. Shown are support-minimal arguments a_1 (left) and a_2 (right) for p, both supported by $\{a\}$. Here, only a_2 is rule-minimal. (This is the smallest such example; other, less 'trivial' ones could be provided.)

$$\begin{array}{cc} p & p \\ | & | \\ p & a \\ | & \\ a & \end{array}$$

Whereas the notion of support-minimal argument is 'global', in that to check whether an argument is support-minimal this needs to be compared with all other arguments, the notion of rule-minimal argument is 'local', in that to check whether an argument is rule-minimal all that is required is a syntactic check of the argument. Moreover, every argument can be transformed into a rule-minimal argument, by means of algorithm 1.[2]

Note that at lines 6 and 9 the algorithm performs non-deterministic choices (of a node/sentence and of a sub-tree, respectively). By making alternative such

---

[2] Here: $rank(N, T)$ returns the length of the path from N to the root of tree T; $rank(T)$ returns the maximum rank of any node in tree T; $path(N, N', T)$ returns the set of nodes on the (unique) path from N to N' (not including N) in tree T; $substitute(T, N, T')$ takes tree T and replaces the sub-tree rooted at N by tree T'; $nodes(T)$, $root(T)$ and $subTrees(T)$ return, respectively, the set of nodes, the root and the set of sub-trees of tree T; $pickOne(S)$ chooses a member of S; $label(N, a)$ returns the label of node N in argument a (this is a member of $\mathcal{L}$ or $\top$, see section 2).

Algorithm 1. *reduce*(a: argument)

1: $r := 0$
2: $seen := \{\}$
3: **while** $r \leqslant rank(\mathsf{a})$ **do**
4:     $nodes := \{N \in nodes(\mathsf{a}) \mid (rank(N, \mathsf{a}) = r) \wedge (label(N, \mathsf{a}) \in \mathcal{L} - \mathcal{A}) \wedge (N \notin seen)\}$
5:     **while** $nodes \neq \{\}$ **do**
6:         $N := pickOne(nodes)$
7:         $s := label(N, \mathsf{a})$
8:         $leafTrees := \{\mathsf{b} \in subTrees(\mathsf{a}) \mid (label(root(\mathsf{b})) = s) \wedge \neg \exists N'[N' \in nodes(\mathsf{b}) - \{root(\mathsf{b})\} \wedge label(N', \mathsf{a}) = s]\}$
9:         $\mathsf{b} := pickOne(leafTrees)$
10:        **for all** $N' \in nodes(\mathsf{a})$ s.t. $label(N', \mathsf{a}) = s \wedge \neg \exists X[X \in path(N', root(\mathsf{a}), \mathsf{a}) \wedge label(X) = s]$ **do**
11:            $\mathsf{a} := substitute(\mathsf{a}, N', \mathsf{b})$
12:        **end for**
13:        $seen := seen \cup \{N \in nodes \mid label(N) = s\}$
14:        $nodes := nodes - seen$
15:     **end while**
16:     $r := r + 1$
17: **end while**
18: **return** a

---

choices different arguments can be obtained, as illustrated next.

Example 4. Given argument a_1 (left), depending on the choice of sub-tree at line 9, the algorithm may return a_2 (middle) or a_3 (right).

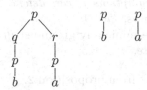

Definition 4. *Given a set of arguments* A, *a reduction of* A *is a set of arguments* B *s.t. (i) for each* b $\in$ B *there is an argument* a $\in$ A *s.t.* b = *reduce*(a)*; (ii) for each argument* a $\in$ A *there exists an argument* b $\in$ B *s.t.* b = *reduce*(a).

In example 4, $\{\mathsf{a}_2\}$, $\{\mathsf{a}_3\}$, $\{\mathsf{a}_2, \mathsf{a}_3\}$ are reductions of $\{\mathsf{a}_1\}$.

In general, given an argument a, algorithm 1 'reduces' it to a rule-minimal argument a′ whose claim is identical to, and whose support is a subset of that of a, as sanctioned by:

Proposition 1. *Let* a *be an argument for* c *supported by* S. *Then* a′ = *reduce*(a) *is a rule-minimal argument for* c *supported by* S′ ⊆ S.

Proof. First, algorithm 1 terminates, since (i) a *is finite and thus rank*(a) *is finite; (ii) there are finitely many nodes at lines 10, 13; (iii) at every iteration of the external while loop the set nodes is smaller. Secondly,* a′ *is a sub-tree of* a *with the same root, and so the same claim and support as* a. *Thirdly, trivially* a′ *is an argument in the ABA sense. Finally, by construction, each sentence in* a′ *is proven by only one rule.*

Then, directly from proposition 1:

Proposition 2. *(i) For every rule-minimal argument for s supported by A there exists an argument of s supported by A. (ii) For every argument for s supported by A there exists a rule-minimal argument of s supported by $A' \subseteq A$.*   ⌟

Clearly, it is computationally advantageous, when determining whether a sentence is acceptable under some semantics, to focus on rule-minimal arguments: there are fewer of them, they are smaller, and they have smaller supports. We define new notions of acceptability w.r.t. rule-minimal arguments, and prove they are equivalent to the original notions.

To extend notions of acceptability for sets of assumptions when focusing on rule-minimal arguments, we define a variant of the notion of attack between sets of assumptions:

Definition 5. *A set of assumptions B* rule-minimally attacks *a set of assumptions A iff there is some rule-minimal argument for $\bar{a}$ supported by some $B' \subseteq B$, for some $a \in A$.*
A set of assumptions is

- rule-minimally admissible *iff it does not rule-minimally attack itself and it rule-minimally attacks every set of assumptions rule-minimally attacking it;*
- rule-minimally complete *iff it is rule-minimally admissible and contains all assumptions it can defend (by rule-minim. attacking all rule-min. attacks against them);*
- rule-minimally grounded *iff it is minimally (w.r.t. $\subseteq$) rule-minimally complete.*   ⌟

Directly from proposition 2:

Proposition 3. *Let $A \subseteq \mathcal{A}$ be a set of assumptions. A is admissible/complete/ grounded iff A is rule-minimally admissible/complete/grounded (respectively).* ⌟

Thus, when deciding whether a set of assumptions is acceptable, one can restrict attention to rule-minimal arguments.

As in the case of standard ABA, we can lift notions of acceptability at the assumption level to the sentence level:

Definition 6. *$s \in \mathcal{L}$ is* rule-minimally admissible/complete/grounded *(optionally, w.r.t. $A \subseteq \mathcal{A}$) iff there are (i) (respectively) a set of assumptions $A \subseteq \mathcal{A}$ s.t. A is rule-minimally admissible or $A \subseteq A' \subseteq \mathcal{A}$ for some rule-minimally complete/grounded A' and (ii) a rule-minimal argument a s.t. claim(a) = s and support(a) $\subseteq A$.*   ⌟

Then, directly from proposition 3:

Proposition 4. *$s \in \mathcal{L}$ is rule-minimally admissible/complete/grounded/iff s is admissible/complete/grounded (respectively).*   ⌟

Rule-minimally acceptable sets of assumptions may still contain redundancies, as illustrated by the following example.

Example 5. Consider the ABA framework with $\mathcal{R} = \{(1) \; p \leftarrow s, r, a; (2) \; s \leftarrow r, a; (3) \; r \leftarrow a; (4) \; p \leftarrow b; (5) \; q \leftarrow d; (6) \; q \leftarrow e\}$; $\mathcal{A} = \{a, b, c, d, e\}$; $\bar{a} = x, \bar{b} = y, \bar{c} = q, \bar{d} = p, \bar{e} = p$. (The rules are numbered for later use.) Then c is (rule-minimally) admissible, complete and grounded, w.r.t. $\{c, a, b\}$, $\{c, a\}$ and $\{c, b\}$. $\{c, a\}$ and $\{c, b\}$ determine a more parsimonious set of arguments, in that p is supported by $\{a\}$ (in the case of $\{c, a\}$) or $\{b\}$ (for $\{c, b\}$).   ⌐

Definition 7. *A set of arguments A is* parsimonious *iff there exist no two different sub-trees* a, b *of any (possibly different) arguments in A such that the root of a and b is labelled by the same sentence.*   ⌐

Every argument in a parsimonious set is rule-minimal. In example 5, the set of assumptions $\{c, a\}$ and $\{c, b\}$ support parsimonious arguments, whereas $\{c, a, b\}$ does not.

It is easy to see that in order to determine acceptability of sentences, it suffices to focus on parsimonious arguments:

Proposition 5. *A sentence s is rule-minimally admissible/complete/grounded iff there are (i) a parsimonious set of arguments A and (ii) a $\in$ A with claim(a) = s s.t. (respectively) A is admissible or A $\subseteq$ A' for some complete/grounded A'.* ⌐

The relevance of this will be seen in the following section. When constructing a set A of proponent arguments (according to the algorithm in Definition 9) starting from some claim s, we can restrict attention to parsimonious A; this is a further efficiency and removal of redundancy.

4   Graph-Based GB-Dispute Derivations

A graph-based GB dispute derivation gradually derives justifications for sentences in a way guaranteed to produce rule-minimal arguments which are parsimonious and grounded. They rely upon arguments defined as graphs, as follows:

Definition 8. *A graph-based argument is an acyclic directed graph (V, E) with $V \subseteq (\mathcal{L} \cup \{\top\})$, and for any $s \in V$:*

- *if $s \in (\mathcal{L} - (\mathcal{A} \cup \{\top\}))$, then for a unique rule $s \leftarrow s_1, \ldots, s_m$ in $\mathcal{R}$, (i) if $n = 0$, then $\{x | (s, x) \in E\} = \{\top\}$; or (ii) if $n > 0$, then $\{x | (s, x) \in E\} = \{s_1, \ldots, s_n\}$;*
- *if $s \in V - (\mathcal{L} - (\mathcal{A} \cup \{\top\}))$, then there are no outgoing edges from s in E;*
- *there is a unique $c \in (V \cap \mathcal{L})$ (the claim) s.t. there is no edge (s, c) in E and there is a path $(c, \ldots, s)$ for any $s \in V$.*   ⌐

It is evident that argument graphs can be 'unravelled' into rule-minimal arguments, as illustrated below for example 5:

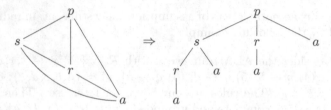

gGB-DDs work over tuples $(\mathcal{P}_i, \mathcal{O}_i, D_i, C_i, JsP_i, JsO_i, Att_i, G_i)$, where $\mathcal{P}_i$ are the sentences the proponent has yet to prove; $\mathcal{O}_i$ contains tuples $(X, Js, \mathbf{C})$ representing partially-completed opponent arguments: $\mathbf{C}$ is the claim, X the sentences supporting the argument yet to be proved, and Js a set of *justifications*–pairs (s, R) where s is a sentence and R is either the body of a rule used to justify s in the context of $(X, Js, \mathbf{C})$, or $*$ if $s \in \mathcal{A}$; D_i and C_i are as in GB-dispute derivations (see section 2); JsP_i contains justifications (pairs (s, R), as above) for the proponent arguments, and JsO contains the justification triples for the opponent arguments; Att_i contains points of attack between proponent and opponent arguments, and G_i records the dependency graph among sentences, grown gradually during the derivation.

Definition 9. *Given a selection function, a gGB-DD of defence set Δ and dialectical structure (JsP, JsO, Att) for a sentence $s \in \mathcal{L}$ is a finite sequence of tuples $(\mathcal{P}_0, \mathcal{O}_0, D_0, C_0, JsP_0, JsO_0, Att_0, G_0), \ldots, (\mathcal{P}_n, \mathcal{O}_n, D_n, C_n, JsP_n, JsO_n, Att_n, G_n)$, where*

$$\mathcal{P}_0 = \{s\}, D_0 = \mathcal{A} \cap \{s\}, \mathcal{O}_0 = C_0 = JsP_0 = JsO_0 = Att_0 = G_0 = \{\}$$
$$\mathcal{P}_n = \mathcal{O}_n = \{\}, \Delta = D_n, JsP = JsP_n, JsO = JsO_n, Att = Att_n$$

and for every i s.t. $0 \leqslant i < n$, only one σ in $\mathcal{P}_i$ or one $(X, Js, \mathbf{C})$ in $\mathcal{O}_i$ is selected, and:

1. *If $\sigma \in \mathcal{P}_i$ is selected then*
   (i) *if $\sigma \in \mathcal{A}$ then*

$$\mathcal{P}_{i+1} = \mathcal{P}_i - \{\sigma\}$$
$$\mathcal{O}_{i+1} = \mathcal{O}_i \cup \{(\{\bar{\sigma}\}, \{\}, \bar{\sigma}) \mid \neg \exists R((\bar{\sigma}, R) \in JsO_i\}$$
$$JsP_{i+1} = JsP_i \cup \{(\sigma, *)\}$$
$$Att_{i+1} = Att_i \cup \{(\bar{\sigma}, \sigma)\}$$
$$G_{i+1} = G_i \cup \{(\bar{\sigma}, \sigma)\}, \text{ and } G_{i+1} \text{ is acyclic}$$

   (ii) *if $\sigma \notin \mathcal{A}$, then (a) there is some $(\sigma, R) \in JsP_i$, and $\mathcal{P}_{new}$ is $\{\}$; or, if not, (b) there exists some $\sigma \leftarrow R \in \mathcal{R}$, $\mathcal{P}_{new}$ is R—and (in both cases) $C_i \cap R = \{\}$ and*

$$\mathcal{P}_{i+1} = (\mathcal{P}_i - \{\sigma\}) \cup \mathcal{P}_{new}$$
$$D_{i+1} = D_i \cup (R \cap \mathcal{A})$$
$$JsP_{i+1} = JsP_{i+1} \cup \{(\sigma, R)\}$$
$$G_{i+1} = G_i \cup \{(x, \sigma) \mid x \in R\}, \text{ and } G_{i+1} \text{ is acyclic}$$

2. If (X, Js, C) is selected in $\mathcal{O}_i$ and σ is selected in X then
   (i) if $\sigma \in \mathcal{A}$, then:
       (a) σ is ignored, i.e. $\mathcal{O}_{i+1} = (\mathcal{O}_i - \{(X, Js, C)\}) \cup \{(X - \{\sigma\}, Js \cup \{(\sigma, *)\}, C)\}$.
       (b) or $\sigma \notin D_i$ and if $\exists R((\bar{\sigma}, R) \in JsP_i)$ then $P_{new} = \{\}$; otherwise, $P_{new} = \{\bar{\sigma}\}$ and

$$P_{i+1} = P_i \cup P_{new}$$
$$\mathcal{O}_{i+1} = \mathcal{O}_i - \{(X, Js, C)\})$$
$$D_{i+1} = D_i \cup (\{\bar{\sigma}\} \cap \mathcal{A})$$
$$C_{i+1} = C_i \cup \{\sigma\}$$
$$JsO_{i+1} = JsO_i \cup \{(X - \{\sigma\}, Js \cup \{(\sigma, *)\}, C)\}$$
$$Att_{i+1} = Att_i \cup \{(\bar{\sigma}, \sigma)\}$$
$$G_{i+1} = G_i \cup \{(\bar{\sigma}, \sigma)\}, \text{ and } G_{i+1} \text{ is acyclic}$$

   (ii) if $\sigma \notin \mathcal{A}$ then
        − if $\exists R((\sigma, R) \in Js)$, let $O_{new} = \{((X - \{\sigma\}) \cup R, Js, C)\}$ and let $G_i* = G_i$;
        − otherwise let $O_{new} = \{((X-\{\sigma\})\cup R, Js\cup \{(\sigma, R)\}, C) \mid (\sigma \leftarrow R) \in \mathcal{R}\}$ and let $G_i* = G_i \cup \{(x, \sigma) \mid \exists(\sigma \leftarrow R) \in \mathcal{R}, \ x \in R\}$ and G_i* is acyclic.
        then: $\mathcal{O}_{i+1} = \mathcal{O}_i \cup O_{new}$ and $G_{i+1} = G_i*$.   ⌟

As an illustration, consider table 1 (Att_i and G_i are omitted for lack of space). The opponent has two arguments attacking the claim c, introduced in step 2 when the incomplete argument for q was developed using rules (4) and (5) (in example 5). The proponent attacks opponent argument $(\{d\}, \{(q, 4)\}, q)$ using rule (1) for p (step 4). Then, when the proponent must attack the second opponent argument $(\{e\}, \{(q, 5)\}, q)$, at step 8, the algorithm notices that $\bar{e} = p$ has already been argued for by the proponent (at case 2(i)(b) in definition 9, the condition which sets P_{new} to $\{\}$), so an argument for p is not developed again (avoiding the possibility that it would be developed using an alternative rule). It is here that we ensure parsimoniousness. The acyclicity check on G_i ensures that this avoidance of recomputation is sound; the final graph G_n is shown below.

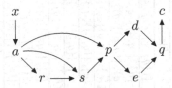

Definition 10. Let J be a set of pairs of the form (s, R); if $s \in \mathcal{A}$ then R is $*$; otherwise there exists some rule $s \leftarrow R \in \mathcal{R}$. The arguments determined by J are those constructible from the ABA framework $(\mathcal{L}', \mathcal{R}', \mathcal{A}', \bar{\ }')$:
   $\mathcal{L}' = \{s \mid \exists(s', R) \in J[s = s' \vee (R \neq * \wedge s \in R)]\}$;
   $\mathcal{R}' = \{s \leftarrow R \mid (s, R) \in J, \ R \neq *\}$;
   $\mathcal{A}' = \{a \mid (a, *) \in J\}$; $\bar{a}' = a$, for all $a \in \mathcal{A}$.   ⌟

Table 1. Sample gGB-DD for c in example 5

	$\mathcal{P}$	O	D	C	JsP	JsO
0	$\{c\}$	$\{\}$	$\{c\}$	$\{\}$	$\{\}$	$\{\}$
1	$\{\}$	$\{(\{q\},\{\},q)\}$	$\{c\}$	$\{\}$	$\{(c,*)\}$	$\{\}$
2	$\{\}$	$\{(\{d\},\{(q,4)\},q), (\{e\},\{(q,5)\},q)\}$	$\{c\}$	$\{\}$	$\{(c,*)\}$	$\{\}$
3	$\{p\}$	$\{(\{e\},\{(q,5)\},q)\}$	$\{c\}$	$\{d\}$	$\{(c,*)\}$	$\{(\{\},\{(d,*),(q,4)\},q)\}$
4	$\{s,a\}$	$\{(\{e\},\{(q,5)\},q)\}$	$\{a,c\}$	$\{d\}$	$\{(c,*),(p,1)\}$	$\{(\{\},\{(d,*),(q,4)\},q)\}$
5	$\{a,r\}$	$\{(\{e\},\{(q,5)\},q)\}$	$\{a,c\}$	$\{d\}$	$\{(c,*),(p,1),(s,2)\}$	$\{(\{\},\{(d,*),(q,4)\},q)\}$
6	$\{a\}$	$\{(\{e\},\{(q,5)\},q)\}$	$\{a,c\}$	$\{d\}$	$\{(c,*),(p,1),(r,3),(s,2)\}$	$\{(\{\},\{(d,*),(q,4)\},q)\}$
7	$\{\}$	$\{(\{e\},\{(q,5)\},q), (\{x\},\{\},x)\}$	$\{a,c\}$	$\{d\}$	$\{(a,*),(c,*),(p,1), (r,3),(s,2)\}$	$\{(\{\},\{(d,*),(q,4)\},q)\}$
8	$\{\}$	$\{(\{x\},\{\},x)\}$	$\{a,c\}$	$\{d,e\}$	$\{(a,*),(c,*),(p,1),(r,3),(s,2)\}$	$\{(\{\},\{(d,*),(q,4)\},q),(\{\},\{(e,*),(q,5)\},q)\}$
9	$\{\}$	$\{\}$	$\{a,c\}$	$\{d,e\}$	$\{(a,*),(c,*),(p,1),(r,3),(s,2)\}$	$\{(\{\},\{(d,*),(q,4)\},q),(\{\},\{(e,*),(q,5)\},q)\}$

It is apparent that where, for any s, there is at most one pair (s, R) in JsP, then the set of arguments determined by JsP is parsimonious. Furthermore, the set JsP can be more compactly visualized as a graph, whose nodes are the sentences mentioned in JsP, and where there is an edge (s, r) iff there is a pair $(s, R) \in JsP$ s.t. $r \in R$. For the gGB-DD in table 1, this visualization is shown below, together with the dialectical relationship with opponent arguments from JsO:

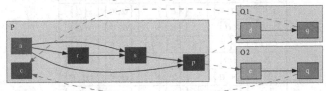

In the diagram, the proponent's justifications are shown in the large box on the left; the opponent's arguments are the two small boxes on the right; and attacks are dashed lines.

Proposition 6. *If there is a gGB-DD for s then there is a GB-DD for s with the same defence set.*

Proof. (Sketch: the details are omitted for reasons of space.) The structure of gGB-DDs precisely mirrors that presented in section 2 for GB-DDs; the sets $\mathcal{P}_i$ are the same, and the members $(X, Js, \mathbf{C})$ of the sets $\mathcal{O}_i$ have components X which precisely correspond to the members of $\mathcal{O}_i$ in GB-DDs. However, because of the checks at steps 1(ii), 2(i)(b) and 2(ii) of gGB-DDs, some steps of a GB-DD may be omitted in a gGB-DD. So, given a gGB-DD $(\mathcal{P}_0, \mathcal{O}_0, D_0, C_0, JsP_0, JsO_0, Att_0, G_0), \ldots, (\mathcal{P}_m, \mathcal{O}_m, D_m, C_m, JsP_m, JsO_m, Att_m, G_m)$ there is a GB-DD $(\mathcal{P}'_0, \mathcal{O}'_0, D'_0, C'_0), \ldots, (\mathcal{P}'_n, \mathcal{O}'_n, D'_n, C'_n)$ with $(m \leqslant n)$, such that to each step $(\mathcal{P}_i, \mathcal{O}_i, D_i, C_i, JsP_i, JsO_i, Att_i, G_i)$ there corresponds a step of the GB-DD $(\mathcal{P}'_j, \mathcal{O}'_j, D'_j, C'_j)$ with $\mathcal{P}'_j = \mathcal{P}, \mathcal{O}'_j = \{X \mid \exists (X, Js, \mathbf{C}) \in \mathcal{O}_i\}, D'_j = D_i, C'_j = C_i$ and s.t. the corresponding steps fall into the same order. ⌐

The table below shows the GB-DD corresponding to the gGB-DD of table 1. The numbers of corresponding steps from the gGB-DD are in brackets.

Proposition 6 also holds in the reverse, 'completeness' direction, with the modification that the defence set may be a subset of that for the corresponding GB-DD.

Proposition 7. *If there is a gGB-DD for s with defence set Δ, then s is grounded, Δ is admissible, and there is $\Delta' \supseteq \Delta$ s.t. Δ' is grounded.*

Proof. By proposition 6, there is a GB-DD for s with defence set Δ; then from Theorem 4.2 of [3], the result is immediate. ⌐

Proposition 8. *If there is a gGB-DD for s with defence Δ, then the arguments determined by JsP are parsimonious.*

Proof. By construction, there are no two pairs $(s, R_1), (s, R_2)$ in JsP with $R_1 \neq R_2$. Thus the arguments determined by JsP can only be parsimonious. ⌐

	$\mathcal{P}$	$\mathcal{O}$	$\mathcal{D}$	$\mathcal{C}$
0 [0]	$\{c\}$	$\{\}$	$\{c\}$	$\{\}$
1 [1]	$\{\}$	$\{\{q\}\}$	$\{c\}$	$\{\}$
2 [2]	$\{\}$	$\{\{d\},\{e\}\}$	$\{c\}$	$\{\}$
3 [3]	$\{p\}$	$\{\{e\}\}$	$\{c\}$	$\{d\}$
4 [4]	$\{s,a\}$	$\{\{e\}\}$	$\{a,c\}$	$\{d\}$
5 [5]	$\{a,r\}$	$\{\{e\}\}$	$\{a,c\}$	$\{d\}$
6 [6]	$\{a\}$	$\{\{e\}\}$	$\{a,c\}$	$\{d\}$
7 [7]	$\{\}$	$\{\{e\},\{x\}\}$	$\{a,c\}$	$\{d\}$
8	$\{p\}$	$\{\{x\}\}$	$\{a,c\}$	$\{d,e\}$
9	$\{s,a\}$	$\{\{x\}\}$	$\{a,c\}$	$\{d,e\}$
10	$\{a,r\}$	$\{\{x\}\}$	$\{a,c\}$	$\{d,e\}$
11	$\{a\}$	$\{\{x\}\}$	$\{a,c\}$	$\{d,e\}$
12 [8]	$\{\}$	$\{\{x\}\}$	$\{a,c\}$	$\{d,e\}$
13 [9]	$\{\}$	$\{\}$	$\{a,c\}$	$\{d,e\}$

5   Experiments

To compare the original GB-DDs to the gGB-DDs of section 4, we implemented both in Prolog. The implementation of the original algorithm (proxdd) used its (equivalent) variant presented in [5], which records the arguments as well as the attack relationships between them as they are constructed. This is appropriate for purposes of comparison, as our algorithm and its implementation (grapharg) record the rule-minimal justification structure as it proceeds.[3]

In comparing the results of the two implementations, it is important to set the same search strategy in each case. Each algorithm has various choice points (indicated by words such as 'selected', or disjunctions), and to compare like with like it is necessary that the selection be done using the same criteria.

Another fact we had to consider was that, for many strategies, the original GB-DDs quickly used up all of Prolog's memory resources. (For such strategies, the gGB-DD implementation, grapharg, typically terminated or timed out.) We therefore used strategies for which memory was typically not exceeded for both implementations.

For the first set of experiments, we randomly generated ABA frameworks $(\mathcal{L}, \mathcal{R}, \mathcal{A}, ^-)$ to use as experimental data. The random generation followed a very simple procedure of choosing contraries to assumptions at random, and populating rule bodies with sentences randomly. The proportions of assumptions to non-assumptions in the language; the minimum and maximum number of sentences per rule body; the minimum and maximim number of rules per sentence serving as rule head—these and similar parameters can all be supplied by the user. In our experiments, the mean language size ($|\mathcal{L}|$) was 126 sentences, and the mean number of rules ($|\mathcal{R}|$) was 178, with a mean of 3.6 sentences in the

---

[3] Both implementations are freely available for download from
http://www.doc.ic.ac.uk/~rac101/proarg/.

body of each rule. For each randomly-selected framework, we randomly selected 10 sentences from the language of the framework to use as queries. We tested each query-framework pair for both implementations, on the same strategy, with a time-out of two minutes. In all cases we asked the implementations to find all possible solutions. The results, for 65 frameworks, are presented in tabular form below (times in secs.):

	grapharg	proxdd
Av. time (both complete)	0.447	6.618
Av. time (overall)	54.716	87.413
percentage timeout	40.871	71.208

We recorded the mean time for query-framework pairs where both implementations completed (first row), as well as the mean time for query-framework pairs that may have reached the chosen time-out of two minutes.

Our algorithm shows a marked improvement in the mean times taken to answer queries, in the two cases where both implementations completed, and when one of them reached time-out. The percentage of time-outs itself was much lower for gGB-DDs. These results are encouraging and confirm our theoretical evaluation.

We were surprised by the comparisons on number of solutions found: in the cases where both implementations completed, the same number of solutions were discovered. One might have expected that the guarantee of rule-minimality in the case of the graph-based algorithm would have meant that fewer solutions would have been produced by the graph-based algorithm, with the non-rule-minimal ones being cut. The fact that the figures are the same in each case is an indication that the ABA frameworks our random-generator produced did not exhibit the scope for non-rule-minimal arguments—for the chosen queries, at least. Finally, the very high number of total solutions found overall for the graph-based algorithm (13,653 vs 217) is owed to one particular randomly-generated query-framework pair, for which grapharg found 13,427 solutions (proxdd found none before time-out). If that particular query-framework pair is left out of account, then the comparison comes to 226 vs 217.

For the experiments based on the breast-cancer study, we used data originally published in [15], and which we have used in the context of experiments on parallel argumentation in [7]. The ABA frameworks represent an ontology of drugs and treatments, and recommendations from 57 papers referred to in the National Cancer Institute's breast cancer guideline [16], as well as hypothetical patient data. In half of the frameworks, we introduced random preferences over the recommendations from the various clinical trials; this simulates the weights which patients or doctors might give to the various clinical trials from which the recommendations are drawn. Further, in half of the frameworks, we flattened the ontology to a set of Prolog facts, rather than retaining the original combination of Prolog facts and rules. The ABA resulting frameworks consist of an average of 947 rules ($|\mathcal{R}|$), and 11 queries were made per framework—each query asking whether a particular regime of chemotherapy or drugs was recommended.

We again made these experiments using our graph-based implementation, `grapharg`, and compared it to the existing best implementation of the standard algorithm, `proxdd`. The results are shown in tabular form below.

	grapharg	proxdd
Av. time (both complete)	0.575	3.827
Av. time (overall)	23.630	46.015
percentage timeout	18.182	36.364

The results are broadly consistent with those obtained for the randomly-generated frameworks in the previous round of experiments, and indicate a similar, increased performance and utility in the case of graph-based dispute derivations.

6   Conclusion

We proposed an equivalent but 'leaner' form of ABA, based on rule-minimal, graph-based arguments, and gave a variant of an existing mechanism for computation under the grounded semantics in ABA, namely GB-dispute derivations [3] (GB-DDs in short), to restrict computation to graph-based arguments only. We have proven theoretically that our graph-Based GB-dispute Derivations (gGB-DDs in short) are sound, under the grounded semantics, and conducted a number of experiments suggesting that our gGB-DDs are more efficient than standard GB-DDs, both in terms of completion time and terminating computations.

Like others, we are concerned with 'efficient' arguments. [11] require arguments to have a minimal support; the analogous notion for us (minimal sets of assumptions as support) is neither implied by, nor implies, that of rule-minimality. Support-minimality needs to be ascertained 'globally', by checking the entire framework for alternative arguments—rule-minimality can be verified without such a global check. Our notion of rule-minimality is close to condition 3 in the definition of argument structure (Def. 3.1) in [10].

Our notion of gGB-DD borrows from the work of [13] the use of a graph whose acyclicity is an essential prerequisite of success. However, whereas [13] provide a computational machinery for abstract argumentation [6], we have focused on structured argumentation in the form of ABA. Moreover, [13] consider several argumentation semantics; we have focused on the grounded semantics.

There is an established completeness result for the derivation algorithm for GB-DDs, from [3], which holds for p-acyclic ABA frameworks. This result is inherited for the algorithms defined in the present paper; this can be shown straightforwardly. We have omitted this for reasons of space in the current paper.

In future work, it would be interesting to see whether our notions of rule-minimal and graph-based arguments could be applied in other frameworks for structured argumentation, e.g. those of [9,10,11,12].

We conducted preliminary experimentation with an implementation of our gGB-DDs and shown that it moderately, but consistently, improves upon an implementation of standard GB-DDs. We plan to further this experimentation to a larger pool of frameworks and queries.

Like us, [7] also focus on obtaining more efficient computational support for ABA in the context of a medical application, but by resorting to parallelisation, where different strategies lead to different threads of execution. It would be interesting to see how parallelisation could further quicken our implementation.

We have focused on the computation of argumentation under the grounded semantics. We have already defined variants of our gGB-DDs to compute the admissible semantics, and implemented that in **grapharg**. We plan also to define and implement a variant for the ideal semantics; using the parametric methodology of [5] this should be straightforward.

References

1. Bondarenko, A., Dung, P.M., Kowalski, R., Toni, F.: An abstract, argumentation-theoretic approach to default reasoning. Artificial Intelligence 93(1-2), 63–101 (1997)
2. Dung, P., Kowalski, R., Toni, F.: Dialectic proof procedures for assumption-based, admissible argumentation. Artificial Intelligence 170, 114–159 (2006)
3. Dung, P., Mancarella, P., Toni, F.: Computing ideal sceptical argumentation. Artificial Intellgence 171(10-15), 642–674 (2007)
4. Dung, P.M., Kowalski, R.A., Toni, F.: Assumption-based argumentation. In: Rahwan, I., Simari, G.R. (eds.) Argumentation in AI, pp. 25–44. Springer (2009)
5. Toni, F.: A generalised framework for dispute derivations in assumption-based argumentation. In: Artificial Intelligence (2012) (in press)
6. Dung, P.: On the acceptability of arguments and its fundamental role in non-monotonic reasoning, logic programming and n-person games. Artificial Intelligence 77, 321–357 (1995)
7. Craven, R., Toni, F., Hadad, A., Cadar, C., Williams, M.: Efficient support for medical argumentation. In: Brewka, G., Eiter, T., McIlraith, S.A. (eds.) Proc. 13th International Conference on Principles of Knowledge Representation and Reasoning, pp. 598–602. AAAI Press (2012)
8. Matt, P.A., Toni, F., Stournaras, T., Dimitrelos, D.: Argumentation-based agents for eprocurement. In: Berger, M., Burg, B., Nishiyama, S. (eds.) Proceedings of the 7th Int. Conf. on Autonomous Agents and Multiagent Systems (AAMAS 2008)-Industry and Applications Track, pp. 71–74 (2008)
9. Modgil, S., Prakken, H.: A general account of argumentation with preferences. In: Artificial Intelligence (2012) (in press)
10. García, A.J., Simari, G.R.: Defeasible logic programming: An argumentative approach. Theory and Practice of Logic Programming 4(1-2), 95–138 (2004)
11. Besnard, P., Hunter, A.: Elements of Argumentation. MIT Press (2008)
12. Amgoud, L.: The outcomes of logic-based argumentation systems under preferred semantics. In: Hüllermeier, E., Link, S., Fober, T., Seeger, B. (eds.) SUM 2012. LNCS, vol. 7520, pp. 72–84. Springer, Heidelberg (2012)
13. Thang, P.M., Dung, P.M., Hung, N.D.: Towards a common framework for dialectical proof procedures in abstract argumentation. Journal of Logic and Computation 19(6), 1071–1109 (2009)

14. Toni, F.: Reasoning on the web with assumption-based argumentation. In: Eiter, T., Krennwallner, T. (eds.) Reasoning Web 2012. LNCS, vol. 7487, pp. 370–386. Springer, Heidelberg (2012)
15. Williams, M., Hunter, A.: Harnessing Ontologies for Argument-Based Decision-Making in Breast Cancer. In: ICTAI (2), pp. 254 261. IEEE Computer Society (2007)
16. NCI: Breast Cancer PDQ (Stage I, II, IIA, and operable IIIC Breast Cancer) (2007)

Argument Schemes for Normative Practical Reasoning

Nir Oren

Department of Computing Science, University of Aberdeen, AB24 3UE, Scotland
n.oren@abdn.ac.uk

Abstract. This paper describes a framework for practical reasoning in the presence of norms. We describe a formal normative model constructed using Action-based Alternating Transition Systems. This model is able to represent goals; obligations and prohibitions and their violation; and permissions, which are used to derogate the former. Inspired by Atkinson's scheme for practical reasoning, we utilise argument schemes and critical questions to both show and reason about how goals and obligations lead to preferences over the possible executions of the system. The model then allows us to determine if sufficient information has been provided in order to perform practical reasoning, identify the best courses of action, and explain *why* specific sequences of actions should be executed by agents within the system.

1 Introduction

The violation of a norm, as expressed through obligations, permissions and prohibitions, can result in sanctions being imposed on an agent. Since such sanctions are undesirable, the agent will typically attempt to comply with its norms while pursuing goals. However, it may be the case that the violation of a norm can yield greater rewards than the cost of sanctions to the agent (e.g. if the violation results in the achievement of an important goal). Norms therefore impose *soft constraints* upon an agent, and when performing practical reasoning, an agent must weigh up the penalties (and rewards) involved in violating (or adhering to) norms against the rewards provided by achieving its goals.

Now while practical reasoning frameworks taking norms into account have been previously proposed (e.g. [4]), explaining the decision processes taken by agents when acting in such a system, particularly to non-experts, is a difficult task. In this paper, we build on the work of Atkinson et al.[1] to propose an argumentation based framework for practical reasoning in the presence of norms, with the longer term aim of investigating how argumentation can be used to contribute to the explanation of the agent's decision processes. While decision and game theory provide processes whereby a rational agent (i.e. one that attempts to maximise some utility, or reach a most preferred state) can identify an optimal sequence of actions, we argue that in the practical reasoning domain, such processes (due to their intrinsically conflicting nature) can be more easily understood through argument schemes. The instantiation of such schemes, and

E. Black, S. Modgil, and N. Oren (Eds.): TAFA 2013, LNAI 8306, pp. 63–78, 2014.
© Springer-Verlag Berlin Heidelberg 2014

their associated critical questions, results in an argument framework which can be evaluated to identify the appropriate action(s) to pursue. These arguments can then be presented to explain why the specific course of action was selected.

In this paper we propose a semantics for norms and goals that can be used to describe the possible executions of a system. The set of all these executions then forms the core of the practical reasoning process. Building on this formal system, we introduce a set of argument schemes together with the appropriate critical questions, which can in turn be used to identify the most preferred system execution path.

In the next section we describe our formal model in detail. Following this, Section 3 introduces the argument scheme and maps it to our formal model. An example of the approach is provided in Section 4, and we discuss related and future work in Section 5, before concluding the paper in Section 6.

2   The Model

In this section we describe our formal model, which is based on action-based alternating transition systems (AATSs) [10]. Such AATSs are intended to encode all possible evolutions of a system due to the actions of all agents within it, representing the various states through which the system can pass through by means of a branching time tree structure. Since this can be described as a Kripke system, we can reason about the possible trajectories of the system by means of a branching time logic. After introducing the basic concepts of AATSs, we detail how goals and norms, as well as more complex concepts such as violations and the derogation of obligations can be specified using the logic.

2.1   Semantics

Definition 1. *(AATS, [10])* *An Action-based alternating transition system (AATS) is a tuple of the form*

$$S = \langle Q, q_0, Ag, Ac_1, \ldots Ac_n, \rho, \tau, \Phi, \pi \rangle$$

Where

- Q *is a finite non-empty set of* states.
- $q_0 \in Q$ *is the* initial state.
- $Ag = \{1, \ldots, n\}$ *is a finite non-empty set of agents.*
- Ac_i, *with* $1 \leq i \leq n$, *is a finite and non-empty set of actions for each agent, where actions for different agents do not overlap.*
- $\rho : Ac_i \to 2^Q$ *is an action precondition function which identifies the set of states from which some action* $\alpha \in Ac_i$ *can be executed*
- $\tau : Q \times J_{Ag} \to Q$ *where* $J_{Ag} = \prod_{i \in Ag} Ac_i$, *is the system transition function identifying the state that results from executing a set of actions from within* J_{Ag} *in some state.*
- Φ *is a finite and non-empty set of atomic propositions*

– $\pi : Q \to 2^{\Phi}$ *is the interpretation function which identifies the set of proposi-*
tions satisfied in each state.

Following [10], we define a computation (also referred to as a path) to be an
infinite sequence of states $\lambda = q_0, q_1, \ldots,$ *where* $q_i \in \tau(q_{i-1}, \alpha)$ *for some* α *for*
which $q_i \in \rho(\alpha)$. *We index a state within a path using array notation. Thus, the*
first element of path λ *can be referenced via* $\lambda[0]$, *while a sub-path of the path*
starting at the second element and consisting of the remainder of the path is
written $\lambda[1, \infty]$.

An AATS encodes the possible states of the world that result from executing
actions, and can be viewed as a Kripke structure with the transition function τ
acting as the accessibility relation. We can therefore represent the AATS using
CTL* operators [7], allowing us to refer to both single paths and groups of paths
in the structure. We define the semantics of CTL* in two stages, first defining
state formulae, following which we describe path formulae. The syntax of CTL*
emerges directly from the semantics and is not detailed due to space constraints.

Definition 2. (State Formulae) *State formulae are evaluated with respect to*
an AATS S and a state $q \in Q$:
   $S, q \models \top$
   $S, q \not\models \bot$
   $S, q \models p$ *iff* $p \in \pi(q)$
   $S, q \models \neg\psi$ *iff* $S, q \not\models \psi$
   $S, q \models \psi \lor \phi$ *iff* $S, q \models \psi$ *or* $S, q \models \phi$
   $S, q \models A\psi$ *iff* $S, \lambda \models \psi$ *for all paths where* $\lambda[0] = q$
   $S, q \models \mathcal{E}\psi$ *iff* $S, \lambda \models \psi$ *for some path where* $\lambda[0] = q$

Definition 3. (Path Formulae) *Path formulae are evaluated with respect to*
an AATS S and a path λ.
   $S, \lambda \Vmodels \psi$ *iff* $S, \lambda[0] \models \psi$ *where* ψ *is a state formula.*
   $S, \lambda \Vmodels \neg\psi$ *iff* $S, \lambda \not\Vmodels \psi$
   $S, \lambda \Vmodels \psi \lor \phi$ *iff* $S, \lambda \Vmodels \psi$ *or* $S, \lambda \Vmodels \phi$
   $S, \lambda \Vmodels \bigcirc\psi$ *iff* $S, \lambda[1, \infty] \Vmodels \psi$
   $S, \lambda \Vmodels \Diamond\psi$ *iff* $\exists u \in \mathbb{N}$ *such that* $S, \lambda[u, \infty] \Vmodels \psi$
   $S, \lambda \Vmodels \Box\psi$ *iff* $\forall u \in \mathbb{N}$ *it is the case that* t $S, \lambda[u, \infty] \Vmodels \psi$
   $S, \lambda \Vmodels \phi\mathcal{U}\psi$ *iff* $\exists u \in \mathbb{N}$ *such that* $S, \lambda[u, \infty] \Vmodels \psi$ *and*
           $\forall v$ *s.t.* $0 \leq v < u,$ $S, \lambda[v, \infty] \Vmodels \phi$

Note that state formulae refer only to a single possible world, or state, within
a path, even in the case when the state operator then refers to a path formula
(c.f. the A and $\mathcal{E}$ operators). Path formulae always refer to entire paths which
begin at some state (e.g. the next state in the case of the $\bigcirc$ operator).

These semantics capture the evolution of a system over time due to agent
actions. However, they say nothing about why one path might be followed by
agents rather than another in order to effect certain actions and therefore lead
to certain states. To capture this notion we define a relation over paths, written
$\succeq^g$ to represent the preferences of some group of agents g with respect to one

group of paths over another. This group of paths is specified by means of a path formula. Thus, for example, $\Diamond a \succeq^{\{\alpha\}} \Diamond \neg a$ captures the preference of agent α for those paths in which a is eventually true over those paths where it is eventually false. When dealing with a single agent, or referring to a group by a label, we write $\succeq^\alpha$ instead of $\succeq^{\{\alpha\}}$. Finally, we write $\lambda \succ^g \lambda'$ to represent the case when $\lambda \succeq^g \lambda'$ and $\lambda' \not\succeq^g \lambda$, and abbreviate the situation where both $\lambda \succeq^g \lambda'$ and $\lambda' \succeq^g \lambda$ hold as $\lambda \sim^g \lambda'$.

Now a question arises as to the origin and form of the preference relation, and we propose that the agent's goals, together with the norms found in the system constrain (but do not fully specify) it. For example, if an agent has a goal, then it should prefer those paths where the goal is achieved to those paths where it is not. However, this goal does not impose any preference ordering between those paths in which the goal is achieved (or indeed between those paths where it is not). In other words, if a goal g is achieved in paths λ_1 and λ_2, but not in paths $\lambda_3 \ldots \lambda_8$, then $\lambda_m \succ^g \lambda_n$ where $m \in \{1, 2\}$ and $n \in \{3 \ldots 8\}$, but we cannot identify a preference between λ_1 and λ_2 (and similarly, cannot specify whether, for example λ_3 is preferred to λ_7).

We begin a more detailed exploration of the preference relationship by examining goals more closely.

2.2   Goals

Goals identify states of affairs in the world that an agent prefers (and should be able to bring about in part due to their action, but we do not formally impose this requirement). In other words, when undertaking practical reasoning, agents prefer those actions forming paths wherein their goals are achieved to those where they are not. We therefore represent goals through path formulae, identifying the state of affairs that must exist for a goal to be considered as *met* or *satisfied*.

We consider both achievement and maintenance goals [9]. The former identifies a state of affairs that must hold at some point in time, while the latter requires some state of affairs to be maintained until some deadline. Both of these goals can be easily represented in our logic, though in this paper we ignore conditional goals (i.e. goals of the form " If X is the case then a goal Y exists").

Definition 4. *(Goals) A formula γ describes a path where an achievement goal is met if it is of the form $\neg d \mathcal{U} x$. It describes a maintenance goal path if it takes the form $(\neg d \wedge x) \mathcal{U} d$.*[1]

x represents the state of affairs that the goal aims to satisfy, while d represents the goal's deadline.

The above definition therefore requires that the deadline d not be in force, and x be in force *until* the deadline d occurs, matching the intuition behind a maintenance goal.

---

[1] The semantics of $\mathcal{U}$ require us to ensure that the deadline does not occur before it actually does.

Since achieving a goal γ is preferred by some agent or group over not achieving the goal, we can identify a preference ordering over possible paths by the simple rule

$$\gamma \succ^g \neg\gamma$$

2.3 Norms

Norms within a system represent obligations, prohibitions and permissions imposed on, or provided to, entities within a society or group. Obligations and prohibitions (respectively) identify the states of affairs that a *target* must ensure do (or do not) occur. If these states of affairs do not (or do) occur, then the norm is *violated*. Following [3,2,6], we treat permissions as exceptions to obligations and prohibitions: in the case of an obligation, if a state of affairs is ordinarily obliged, but a permission not to achieve the state exists, then even if the state of affairs is not achieved, no violation occurs. Furthermore, we treat prohibitions as obligations *not* to have some state of affairs hold.

Now we view norms primarily as *social* constructs. That is, an obligation (for example) specifies *who* should behave in some way (i.e. it has a set of target agents), and also identifies which agent — or set of agents — desires that this behaviour occur. The latter form the norm's *creditors* (c.f. the social commitments of Singh [16]).

Following this perspective, we view a norm as expressing a preference over a state of affairs *for its creditors* rather than its target. That is, a creditor prefers those situations in which a norm is not violated to one where it is. Now this implies that a norm, in isolation, has no direct effect on its target's behaviour. Instead, we believe that such behaviour regulation stems from two sources. First, the violation of a norm could (via contrary-to-duties [5]) permit a sanction to be imposed on the violator. Second, social ties could mean that a norm's target takes the norm creditor's preferences into account (e.g. I may fulfil my obligations to my friends because I care about their feelings rather than any threat of sanctions). Note however that in our argument framework, we merge all individual agent preferences into a global preference, limiting the effects of this approach; investigating a more "local" view of preferences forms part of our future work.

Next, we provide a high level overview of the different norm types, before proceeding to formalise them.

Obligations and Prohibitions. As mentioned above, obligations identify states of affairs that should be achieved by the *target* of the obligation. Obligations are imposed by some group (the *creditor*) on the target[2]. Furthermore, if an obligation is not fulfilled, then the creditor could potentially sanction the obligation's target. An obligation therefore encodes two concepts, namely the preference by the creditor for paths wherein the obligation is fulfilled over those

---

[2] Note that this creditor could be the entire society of agents.

where it is not. Second, if an obligation is not fulfilled, then a record must be kept that it has been *violated* in order to enable sanctions to be put into place.

In line with goals, we consider two distinct types of obligations (c.f. [8]), namely *achievement* obligations, which require the target to see to it that some state of affairs holds at some point before some *deadline* occurs, and *maintenance* obligations, which require the target to ensure that the state of affairs holds at all points before the deadline. Before formally defining obligations, we must examine the notion of a permission, which acts as an exception to an obligation.

Permissions. A permission acts as an exception to an obligation (or a prohibition). In other words, given an obligation to achieve some state of affairs, and a permission not to achieve it, not achieving this state of affairs will not result in a violation. As discussed previously, we model prohibitions as negated obligations, and therefore concentrate on the interactions between permissions and obligations. Like other modalities, a permission is given by some creditor to a target, and affects the creditor's concept of a violation. Similarly, permissions identify some (permitted) state of affairs, and a deadline.

Clearly, interpreting a permission in this way makes little sense without an obligation or prohibition being present, and we therefore encode permissions through the presence of a permission proposition, with one such unique proposition being defined for every combination of creditor, target and state of affairs. Since our AATS has only a finite number of agents and propositions, there are a finite number of such proposition symbols. More precisely, we use the proposition $\mathcal{P}^g_{a,x}$ to indicate that agent a has obtained permission from g to see that the state of affairs x *is not the case* in the state where the proposition is true. We can now define a permission through the use of a formula in our logic, writing $P^g_a(x|d)$ as an abbreviation of the formula

$$\mathcal{AP}^g_{a,x}\mathcal{U}d$$

This formula ensures that a permission is in force over all possible paths in the system until deadline d. Since we must ensure that the permission predicate does not hold when no permission is in force, we require the following axiom in the system:

$$\mathcal{A}\square(\neg P^g_a(x|d) \rightarrow \neg \mathcal{P}^g_{a,x})$$

Note that a permission can exist while an obligation is not present. However, in such a situation, the permission will have no effect on the system.

Formalising Obligations. Obligations identify states of affairs that should hold, and a failure to abide by the requirements of an obligation leads to a violation. We encode such a violation through a violation proposition (as done in, for example [17]), in a manner similar to the permission proposition. In other words, the proposition $\mathcal{V}^g_{a,x,d}$ represents a violation by the target a of the obligation, with respect to a creditor g, to see to it that state of affairs x was the case with respect to a deadline d.

An achievement obligation, abbreviated $O_a^g(x|d)$ requiring the target a to ensure that some state of affairs x holds before a deadline d towards a creditor g is represented as follows:

$$\mathcal{A}(\neg \mathcal{V}_{a,x,d}^g \wedge \neg d \wedge \neg x)\mathcal{U}\;(((\neg x \wedge d \wedge \neg \mathcal{P}_{a,x}^g \wedge \mathcal{V}_{a,x,d}^g) \vee$$
$$(\neg x \wedge d \wedge \mathcal{P}_{a,x}^g \wedge \neg \mathcal{V}_{a,x,d}^g)) \vee$$
$$(x \wedge \neg \mathcal{V}_{a,x,d}^g))$$

This obligation therefore requires the following conditions to be met on all possible paths:

1. Before either the deadline or x occurs, the obligation is not considered violated (the first line of the obligation following the $\mathcal{U}$).
2. If the deadline occurs and x is not the case, then if there is no permission allowing this to occur, a violation is recorded. Alternatively, if such a permission exists, then no violation is recorded (this is encoded by the second line of the proposition).
3. Finally, if x is achieved (before the deadline), then no violation is recorded (this is captured by the final line of the proposition).

Therefore, our encoding of an obligation essentially states that if an obligation is in force, it is only violated if the deadline is reached without the desired state of affairs being achieved, assuming that no permission exists allowing the obligation to be ignored. However, nothing in this definition prevents a violation from existing in a state of affairs without an associated obligation. We therefore require that the following axiom hold:

$$\mathcal{A}\square(\neg O_a^g(x|d) \rightarrow \neg \mathcal{V}_{a,x,d}^g)$$

Maintenance obligations requires that a state of affairs be maintained until some deadline[3]. We abbreviate a maintenance obligation on a from g requiring x be the case until deadline d as $O_a^g(m:d)$. This stands for the following formula.

$$\mathcal{A}\,((\neg x \wedge \neg d \wedge (\neg \mathcal{P}_{a,x}^g \wedge \mathcal{V}_{a,x,d}^g) \vee$$
$$(\mathcal{P}_{a,x}^g \wedge \neg \mathcal{V}_{a,x,d}^g)) \vee (x \wedge \neg d))\mathcal{U}d$$

In other words, before the deadline, either x is maintained, or x is not maintained, in which case the obligation is violated if an associated permission does not exist.

The requirement for the lack of a violation, as stated above, is repeated for maintenance obligations:

$$\mathcal{A}\square(\neg O_a^g(x:d) \rightarrow \neg \mathcal{V}_{a,x,d}^g)$$

In discussing obligations so far, we have identified the situations in which they are violated. Detecting these situations allows for the modelling of *contrary to*

---

[3] We assume that this maintenance requirement comes into force with the obligation, ignoring obligations of the form "maintain x between 5pm and 8pm tomorrow".

duty obligations, which come into force when a violation occurs. Such contrary to duties are a form of conditional obligation, which comes into force only when some state of affairs holds in the environment, and generally, such conditionals can be represented via an axiom utilising an implication relation, e.g.

$$\mathcal{A}(\mathcal{V}_{a,x,d}^{g} \to O_{a}^{g}(x'|d'))$$

We now turn our attention to the second aspect of obligations, namely their interactions with preferences over paths through the system. Informally, the presence of an obligation or prohibition imposed by some creditor leads to that creditor preferring those paths through the system where the obligation is complied with (i.e. not violated) over those where it is violated. This leads to the following rule within our system:

$$\Box \neg \mathcal{V}_{a,x,d}^{g} \succ^{g} \Diamond \mathcal{V}_{a,x,d}^{g}$$

Note that we do not prefer fewer violations over more violations, as other preferences, for example regarding the interval length of a violation, could affect the preference ordering.

Having formalised permissions and obligations, we now consider prohibitions. In this work we consider only achievement prohibitions, that is, prohibitions on seeing to it that a state of affairs holds (until the prohibition's deadline occurs). Such a prohibition can in fact be modelled as a maintenance obligation — a prohibition on achieving x until some deadline is a maintenance obligation $O_{a}^{g}(\neg x : d)$, requiring the target to ensure x holds until the deadline.

We conclude this section by making several observations regarding our normative system. Unlike models such as [8], violations in our model do not persist. That is, a violation identifies a single, specific point in time at which an obligation was violated, and is associated with the violated obligation via x and d, the creditor (g) and target (a). Violations are represented as unique propositions in our language.

It should also be noted that our representation of obligations means that an achievement obligation ceases to have force (in the sense of implying a violation) at the moment of deadline; work such as [8] instead specifies that an obligation must still be fulfilled even after it has been violated, and we will investigate this interpretation in future work.

Also note that our preference relation over obligations implies that agents/social groups are, in a sense, "honest", that is, they prefer the outcome implied by compliance with the obligation over one where the obligation is violated.

3   Practical Reasoning via Argumentation

Our formal model contains two distinct aspects. The first aspect consists of the AATS, which identifies all possible evolutions of the system, while the second aspect is associated with the preferences over paths (i.e. sequence of actions) that agents hold. Our aim is to identify whether a most preferred path through the system exists, and explain *why* this is the case. In order to do so, we make use of *argument schemes* [18], defeasible rules expressed in natural language which can be used to justify some conclusion. An argument scheme is associated with a set of *critical questions*, which are used to prevent the inferences of the rule from being made.

The argument schemes we define in the next section are instantiated as arguments within an extended argument framework (EAF) [12]. The evaluation of such an EAF according to a specific argumentation semantics results in a set of *extensions*, each containing a set of arguments. Each of these sets of arguments is, in some sense, justified. We begin by describing our argument schemes in more detail, following which we describe EAFs and the extension evaluation procedure.

3.1 Argument Schemes

The first scheme we consider puts forth the argument that any sequence of actions through the AATS can be justified. Each path through the AATS thus results in a unique argument which is an instantiation of the following argument scheme.

AS1: In situation S, the sequence of joint actions $A_1, \ldots A_n$ should be executed.
This argument scheme is associated with two critical questions:

CQ1-1. Does some other sequence of actions exist that can be executed?
CQ1-2. Is there a more preferred sequence of actions to this one?

The first critical question will result in symmetric attacks between all instantiations of AS1 for all possible paths (which are instantiations of the sequence of actions) through the system. The second critical question will lead to an asymmetric attack from another AS identifying the more preferred sequence of actions to the less preferred sequence of action. Now a reason for one sequence of actions to be preferred over another is that it achieves a goal, or complies with a norm that is important to the agent. We therefore introduce several additional argument schemes capturing these possible reasons.

AS2: The sequence of joint actions $A_1, \ldots, A_n$ is preferred over $A'_1, \ldots A'_n$ as the former achieves a goal which the latter does not.
Critical questions here are as follows:

CQ2-1. Is there some other sequence of actions which achieves a more preferred goal than the one achieved by this action sequence?
CQ2-2. Does the sequence of actions lead to the violation of a norm?

AS3 and AS4 are argument schemes that deal with obligations and permissions:
AS3: The sequence of actions $A_1, \ldots A_n$ should be less preferred than sequence $A'_1, \ldots A'_n$ as, in the absence of permissions, the former violates a norm while the latter does not.

CQ3-1. Is the goal resulting from the sequence of actions more preferred than the violation?

CQ3-2. Does the violation resulting from this norm result in some other, more important violation not occurring?

CQ3-3. Is there a permission that derogates the violation?

AS4: There is a permission that derogates the violation of an obligation. Note that the separation between AS3 and AS4 is intended purely for explanatory purposes; conceptually, it would be possible to merge both of these schemes into one by considering an argument scheme which deals with violation once permissions are considered.

Finally, we can identify several simple argument schemes that allow an agent to associate preferences between different goals and norms, thereby enabling the instantiation of the critical questions for AS2 and AS3.

AS5: Agent α prefers goal g over goal g'

AS6: Agent α prefers achieving goal g to not violating n

AS7: Agent α prefers not achieving goal g to violating n

AS8: Agent α prefers violating n to violating n'

AS9: Agent α prefers situation A to B

This last argument scheme is intended to allow an agent to express individual preferences with regards to outcomes.

3.2   Argument Scheme Semantics

We now provide a brief formalisation of the argument schemes and critical questions based on our AATS semantics. Above, our argument schemes referred to sequences of actions, which are equivalent to paths through the AATS. As done previously, we label this AATS S below. Our formalisation makes use of the formulae obtained from goals and norms to express preferences over paths. That is, given S, and preferences expressed using CTL* formula ϕ and ψ of the form $\phi \succeq^a \psi$, We specify a set of *path preferences* $\lambda \geq^a \lambda'$ for any paths λ, λ' where $S, \lambda \models \phi$ and $S, \lambda' \models \psi$.

Given a sequence of actions $j_1, \ldots, j_n$, we can obtain a path λ as the path beginning in the initial state $q_0 \in Q$, and for which for all $i = 1 \ldots n, \tau(q_{i-1}, j_i) = q_i$.

Given an AATS, we can then identify valid instantiations of the argument schemes and critical questions, resulting in an argument framework whose evaluation allows us to determine justified action sequences[4].

AS1: There is a path λ obtained from the sequence of actions $j_1, \ldots j_n$.

AS2: There is a goal γ and two paths λ, λ' obtained from the sequence of joint actions , $j_1, \ldots j_n$ and $j'_1, \ldots j'_m$ respectively, and it is the case that $S, \lambda \models \gamma$ and $S, \lambda' \not\models \gamma$.

---

[4] Note that for AS2-4, the natural language version of the scheme refers to preferences. These are left implicit in the formalisation, as such preferences emerge from our definition of goals and obligations, as per Sections 2.2 and 2.3.

AS3: There exist two paths λ, λ' obtained from the sequence of joint actions $j_1, \ldots j_n$ and $j'_1, \ldots j'_m$ respectively, and it is the case that $S \backslash \mathcal{P}^g_{a,x}, \lambda \models \mathcal{V}^g_{a,x,d}$ and $S \backslash \mathcal{P}^g_{a,x}, \lambda' \not\models \mathcal{V}^g_{a,x,d}$

AS4: There is a path λ obtained from the sequence of joint actions $j_1, \ldots j_n$, and $S \backslash \mathcal{P}^g_{a,x}, \lambda \models \mathcal{V}^g_{a,x,d}$ but $S, \lambda \not\models \mathcal{V}^g_{a,x,d}$.

AS5-AS9 express individual agent preferences between goals, and violations. For example, an agent may prefer to achieve one goal over another (AS5), or avoid achieving a goal if it means violating a norm (AS7).

AS5: There are goals γ, γ' where $S, \lambda \models \gamma$ and $S, \lambda' \models \gamma'$ and $\gamma \succeq^\alpha \gamma'$

AS6: There is a goal γ and violation $\mathcal{V}^g_{a,x,d}$ such that $\gamma \succeq^\alpha \neg \mathcal{V}^g_{a,x,d}$

AS7: There is a goal γ and violation $\mathcal{V}^g_{a,x,d}$ such that $\neg\gamma \succeq^\alpha \mathcal{V}^g_{a,x,d}$

AS8: There are two violations $\mathcal{V}^g_{a,x,d}, \mathcal{V}^h_{b,y,e}$ such that $\mathcal{V}^g_{a,x,d} \succeq^\alpha \mathcal{V}^h_{b,y,e}$

AS9: $A \succeq^\alpha B$ where A, B are formulae in our language.

Now let us turn our attention to the critical questions, using the same definitions as above.

CQ1-1: There is a sequence of joint actions $j'_1, \ldots j'_n$ such that for some $i \in 1 \ldots n$ $j_i \neq j'_i$.

CQ1-2: There is an instance of AS2 or AS3 whose path λ is created by the sequence of joint actions of this AS1. Alternatively, there is an instance of AS9 whose path B is equivalent to λ created by the sequence of joint actions of this AS1.

CQ2-1: There an instance of AS5 whose less preferred goal is the one identified by this instantiation of AS2.

CQ2-2: There is an instance of AS3 whose path λ is the λ path for AS2.

CQ3-1: There is an instance of AS6 for $S, \lambda \models \gamma$ and $S, \lambda \models \mathcal{V}^g_{a,x,d}$, where λ is the first path of AS3.

CQ3-2: There is an instantiation of AS8 for which this instantiation of AS3 means that $S \backslash \mathcal{P}^g_{a,x}, \lambda \models \mathcal{V}^g_{a,x,d}$ and $S \backslash \mathcal{P}^g_{a,x}, \lambda \not\models \mathcal{V}^h_{b,y,e}$

CQ3-3: There is an instantiation of AS4 referring to a permission $\mathcal{P}^g_{a,x}$ which refers to the same path λ as this instantiation of AS3.

3.3 Instantiating the Framework

We instantiate the framework described above using Modgil's extended argument frameworks (EAF) [12]. Formally, an EAF is defined as follows:

Definition 5. *(Extended Argument Framework)* *An EAF is a tuple* $(Args, R, D)$ *such that Args is a set of arguments,* $R \subseteq Args \times Args$, *and* $D \subseteq Args \times R$ *subject to the constraint that if* $(C, (A, B)), (C', (B, A)) \in D$, *then* $(C, C'), (C', C) \notin R$

Each instantiation of any of the argument schemes is associated with an argument within our EAF, and each critical question is associated with an attack on the argument scheme instantiation to which this critical question belongs. The constraint imposed on EAFs causes additional attacks to appear that are not described by the critical questions. We describe the process of EAF instantiation informally due to both space concerns and its simplicity.

CQ1-1 arises since only one sequence of actions can ultimately be executed, and results in symmetric attacks being inserted into R between every pair of nodes instantiating $AS1$. CQ1-2 refers to preferences between actions and following [13], is captured via an attack from the node representing the argument to the appropriate attacking edge.

CQ2-1, CQ2-2, CQ3-1 and CQ3-2 capture preferences over goals and norms. That is, they are used to represent the fact that one goal (or norm) is preferred over some other goal (or norm) by entities in the system. All of these link the appropriate argument, as instantiated by AS5-8 via an attack, on the attack from the argument instantiated by the appropriate AS2 or AS3.

Finally, CQ3-3 encompasses the possibility of a violation being derogated by a permission, and in instantiated as an attack from AS8 to the appropriate AS3.

Given the above, CQ1-1 and CQ3-3 result in attacks added to R, while the remaining critical questions result in attacks added to D. Together with the attacks added by the constraint, these attacks between the arguments instantiated from the application of the argument schemes fully specify our EAF.

Given an EAF instantiated as above, all the preferred extensions of the EAF will contain a single argument from argument scheme AS1 for some specific action sequence to be executed iff this action sequence is most preferred by all agents in the system. This sequence of actions is the dominant strategy for all agents in the system. Therefore, each preferred extension of the EAF identifies a single most preferred sequence of action.

The presence of multiple preferred extensions indicates that there are multiple most preferred sequences of action. In most multi-agent situations, this is an undesirable situation, as additional coordination is then required between the agents to ensure that a most desired sequence of joint actions is executed. This would require more refined reasoning about plans (e.g. [11]) to take place.

Finally, an empty set of extensions indicates that there is a preference conflict that must be resolved before a course of action can be agreed on.

Our system has several levels of argument schemes capturing arguments about paths, norms and goals; the former are in effect the object language, while the latter, together with argument schemes about preferences over norms and goals, represent a meta-language and a meta-meta-language. The use of an EAF therefore allows us to separate out these different levels, in a manner similar to [13]).

4   Example

In this section, we provide a brief example of the framework in action. Due to space constraints, we do not present all details of the system in our example, but instead concentrate on the most important aspects of the system's operation.

Consider two agents, α and β. α can undertake two actions, namely to visit her ill mother in hospital (V), or go to work (W). β, who is α's boss, has two possible actions, namely to fire α (F), or not fire her (N). α has two (conflicting) goals: to visit her mother (vm), and to keep her job (kj), while β would like to see some work done (wd), which can only occur if α goes to work. Finally, β has

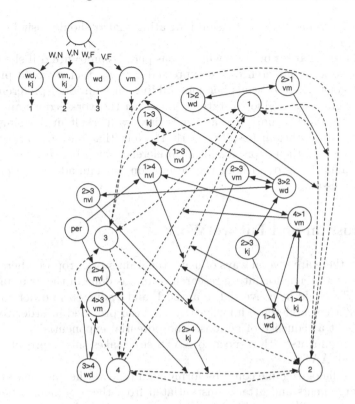

Fig. 1. The AATS (top left) and EAF (main figure) of the example

an obligation to not fire α, but has permission to do so if α does not come to work.

The AATS for this example is shown in the top left of Figure 1, and instantiating the EAF results in the main graph of Figure 1. Within this graph, paths from the AATS are indicated through nodes containing the path number; preference information is encoded through the propositions true in the state (e.g. $1 > 3$ kj indicate that path 1 is preferred to path 3 due to α's preference to keep her job; the permission to fire is indicated via the *per* node, and *nvl* identifies preference nodes instantiated through the prohibition on firing α. Dashed lines indicate attacks due to actions being mutually exclusive, while solid lines capture preference based attacks.

Evaluating the preferred extension of this EAF indicates that multiple actions are possible; for example, paths 1 and 2 are present in two of the extensions. This means that the system's preferences are underspecified. Looking at the situation more closely, this occurs for several reasons. First, α does not have any preferences encoded between going to the hospital or keeping her job; prioritising one of these (by adding attacks on edges between kj and vm via an instantiation of AS9) reduces the number of extensions, for example, if vm is preferred over kj, only path 2 remains in the extension indicating that α should visit her mother and keep her job.

This odd result arises because while β has permission to fire α if she does not turn up to work, no preferences are expressed over whether β would prefer this situation to one where α keeps her job. Adding an additional preferences over paths, through a new goal for β stating that either the work is done and α keeps her job, or the work is not done and α is fired, will result in α losing her job if she visits her mother in hospital (path 4). Note that due to the permission, there is no need to then express another preference for β between this goal and the norm on not firing α; without the permission, such an additional preference would be necessary.

5   Discussion and Future Work

In practice, there are several ways of using the framework proposed here, each of which poses an avenue for future research. First, as done in the example above, a given AATS could be converted to an EAF and evaluated in order to identify whether sufficient preference information has been provided in order to reach a decision about a sequence of actions. The potential exponential growth in the number of arguments with respect to AATS size makes this approach practical for only small AATSs.

Second, a dialogue game could be formulated (and verified against an AATS) based on arguments and attacks instantiated from the argument schemes and critical questions. This would involve agents arguing for why some course of action should be taken via utterances regarding their goals, norms and preferences.

Third, and perhaps most novel, an instantiated EAF could be used as the basis of a process to explain why some sequence of actions was followed given agents with some goals and norms. A user could, for example, understand that an action was executed as while a norm was violated, the goal achieved was more important to the agents in the system than the violation.

While norms can in general refer to both actions or states of the world (e.g. you are obliged to open the door, or you are obliged to have the door open respectively), in this paper we considered only norms that refer to environmental states. This restriction can be worked around by introducing so called *action predicates* which evaluate to true if some specific action executed in the previous state, causing a transition to the state where the action predicate is true.

Our work borrows several ideas from Atkinson's argument scheme for practical reasoning based on values [1]. Atkinson's approach puts both goals and values at the centre of the argumentation scheme, stating that "in situation S, action A should be pursued in order to achieve goal G while promoting values V". This argument scheme is encoded through a VAF, which is used to represent the preferences of different audiences over values. Each argument within the VAF can be associated with several values, but an audience's value ordering must be fully specified and consistent (see [14] for work which attempts to relax this assumption).

In the current work, preferences (which have a similar role to Atkinson's values) are associated with different sequences of action due to the goals that these sequences achieve for the agents as well as the norms violated or complied with by the sequence. Given this, our AS1 argument scheme is much simpler than Atkinson's, stating that (by default) some sequence of actions should be executed, and requiring all possible sequences of actions to be mutually exclusive with each other. Deciding how to act then requires identifying the most preferred sequence of actions. While our approach bears many similarities to [1], our work explicitly considers norms in practical reasoning, and considers all possible interactions between norms and goals.

Our representation of preferences within an EAF is based on [13], which applied EAFs to VAFs. While there are many similarities between our instantiation and the VAF instantiation, the requirement of VAFs to have a single consistent preference ordering makes them unsuitable for our needs; as shown above, we explicitly concern ourselves with detecting inconsistent preference orderings.

In one sense, the work presented here takes a global view of norms and actions. We consider joint actions, and require that all agents agree on a path. Such an approach ignores an important nuances of practical reasoning: agents may be force to pursue sub-optimal goals due to the actions of other agents. Thus, while our approach currently finds dominant strategies, it is unable to find other game theoretic solution concepts (e.g. Nash equilibria); we believe that capturing these additional solution concepts is critical, and are currently investigating how these concepts can be captured using our approach ([15] begins this work, but ignores the argumentation aspect of our approach). This will make more extensive use of the notion of a norm's creditor and target, and the preferences of each with regards to specific outcomes.

Another interesting avenue of future work involves considering a more dynamic system where new obligations, permissions and prohibitions can be created and removed as the system executes, and agents goals can change over time.

Finally, integrating practical reasoning over norms with reasoning over values would also be useful. This, in combination with the already present capability to reason over goals, should provide an end-to-end practical reasoning formalism.

6   Conclusions

In this paper we proposed a representation for norms built on top of an AATS. Using this representation we described how arguments over norms can be constructed, allowing for the detection of inconsistencies when performing practical reasoning, the explanation of *why* some action was taken, and making a decision about how to act in the presence of both goals and norms.

Acknowledgements. I would like to thank the anonymous reviewers for their very detailed and insightful comments.

References

1. Atkinson, K., Bench-Capon, T.J.M.: Practical reasoning as presumptive argumentation using action based alternating transition systems. Artif. Intell. 171(10-15), 855–874 (2007)
2. Boella, G., van der Torre, L.: Institutions with a hierarchy of authorities in distributed dynamic environments. Artificial Intelligence Law 16, 53–71 (2008)
3. Boella, G., van der Torre, L.: Permissions and obligations in hierarchical normative systems. In: Proceedings of ICAIL 2003, Edinburgh, Scotland (2003)
4. Broersen, J., Dastani, M., Hulstijn, J., Huang, Z., van der Torre, L.: The BOID architecture: conflicts between beliefs, obligations, intentions and desires. In: Müller, J.P., Andre, E., Sen, S., Frasson, C. (eds.) Proceedings of the Fifth International Conference on Autonomous Agents (AAMAS 2001), Montreal, Canada, pp. 9–16 (2001)
5. Carmo, J., Jones, A.: Deontic logic and contrary-to-duties. In: Gabbay, D., Guenthner, F. (eds.) Handbook of Philosophical Logic, vol. 8, pp. 265–343. Springer, Netherlands (2002)
6. Croitoru, M., Oren, N., Miles, S., Luck, M.: Graphical norms via conceptual graphs. Knowledge-Based Systems 29, 31–43 (2012)
7. Emerson, E.A., Halpern, J.Y.: 'Sometimes' and 'not never' revisited: on branching versus linear time temporal logic. J. ACM 33(1), 151–178 (1986)
8. Governatori, G., Hulstijn, J., Riveret, R., Rotolo, A.: Characterising deadlines in temporal modal defeasible logic. In: Orgun, M.A., Thornton, J. (eds.) AI 2007. LNCS (LNAI), vol. 4830, pp. 486–496. Springer, Heidelberg (2007)
9. Hindriks, K.V., van Riemsdijk, M.B.: Satisfying maintenance goals. In: Baldoni, M., Son, T.C., van Riemsdijk, M.B., Winikoff, M. (eds.) DALT 2007. LNCS (LNAI), vol. 4897, pp. 86–103. Springer, Heidelberg (2008)
10. van der Hoek, W., Roberts, M., Wooldridge, M.: Social laws in alternating time: effectiveness, feasibility, and synthesis. Synthese 156, 1–19 (2007)
11. Medellin-Gasque, R., Atkinson, K., McBurney, P., Bench-Capon, T.: Arguments over co-operative plans. In: Modgil, S., Oren, N., Toni, F. (eds.) TAFA 2011. LNCS (LNAI), vol. 7132, pp. 50–66. Springer, Heidelberg (2012)
12. Modgil, S.: Reasoning about preferences in argumentation frameworks. Artificial Intelligence 173(9-10), 901–934 (2009)
13. Mogdil, S., Bench-Capon, T.: Integrating object and meta-level value based argumentation. In: Proceedings of COMMA 2008 Conference on Computational Models of Argument, pp. 240–251. IOS Press, Amsterdam (2008)
14. Oren, N., Atkinson, K., Li, H.: Group persuasion through uncertain audience modelling. In: Proceedings of the 4th International Conference on Computational Models of Argument, pp. 350–357 (2012)
15. Oren, N., van Riemsdijk, M.B., Vasconcelos, W.W.: Preferences, paths, power, goals and norms. In: Proceedings of the 25th Benelux Conference on Artificial Intelligence (2013)
16. Singh, M.P.: An ontology for commitments in multiagent systems: Toward a unification of normative concepts. Artificial Intelligence and Law 7, 97–113 (1999)
17. van der Torre, L., Tan, Y.H.: Diagnosis and decision making in normative reasoning. Artificial Intelligence and Law 7, 51–67 (1999)
18. Walton, D.N.: Argumentation Schemes for Presumptive Reasoning. Erlbaum (1996)

Argumentation Accelerated Reinforcement Learning for RoboCup Keepaway-Takeaway

Yang Gao and Francesca Toni

Department of Computing, Imperial College London

Abstract. Multi-Agent Learning (MAL) is a complex problem, especially in real-time systems where both cooperative and competitive learning are involved. We study this problem in the RoboCup Soccer Keepaway-Takeaway game and propose Argumentation Accelerated Reinforcement Learning (AARL) for this game. AARL incorporates heuristics, represented by arguments in Value-Based Argumentation, into Reinforcement Learning (RL) by using Heuristically Accelerated RL techniques. We empirically study for a specific setting of the Keepaway-Takeaway game the suitability of AARL, in comparison with standard RL and hand-coded strategies, to meet the challenges of MAL.

1 Introduction

Multi-agent Learning (MAL) is widely recognised as a complex problem and has attracted much attention. Research on MAL roughly fall into two categories: *cooperative MAL*, where multiple learning agents share the same goal (e.g. [5,12,11,15]), and *competitive MAL*, where different learning agents have different or even opposite goals (e.g. [16,13]). Argumentation [7], studying the concept of 'good' arguments among conflicting arguments, is widely viewed as a powerful tool in solving conflicts and reaching agreement (see, e.g., [8]), and has been successfully incorporated within learning [18,10]. We investigate the use of argumentation in MAL where both cooperative and competitive learning are involved, focusing on the RoboCup Soccer Keepaway-Takeaway (*KATA*) game, an integration of two popular testbeds for MAL [21,14] where there are two competing teams of agents, keepers and takers, collaborating within the teams.

We focus on *Reinforcement Learning* (RL), because it allows agents to learn by interacting with the environment and has been shown to be a generic and robust learning algorithm for MAL [19]. However, when both competitive and cooperative learning are involved in a MAL, the effectiveness of RL could be seriously reduced due to the instability of the environment [22]. To solve this problem, we propose, in the context of KATA games, *Argumentation Accelerated RL* (AARL), which incorporates Value-Based Argumentation [1] into RL by using *Heuristically Accelerated RL* (HARL) techniques [3], so that, when making decisions, agents rely not only on their interacting experiences with the environment, but also domain knowledge in the form of arguments. Further, we test the effectiveness of AARL in the specific setting of 3-keeper-2-taker KATA games.

E. Black, S. Modgil, and N. Oren (Eds.): TAFA 2013, LNAI 8306, pp. 79–94, 2014.
© Springer-Verlag Berlin Heidelberg 2014

Concretely, we test AARL for keepers and takers against two different strategies for each type of agent and perform a round-robin style experiment(where each strategy meets all strategies in turn). Our experiments suggest that the AARL-based strategies are competitive in terms of stability, average convergence time and average optimal performance. This work is an extension of our previous work on single-agent Argumentation-Based Reinforcement Learning (ABRL) [10].

The paper is organised as follows: Section 2 gives background. Section 3 describes how to apply AARL to TAKA games and Section 4 presents empirical results. Section 5 describes related works and Section 6 concludes.

2 Background

First we give fundamentals of value-based argumentation. Then we describe *Markov Decision Process* – a popular mathematical model of RL, focusing on the SARSA(λ) algorithm that we use, followed by an introduction of HARL, by means of which we integrate arguments into RL. Finally, we describe the RoboCup Soccer Keepaway-Takeaway games.

2.1 Argumentation Frameworks

An *abstract argumentation framework* (AF) [7] is a pair (*Arg, Att*) where *Arg* is a set of *arguments* and $Att \subseteq Arg \times Arg$ is a binary relation ((A, B) $\in Att$ is read '*A* attacks *B*'). $S \subseteq Arg$ attacks $B \in Arg$ iff some member of S attacks B. $S \subseteq Arg$ is *conflict-free* iff S attacks none of its members. If $S \subseteq Arg$ attacks all arguments attacking $B \in Arg$, then S *defends* B . Semantics of AFs are defined as sets of "rationally acceptable" arguments (*extensions*), e.g. (given some F = (*Arg, Att*) and $S \subseteq Arg$):

– S is a *complete extension* for F iff S is conflict-free and $S = \{a|S$ defends $a\}$;
– S is the *grounded extension* for F iff S is minimally (wrt $\subseteq$) complete for F.

The grounded extension is guaranteed to be unique, consisting solely of uncontroversial arguments and being thus "sceptical".

In some contexts, the attack relation is not enough to decide what is rationally acceptable, and the "values" promoted by arguments must be considered. *Value-based argumentation frameworks* (VAFs) [1] incorporate values as well as preferences over them into AFs. The key idea is to allow for attacks to succeed or fail, depending on the relative worth of the values promoted by the competing arguments. Given a set V of values, an *audience Valpref* is a strict partial order over V (corresponding to the preferences of an agent), and an *audience-specific VAF* is a tuple (*Arg, Att, V, val, Valpref*), where (*Arg, Att*) is an AF and $val : Arg \to V$ gives the values promoted by arguments. *Valpref*, the audience, is a strict partial order over V. We denote (X, Y) $\in Valpref$ by $X >_v Y$.

In VAF, *Valpref* is taken into account in the definition of extensions. The *simplification* of an audience-specific VAF is the AF (*Arg, Def*), where (A, B) $\in$ *Def* iff (A, B) $\in Att$ and $val(B) \not>_v val(A)$. (A, B) $\in$ *Def* is read '*A* defeats *B*'.

Then, (acceptable) extensions of a VAF are defined as (acceptable) extensions of its simplification (*Arg, Def*). We refer to (*Arg, Def*) as the *simplified AF derived from* (*Arg, Att, V, val, Valpref*).

2.2   Markov Decision Process

The Markov Decision Process (MDP) is one of the most widely used model for RL and has several variants [22]. An MDP is a tuple (S, A, T, R), where S is the *state space*, A is the *action space*, $T(s, a, s') = Pr(s'|s, a)$ is the *transition probability* of moving from state s to state s' by executing action a, and $R(s, a, s')$ gives the immediate *reward* received when action a is taken in state s, moving to state s'. In many real problems, e.g. RoboCup Keepaway/Takeaway games (see Section 2.4), actions may take variable amount of time. In these cases, Semi-MDP [4] are used to model temporally-extended courses of actions. We use the SMDP version of SARSA(λ) [22] learning algorithm extended, in order to improve the learning speed, with *replacing eligibility traces* [20], outlined as Algorithm 1 below.

Algorithm 1. SARSA(λ) with replacing eligibility traces (adjusted from [22])

Initialise $Q(s, a)$ arbitrarily for all states s and actions a
Repeat (for each episode):
   Initialise $e(s, a) = 0$ for all s and a
   Initialise current state s_t
   Choose action a_t from s_t using the ε-greedy policy
   Repeat until s_t is the terminal state:
      Execute action a_t, observe reward r_t and new state s_{t+1}
      Choose a_{t+1} from s_{t+1} using the ε-greedy policy
      $\delta \leftarrow r_t + \gamma Q(s_{t+1}, a_{t+1}) - Q(s_t, a_t)$
      $e(s_t, a_t) \leftarrow 1$
      For all s, a:
         $Q(s, a) \leftarrow Q(s, a) + \alpha \delta e(s, a)$
         $e(s, a) \leftarrow \gamma \lambda e(s, a)$
      $s_t \leftarrow s_{t+1}; a_t \leftarrow a_{t+1}$

In this algorithm, $Q(s, a) \in \mathbb{R}$ represents the value of performing action a in state s. α is the *learning rate*, γ is the *discount factor* governing the weight placed on the future rewards, e represents eligibility traces, which store the credit that previous action choices should receive for current rewards, while λ governs how much credit is delivered back to them. ε-*greedy* is a widely used (action-selection) policy, which selects the action with highest $Q(s, a)$ value for a proportion $1 - \varepsilon$ of the trials; for the other ε proportion, actions will be selected randomly. Formally, this policy is defined as:

$$\pi(s_t) = \begin{cases} \arg\max_{a_t} Q(s_t, a_t) & \text{if } q \leq \varepsilon \\ a_{random} & \text{otherwise} \end{cases} \tag{1}$$

where q is a random value uniformly distributed over $[0, 1]$. a_{random} is an action randomly chosen among all those available in state s_t.

2.3 Heuristically Accelerated RL

HARL [3] is a way to solve a MDP problem by explicitly incorporating heuristics within RL. By using HARL, a learning agent's choice of actions is influenced so that more promising actions are more likely to be performed. HARL influences a RL process by overriding the action-selection policy. For example, if we are using the ε-greedy policy (see Equation 1) in the original RL, by using HARL, the policy will be changed as:

$$\pi^H(s_t) = \begin{cases} \arg\max_{a_t}[Q(s_t, a_t) + H_t(s_t, a_t)] & \text{if } q \leq \varepsilon \\ a_{random} & \text{otherwise} \end{cases} \quad (2)$$

where $H_t(s_t, a_t)$ is the *heuristic function* which is defined by the domain expert. For a state-action pair (s_t, a_t), the higher the value of $H_t(s_t, a_t)$, the more promising performing action a_t in state s_t. As for q and ε, they have the same meaning as in Equation 1. Note that HARL only provides the more promising state-action pairs with higher priority to be explored, but does not change the convergence of the original RL algorithm [2]. The heuristic function H_t can be defined a priori or at any moment during learning, and can be updated at any time throughout learning. Later in Section 3.3, we will give the argumentation-based definition of HARL.

2.4 RoboCup Soccer Games

RoboCup Soccer is an international project which aims at providing an experimental framework in which various technologies can be integrated and evaluated[1]. In order to facilitate RL research in this application, two simplified tasks have been developed: the *Keepaway* game [21], and the *Takeaway* game [14]. The basic settings of these games are the same: $N + 1$ ($N \in \mathbb{N}$, $N \geq 1$) *keepers* are competing with N *takers* on a fixed-size court. Keepers are trying to keep possession of the ball within their team for longer time, whereas takers are trying to win possession. The games consist of a series of *episodes*: at the start of each episode, the keeper in the top-left corner holds the ball, while all other keepers are on the right. All takers are initially in the bottom-left corner. An episode ends when the ball goes off the court or any taker gets the ball, and a new episode starts immediately with all the players reset.

In Keepaway, only the keeper holding the ball is learning. All the other keepers and takers are playing in accordance with hand-coded strategies. In Takeaway, however, all takers are learning independently while all keepers are playing in accordance with hand-coded strategies. So Takeaway is a cooperative MAL problem whereas Keepaway is a single-agent learning problem which takes place in

---

[1] See http://www.robocup.org/ for more information.

a multi-agent scenario. In this paper, we endow both keeper and takers with learning ability, and we call a game with $N + 1$ learning keepers and N learning takers a N-Keepaway-Takeaway (N-KATA) game.

In the RoboCup simulation platform, only primitive actions and coordinate positions are available. However, RL cannot *effectively* use this low-level information in Keepaway [21] or Takeaway [14]. So *macro actions* were proposed originally by [21] for Keepaway, and then adjusted by [14] for Takeaway. In particular, there are 2 macro actions for Keepaway:

HoldBall(): stay still while keeping the ball;
PassBall(i): kick the ball towards keeper K_i;
and 2 macro actions for Takeaway:
TackleBall(): move towards the ball to tackle it
MarkKeeper(i): go to mark keeper K_i, $i \neq 1$

where K_i represents the ith closest keeper to the ball - so that K_1 is the keeper in possession of the ball. Takers are indexed in the same way. When a taker marks a keeper, the taker blocks the path between the ball and that keeper. Thus, a taker is not allowed to mark the ball holder, and the action set in N-Takeaway consists of $N + 1$ actions. In addition, *state variables* are proposed by [21] to facilitate the state representation in Keepaway games. In particular, a state is represented by a *state vector* which consists of elements, known as *state variables*, that can be directly used in the agent's decision making. The state variables for the Keepaway games are shown in Table 1. For example, the distances between takers and the ball holder are state variables, because the holder could use this information to decide when to pass the ball and where to pass the ball. As we can see, all state variables are collected in the perspective of the ball holder, because the ball holder is the only learner in Keepaway. We call these state variables *holder-oriented*.

Most existing research on Takeaway uses the holder-oriented state variables (e.g. [14,17,6]). However, a taker's *self-oriented* state variables would be more helpful. Also, since multiple takers are learning independently in Takeaway, the state variables should also facilitate coordination between takers. We combine taker's *self-oriented* and some holder-oriented state variables, and use the new state variables in Table 2. Later in Section 5 we will show that compared with the learning takers that use the holder-oriented state variables, the takers using our new state variables have significantly better performance.

3   Argumentation for RoboCup Soccer

In Section 3.1 we give arguments and values for keepers and takers. Then, in Section 3.2, we define the defeat relationship among arguments, by taking the ranking of values into account. As a result, we instantiate VAFs (seen in Section 2.1) for keepers and takers. Acceptable arguments (in the grounded extenstion) for these VAFs recommend actions. Finally, in Section 3.3, we integrate this action recommendation into RL by using HARL techniques.

Table 1. State variables for learning keeper K_1 in a N-KATA game. $(i, j \in \mathbb{N})$.

State Variable(s)	Description
$dist(K_i, C)$, $\quad i \in [1, N+1]$	Distance between keepers and the centre of the court.
$dist(T_j, C)$, $\quad j \in [1, N]$	Distance between takers and the centre of the court.
$dist(K_1, K_i)$, $\quad i \in [2, N+1]$	Distance between K_1 and the other keepers.
$dist(K_1, T_j)$, $\quad j \in [1, N]$	Distance between K_1 and the takers.
$\min\limits_{j \in [1,N]} dist(K_i, T_j)$, $\quad i \in [2, N+1]$	Distance between K_i and its closest taker.
$\min\limits_{j \in [1,N]} ang(K_i, T_j)$, $\quad i \in [2, N+1]$	The smallest angle between K_i and the takers with vertex at K_1.

3.1 Arguments and Values

Arguments are of the form:

$$con(A) \quad \text{IF} \quad pre(A)$$

where $con(A)$ (the *conclusion* of A) is the recommended action and $pre(A)$ (the *premise* of A) describes under which conditions argument A is applicable.

Arguments and values for keepers. For the learning keeper, we use the same arguments as described in [10], which are designed based on a successful hand-coded strategy for the keeper described in [21]:

- **HD: HoldBall()** IF $\min\limits_{1 \leq j \leq N} dist(K_1, T_j) \geq 7$
- **F(i): PassBall(i)** IF $\min\limits_{1 \leq j \leq N} dist(K_i, T_j) \geq 15$
- **O(i): PassBall(i)** IF $\min\limits_{1 \leq j \leq N} ang(K_i, T_j) \geq 15$

where $i, j \in \mathbb{N}$. We say that these arguments *belong to* the keeper K_1. Note that the thresholds used above, i.e. 7 and 15, are proposed based on empirical results or thresholds used in the hand-coded strategy. Overall, there are $2N + 1$ candidate arguments for K_1 [2]. These arguments can be interpreted as:

- **HD**: hold the ball because all takers are "far": the distance between each taker and K_1 is larger than 7;
- **F(i)**: pass the ball to K_i because K_i is "far": the distance between K_i and the K_1 is larger than 15;
- **O(i)**: pass the ball to K_i because K_i is "open": the angles between K_i and all the takers, with vertex at K_1, are over 15°.

---

[2] **HD** generates one argument. **F(i)** and **O(i)** generate N arguments each.

Table 2. State variables for learning taker T_1 in a N-KATA game. State variables of other takers can be obtained similarly. $(i, j \in \mathbb{N})$. The top 3 rows describe self-oriented variables, and the others describe variables about the keepers relative layout.

State Variable(s)	Description
$dist(K_i, Me)$, $\quad i \in [1, N+1]$	Distance between keepers and myself.
$dist(T_j, Me)$, $\quad j \in [2, N]$	Distance between other takers and myself.
$ang(K_i, Me)$, $\quad i \in [2, N+1]$	The angle between the free keepers and myself, with vertex at K_1.
$dist(K_i, K_1)$, $\quad i \in [2, N+1]$	Distance between K_1 and the other keepers.
$dist(T_j, K_1)$, $\quad j \in [2, N]$	Distance between K_1 and the other takers.
$\min\limits_{j \in [1,N]} ang(K_i, T_j)$, $\quad i \in [2, N+1]$	The smallest angle between K_i and the takers with vertex at K_1.

The arguments are promoting values:

- **RM**: reduce the risk of teammates being marked;
- **RI**: reduce the risk of the ball being intercepted;
- **RT**: reduce the risk of the ball being tackled;

where $val(\mathbf{HD}) = \mathbf{RM}$, $val(\mathbf{F}(i)) = \mathbf{RT}$ and $val(\mathbf{O}(i)) = \mathbf{RI}$ with $\mathbf{RM} >_v \mathbf{RI} >_v \mathbf{RT}$. Note that in standard Keepaway, takers are always trying to tackle the ball. All arguments and values described above are designed based on this assumption. However, in KATA games, takers can not only tackle the ball, but also mark keepers. In other words, these arguments and values inevitably have errors when applied to KATA games. In Section 4, we will make a deeper analysis of the effects of this imperfect domain knowledge on the learning performance.

Arguments and Values for Takers. As for takers, the arguments should not only instruct takers to compete with keepers, but also coordinate takers. We propose the following categories of candidate arguments that *belong to* the taker T_j:

- $T_j\mathbf{TK}$: **TackleBall()** IF $j = \arg \min\limits_{1 \leq t \leq N} dist(K_1, T_t)$
- $T_j\mathbf{O}(i)$: **MarkKeeper(i)** IF $\min\limits_{1 \leq t \leq N} ang(K_i, T_t) \geq 15$
- $T_j\mathbf{F}(i)$: **MarkKeeper(i)** IF $\min\limits_{1 \leq t \leq N} dist(K_i, T_t) \geq 15$
- $T_j\mathbf{A}(i)$: **MarkKeeper(i)** IF $j = \arg \min\limits_{1 \leq t \leq N} ang(K_i, T_t)$
- $T_j\mathbf{C}(i)$: **MarkKeeper(i)** IF $j = \arg \min\limits_{1 \leq t \leq N} dist(K_i, T_t)$

where $i, j, t \in \mathbb{N}$. For $T_j\mathbf{O}(i), T_j\mathbf{F}(i), T_j\mathbf{A}(i), T_j\mathbf{C}(i)$, $i \in \{2, \cdots, N+1\}$, because K_1 cannot be marked. The intuition behind these arguments is as follows:

- $T_j\mathbf{TK}$: T_j should tackle the ball if T_j is the closest to the ball holder (K_1) among all the takers;
- $T_j\mathbf{O}(i)$: T_j should mark keeper K_i if K_i is quite "open": the angles between K_i and all the takers, with vertex at K_1, are over $15°$;
- $T_j\mathbf{F}(i)$: T_j should mark keeper K_i if K_i is "far": its distances to all takers are larger than 15;
- $T_j\mathbf{A}(i)$: T_j should mark keeper K_i if the angle between T_j and K_i, with vertex at K_1, is the smallest;
- $T_j\mathbf{C}(i)$: T_j should mark keeper K_i if T_j is closest to K_i.

Overall, in a N-KATA game, there are $4N^2 + N$ arguments for takers[3]. These arguments are promoting values:

- **VT**: The ball should be tackled as quickly as possible;
- **VO**: If the ball holder decides to pass, it is very likely to pass the ball to an "open" keeper;
- **VF**: If the ball holder decides to pass, it is very likely to pass to a keeper far from all takers;
- **VA**: The taker with the smallest angle to a keeper is most likely to intercept the ball passed to that keeper;
- **VC**: The taker closest to a keeper can mark it most quickly.

We set $val(T_j\mathbf{TK}) = \mathbf{VT}$, $val(T_j\mathbf{O}(i)) = \mathbf{VO}$, $val(T_j\mathbf{F}(i)) = \mathbf{VF}$, $val(T_j\mathbf{A}(i)) = \mathbf{VA}$, $val(T_j\mathbf{C}(i)) = \mathbf{VC}$. Further, we set $\mathbf{VT} >_v \mathbf{VA} = {}_v\mathbf{VC} >_v \mathbf{VO} >_v \mathbf{VF}$[4]. Note that, for simplicity, we assume the same ranking of values throughout the game, but our technique can be applied with value rankings that change over time.

Applicable arguments. The arguments given so far are candidate arguments that may not be applicable at all times. Indeed, in KATA games, the environment is constantly changing and in each state, an agent has to select the applicable arguments by checking all candidate arguments to see whether their premises hold true in that state. Since takers need to coordinate, we assume that each taker is aware of all other takers' applicable arguments.[5]

For example, consider the scenario in Figure 1. With respect to the learning keeper, since the distances between all takers and K_1 are larger than 7, the argument **HD** is applicable. Also, because the distance between K_3 and K_1 is larger than 15, $\mathbf{F}(3)$ is applicable. The premises of other candidate arguments are not satisfied in this scenario, so they are not applicable. Similarly, we get the applicable arguments for takers: $T_1\mathbf{TK}$, $T_1\mathbf{A}(2)$, $T_1\mathbf{A}(3)$, $T_1\mathbf{C}(2)$, $T_2\mathbf{C}(3)$.

---

[3] Indeed, for taker T_j, $T_j\mathbf{TK}$ gives 1 argument and the other four categories of arguments each give N arguments.

[4] $V_1 =_v V_2$ stands for $(V_1 >_v V_2) \wedge (V_2 >_v V_1)$

[5] This is in line with all existing research on Keepaway/Takeaway games, building upon the assumption that an agent is aware of all agents' locations and the ball's location, i.e. each agent has a *perfect world view*.

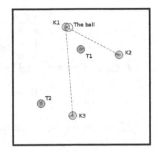

Fig. 1. A scenario of 2-KATA. The size of the court is 40×40.

3.2   Defeat Relation and Simplified AFs

For any two arguments P and Q, $val(P) = V_1$ and $val(Q) = V_2$, P *defeats* Q iff $V_1 >_v V_2$ and one of the following two conditions holds:

- P and Q belong to different agents but recommend the same action (i.e. $con(P) = con(Q)$);
- P and Q belong to the same agent but recommend different actions (i.e. $con(P) \neq con(Q)$).

Given the applicable arguments and the defeat relation, we obtain simplified AFs (see Section 2.1) for keepers and takers. For example, consider again the scenario in Figure 1. For the keeper, **HD** and **F**(3) belong to the same agent but support different actions, and the value promoted by **HD**: **RM**, is more preferred than the value promoted by **F**(3): **RT**, so **HD** defeats **F**(3). The simplified AF for keeper and takers are shown in Figure 2(a) and Figure 2(b), respectively.

3.3   Argumentation Accelerated RL (AARL)

We use the grounded extension (see Section 2.1) to select the *recommended action* for each agent, because this extension is always unique and, as a result, will not recommend different actions to an agent. For example, consider again the scenario in Figure 1. The grounded extension of the keeper's argumentation framework is {**HD**}, so the recommended action for K_1 is **HoldBall()**. The grounded extension of the takers' argumentation framework is {T_1**TK**}, so T_1 is recommended to **TackleBall()**. Note that the grounded extension of takers does not include arguments belonging to T_2. This means that given the current state and our domain knowledge no action is recommended to T_2. Note that in some scenarios, the grounded extension can be empty, which means that based on the current domain knowledge, there is no convincing enough recommendation can be drawn in this scenario. So additional domain knowledge should be added; otherwise, no actions are recommended and agents will choose actions solely based on the values of each state-action pairs (Q-values, see Section 2.2)

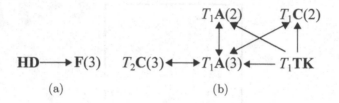

(a)   (b)

Fig. 2. Simplified AFs for Figure 1: for keeper(2(a)) and takers (2(b))

AARL amounts to integrating these recommended actions into RL by using HARL (see Section 2.3) to give these actions higher probabilities to be explored. Because all the arguments and values are designed based on the domain knowledge and are not updated during learning, we define the heuristic function a priori and keep it fixed throughout the learning. In particular, we set the heuristic function of agent A_i as:

$$H(s,a) = \begin{cases} \eta & \text{if } a \text{ is recommended to } A_i \\ 0 & \text{otherwise} \end{cases}$$

where an action a is recommended to A_i iff a is recommended by an argument in the grounded extension of A_i's simplified AF. Because all Q-values are initialised as 0, the heuristic value for the recommended action is the value of η. If an agent does not have any recommended actions, then it uses the standard ε-greedy policy (see Section 2.2). Note that the heuristic function, states and actions have no time index, because they can be applied to any state-action pair.

4   Empirical Results

Our learning algorithm is shown in Algorithm 1) We use the same setting as in [21] for SARSA(λ) and we set $\eta = 2$. For the learning keeper, we use the same rewarding scheme as in [21]:

$$r = CurrentTime - LastActionTime$$

where r is the reward, *CurrentTime* is the time when a keeper holds the ball or an episode ends, and *LastActionTime* is the time when a keeper selected the last action. As a result, if the last action was **HoldBall()**, the reward r must be equal to the duration of an episode; if the last action was **PassBall()**, then the farther the target keeper is, the larger the reward will be. So, roughly speaking, this reward system is *distance-oriented*: passing the ball to farther keepers is more encouraged. For takers, the reward is 10 for the last cycle[6] of each episode and -1 for all the other cycles. In order to prevent possible oscillations of the strategy, a taker updates its policy and makes new decisions every 5 cycles (called a *trail*). We conduct one experiment on each combination of strategies. All the

---

[6] In the RoboCup Soccer Simulator, each second is divided into 20 equal-length time slots, called *cycles*.

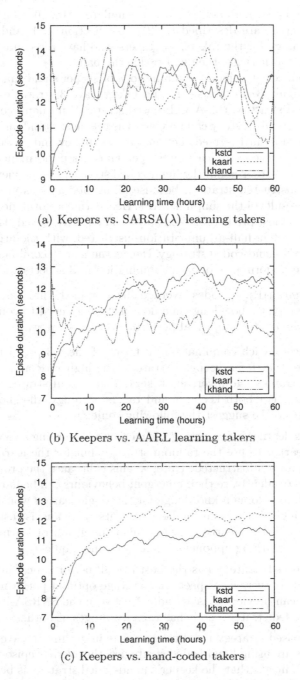

(a) Keepers vs. SARSA(λ) learning takers

(b) Keepers vs. AARL learning takers

(c) Keepers vs. hand-coded takers

Fig. 3. Performances of different learning algorithms for 2-KATA games on a 40×40 court. Each curve represents the performance of a single test. Note that when both keepers and takers are using the hand-coded strategies, the performance is stable and, as a result, we present its average value here (the straight line in 3(c)).

experiments are done in RoboCup Soccer Simulator v15.1.0[7]. The hand-coded strategies of keepers are described in [21] (see Section 3.1), and we design a hand-coded strategy for the takers, s.t. takers who have a recommended action would perform it; otherwise, they will tackle the ball.

The performances of different combinations of keeper's and takers' strategies are shown in Figure 3. Both keepers and takers have 3 strategies, namely the SARSA(λ)-based strategy, the AARL-based strategy and hand-coded strategy. The SARSA(λ)-based strategy can be viewed as the most "random" strategy, because it uses the standard ε-greedy action selection policy and randomly searches the action space in the early learning stage. Thus, its performance is most unpredictable. On the other hand, the hand-coded strategy can be viewed as a fully argumentation-instructed strategy, because all agents' actions are strictly constrained by the results of the simplified AFs. Hence, the performance of the hand-coded strategy is most predictable and stable. The AARL-based strategy can be viewed as half-random-half-argumentation-instructed, with the arguments used the same as for the hand-coded strategy. Hence, there are 9 combinations overall. We evaluate the performance of each combination in 3 aspects:

initial performance (IP): episodes' average duration in the first hour of learning;
convergence time (CT): how long time does a strategy need to converge;
optimal performance (OP): optimal performance of a strategy.

The performance of each combination, in terms of these 3 properties, is shown in Table 3. Note that for a keeper's strategy, the higher IP and OP, the more successful the strategy. However, for takers, a successful strategy should have lower IP and OP. For both keeper's and takers' strategy, the shorter CT, the better the strategy. We suggest the following conjectures:

1. When a single learner is competing with a group of learning agents, it is better for the single learner to use the random strategy, but for the learning group to use the argumentation-instructed strategy. This is because the group of learners are learning independently, so their emergent behaviours can be hardly predicted and, as a result, any domain knowledge for the single learner would be helpless. Instead, if the single learner is using heuristics, its behaviour is easier to predict. On the other hand, the heuristics would help the group of learning agents to predict the single learning opponent's behaviour more quickly.

2. The AARL-based strategy has the best overall performance, in terms of the stability, average convergence speed and average optimal performance. This is because AARL can be viewed as a tradeoff between the SARSA-based strategy and the hand-coded strategy, so it has the advantages of both.

3. The AARL-based strategy is robust to errors in arguments. We can see that when both sides are using hand-coded strategies, the average episode duration is very high, which means that the keeper's hand-coded strategy is better than the takers'. However, with respect to takers, the performance of the AARL-based strategy is always better than the SARSA-based strategy.

---

[7] http://sourceforge.net/projects/sserver/

Table 3. Summary of performances. Each entry consists of three numbers (in seconds): initial performance, convergence time and optimal performance.

		Keeper		
		SARSA	AARL	Hand-coded
Takers	SARSA	9.2, 15, 12.7	9.2, 22, 12.7	13.9, > 60, unknown
	AARL	7.9, 20, 12.3	8.1, 22, 12.0	12.3, 10, 10.2
	Hand-coded	7.1, 30, 11.1	8.1, 21, 12.1	14.8, 0, 14.8

4. When a group of randomly learning agents are competing with a hand-coded opponent, the convergence speed can be very slow, even slower than when the opponent is using a learning strategy. The reason could be that when using the AARL-based or the hand-coded strategy, the learning group have some coordination schemes so their group behaviours can converge faster; when both sides are using learning strategies, they are pushing each other to achieve a Nash Equilibrium[16] [8], so the convergence time can by quicker.

5   Related Works

There is research on improving machine learning by argumentation. Mozina et al. [18] proposed argumentation based machine learning, which combines arguments with the original examples of CN2 algorithm to form argumented examples. The use of arguments significantly improves the performance of CN2. However, the relationships between different arguments are not taken into account in their technique, which restricts the effect argumentation should have. Also, the machine learning technique they considered, CN2, is supervised and fundamentally different from RL. Research has also been devoted to incorporating domain knowledge into RL to improve its performance in Keepaway games. For example, [6] used potential-based reward shaping in Takeaway games and showed that the convergence time can be reduced and group performance can be altered. However, their work does not explicitly consider the domain knowledge representation. Moreover, under the same game settings, their average episode durations are almost twice as long as ours.

With respect to cooperative RL, [5] distinguished and compared two forms of multi-agent RL: *independent learners* (ILs), who only consider its own Q-values when choosing actions, and *joint action learners*, who search the exponential joint action space to maximise the sum of all agents' Q-values. However, the performance of these two learners are almost the same. Our agents can be seen as ILs. [12] used *coordination graph* to restrain the coordination relationships between actions. Actions are selected to maximise the sum of Q-values of only

---

[8]   The KATA game can be viewed as a zero-sum game because the goal of the two sides are opposite. However, since our application and algorithm is very different from those in [16], we cannot guarantee a Nash Equilibrium can be achieved. The difference between our research and [16] are discussed in Section 5.

related agents. So in order to know the Q-values of all related teammates, each agent has to compute all these Q-values or get them by communication. This technique is not suitable for real-time applications where computational time is strictly constrained and communication is forbidden, e.g. Takeaway. Some have also explored using Hierarchical RL (HRL) to guide coordination. For example, [11] proposed *Cooperative HRL*, in which coordination is only learnt in predefined *cooperative subtasks* (CSs), defined by domain experts as subtasks where coordination would significantly improve the performance of the whole team. [15] modelled the coordination among agents as *coordination constraints* and used these to limit the joint action space for exploration. In all these HRL approaches, domain knowledge is in the form of hard constraints and the action exploration is strictly constrained by them. Hence, the learning process cannot correct errors contained in the domain knowledge and the performances of these techniques, as a result, are highly sensitive to the quality of the domain knowledge. Note that there are also research about using argumentation to coordinate cooperative agents [9,23]. However, their agents do not learn.

For competitive RL, [16] proposed the *minimax-Q-Learning* algorithm for two-player zero-sum Markov game. Based on Littman's work, [13] developed a more general algorithm for n-player general-sum Markov games. Both these approaches are guaranteed to converge to a Nash equilibrium under certain conditions. However, in the Keepaway/Takeaway games, keepers and takers are making decisions asynchronously, i.e. the keeper is making a decision at each time slot whereas takers are making decisions every 5 time slots (see Section 4), and the actions of opponent(s) are difficult or even impossible to identify. For these reasons, the payoff matrices, which are the bases of these approaches, can hardly be built in Keepaway/Takeaway. Another fact worth mentioning is that the application domains of all these cooperative/competitive RL techniques above are simple problems, such as matrix games or 'grid world' where there are finite number of discrete states. However, KATA games are real-time large-scale problems which take place in continuous space, and both cooperative learning and competitive learning are involved. Thus, the application domain we are using is more realistic and complex than most existing research.

6 Conclusions

We presented *Argumentation-Accelerated RL* (AARL) for the 2-KATA game. This is a new approach to RL where domain knowledge is represented and organised as an argumentation framework. We implement AARL using the SARSA(λ) algorithm and conduct experiments in 2-KATA games. The results of our experiments suggest that AARL is competitive with respect to stability, average convergence time and average optimal performance. Further experiments are needed to consolidate our conclusions.

This work is preliminary research on using arguments to solve multi-agent cooperative-competitive learning. Since the arguments we are using (see Section 3) are independent of any specific learning algorithm, we believe that our approach can in principle be integrated within other learning algorithms (not limited to RL) or within RL via other techniques (not limited to HARL). However, as we have mentioned in Section 3.1, the arguments we are using contain obvious faults and have a huge space for improvement. So future work can be done to try out our methodology with other learning methods and more sophisticated arguments. In addition, since the conclusions are based on one specific game and limited experiments, more experiments on more games should be performed so as to test our conclusions more generally.

References

1. Bench-Capon, T.: Persuasion in practical argument using value-based argumentation frameworks. J. Log. Comput. 13(3), 429–448 (2003)
2. Bianchi, R.: Using heuristics to accelerate reinforcement learning algorithms. Ph.D. thesis, University of São Paulo (2004) (in Portuguese)
3. Bianchi, R., Ribeiro, C., Costa, A.: Accelerated autonumous learning by using heuristic selection of actions. Journal of Heuristics 14, 135–168 (2008)
4. Bradtke, S., Duff, M.: Reinforcement learning methods for continuous-time markov decision problems. Advances in Neural Information Processing Systems 7, 393–400 (1995)
5. Claus, C., Boutilier, C.: The dynamics of reinforcement learning in cooperative multiagent systems. In: The Proc. of AAAI (1998)
6. Devlin, S., Grzes, M., Kudenko, D.: An empirical study of potential-based reward shaping and advice in complex, multi-agent systems. Advances in Complex Systems 14, 251–278 (2011)
7. Dung, P.M.: On the acceptability of aruguments and its fundamental role in non-monotonic reasoning, logic programming and n-person games. Artificial Intelligence 77(2), 321–357 (1995)
8. Fan, X., Toni, F.: Argumentation dialogues for two-agent conflict resolution. In: Proc. of COMMA (2012)
9. Ferretti, E., Errecalde, M., García, A., Simari, G.: An application of defeasible logic programming to decision making in a robotic environment. In: LPNMR (2007)
10. Gao, Y., Toni, F., Craven, R.: Argumentation-based reinforcement learning for robocup soccer keepaway. In: Proc. of ECAI (2012)
11. Ghavamzadeh, M., Mahadevan, S., Makar, R.: Hierarchical multi-agent reinforcement learning. Autonomous Agents and Multi-Agent Systems 13, 197–229 (2006)
12. Guestrin, C., Lagoudakis, M., Parr, R.: Coordinated reinforcement learning. In: Machine Learning International Workshop Then Conference (2002)
13. Hu, J., Wellman, M.P.: Multiagent reinforcement learning: Theoretical framework and an algorithm. In: Proc. of ICML (1998)
14. Iscen, A., Erogul, U.: A new perspective to the keepaway soccer: The takers (short paper). In: Proc. of AAMAS (2008)
15. Lau, Q.P., Lee, M.L., Hsu, W.: Coordination guided reinforcement learning. In: Proc. of AAMAS (2012)
16. Littman, M.L.: Markov games as a framework for multi-agent reinforcement learning. In: Proc. of ICML (1994)
17. Min, H.Q., Zeng, J.A., Chen, J., Zhu, J.H.: A study of reinforcement learning in a new multiagent domain. In: 2008 IEEE/WIC/ACM International Conference on Web Intelligence and Intelligent Agent Technology (2008)

18. Mozina, M., Zabkar, J., Bratko, I.: Argument based machine learning. Artificial Intelligence 171, 922–937 (2007)
19. Sen, S., Sekaran, M., Hale, J.: Learning to coordinate without sharing information. In: Proc. of AAAI (1994)
20. Singh, S.P., Sutton, R.S.: Reinforcement learning with replacing eligibility traces. Machine Learning 22, 123–158 (1996)
21. Stone, P., Sutton, R., Kuhlmann, G.: Reinforcement learning for robocup soccer keepaway. Adaptive Behavior 13, 165–188 (2005)
22. Sutton, R., Barto, A.: Reinforcement Learning. MIT Press (1998)
23. Tambe, M., Jung, H.: The benefits of arguing in a team. AI Magzine 20(4), 85–92 (1999)

Towards Agent Dialogue as a Tool for Capturing Software Design Discussions

Elizabeth Black, Peter McBurney, and Steffen Zschaler

Department of Informatics, King's College London
{elizabeth.black,peter.mcburney,steffen.zschaler}@kcl.ac.uk

Abstract. Software design is an important creative step in the engineering of software systems, yet we know surprisingly little about how humans actually do it. While it has been argued before that there is a need for formal frameworks to help capture design dialogues in a format amenable to analysis, there is almost no work that actually attempts to do so. In this paper, we take a first step in this direction by exploring the application of concepts from agent dialogues to the description of actual design dialogues between human software designers. We have found that this can be done in principle and present a set of dialogue moves that we have found useful in the coding of an example dialogue. Through this formulation of the dialogue, we were able to identify some interesting patterns of moves and dialogue structures. More importantly, we believe that such a representation of design dialogues provides a good basis for a better understanding of how designers interact.

1 Introduction

Collaborative software design is a process that is little understood. Although there are good arguments (e.g., [1]) that there is a need for formal description frameworks that allow design processes to be modelled and analysed, there is little work that addresses this need.

Here, we take an agent dialogue approach to the problem. We have studied a recording and transcript of a pair of designers working together to determine a software design that meets a high-level requirements specification that they have been provided with.[1] Based on this initial study, we have defined a set of moves for capturing software design dialogues; we have considered what the effects of making the different types of move are and the conditions that we expect to see satisfied when each type of move is made. Table 1 shows an excerpt of the original transcript to give an idea of the material we have worked with. It also includes some examples of the kinds of moves we have identified.

We have modelled the collaborative software design as an argumentative process, where the participants exchange arguments in order to reach an agreement on the design specification that should be implemented. Existing dialogue systems about how to act

---

[1] Results described in this paper are based upon videos and transcripts initially distributed for the 2010 international workshop "Studying Professional Software Design", as partially supported by NSF grant CCF-0845840.

E. Black, S. Modgil, and N. Oren (Eds.): TAFA 2013, LNAI 8306, pp. 95–110, 2014.
© Springer-Verlag Berlin Heidelberg 2014

Table 1. Interrupted move by Male 2

[0:05:29.7]	
Male 1: Well, I want to start by hearing your summary of this	(1, p1, question, Feature, G, your-summary, null)
[0:05:36.4]	
Male 2: Gotcha, well. Looks like basically two pieces: the interaction and the code for map that's able to manipulate road systems with a whole bunch of details.	(2, p2, propose, Feature, G, interaction, 1) (3, p2, propose, Feature, G, map, 1)
What accounts for that to me is, be able to accommodate at least six intersections, be able to control lights at an individual level, so timing, how to get set off at each individual intersection.	(4, p2, justify, Feature, G, map-since-needed-to-accommodate-intersections, 3)
Sounds like at each individual lane.	(5, p2, propose, Feature, G, individual-lanes, null)

focus on *deliberation,* where agents want to agree on an action to achieve a shared goal but each may aim to influence outcome of decision in their favour (e.g. [2, 3]), *negotiation,* where there is some set of scarce resources that needs to be divided (e.g. [4]), or they may be *command dialogues,* where there is some authority relationship between participants (e.g. [5]). Software design discussions have a different focus. The main aim is to reach agreement on what the requirements of the system really are and what features should be implemented in order to meet these requirements.

Our limited analysis of a single software design discussion does not allow us to make any claims about the completeness or correctness of the dialogue moves that we propose for describing the software design process; nevertheless, we feel it is a valuable first step in developing a formal model for capturing and analysing design dialogues and we are encouraged by the variety of patterns and structures we have already identified with our framework.

Our paper is structured as follows: Section 2 presents the argument model we are using; in Section 3 we present the methodology that we followed in defining the dialogue moves; Section 4 presents our initial attempt at defining a dialogue framework to capture software design dialogues; Section 5 gives a discussion of our experience in annotating the transcript, highlighting some patterns and challenges that we found; related work is discussed in Section 6; Section 7 gives some conclusions.

2   Practical Arguments

The high level goal of a software design dialogue is to reach an agreement on a design specification that allows creation of an artefact that meets the system requirements. The main focus is not on what should be believed (although this may play a part) but on what states of the world should be brought about and how: what requirements should be met and what features should be implemented to meet those requirements.

With this in mind, we use the **practical reasoning argument scheme** of Atkinson *et al.* [6] to capture software design arguments.

In current circumstances $\mathbb{R}$, we should perform action α, which will result in new circumstances $\mathbb{S}$, which will achieve goal $\mathbb{G}$, which will promote value $\mathbb{V}$.

In software design terms:

- $\mathbb{R}$ represents the designers' beliefs about the world, including beliefs about the stakeholders' preferences and any requirements specification they have been given;
- α refers to the actual code to be written and steps that need to be taken to produce this code;
- $\mathbb{S}$ sets out the features that the code must implement, i.e. the design of the system;
- $\mathbb{G}$ captures the requirements of the system;
- $\mathbb{V}$ refers to values that may be held by the designers or the stakeholders.

By arguing about the different elements of the practical reasoning argument scheme, the designers aim to reach an agreement on $\mathbb{S}$.

3 Methodology

Our empirical work is based on videos originally recorded for the 2010 International Workshop on "Studying Professional Software Design" and subsequently made available to the research community. These are videos (and transcripts) of pairs of designers working out a software design based on a short design prompt giving a high-level requirements specification. Three videos have been made available, but for the purpose of this paper, we have focused on one of these only; specifically the video called `anonymous-video`. This is intentional, as it gives us the opportunity to use the remaining two videos for further validation and refinement of our framework in a next research stage.

Based on these videos, we have adopted a framework-based analysis methodology as follows:

1. We started by watching the entire video, followed by a high-level discussion of points of interest, this led to us identifying agreement on $\mathbb{S}$ (of the practical reasoning argument scheme) as the main goal of the dialogue;
2. We developed an initial framework of dialogue moves, this was based on a high-level categorisation of the dialogue kind based on our previous experience defining dialogue systems;
3. We annotated the transcript of the design dialogue up to timestamp 0:18:19.4 using the moves identified, making note of any problematic or irregular cases;
4. We developed a simple semantics in terms of the effects of making a move and the expectations we felt should be met when making a move;
5. Based on this initial semantics and the problematic or irregular cases identified, we revised the set of dialogue moves;
6. We re-annotated the transcript up to timestamp 0:18:19.4 using the revised set of dialogue moves, again noting any problematic or irregular cases;
7. We repeated steps 4-6.

In the next section, we present the resulting set of dialogue moves.

4 Dialogue Moves for Design Dialogues

In this section, we present our current version of the dialogue moves for design dialogues, produced by following the methodology in the previous section. We assume
for simplicity exactly two participants in the dialogue ($p1$ and $p2$); we believe it would
be straightforward to extend it to more participants. These participants make **moves**
throughout the dialogue, which affect one of five different **dialogue stores** that we associate with a design dialogue.

In Section 4.1 we first present the format of dialogue moves. Section 4.2 describes the
different dialogue stores those moves may affect. In Section 4.3, we detail what **effect**
the different types of move have on those stores and whether there are any conditions
that we expect to be satisfied when a particular move is made; note, since we are aiming
for a descriptive model, we refer to these conditions that we expect to be satisfied as the
expectations of a move (rather than preconditions).

4.1 Dialogue Moves

Dialogue moves have the following format

$$(ID, Sender, Type, Scope, Focus, Content, Target)$$

where:

- $ID \in \mathbb{N}$ uniquely identifies the move in the dialogue;
- $Sender \in \{p1, p2\}$ uniquely identifies the dialogue participant making the move;
- $Type \in \{propose, question, challenge, justify, withdraw, accept, reject,$
  $commit, uncommit\}$ is the **type** of the move;
- $Scope \in \{\text{FEATURE}, \text{RATING}, \text{CRITERIA}, \text{TOPIC}\}$ indicates whether the move re-
  lates to features of the system to be designed (FEATURE), an assessment of those
  features (RATING), the criteria that features should be assessed on (CRITERIA), or
  is suggesting topics for discussion (TOPIC) and so part of a meta-dialogue;
- $Focus \in \{\mathbb{R}, \alpha, \mathbb{S}, \mathbb{G}, \mathbb{V}\}$ denotes which part of the practical reasoning argument
  scheme the move refers to;
- $Content$ is a string derived from the locution uttered by the participant;
- $Target \in \mathbb{N} \cup \{null\}$ uniquely identifies an earlier move in the dialogue that this
  move refers to, if there is such a move, or is $null$ if there is no such move.

During the dialogue, the moves that the participants make cause things to be added
or removed from the different dialogue stores that we associate with a design dialogue.

4.2 Dialogue Stores

The format of the elements that make up each of the different types of dialogue store is
given in Table 2.

The **proposal store**, $\mathcal{P}$, keeps track of the proposals being discussed in the dialogue.
If something is present in the proposal store, then the participants aim to decide whether

it should be added to the commitment store or not. A single agent can add something to the proposal store (with a propose move), but all participants must agree in order to remove something from the proposal store (with a reject move made by one participant targeted by an accept move made by the other participant).

The **question store**, $\mathcal{Q}$, keeps track of questions that have been posed during the dialogue. A single participant can add something to the question store (with a question move). A single participant can remove something from the question store by answering a question with a propose move or with a withdraw move if it was the participant that posed the original question. Elements in the question store have to keep track of who posed them ($Sender$), since only the same participant can withdraw that question.

The **challenge store**, $\mathcal{CH}$, keeps track of proposals and commitments that have been challenged during the dialogue. A single participant can add something to the challenge store (with a challenge move). A single participant can remove something from the challenge store by answering a challenge with a justify move, or with a withdraw move but only if it was the participant that made the original challenge move. Elements in the challenge store have to keep track of who posed them ($Sender$), since only the same participant can withdraw that question.

The **commitment store**, $\mathcal{CO}$, keeps track of the commitments the participants have made during the dialogue. All participants must agree in order to add something to the commitment store (with a commit move made by one participant targeted by an accept move made by the other participant). Elements in the commitment store record the ID of the move that first put forward the commitment, rather than of the move that accepted it. All participants must agree in order to remove something from the commitment store (with an uncommit move made by one participant targeted by an accept move made by the other participant).

The **argument store**, $\mathcal{A}$, keeps track of the arguments that the participants have made during the dialogue. A single participant can add something to the argument store (with a justify move). Things are not removed from the argument store, the idea being that inconsistencies can be dealt with by applying an argumentation semantics (e.g. [7]) to evaluate the dialectical acceptability of the arguments in the store.

4.3 Effects and Expectations of Moves

Each type of move has **effects**, i.e. what is added and removed from the different stores, and also some **expectations**, i.e. what we expect to see when a particular type of move is made in terms of the different elements of the move and contents of the different stores. The effects and expectations of each of the different types of move are given in Table 3. Note that we are using the notion of an **expectation** rather than a pre-condition to highlight the fact that these operators are used to record observed human behaviour, which invariably will invalidate some of these expectations. We hope, however, that in future work we may be able to learn a set of reasonable expectations from examples of good design dialogues and use these to help us identify good or less promising cases of design dialogues.

Propose moves may have no target or may target a previous question. If a propose move targets a previous question, it causes that question to be removed from the question store. All propose moves cause an item to be added to the proposal store.

Table 2. Format of elements in the dialogue stores; first column gives the type of dialogue store, second column gives the format of an element in that type of dialogue store, third column gives an explanation of the different parameters of the element

Dialogue store	Format of element	Description
Proposal store, $\mathcal{P}$	$(ID, Scope, Focus, Content)$	ID is the identifier of the move that made the proposal; $Scope, Focus$ and $Content$ give the details of the proposal.
Question store, $\mathcal{Q}$	$(ID, Sender, Scope, Focus, Content)$	ID is the identifier of the move that made the question; $Sender$ is the identifier of the participant who made that move; $Scope, Focus$ and $Content$ give the details of the question.
Challenge store, $\mathcal{CH}$	$(ID, Sender, Target)$	ID is the identifier of the move that made the challenge; $Sender$ is the identifier of the participant who made that move; $Target$ identifies the previous move that is being challenged.
Commitment store, $\mathcal{CO}$	$(ID, Scope, Focus, Content)$	ID is the identifier of the move that first put forward the commitment; $Scope, Focus$ and $Content$ give the details of the commitment.
Argument store, $\mathcal{A}$	$(ID, Scope, Focus, Content, Target)$	ID is the identifier of the move that put forward the justification; $Scope, Focus$ and $Content$ give the details of the argument; $Target$ identifies what (if anything) is being justified.

Question moves do not target a previous move and have the effect of adding an item to the question store.

We expect a **challenge** move to target either a previous proposal or a previous commitment made; this is reflected by our annotation of the transcript. Making a challenge move causes an item to be added to the challenge store.

In our first iteration of defining the move semantics, we felt that a **justify** move would always target a previous propose move. In fact, we have identified justify moves that target previous question moves, commit moves, reject moves and that have no target; thus we have currently no expectations of a justify move. When a justify move is made it causes an item to be added to the argument store. If a justify move is made that targets a previous proposal that is also the target of a previous challenge, it causes that challenge to be removed from the challenge store.

A **commit** move has no effect on its own, since it must be explicitly targeted by a subsequent accept move made by the other participant to cause an item to be added to the commitment store. We initially felt that a commit move would always target a previous proposal. In fact, we identified very few commit moves: one that targeted a previous proposal, one that targeted a previous question and two that had no target, thus there are no expectations of commit moves.

Table 3. The effects and expectations of making a move ($ID, Sender, Type, Scope, Focus, Content, Target$); the first column gives the *Type* of move being made, the second column gives the effects of making a move of that *Type*, the third column gives the expectations of a move of that *Type*. Note: $\overline{Sender} = p1$ iff $Sender = p2$; $\overline{Sender} = p2$ iff $Sender = p1$.

Type	Effects	Expectations
propose	$(ID, Scope, Focus, Content)$ added to $\mathcal{P}$ If present, $(Target, -, Scope, Focus, -)$ removed from $\mathcal{Q}$	If $Target \neq null$, then $(Target, -, Scope, Focus, -) \in \mathcal{Q}$
question	$(ID, Sender, Scope, Focus, Content)$ added to $\mathcal{Q}$	$Target = null$
challenge	$(ID, Sender, Target)$ added to $\mathcal{CH}$	$Target \neq null$ $(Target, Scope, Focus, Content) \in \mathcal{P} \cup \mathcal{CO}$
justify	$(ID, Scope, Focus, Content, Target)$ added to $\mathcal{A}$ If present, $(-, -, Target)$ removed from $\mathcal{CH}$	None
commit	None	None
reject	None	$(Target, Scope, Focus, Content) \in \mathcal{P}$
uncommit	None	$(Target, Scope, Focus, Content) \in \mathcal{CO}$
accept	If there exists a previous dialogue move $(Target, \overline{Sender}, Type', Scope, Focus, Content, Target')$, then: - if $Type' = reject$, then $(Target', Scope, Focus, Content)$ removed from $\mathcal{P}$; - if $Type' = commit$, then $(Target', Scope, Focus, Content)$ added to $\mathcal{CO}$; - if $Type' = uncommit$, then $(Target', Scope, Focus, Content)$ removed from $\mathcal{CO}$.	$Target \neq null$
withdraw	If present, $(Target, Sender, Scope, Focus, Content)$ removed from $\mathcal{Q}$ If present, $(Target, Sender, -)$ removed from $\mathcal{CH}$	Either $(Target, Sender, -) \in \mathcal{CH}$ or $(Target, Sender, Scope, Focus, Content) \in \mathcal{Q}$

Table 4. Interrupted move by Male 2

And the left-hand, this kind of implies- **[0:10:28.6]** Male 2: Really, it's just a- **[0:10:30.7]** Male 1: Two-two lanes? Is there a left-turn lane, or is it a suicide left?   *(31, p1, question, Feature, G, left-turn-lane, null)*

We expect that a **reject** move may target either a previous proposal or a previous commitment. We have seen only one reject move in our annotation of the transcript, which targets a proposal. Making a reject move on its own has no effect, since it must be explicitly targeted by a subsequent accept move made by the other participant in order to cause something to be removed from the proposal store.

Initially we felt that **accept** moves would target only reject, commit, or uncommit moves made by the other participant; in these cases they act as an explicit confirmation that an item is to be removed from the proposal store (when targeting a reject move), added to the commitment store (when targeting a commit move), or removed from the commitment store (when targeting an uncommit move). We found, however, that accept moves are also made that targeted challenge moves, justify moves and commit moves; in our current model, such accept moves have no effect, since the targeted moves do not need explicit acceptance to affect their respective store. We expect that an accept move targets some previous move.

We expect that a participant may **withdraw** something that they themselves have posed as a challenge or a question from either the challenge or question store. We have so far only identified one instance of a withdraw move, where the participant withdraws a previous challenge they made.

5   Discussion

While we have used a relatively fine-grained approach to annotating the discussion transcript with our operators, such an annotation necessarily leads to a level of abstraction; that is, some details of the dialogue are lost in the encoding. For example, we have chosen not to annotate moves that seemed to be interrupted (e.g., the interrupted Male-2 move in Table 4). In the transcript we have looked at for this paper, the interrupted move seems indeed inconsequential for the further dialogue; the other participant just continues his own train of thought. However, in other dialogues this may not be the case: For example, the interruption may occur because the partial move has triggered an idea in the other participant. In these cases it may become necessary to define additional annotations to encode interrupted or partial moves.

More importantly perhaps, our annotations abstract completely from how each move was implemented by the respective participant. It would perhaps also be of interest to understand how particular kinds of moves are signalled by human designers; however this is out of scope for our study. We take a more symbolic-interactionist approach as we are primarily interested in understanding the 'protocol' of design dialogues. As

Table 5. Male 2 challenging his own proposal

[0:13:15.9]
Male 2: I think we have-we can probably
numerate the rules we're going to need too. *(59, p2, propose, enumerate-rules, Topic, S, null)*
Or do we care?   *(60, p2, challenge, enumerate-rules, Topic, S, 59)*

a consequence, in some cases we have even annotated moves that are not explicitly present in the transcript. These are derived from the definitions of our dialogue moves: it appears that some moves happen implicitly. For example, a commit move may be accepted implicitly by not challenging it.

Our analysis currently only looks at the spoken conversation as captured in the transcript. We did, in a number of instances, refer to the video-recorded design session to disambiguate a particular move, but in general almost no information beyond the spoken text was used. In particular, we have not encoded the designers' interactions at and with the white board and their use of this as a (temporary) store of knowledge. It seems obvious, that this is an important dimension of the design dialogue that bears further analysis. However, it is not entirely clear whether and how the use of the whiteboard could be fit into our current model. Some initial work on whiteboard usage exists [8], but this takes a more conversation-analytic approach focussed on the mechanics of interaction. As a result Mangano *et al.* have developed a novel tool for intelligent whiteboards to support some of the specific interaction styles observed.

Beyond these methodological issues, we have also identified a number of features in the interaction between the designers. This seems to be a key benefit of the encoding that we have defined, in that it lets us focus on such interaction features / patterns in order to extract protocols of interesting forms of interaction. In particular, we have found the following features:

- **Self-challenge.** Commonly in argumentation dialogues, we might expect that a proposal can only be challenged by the other participant. However, interestingly, in the dialogue we have analysed we have found situations in which one participant seems to be challenging his own proposal (e.g., Table 5).
- **Vagueness of commit.** It is not always clear from the transcript or actual video whether a particular move is a proposal or a commit move. For example, moves 45 and 49 shown in Table 6 are such ambiguous cases. It would be interesting to see whether the designers themselves have a clear idea of what they have committed to. If yes, then we need further research to understand better how commits are expressed. If they do not agree what they have committed to, there may be some benefit in tooling that can assist in making commitments explicit without interrupting the flow of interaction too much.
- **Non-strict protocol.** We have defined previously that a propose move in response to a question move removes that question from the question store. This assumes that every question can be answered with a single proposal. However, we can find cases where more than one proposal move occurs in response to a question move (e.g., moves 2 and 3 both answer move 1, see Table 7). This seems to indicate that a different protocol would be more appropriate, whereby questions are not

Table 6. Ambiguous commits: Should Move 45 be a propose? Should Move 49 be a commit?

[0:11:56.3]	
Male 1: Do we want to assume one lane of traffic coming in, and?	*(45, p1, commit, roads-should-not-have-lanes, Feature, G, 38)*
...	
[0:12:12.9]	
Male 1: So we have a model of behavior where we have these cars turning left, these stopped, these cars going straight, and then when this stops these cars can then go	*(49, p1, propose, details-intersection-protected-left-turn, Feature, G, null)*

Table 7. Non-strict protocol: Multiple proposals in response to a question

[0:05:29.7]	
Male 1: Well, I want to start by hearing your summary of this	*(1, p1, question, Feature, G, your-summary, null)*
[0:05:36.4]	
Male 2: Gotcha, well. Looks like basically two pieces: the interaction and the code for map that's able to manipulate road systems with a whole bunch of details.	*(2, p2, propose, Feature, G, interaction, 1)* *(3, p2, propose, Feature, G, map, 1)*

removed from the question store by a propose move. Instead, a question can be considered answered if the proposal store contains at least one proposal referencing the question move.

– **Missing move types.** We have found some types of moves that did not fit well into our framework. For example, the designers occasionally follow the consequences of a proposal by talking through the logical implications (see for example minute 15:38.5). This has been called mental modelling before and it would be good to be able to capture this kind of move as well. Similarly, in some cases the participants make meta-moves to control the structure of the dialogue beyond simply proposing or rejecting new topics. For example, in Table 8, the participants seem to agree on delaying the discussion of a particular topic without actually removing it from the topic list. Finally, there are some moves that we have classified as questions, but which actually seem to be used as proposals. This could be the participant's way of expressing that some ideas are more tentative than others (see also [9]).

– **Patterns of interaction.** Some interesting patterns can already be established from our initial work. A particularly interesting one occurs from move 78 to move 85, where the same proposal is justified in a number of different ways by the two participants although they already seem to have accepted the proposal very early on in the interaction (see Table 9).

We have found a number of other interesting things, which we are not discussing here as the space is limited. It seems clear that agent dialogue techniques can be used in principle to capture design dialogues. At the same time, however, this can only be the

Table 8. Delaying a topic

[0:15:30.1]	
...	
Concerned with too much detail before we even-otherwise we're going to cut stuff out.	*– proposal of delay –*
[0:15:38.5]	
Male 1: Sure, yeah, yeah. Let's look for *(error)*erm.	*(74, p1, accept, ??, Topic, G, ??)*

Table 9. Chains of justification

[0:16:32.6]	
Male 2: It sounds like more and more like the intersection is kind of [inaudible] because basically it's going to have given	*(78, p2, accept, intersection-controls-signals, Feature, S, 75)*
S1 goes green, it's going to have to delegate the actions of what S2 and S3 are; is it safe from stuff like that	*(79, p2, justify, intersection-controls-signals-since-delegate-actions, Feature, S, 75)*
[0:16:41.1]	
Male 1: Exactly, exactly.	*(80, p1, accept, intersection-controls-signals-since-delegate-actions, Feature, S, 79)*
Somebody is controlling the interactions. If you think of this as kind of an encapsulated entity then it's not going to know about this.	*(81, p1, justify, intersection-controls-signals-since-somebody-controls-interactions, Feature, S, 75)*
[0:16:51.0]	
Male 2: Exactly, yeah exactly.	*(82, p2, accept, intersection-controls-signals-since- somebody-controls-interactions, Feature, S, 81)*
So how do you share that information across all the signals.	*(83, p2, justify, intersection-controls-signals-since-alllows-share-information-across-signals, Feature, S, 75)*
[0:16:55.6] Male 1: Exactly.	*(84, p1, accept, intersection-controls-signals-since-alllows-share-information-across-signals, Feature, S, 83)*
[0:16:56.4]	
Male 2: Because at that point the rules more apply to the intersection itself as opposed to any one individual signal.	*(85, p2, justify, intersection-controls-signals-since-rules-apply-to-intersection-not-signal, Feature, S, 75)*

foundation for more in-depth research into the different patterns of interaction used in these dialogues.

6 Related Work

In his panel contribution [1], Finkelstein was the first, as far as we can identify, to propose that there is a need for formal representations of design dialogues (considering this term in the widest sense to also include, for example, requirements-analysis dialogues). Together with Fuks, in [10] he provides a first proposal of such a formalisation based on argumentation theory. However, while this is an interesting early proposal of an agent-dialogue protocol, it is less clear how faithfully it represents actual human dialogues. In particular, it would appear that the operators and protocol rules are based on generalisations drawn from the authors' considerable experience with requirements analysis rather than specific observations and annotations of transcripted dialogues. In contrast, our work is based entirely on transcripts taken from video-taped design dialogues. Moreover, the model of Finkelstein and Fuks adopts the dialogue system *DC* of James MacKenzie [11], a system developed by philosophers of argumentation for analyzing fallacious or apparently fallacious arguments over beliefs; this purpose would seem to be inappropriate for representing dialogues over design, dialogues which presumably have as their end-purpose some actions or some plans for actions.

Several works have considered the application of argumentation theory to the process of requirements engineering. For example, both [12] and [13] propose argumentation as a tool for identifying and analysing inconsistencies in requirements. An argumentation-based method for reasoning about the implications of security risks and the satisfaction of security requirements is given in [14]. [15] uses the Argument Interchange Format [16] to represent information from a discussion on the relative validity of a requirements engineering artifact and provides a mechanism for determining the acceptability of the artifact based on this information. These works all propose the use of argumentation as a tool for supporting the requirements engineering process but do not aim to capture possible dialogues for requirements elicitation. We hope, in the future, to complement the work we present here with the proposal of an agent-dialogue model of the requirements elicitation process. It will be interesting to see whether any of these existing works can be used as the underlying argumentation model.

As we have mentioned before, the videos that form the basis of our work, have been captured as part of a workshop on "Studying Professional Software Design". Other researchers have also studied these videos from a variety of perspectives, leading to a number of special issues of journals [17,18]. The work collected in these special issues and in other venues has looked at the videos from a variety of perspectives—including, for example, conversation analysis [9], decision-making in product design [19,20], topic analysis [21], and others.

To the best of our knowledge, there is no work that attempts to provide a formalised representation of design dialogues using, for example, dialogue systems. The works that come, perhaps, closest to ours are [19,20]. In [19], the authors attempt a description of the strategies used by the designer in the three videos. However, their framework is much more coarse-grained and is not based on an annotation of individual statements.

Consequently, while it enables a high-level classification of design dialogues, it is less useful for identifying recurring patterns in the interaction. The work in [20] is based on a much more detailed coding of the design dialogues, much closer to our use of dialogue moves. Their evaluation, however, again focuses on the macro level of design strategies rather than the micro level of individual design interactions.

Within the academic community that studies artefact design, the closest work to our paper is the book by the architect Andrew Dong [22]. Drawing on speech act theory (e.g., [23]), Dong presents a theory of successful collaborative design dialogues which involves a three-stage model of interaction (summarized in [22, Chapter 7]). In Stage 1, *Aggregation*, the participants gather materials to form a frame or a collection of constraints and objectives for the design concept. In the software engineering domain, such constraints would include the system specification and requirements. In Stage 2, *Accumulation*, the participants jointly and incrementally reify and materialize the design concept; i.e., they flesh out the design. In Stage 3, *Appraisal*, the participants assess, from their potentially differing and subjective perspectives, the concept and its realization. These stages are abstractions, of course, and in real design interactions participants may move between them many times as the interaction progresses [20]. Although he does consider the performative nature of utterances in materializing a design concept (i.e., for Stage 2), his framework remains at a much higher level of abstraction than our work here. Despite this, it is easy to see that the utterance annotation we have presented here could be readily categorized by Dong's three stages.

Within the field of agent communications and agent argumentation, considerable recent work over the last decade has explored formal dialogues, and particularly dialogues over actions (see [24] for a review). McBurney *et al.* presented a formal framework for agent deliberation dialogues—dialogues about what to do in some situation— in [25]. Atkinson *et al.* [6] proposed an argumentation scheme and associated critical questions for proposals over actions, which has been influential in later work. Atkinson and Bench-Capon, for example, gave this schema a novel semantics [26]; Black and Atkinson [2] considered the strategic selection of utterances in dialogues over action; Atkinson *et al.* [5] considered dialogues involving commands; and Medellin *et al.* [27] considered dialogues between agents co-ordinating separate plans. Since [6], these works all have in common a representational structure we have also drawn upon in Section 2: actions are understood as taking us from some initial (or present) state to some future, successor state, in which latter state certain propositions are true; being true, these propositions promote or demote certain values. The true propositions are objectively true (i.e., agreed by all, at least in principle), while any subjective assessment of the future state arising from the successful execution of the action is confined to the values and their preference ordering. In all the works cited, the focus of attention in the dialogues being modeled or presented is on the possible actions, and how participants may or should compare and assess alternative actions.

In our current work, however, we notice that the participants to the software design dialogue seem to take the actual actions they will select for granted. Being experienced software developers they each know what specific actions are needed to produce any desired software outputs (at least within the range of outputs covered by the design brief), and they know (or they assume) that each other participant knows this too.

Consequently, the dialogue between them can ignore the specific actions, and focus on the outcomes of the action; that is, on the successor state and the propositions which will be true in that state, and (to a lesser extent) on the values promoted or demoted by those outcomes. It may be that, having agreed the desired outcomes, they may turn their attention to the specific actions required to achieve these outcomes. We believe this different focus marks out such design dialogues as a specific sub-type of deliberation dialogues: they are collaborative dialogues about what actions to take, where the agreed intended purpose of the actions is the joint creation of an artefact.

7 Conclusions

We have presented an initial study exploring the use of ideas from agent dialogues to formally describe dialogues between designers of software systems. The overall goal of this research is to provide ways in which such design dialogues can be captured for further analysis—for example, it may be possible to understand common problems and provide tool support to alleviate them or we may be able to learn strategies of successful designers and teach them to novice designers.

In this paper, we have studied one transcript from a design dialogue captured as part of the "Studying Professional Software Design" workshop held in 2010. We have shown that it is indeed feasible to capture key elements of design dialogues using the notion of moves from agent dialogues and have proposed a specific schema of moves to do so. We feel that this is a promising application of agent-dialogue ideas as it opens a range of different research directions—for example:

- How do designers keep track of the various stores, and in particular of committed decisions? Even from the relatively limited study reported here it seems that they may loose track of some of the decisions made earlier. If this is indeed the case, can we make use of the representation of design dialogues proposed to provide some form of tool support to software designers?
- What are typical strategies of design dialogues? Are there some strategies which are more often seen in successful design dialogues? One way of capturing good design dialogues may be through a refinement of the notion of expectations that we have introduced in Sect. 4.3: These may be able to model the way experienced designers work. When we find that expectations are frequently not valid in a design dialogue, this may then be a sign of a less experienced designer and there may be ways in which support can be derived from this observation.

Similarly, we believe that design dialogues are a novel form of dialogue, not previously discussed in the literature on agent dialogues. The focus here is less on bringing together knowledge distributed over a set of agents nor on deciding on a particular course of action. Instead, design dialogues aim for a balance between agreeing on the overall goals and values as well as actions towards a set of new circumstances (the implementation), all of which are up for discussion. Interestingly, the specific actions seem of least interest in the software-design dialogues as they are implied by the implementation details chosen.

References

1. Finkelstein, A.: Modeling the software process: "not waving but drowning": Representation schemes for modelling software development (panel session). In: Proc. 11th Int'l Conf. on Software Engineering (ICSE 1989), pp. 402–404. ACM, New York (1989)
2. Black, E., Atkinson, K.: Choosing persuasive arguments for action. In: Proceedings of the Tenth International Conference on Autonomous Agents and Multi-Agent Systems (2011)
3. Hitchcock, D., McBurney, P., Parsons, S.: A framework for deliberation dialogues. In: 4th Biennial Conf. of the Ontario Society for the Study of Argumentation (2001)
4. Rahwan, I., Ramchurn, S.D., Jennings, N.R., McBurney, P., Parsons, S., Sonenberg, E.: Argumentation-based negotiation. Knowledge Engineering Review 18(4), 343–375 (2003)
5. Atkinson, K., Girle, R., McBurney, P., Parsons, S.: Command dialogues. In: Rahwan, I., Moraitis, P. (eds.) Proceedings of the Fifth International Workshop on Argumentation in Multi-Agent Systems (ArgMAS 2008), pp. 9–23 (2008)
6. Atkinson, K., Bench-Capon, T., McBurney, P.: Computational representation of practical argument. Synthese 152(2), 157–206 (2006)
7. Dung, P.M.: On the acceptability of arguments and its fundamental role in nonmonotonic reasoning, logic programming and n-person games. Artificial Intelligence 77, 321–357 (1995)
8. Mangano, N., van der Hoek, A.: The design and evaluation of a tool to support software designers at the whiteboard. Automated Software Engineering 19(4), 381–421 (2012)
9. McDonnell, J.: Accommodating disagreement: A study of effective design collaboration. Design Studies 33(1), 44–63 (2012)
10. Finkelstein, A., Fuks, H.: Multiparty specification. SIGSOFT Softw. Eng. Notes 14(3), 185–195 (1989)
11. MacKenzie, J.D.: Question-begging in non-cumulative systems. Journal of Philosophical Logic 8, 117–133 (1979)
12. Bagheri, E., Ensan, F.: Consolidating multiple requirement specifications through argumentation. In: Chu, W.C., Wong, W.E., Palakal, M.J., Hung, C.C. (eds.) SAC, pp. 659–666. ACM (2011)
13. Mirbel, I., Villata, S.: Enhancing goal-based requirements consistency: An argumentation-based approach. In: Fisher, M., van der Torre, L., Dastani, M., Governatori, G. (eds.) CLIMA XIII 2012. LNCS (LNAI), vol. 7486, pp. 110–127. Springer, Heidelberg (2012)
14. Franqueira, V.N., Tun, T.T., Yu, Y., Wieringa, R., Nuseibeh, B.: Risk and argument: A risk-based argumentation method for practical security. In: 2011 19th IEEE International Conference on Requirements Engineering (RE), pp. 239–248. IEEE (2011)
15. Jureta, I., Mylopoulos, J., Faulkner, S.: Analysis of multi-party agreement in requirements validation. In: 17th IEEE International Conference on Requirements Engineering, RE 2009, pp. 57–66. IEEE (2009)
16. Chesñevar, C., McGinnis, J., Modgil, S., Rahwan, I., Reed, C., Simari, G., South, M., Vreeswijk, G., Willmott, S.: Towards an argument interchange format. Knowl. Eng. Rev. 21(4), 293–316 (2006)
17. Petre, M., van der Hoek, A., Baker, A.: Editorial. Design Studies: Special Issue Studying Professional Software Design 31(6), 533–544 (2010)
18. Baker, A., van der Hoek, A., Ossher, H., Petre, M.: Guest editors' introduction: Studying professional software design. IEEE Software 29(1), 28–33 (2012)
19. Christiaans, H., Almendra, R.A.: Accessing decision-making in software design. Design Studies: Special Issue Studying Professional Software Design 31(6), 641–662 (2010)
20. Tang, A., Aleti, A., Burge, J., van Vliet, H.: What makes software design effective? Design Studies 31(6), 614–640 (2010); Special Issue Studying Professional Software Design

21. Baker, A., van der Hoek, A.: Ideas, subjects, and cycles as lenses for understanding the software design process. Design Studies: Special Issue Studying Professional Software Design 31(6), 590–613 (2010)
22. Dong, A.: The Language of Design: Theory and Computation. Springer, Berlin (2008)
23. Austin, J.L.: How To Do Things with Words. Oxford University Press, Oxford (1962); (Originally delivered as the William James Lectures at Harvard University in 1955.)
24. McBurney, P., Parsons, S.: Dialogue games for agent argumentation. In: Rahwan, I., Simari, G. (eds.) Argumentation in Artificial Intelligence, pp. 261–280. Springer, Berlin (2009)
25. McBurney, P., Hitchcock, D., Parsons, S.: The eightfold way of deliberation dialogue. International Journal of Intelligent Systems 22(1), 95–132 (2007)
26. Atkinson, K., Bench-Capon, T.J.M.: Practical reasoning as presumptive argumentation using action based alternating transition systems. Artificial Intelligence 171(10-15), 855–874 (2007)
27. Medellin-Gasque, R., Atkinson, K., Bench-Capon, T., McBurney, P.: Strategies for question selection in argumentation about plans. Argument and Computation (2013) (in press)

On the Maximal and Average Numbers of Stable Extensions

Ringo Baumann and Hannes Strass

Computer Science Institute, Leipzig University

Abstract. We present an analytical and empirical study of the maximal and average numbers of stable extensions in abstract argumentation frameworks. As one of the analytical main results, we prove a tight upper bound on the maximal number of stable extensions that depends only on the number of arguments in the framework. More interestingly, our empirical results indicate that the distribution of stable extensions as a function of the number of attacks in the framework seems to follow a universal pattern that is independent of the number of arguments.

1 Motivation

Stable extensions constitute one of the most important and well-researched semantics for abstract argumentation frameworks (AFs). Dung used the stable extension semantics in his original paper to relate AFs to Reiter's default logic, different forms of logic programming, and to solve the stable marriage problem, among others [1]. Alas, there are some fundamental questions to be asked about stable extension semantics which have yet remained unanswered.

Given an abstract argumentation framework for which the only thing we know is that it has n arguments and x attacks, how many stable extensions does it have at most? How many on average?

For $x = 0$, without attacks, the case is quite clear – there will be exactly one stable extension, the set of all arguments. For $x = n^2$, the AF contains all possible attacks, in particular all self-attacks, and there will be no stable extension. But what happens in between, when $0 < x < n^2$?

This paper takes a step towards analytical and empirical answers to these questions. In particular, we develop predictions on the maximal and average number of stable extensions when only the number of arguments and attacks are known (and finite).

In the considerable zoo of semantics for abstract argumentation, stable extension semantics is the only one for which extension existence is not guaranteed for finite AFs. While this is usually regarded as a weakness, there is an obvious benefit to it when AFs are used to model NP-complete problems, which do not necessarily possess a solution. In this setting, the fact that an NP problem instance encoded as an AF has no stable extension elegantly reflects the fact that the problem instance has no solution. Using other semantics, unsolvability would have to be represented by introducing new (meta-)language constructs.

E. Black, S. Modgil, and N. Oren (Eds.): TAFA 2013, LNAI 8306, pp. 111–126, 2014.
© Springer-Verlag Berlin Heidelberg 2014

NP problems typically have elements that are generating (that is, generate possible solution candidates) and elements that are constraining (that is, eliminate possible solution candidates). The classical example of an NP-complete problem is of course deciding the satisfiability of a given propositional formula in conjunctive normal form, the SAT problem. There, the propositional variables are the generating elements (since solution candidates are among all interpretations for the variables) while the disjunctive clauses are the constraining elements (they remove those interpretations not satisfying some clause).

Can the same be said about arguments and attacks? Surely, arguments are generating, since extension candidates are sets of arguments. But are attacks always constraining?

Consider the argumentation framework on the right where a_1 attacks a_2, and two specific ways to add an attack to this framework: (1) adding an attack from a_2 to a_1 (middle), and (2) adding an attack from a_1 to itself (below). AF (1) has two stable extensions, while AF (2) has no stable extension. So while adding a clause to a CNF may never increase the number of models, adding attacks to an AF may in general both increase or decrease the number of stable extensions.

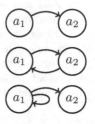

Roughly, to be a stable extension, a set has to satisfy two properties. It has to be conflict-free, and has to attack all arguments not in the set. Intuitively, the number of attacks in an AF correlates negatively with the number of conflict-free sets – the more attacks (that is, conflicts) there are, the less conflict-free sets are found. At the same time, the number of attacks correlates positively with the number of sets which attack all outsiders. So how will these two interleaved and counteracting forces come to terms in general?

The paper is structured as follows. We next introduce the necessary background in graph theory and Dung's abstract argumentation frameworks. Then Section 3 presents our analytical results; Section 4 describes the results we obtained empirically. We conclude with a discussion of the results and give some perspectives on future work.

2   Background

Throughout the paper we assume some familiarity with standard analysis, combinatorics and statistics. For a set X, a *(binary) relation* over X is any set $R \subseteq X \times X$. Special among these relations is the *identity* $\mathrm{id}_X = \{(x, x) \mid x \in X\}$. A relation R over X is *irreflexive* iff $R \cap \mathrm{id}_X = \emptyset$, that is, for each $x \in X$ we have $(x, x) \notin R$. It is *symmetric* iff for each $(x, y) \in R$ we have $(y, x) \in R$. The *inverse* of a relation R is given by $R^{-1} = \{(y, x) \mid (x, y) \in R\}$.

2.1   Graph Theory

A *directed graph* is a pair (V, E) where V is a finite set and E a binary relation over V. The elements of V are called *nodes* and those of E are called *edges*.

A directed graph is *symmetric* iff its edge relation E is symmetric. For a directed graph $G = (V, E)$, we denote by $sym(G) = (V, E \cup E^{-1})$ its symmetric version. Similarly, the irreflexive version of a graph $G = (V, E)$ is defined as $irr(G) = (V, E \setminus \text{id}_V)$.

An *undirected graph* is a pair (V, F) where V is as above and $F \subseteq \binom{V}{2} \cup \binom{V}{1}$ is a set of 2- and 1-element subsets of V, which represent the undirected edges. For a directed graph $G = (V, E)$, we denote by $und(G) = (V, \{\{u, v\} \mid (u, v) \in E\})$ its associated undirected graph. An undirected graph (V, F) is *simple* iff $F \subseteq \binom{V}{2}$. We denote by $\mathcal{G}_n$ the set of all simple graphs with n nodes.

For a simple graph $G = (V, F)$, a set $M \subseteq V$ is *independent* iff for all $u, v \in M$ we have $\{u, v\} \notin F$. A set $M \subseteq V$ is *maximal independent* iff it is independent and there is no proper superset of M which is independent. The set of all maximal independent sets of a simple graph G is denoted by $MIS(G)$.

2.2 Abstract Argumentation

An *argumentation framework (AF)* $\mathcal{F} = (A, R)$ is a directed graph; the elements of A are also called *arguments* and the elements of R are also called *attacks*. All other graph theoretic notions carry over to AFs. A *full AF* is of the form $(A, A \times A)$ for some set A.

For the purposes of this paper, we denote by $\mathcal{A}_n$ the set of all AFs with n arguments, and by $\mathcal{A}_{n,x}$ the set of all AFs with n arguments and x attacks. There, not the precise arguments are of interest to us but only the *number* of arguments; we will implicitly assume that the n arguments can be numbered by $1, \ldots, n$. Once the arguments are fixed, however, we consider two AFs the same if and only if they have the same attack relation. So the AF with two arguments $1, 2$ where 1 attacks 2 is different from the AF with two arguments $1, 2$ where 2 attacks 1, although the two are isomorphic in a graph theoretic sense. This guarantees that all possible scenarios, that is, any arrangement of attacks for fixed numbers of arguments and attacks is considered.

The semantics of AFs is defined by determining those subsets $S \subseteq A$ which are acceptable according to specific criteria, so-called *extensions*. Among the various semantics from the literature, we are only interested in the stable semantics: a set $S \subseteq A$ is a *stable extension* for (A, R) iff (1) there are no $a, b \in S$ with $(a, b) \in R$, and (2) for all $a \in A \setminus S$, there is a $b \in S$ with $(b, a) \in R$. For an AF $\mathcal{F}$, the set of its stable extensions is denoted by $\mathcal{E}_{st}(\mathcal{F})$.

Interpreting the attack relation as denoting some kind of directed conflict between arguments, a stable extension can be seen as a set of arguments that is without internal conflict and attacks all arguments not contained in it. We call an argumentation framework a *y-AF* iff it has exactly y stable extensions. For the purpose of illustration consider the following example AF $\mathcal{F}$:

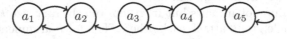

$\mathcal{F}$ has two stable extensions – $\mathcal{E}_{st}(\mathcal{F}) = \{\{a_1, a_4\}, \{a_2, a_4\}\}$ – thus $\mathcal{F}$ is a 2-AF.

3   Analytical Results

Baroni et al. [2] showed that counting the number of stable extensions of an argumentation framework is a computationally hard problem. The analysis of counting techniques may yield upper bounds for algorithms computing extensions. Furthermore, a fast counting algorithm gives a first advice on how controversial the information represented in an AF is. In this section, we contribute some analytical results to this direction of research.

For a fixed number n of arguments there are $|\mathcal{A}_n| = 2^{n^2}$ different AFs, since any attack relation whatsoever is possible and significant. Furthermore, if we additionally know that the AF in question possesses x attacks, then the total number of possibilities equals $|\mathcal{A}_{n,x}| = \binom{n^2}{x}$, the number of x-element subsets of an n^2-element set. This means that in principle, one may obtain numerically precise results by brute force for classes of AFs possessing a certain number of arguments and attacks. For example, specific classes of AFs could be enumerated and each element analysed separately. But obviously, such an approach cannot provide a solution which is parametric in the numbers of arguments and attacks.

3.1   Maximal Number of Stable Extensions

What is the maximal number of stable extensions given an AF $\mathcal{F} = (A, R)$ with $|A| = n$ arguments? Since argumentation semantics choose their extensions from the set of subsets of A, we have $\mathcal{E}_{st}(\mathcal{F}) \subseteq 2^A$. This yields an immediate upper bound on the number of extensions for any semantics, namely $|\mathcal{E}_{st}(\mathcal{F})| \leq |2^A| = 2^n$. Can this quite naive bound be improved? In case of semantics satisfying I-maximality the answer is "yes." For short, I-maximality is fulfilled if no extension can be a proper subset of another [3]. In other words, the cardinality of one of the largest $\subseteq$-antichains S being a subset of an n-element set gives a further upper bound on the number of extensions.[1] The maximal cardinality of such antichains is given by Sperner's theorem [4], namely $|S| = \binom{n}{\lfloor \frac{n}{2} \rfloor}$. By a straightforward calculation one may show that $\binom{n}{\lfloor \frac{n}{2} \rfloor} \leq \frac{2^n}{n}$. Without any further knowledge about the considered semantics it is impossible to find better bounds.

Let us turn to stable semantics. In any case, we can achieve a high number of stable extensions by grouping. For instance, the maximal number of stable extensions for an AF possessing an even number $n = 2m$ of arguments is at least $2^m = 2^{\frac{n}{2}}$. Such a framework is given by grouping the arguments in pairs that mutually attack each other:

$$\mathcal{F} = (\{a_i, b_i \mid 1 \leq i \leq m\}, \{(a_i, b_i), (b_i, a_i) \mid 1 \leq i \leq m\})$$

Is grouping in pairs the best we can do?

Assume we group not in pairs but in groups of arbitrary size k such that all members of a single group attack each other. Then for n arguments the number

---

[1] A $\subseteq$-antichain is a set of sets of which any two are mutually $\subseteq$-incomparable.

of stable extensions is given by the following function:

$$f : \mathbb{N} \to \mathbb{N} \text{ where } f(k) = k^{\lfloor \frac{n}{k} \rfloor}$$

To approximate the maximum of $f(k)$ we calculate the extrema of the associated real-valued function

$$g : \mathbb{R} \to \mathbb{R} \text{ where } g(k) = k^{\frac{n}{k}} = e^{\frac{n}{k} \cdot \ln(k)}$$

For that, we have to solve the following equation:

$$k^{\frac{n}{k}} \left(-\frac{n}{k^2} \cdot \ln(k) + \frac{n}{k^2} \right) = k^{\frac{n}{k}} \cdot \frac{n}{k^2} \cdot (1 - \ln(k)) = 0$$

The only solution for this equation is that k equals Euler's number e. Of course, it is very difficult to arrange in groups of e when dealing with arguments. Nevertheless, the obtained result provides an upper bound for the initial problem – namely the value $g(e) = e^{\frac{n}{e}}$ – assuming that grouping is the best. We will see that the exact value is not far away.

On the path to the main theorem we start with two simple observations which hardly need a proof. Being aware of this fact, we still present them in the form of a proposition to be able to refer to them later on. For one, whenever a set E is a stable extension of $\mathcal{F}$, then E is also a stable extension in the symmetric and self-loop free version of $\mathcal{F}$. Observe that the converse is not true in general.

Proposition 1. *For any argumentation framework $\mathcal{F} = (A, R)$ and any $E \in \mathcal{E}_{st}(\mathcal{F})$ we have $E \in \mathcal{E}_{st}(sym(irr(\mathcal{F})))$.*

For another, the second proposition establishes a simple relationship between stable extensions in symmetric AFs without self-loops and maximal independent sets in undirected graphs.

Proposition 2. *For any symmetric and irreflexive argumentation framework $\mathcal{F} = (A, R)$ we have: $E \in \mathcal{E}_{st}(\mathcal{F})$ iff $E \in MIS(und(\mathcal{F}))$.*

Now we turn to the main theorem which is mainly based on a graph theoretical result by J.W. Moon and L. Moser from 1965 [5].[2] The theorem establishes a tight upper bound for the number of stable extensions of an AF with n arguments. The upper bound is obtained as a function $\sigma_{\max}$ of n.

Theorem 1. *For any natural number n, it holds that*

$$\max_{\mathcal{F} \in \mathcal{A}_n} |\mathcal{E}_{st}(\mathcal{F})| = \sigma_{\max}(n)$$

where the function $\sigma_{\max} : \mathbb{N} \to \mathbb{N}$ is defined by

$$\sigma_{\max}(n) = \begin{cases} 1, & \text{if } n = 0 \text{ or } n = 1, \\ 3^s, & \text{if } n \geq 2 \text{ and } n = 3s, \\ 4 \cdot 3^{s-1}, & \text{if } n \geq 2 \text{ and } n = 3s + 1, \\ 2 \cdot 3^s, & \text{if } n \geq 2 \text{ and } n = 3s + 2. \end{cases}$$

---

[2] Note that the original work deals with maximal cliques. The result can be equivalently formalised in terms of maximal independent sets as done by Wood [6].

Proof. The cases $n = 0$ and $n = 1$ are obvious; let $n \geq 2$.

"$\leq$": We already observed that for any AF $\mathcal{F}$ we have $\mathcal{E}_{st}(\mathcal{F}) \subseteq \mathcal{E}_{st}(sym(irr(\mathcal{F})))$ (Proposition 1). Consequently, $|\mathcal{E}_{st}(\mathcal{F})| \leq |\mathcal{E}_{st}(sym(irr(\mathcal{F})))|$ follows and

$$\max_{\mathcal{G} \in \mathcal{A}_n} |\mathcal{E}_{st}(\mathcal{G})| \leq \max_{\mathcal{G} \in \mathcal{A}_n} |\mathcal{E}_{st}(sym(irr(\mathcal{G})))|$$

In the light of Proposition 2 we get

$$\max_{\mathcal{G} \in \mathcal{A}_n} |\mathcal{E}_{st}(sym(irr(\mathcal{G})))| = \max_{\mathcal{G} \in \mathcal{A}_n} |MIS(und(sym(irr(\mathcal{G}))))|$$

Observe that the functions $irr(\cdot)$, $sym(\cdot)$ and $und(\cdot)$ do not change the number of nodes (respectively arguments). Consequently, we may estimate thus:

$$\max_{\mathcal{G} \in \mathcal{A}_n} |MIS(und(sym(irr(\mathcal{G}))))| \leq \max_{\mathcal{U} \in \mathcal{G}_n} |MIS(\mathcal{U})|.$$

This means, the value $\sigma_{\max}(n)$ does not exceed the maximal number of maximal independent sets of simple undirected graphs of order n. Due to Theorem 1 in [5] these values are exactly given by the last three lines of the claimed value range of $\sigma_{\max}(n)$.

"$\geq$": We define the following AFs.
- $A_2(i) = \{a_i, b_i\}$ and $A_3(i) = \{c_i, d_i, e_i\}$,
- $\mathcal{F}_2(i) = irr(A_2(i), A_2(i) \times A_2(i))$ and $\mathcal{F}_3(i) = irr(A_3(i), A_3(i) \times A_3(i))$.
- For $n = 3s$ consider $\mathcal{F}_{3s} = \bigcup_{i=1}^{s} \mathcal{F}_3(i)$.
- For $n = 3s + 1$ consider $\mathcal{F}_{3s+1} = (\bigcup_{i=1}^{2} \mathcal{F}_2(i)) \cup (\bigcup_{i=1}^{s-1} \mathcal{F}_3(i))$.
- Finally, in case of $n = 3s + 2$ consider $\mathcal{F}_{3s+2} = \mathcal{F}_2(1) \cup (\bigcup_{i=1}^{s} \mathcal{F}_3(i))$.

It is straightforward to verify that $|\mathcal{E}_{st}(\mathcal{F}_{3s})| = 3^s$, $|\mathcal{E}_{st}(\mathcal{F}_{3s+1})| = 4 \cdot 3^{s-1}$ and $|\mathcal{E}_{st}(\mathcal{F}_{3s+2})| = 2 \cdot 3^s$. $\qquad\square$

For illustration we present here an instantiation of the presented prototypes, namely $\mathcal{F}_{10} = \mathcal{F}_{3 \cdot 3 + 1} = (\bigcup_{i=1}^{2} \mathcal{F}_2(i)) \cup (\bigcup_{i=1}^{2} \mathcal{F}_3(i))$ which is graphically represented by the following figure:

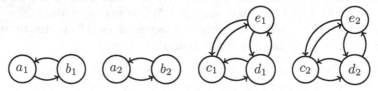

Observe that $|\mathcal{E}_{st}(\mathcal{F}_{10})| = |\mathcal{E}_{st}(\mathcal{F}_{3 \cdot 3 + 1})| = 4 \cdot 3^2$. In general, the function $\sigma_{\max}$ looks more complicated than it is, because the numbers are slightly different depending on the remainder of n on division by 3. Here is a much simpler version.

Corollary 1 (Upper bound short cut). *For any natural number n, we find:*

$$\sigma_{\max}(n) \leq 3^{\frac{n}{3}} \leq 1,4423^n.$$

As a final note we want to mention that it does not make much sense to ask for the minimal number of stable extensions, since for any $n > 0$ and $0 < x \leq n^2$ there are always AFs without stable extensions.

3.2   Average Number of Stable Extensions

What is the average number of stable extensions of argumentation frameworks with n arguments and x attacks?

As in the case of the maximal number of stable extensions, the precise value is computable in principle. This is immediate from its formal definition:

Definition 1. *The function $\bar{\sigma}(n, x)$ returns the average number of stable extensions of all AFs with n arguments and x attacks, and is defined thus:*

$$\bar{\sigma} : \mathbb{N} \times \mathbb{N} \to \mathbb{R} \ where \ \bar{\sigma}(n, x) = \frac{\sum_{\mathcal{F} \in \mathcal{A}_{n,x}} |\mathcal{E}_{st}(\mathcal{F})|}{\binom{n^2}{x}}$$

While this definition makes it precise what we mean by "average number of stable extensions," it does not give any clue how to efficiently compute this number for given n and x. (It only suggests the brute force method of enumerating all AFs from $\mathcal{A}_{n,x}$ and counting their stable extensions.)

But we are looking for a way to heuristically predict the number of stable extensions of a given single AF *without actually inspecting the AF* except for determining the parameters n and x. This would be useful since the number n of arguments and the number x of attacks can be determined in linear time, and knowing $\bar{\sigma}(n, x)$ gives some guidance on how many extensions a given AF $\mathcal{F} \in \mathcal{A}_{n,x}$ will have.

The best-case scenario would be the specification of a closed-form function that returns the exact values of $\bar{\sigma}(n, x)$. Unfortunately, the combinatorial blowup even in case of small numbers of attacks turns this endeavour into a challenging task. Nevertheless, we were able to specify certain values. The following proposition presents some exact values of $\bar{\sigma}(n, x)$ given that the number of attacks x is close to 0 or close to n^2.

Proposition 3. *For any $n \in \mathbb{N}$, we have*

$$\bar{\sigma}(n, 0) = 1 \qquad\qquad \bar{\sigma}(n, n^2 - 3) = \begin{cases} \frac{3 \cdot (n^2 - n - 1)}{(n+1) \cdot (n^2 - 2)}, & \text{if } n \geq 3, \\ 1 - \frac{1}{n}, & \text{if } n = 2 \\ 0, & \text{otherwise} \end{cases}$$

$$\bar{\sigma}(n, 1) = \begin{cases} 1 - \frac{1}{n}, & \text{if } n \geq 1, \\ 0, & \text{otherwise} \end{cases} \qquad \bar{\sigma}(n, n^2 - 2) = \begin{cases} \frac{2}{n+1}, & \text{if } n \geq 2, \\ 0, & \text{otherwise} \end{cases}$$

$$\bar{\sigma}(n, 2) = \begin{cases} 1 - \frac{2n-2}{n^2+n}, & \text{if } n \geq 2, \\ 0, & \text{otherwise} \end{cases} \qquad \bar{\sigma}(n, n^2 - 1) = \begin{cases} \frac{1}{n}, & \text{if } n \geq 1, \\ 0, & \text{otherwise} \end{cases}$$

$$\bar{\sigma}(n, n^2) = \begin{cases} 1, & \text{if } n = 0, \\ 0, & \text{otherwise} \end{cases}$$

Proof. The values of $\bar{\sigma}(n, 0)$ and $\bar{\sigma}(n, n^2)$ are obvious. Consider $\bar{\sigma}(n, 1) = 1 - \frac{1}{n}$. This can be seen as follows: If the belonging attack is a self-loop, then we have no extensions. If it is not, then we have exactly one extension which is the union of all unattacked arguments. Obviously, we have $|\mathcal{A}_{n,1}| = \binom{n^2}{1} = n^2$ and furthermore, there are n different AFs in $\mathcal{A}_{n,1}$ possessing exactly one loop. Thus $\bar{\sigma}(n,1) = \frac{n^2-n}{n^2} = 1 - \frac{1}{n}$. Analogously one may prove $\bar{\sigma}(n, n^2-1) = \frac{1}{n}$.

We want to emphasise that the other values are non-trivial. To get an idea of the complexity of the remaining proofs we consider the value $\bar{\sigma}(n, n^2 - 3)$. W.l.o.g. we may assume $n \geq 2$ since the number of attacks has to be non-negative. Furthermore we may even assume that $n \geq 3$ because if $n = 2$, then $\bar{\sigma}(n, n^2-3) = \bar{\sigma}(n,1)$ which is already solved. An AF $\mathcal{F} \in \mathcal{A}_{n,n^2-3}$ can be seen as the result of the following process: One starts with a full AF with n arguments. We then stepwise delete 3 attacks which are either loops or non-loops. We list now the probabilities to end up in an AF where k loops are deleted.

$$P(k = 3) = 1 \cdot \frac{n}{n^2} \cdot \frac{n-1}{n^2-1} \cdot \frac{n-2}{n^2-2}$$

$$P(k = 2) = 3 \cdot \frac{n}{n^2} \cdot \frac{n-1}{n^2-1} \cdot \frac{n^2-n}{n^2-2}$$

$$P(k = 1) = 3 \cdot \frac{n}{n^2} \cdot \frac{n^2-n}{n^2-1} \cdot \frac{n^2-n-1}{n^2-2}$$

We omit the consideration of $P(k = 0)$ since such kind of frameworks do not possess an extension and thus does not contribute anything to $\bar{\sigma}(n, n^2 - 3)$. We list now the average number of extensions of AFs in $\mathcal{A}_{n,n^2-3}$ where k loops are deleted.

$$av(k = 3) = 3$$

$$av(k = 2) = 1 \cdot \frac{2(n-1)}{n^2-n} + 2 \cdot \frac{(n^2-n) - 2(n-1)}{n^2-n}$$

$$= 2 \cdot \left(1 - \frac{1}{n}\right)$$

$$av(k = 1) = 1 - \left(\frac{n-1}{n^2-n} + \frac{(n^2-n) - (n-1)}{n^2-n} \cdot \frac{n-1}{n^2-n-1}\right)$$

$$= \frac{n^2 - 3n + 2}{n^2 - n - 1}$$

The average numbers can be seen as follows. If we delete exactly three loops we end up in an AF with 3 stable extensions, namely the singletons of the non-looping arguments. Consequently, $av(k = 3) = 3$. If we delete 2 loops and 1 non-loop we either end up with 1 extension, namely if the deleted non-loop starts by an self-loop free argument or 2 extensions otherwise. The probability of the former is $\frac{2(n-1)}{n^2-n}$. Since both cases are mutual exclusive and exhaustive we derive a probability of $\frac{(n^2-n)-2(n-1)}{n^2-n}$ for the latter case proving the claimed value of $av(k = 2)$.

Consider now av(k = 1). Observe that the maximal number of extensions equals 1 because only 1 self-loop is deleted. In the following we call this argument arg. We specify now the probability that we end up in AF with zero stable extension. This is the case if at least one deleted non-loop starts by arg. The probability for the "first" non-loop is $\frac{n-1}{n^2-n}$. Furthermore, the probability for the "second" deleted non-loop to start by arg providing that the first one does not started by arg is given by $\frac{(n^2-n)-(n-1)}{n^2-n} \cdot \frac{n-1}{n^2-n-1}$. Thus, the claimed value for av(k = 1) follows. Finally, we have to sum up, that is,

$$\bar{\sigma}(n, n^2 - 3) = \sum_{i=1}^{3} P(k = i) \cdot av(k = i) = 3 \cdot \frac{n^2 - n - 1}{(n+1)(n^2 - 2)}$$

We omit the consideration of $\bar{\sigma}(n, 2)$ and $\bar{\sigma}(n, n^2 - 2)$ since their treatment is similar in style to the above proof.   □

It can be seen that the values of $\bar{\sigma}(n, 1)$ and $\bar{\sigma}(n, 2)$ do not give any indication on how $\bar{\sigma}(n, 3)$ could look like, not even qualitatively. The same holds for $\bar{\sigma}(n, n^2 - 2)$ and $\bar{\sigma}(n, n^2 - 3)$, and potential informed guesses about $\bar{\sigma}(n, n^2 - 4)$.

But having these exact values at hand we may consider the limit values for AFs with an increasing number of arguments. We have

$$\lim_{n\to\infty} \bar{\sigma}(n, 0) = \lim_{n\to\infty} \bar{\sigma}(n, 1) = \lim_{n\to\infty} \bar{\sigma}(n, 2) = 1$$

On the other hand, we obtain

$$\lim_{n\to\infty} \bar{\sigma}(n, n^2) = \lim_{n\to\infty} \bar{\sigma}(n, n^2 - 1) = \lim_{n\to\infty} \bar{\sigma}(n, n^2 - 2) = \lim_{n\to\infty} \bar{\sigma}(n, n^2 - 3) = 0$$

This means that for increasing numbers of arguments, the average number of stable extensions in the case of very small numbers of attacks approaches from below to 1. In the case of very large numbers of attacks we have a convergence to 0 from above. So far, so good; but it is still unclear how many extensions there usually are in between. With an increasing number of attacks, does the average number of stable extensions just decrease in a monotone fashion? It turns out that this is a really hard problem.[3]

Of course, we can look at simple special cases. For example, for $n = 2$, Proposition 3 yields the precise values for all possible numbers of attacks $0 \le x \le n^2 = 4$: an AF with 2 arguments and $0, 1, 2, 3, 4$ attacks will have an average number of $1, \frac{1}{2}, \frac{2}{3}, \frac{1}{2}, 0$ stable extensions, respectively. So while the number of attacks linearly increases, the average number of extensions first decreases, then increases and then decreases again. Qualitatively speaking, this means that for a fixed number of arguments, there are certain numbers of attacks where the average number of extensions is locally maximal or minimal, respectively.

---

[3] We therefore introduce the "average-number-stable-challenge" which is: present a closed-form function for $\bar{\sigma}(n, x)$ or at least specific values like $\bar{\sigma}(n, n^2-n)$ or $\bar{\sigma}(n, 2n)$. The prize is a hot or cold drink with the authors.

We have seen in the proofs of the results above that already the closed-form solutions for values of $\bar{\sigma}(n, 2)$ and $\bar{\sigma}(n, n^2 - 3)$ are quite hard to obtain. To nevertheless get an inkling of the characteristic distribution of stable extensions, we have set out to study the problem in an empirical way.

4   Empirical Results

As we have seen, combinatorial explosion stood in our way of mathematically analysing the average number of stable extensions. While the same combinatorial explosions prevent us from an exhaustive empirical analysis of the average number of stable extensions, we can still use methods from descriptive statistics to draw some meaningful conclusions.

The basic idea is simple: instead of computing the average number of stable extensions for *all* AFs in some class such as $\mathcal{A}_{n,x}$, we only analyse a uniformly drawn random sample $S \subseteq \mathcal{A}_{n,x}$ of a fixed size $|S|$. We thereby obtain a point estimation of the actual (hidden) parameter $\bar{\sigma}(n, x)$.

4.1   Experimental Setup

We wrote a program that randomly samples AFs with specific parameters and determines how many stable extensions they have. To create a random AF, we first set $A = \{1, \ldots, n\}$. To create attacks we then randomly select x elements from the set $A \times A$ with equal probability for each pair. Thus we obtain an AF $\mathcal{F} = (A, R) \in \mathcal{A}_{n,x}$. For a given n, this process is repeated for all $0 \leq x \leq n^2$. Now for each AF thus created, we determine the number of stable extensions as follows: We use the translation of Dung [1, Section 5] to transform the AF into a logic program. By [1, Theorem 62], the stable models of this logic program and the stable extensions of the AF are in one-to-one-correspondence. Using the answer set solver `clingo` [7], we determine the number of stable models of the program and thus the number of stable extensions of the AF. So for a given n, we can empirically estimate the average number of stable extensions in each sample set of AFs with n arguments and x attacks for all $0 \leq x \leq n^2$.

4.2   Average Number of Stable Extensions

To check the experimental setup, we first ran the experiment with $n = 2$ and observed that the empirical results agreed with the predictions of Section 3.2. The results for $n = 20$ are depicted in a scatter plot, in Figure 1 on page 121; the results for $n = 50$ are plotted likewise in Figure 2, page 122.

The empirical data clearly vindicate our analytical predictions for very small and very large numbers of attacks. In between, the data furthermore confirm our predictions about the emergence of local minima and maxima. In addition to the experiments that are graphically depicted, we present the positions of these empirically obtained minima and maxima for several additional small n in Table 1.

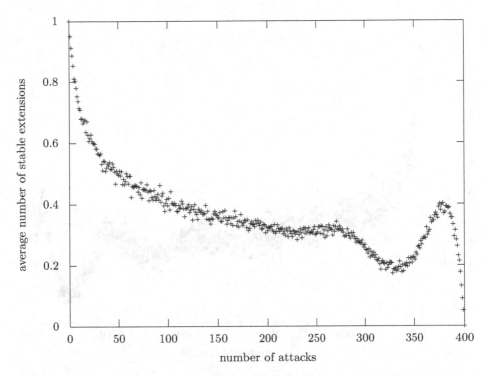

Fig. 1. Average number of stable extensions of AFs with $n = 20$ arguments. The values have been obtained from a random sample of size 2500 for each possible number $0 \leq x \leq 400$ of attacks. (So the total sample size is $1\,002\,500$.) We can see that there is a significant local minimum at $x_{\min} \approx 330$ and a local maximum at $x_{\max} \approx 380$.

For the local minimum and for small n, an approximation of the position $x_{\min}$ of the local minima from below is given by $n^2 - n \cdot \sqrt{n}$. More precisely – and astonishingly –, the position of the local maximum *always* coincides with $n^2 - n$. On an intuitive level, this suggests that removing n attacks from a full AF with n arguments quite probably leads to AFs for which *both adding and removing* attacks leads to a *decrease* in the number of stable extensions. To investigate this issue somewhat deeper, we next analysed how the average number of stable extensions came about.

4.3   Number of AFs with at Most One Stable Extension

The point estimator *sample mean* we used for approximating $\bar{\sigma}(n, x)$ does not per se tell us anything about the distribution of 0-AFs, 1-AFs, ..., y-AFs among the AFs sampled.[4] In principle, an average number of 0.5 stable extensions could be obtained by a 50/50-ratio of 0-AFs to 1-AFs, or likewise by a 75/25-ratio of 0-AFs to 2-AFs. To find out what is the case, we extracted the absolute frequency

---

[4] Recall that a y-AF is an AF with exactly y stable extensions.

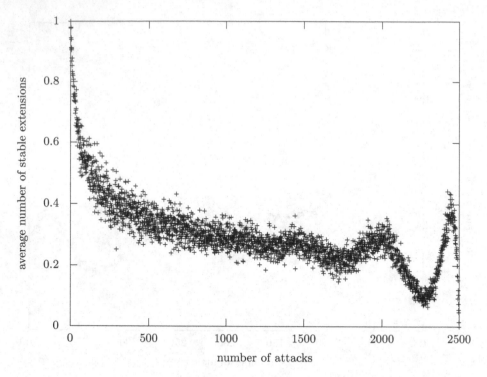

Fig. 2. Average number of stable extensions of AFs with $n = 50$ arguments and sample size 400 for each $0 \leq x \leq 2500$. Again, there are significant extrema: a local minimum at $x_{\min} \approx 2250$ and a local maximum at $x_{\max} \approx 2450$. It even seems that there is another local maximum at $x'_{\max} \approx 2000$ and another local minimum before that, but the data are unreliable. (Recall that for $x = 2000$ the number of AFs to sample from is $|\mathcal{A}_{50,2000}| = \binom{2500}{2000} \geq \left(\frac{2500}{2000}\right)^{2000} \approx 6.6 \cdot 10^{193}$.)

of 0-AFs and 1-AFs from our results for $n = 50$ and plotted them in the stacked histogram (Figure 3) on page 124.

The stacked histogram for $n = 20$ looks alike, indeed as much as the scatter plots in Figures 1 and 2 do. This suggests that there are certain recurring features in this distribution that are independent of the number n of arguments.

It cannot be seen in the histogram, but we also observed that for any set of sampled AFs from $\mathcal{A}_{50,x}$ with $0 \leq x \leq 50^2$, there are typically more 1-AFs than 2-AFs, more 2-AFs than 3-AFs, and so on. This gives some hints about the sizes of the subclasses of 1-AFs, 2-AFs, ... in a given class $\mathcal{A}_{n,x}$.

We close the empirical section by presenting two conjectures supported by the obtained results. The first one is concerned with the cardinality of y-AFs for a fixed number n of arguments.

Conjecture 1. For any natural numbers n, k and l with $0 < k < l \leq n$ we have:

$$|\{\mathcal{F} \mid \mathcal{F} \in \mathcal{A}_n, \ \mathcal{F} \text{ is a } k\text{-AF}\}| \geq |\{\mathcal{G} \mid \mathcal{G} \in \mathcal{A}_n, \ \mathcal{G} \text{ is an } l\text{-AF}\}|.$$

Table 1. Positions (at a specific number x of attacks) of empirically observed local minima (denoted by x_{min}) and maxima (x_{max}) of the average number of stable extensions of AFs with n arguments. We additionally present the values of our analytical estimations. To approximate the position of the minima, we devised the function $n^2 - n \cdot \sqrt{n}$; for the maxima we obtained $n^2 - n$. The rows labelled by e_{abs} and e_{rel} show the absolute and relative error of these estimates.

n	2	3	4	5	6	7	8	9	10
x_{min}	1	4	9	15	23	32	45	57	73
$n^2 - n \cdot \sqrt{n}$	1.17	3.80	8	13.82	21.30	30.48	41.37	54	68.38
e_{abs}	0.17	0.2	1	1.18	1.7	1.52	3.63	3	4.62
e_{rel}	0.17	0.04	0.11	0.08	0.07	0.05	0.08	0.05	0.06
x_{max}	2	6	12	20	30	42	56	72	90
$n^2 - n$	2	6	12	20	30	42	56	72	90
$e_{abs} = e_{rel}$	0	0	0	0	0	0	0	0	0

The second conjecture claims that the average number of stable extensions of AFs is always located in between 0 and 1. Here is the precise formulation.

Conjecture 2. For any natural numbers n and x with $0 < x < n^2$ we have:

$$0 < \bar{\sigma}(n, x) < 1$$

5   Discussion

We have conducted a detailed analytical and empirical study on the maximal and average numbers of stable extensions in abstract argumentation frameworks. First of all, we have proven a tight upper bound on the maximal number of stable extensions. For specific numbers of attacks, we have also given the precise average number of stable extensions in terms of closed-form expressions. As the calculation of these analytical values tends to be quite complex, we turned to studying the problem empirically. There, we obtained data about the distribution of stable extensions in samples of AFs which were randomly drawn with

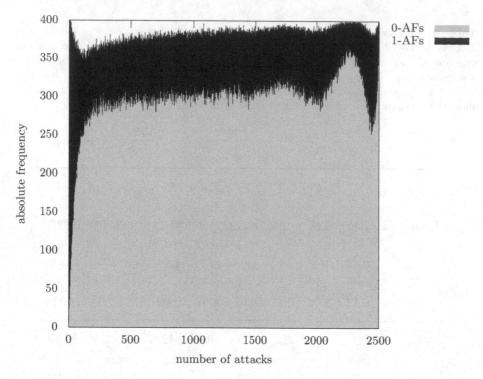

Fig. 3. Absolute frequencies of 0-AFs (grey) and 1-AFs (black) among all AFs with $n = 50$ arguments and x attacks for $0 \leq x \leq n^2 = 2500$ with a total sample size of $1\,000\,400$. It is obvious from the histogram that the majority (at least two thirds) of all sampled AFs have no stable extension. Additionally, almost all AFs have at most one stable extension. The white area at the top consequently depicts the y-AFs for $y \geq 2$. For $x \approx 100 = 2n$, there is a meaningful number of such y-AFs, which however decreases with increasing x. (Note that the extremal graphs defined in Theorem 1 have n arguments and $2n$ attacks.) At $x \approx 2250$, where the average number of stable extensions has a local minimum, the absolute frequency of 0-AFs has a local maximum; furthermore at this position there are almost no y-AFs for $y \geq 2$. Conversely, at $x \approx 2450$ where the average number of stable extensions has a local maximum, the absolute frequency of 0-AFs has a local minimum; furthermore there are yet again y-AFs for $y \geq 2$.

a uniform probability. Our empirical results offer new insights into the average number and also the distribution of stable extensions for AFs, given only the parameters n (number of arguments) and x (number of attacks).

We could not provide exhaustive theoretical explanations for the many empirical observations we have made, and consider this as one of the major future directions of this research. First and foremost we consider it important to work on proving or disproving the conjectures we explicitly formulated at the end of the previous section. Also the conjectured local maximum of the average number of stable extensions at $n^2 - n$ attacks deserves some attention. A possible way to tackle these conjectures may be to look at subclasses of AFs with special structural properties, such as having no self-loops, or more generally no cycles, those being symmetric, or the ones with a specific average connectivity. Finally, it is clear that many of the questions we asked about stable extension semantics can be asked about the other standard semantics.

Note that our results are not only of interest to the argumentation community: We have seen in the proof of Theorem 1 that there is a close relationship between stable extensions of AFs and maximal independent sets of undirected graphs.[5] In a sense, stable extensions represent a directed generalisation of maximal independent sets, where the $\subseteq$-maximality condition has been replaced by the condition that all nodes not in the set must be reached by a directed edge from the set. So there is also a graph theoretical significance to our results.

For abstract argumentation, our results show that – in the context of stable semantics – attacks cannot simply be thought of as constraining: adding an attack may sometimes increase and sometimes decrease the number of stable extensions. Although this might be obvious in general to argumentation researchers (AFs are, after all, a nonmonotonic formalism), for the first time we were able to present some precise numerical figures around this phenomenon.

The present paper is also related to recent work on realisability in abstract argumentation [8]. Realisability addresses the following question: given a set X of sets of arguments, is there an argumentation framework whose set of extensions exactly coincides with X? From the results of this paper, we immediately know that the answer is "no" if X involves n distinct arguments and the cardinality of X is greater than $3^{\frac{n}{3}}$. I-maximality and Sperner's theorem do not tell us that much: with $n = 6$ arguments, for example, I-maximality only guarantees that at least $2^{\frac{6}{2}} = 8$ extensions can be realised, while our construction shows that $3^{\frac{6}{3}} = 9$ is perfectly possible *and more than that is impossible*. Conversely, the cardinality of the extension-set X gives an indication of the minimal number of arguments needed to realise the extensions in X. For example, if there are 10 extensions to realise, we immediately know that we will need at least 7 arguments to do so.

Our current results on the average number of stable extensions regard all possible AFs to occur equally likely. In future research, we want to look at AFs that occur "in practice," that is, from instantiations of more concrete argumentation languages. In Section 1.5 of [9], the authors acknowledge the need for a benchmark library in abstract argumentation. In particular, they mention that the library should contain benchmarks "that arise from real-world instantiations of argumentation." We consider the development of such a benchmark collection an important prerequisite for analysing empirical properties of their instances.

---

[5] Indeed, maximal independent sets are sometimes called "stable sets" in the graph theory literature.

References

1. Dung, P.M.: On the Acceptability of Arguments and its Fundamental Role in Non-monotonic Reasoning, Logic Programming and n-Person Games. Artificial Intelligence 77, 321–358 (1995)
2. Baroni, P., Dunne, P.E., Giacomin, M.: On extension counting problems in argumentation frameworks. In: Proceedings of COMMA, pp. 63–74 (2010)
3. Baroni, P., Giacomin, M.: On principle-based evaluation of extension-based argumentation semantics. Artificial Intelligence 171(10-15), 675–700 (2007)
4. Sperner, E.: Ein Satz über Untermengen einer endlichen Menge. Mathematische Zeitschrift 27(1), 544–548 (1928)
5. Moon, J., Moser, L.: On cliques in graphs. Israel Journal of Mathematics 3(1), 23–28 (1965)
6. Wood, D.: On the number of maximal independent sets in a graph. Discrete Mathematics & Theoretical Computer Science 13(3), 17–20 (2011)
7. Gebser, M., Kaminski, R., Kaufmann, B., Ostrowski, M., Schaub, T., Schneider, M.: Potassco: The Potsdam Answer Set Solving Collection. AI Communications 24(2), 105–124 (2011), http://potassco.sourceforge.net
8. Dunne, P.E., Dvořák, W., Linsbichler, T., Woltran, S.: Characteristics of multiple viewpoints in abstract argumentation. In: Proceedings of the Fourth Workshop on Dynamics of Knowledge and Belief, DKB 2013 (2013)
9. Modgil, S., Toni, F., Bex, F., Bratko, I., Chesñevar, C., Dvořák, W., Falappa, M., Fan, X., Gaggl, S.A., García, A.J., González, M.P., Gordon, T.F., Leite, J., Možina, M., Reed, C., Simari, G.R., Szeider, S., Torroni, P., Woltran, S.: The Added Value of Argumentation. In: Ossowski, S. (ed.) Agreement Technologies. Law, Governance and Technology Series, vol. 8, pp. 357–403. Springer, Netherlands (2013)

Decision Making with Assumption-Based Argumentation

Xiuyi Fan and Francesca Toni

Imperial College London, London, United Kingdom
{xf309,ft}@imperial.ac.uk

Abstract. In this paper, we present two different formal frameworks for representing decision making. In both frameworks, decisions have multiple attributes and meet different goals. In the second framework, decisions take into account preferences over goals. We also study a family of decision functions representing making decisions with different criteria, including decisions meeting all goals, most goals, goals no other decisions meet, and most preferred achievable goals. For each decision function, we define an argumentation-based computational mechanism for computing and explaining the selected decisions. We make connections between decision making and argumentation semantics, i.e., selected decisions in a decision making framework are admissible arguments in the corresponding argumentation framework. The main advantage of our approach is that it not only selects decisions but also gives an argumentation-based justification of selected decisions.

1 Introduction

Argumentation based decision making has attracted considerable research interest in recent years [1,8,7,10]. In this paper, we give a formal treatment of two forms of decision making with argumentation. We view decision making as concerned with three related processes: (I) agents represent information that is relevant to the decision making; (II) agents choose a decision criteria to represent "good" decisions; and (III) agents compute and explain the desired decision based on the selected criteria. We realise these three components formally.

We give formal definitions for *decision frameworks*, used to model the agents' knowledge bases to support I. We allow a decision framework to have multiple *decisions* and a set of *goals*, such that each decision can have a number of different *attributes* and each goal can be satisfied by some attributes. With decision frameworks defined, we model different decision criteria with *decision functions*. Given a decision framework, decision functions return a set of *selected* decisions, representing decisions that meet the decision criteria underpinning the decision function. To compute and explain the desired decisions, we map decision frameworks and decision functions into assumption-based argumentation (ABA) frameworks [3]. We prove that selected decisions w.r.t. a given decision function are claims of admissible arguments in the corresponding ABA framework. The

E. Black, S. Modgil, and N. Oren (Eds.): TAFA 2013, LNAI 8306, pp. 127–142, 2014.
© Springer-Verlag Berlin Heidelberg 2014

main advantage of our approach is that while finding the "good" decisions, it gives an argumentation-based justification of selected decisions.

This paper is organised as follows. We briefly introduce ABA in Section 2. We define decision frameworks and decision functions in Section 3. We present ABA representation of decision frameworks and functions in Section 4. We introduce decision making with preference over goals in Section 5. We review a few related work in Section 6. We conclude in Section 7.

2   Background

An ABA framework [3,5] is a tuple $\langle \mathcal{L}, \mathcal{R}, \mathcal{A}, \mathcal{C} \rangle$ where

- $\langle \mathcal{L}, \mathcal{R} \rangle$ is a deductive system, with $\mathcal{L}$ the *language* and $\mathcal{R}$ a set of *rules* of the form $s_0 \leftarrow s_1, \ldots, s_m (m \geq 0)$;
- $\mathcal{A} \subseteq \mathcal{L}$ is a (non-empty) set, referred to as *assumptions*;
- $\mathcal{C}$ is a total mapping from $\mathcal{A}$ into $2^{\mathcal{L}}$, where $\mathcal{C}(\alpha)$ is the *contrary* of $\alpha \in \mathcal{A}$.

When presenting an ABA framework, we omit presenting $\mathcal{L}$ explicitly as we assume $\mathcal{L}$ contains all sentences appearing in $\mathcal{R}$, $\mathcal{A}$ and $\mathcal{C}$. Given a rule $s_0 \leftarrow s_1, \ldots, s_m$, we use the following notation: $Head(s_0 \leftarrow s_1, \ldots, s_m) = s_0$ and $Body(s_0 \leftarrow s_1, \ldots, s_m) = \{s_1, \ldots, s_m\}$. As in [3], we enforce that ABA frameworks are *flat*, namely assumptions do not occur in the head of rules.

In ABA, *arguments* are deductions of claims using rules and supported by assumptions, and *attacks* are directed at assumptions. Informally, following [3]:

- an *argument for (the claim)* $c \in \mathcal{L}$ supported by $S \subseteq \mathcal{A}$ ($S \vdash c$ in short) is a (finite) tree with nodes labelled by sentences in $\mathcal{L}$ or by the symbol τ^1, such that the root is labelled by c, leaves are either τ or assumptions in S, and non-leaves s have as many children as elements in the body of a rule with head s, in a one-to-one correspondence with the elements of this body.
- an *argument* $S_1 \vdash c_1$ attacks an argument $S_2 \vdash c_2$ iff $c_1 = \mathcal{C}(\alpha)$ for $\alpha \in S_2$.

Attacks between arguments correspond in ABA to attacks between sets of assumptions, where *a set of assumptions* A attacks *a set of assumptions* B iff an argument supported by $A' \subseteq A$ attacks an argument supported by $B' \subseteq B$.

When there is no ambiguity, we also say a sentence b attacks a sentence a when a is an assumption and b is a claim of an argument $\mathtt{Arg'}$ such that a is in the support of some argument $\mathtt{Arg}$ and $\mathtt{Arg'}$ attacks $\mathtt{Arg}$.

With argument and attack defined, standard argumentation semantics can be applied in ABA [3]. We focus on the admissibility semantics: *a set of assumptions is admissible* (in $\langle \mathcal{L}, \mathcal{R}, \mathcal{A}, \mathcal{C} \rangle$) iff it does not attack itself and it attacks all $A \subseteq \mathcal{A}$ that attack it; *an argument* $S \vdash c$ belongs to an admissible extension supported by $\Delta \subseteq \mathcal{A}$ (in $\langle \mathcal{L}, \mathcal{R}, \mathcal{A}, \mathcal{C} \rangle$) iff $S \subseteq \Delta$ and Δ is admissible. When there is no ambiguity, we also say an argument $\mathtt{Arg}$ is admissible if $\mathtt{Arg}$ belongs to an admissible extension supported by some Δ.

---

[1] As in [3], $\tau \notin \mathcal{L}$ stands for "true" and is used to represent the empty body of rules.

3   Decision Frameworks and Decision Functions

In this paper, we consider the following form of decision: there are a set of possible decisions D, a set of attributes A, and a set of goals G, such that a decision $d \in$ D may *have* some attributes $A \subseteq$ A, and each goal $g \in$ G is *satisfied* by some attributes $A' \subseteq$ A. Then decisions can be selected based on a certain *decision function*. The relations between decisions and attributes and between goals and attributes jointly form a *decision framework*, which can be represented as two tables, as follows:

Definition 1. *A decision framework is a tuple* $\langle$D, A, G, T$_{DA}$, T$_{GA}\rangle$, *consisting of:*

- *a set of decisions* D $= \{d_1, \ldots, d_n\}, n > 0,$
- *a set of attributes* A $= \{a_1, \ldots, a_m\}, m > 0,$
- *a set of goals* G $= \{g_1, \ldots, g_l\}, l > 0,$ *and*
- *two tables:* T$_{DA}$, *of size* $(n \times m)$, *and* T$_{GA}$, *of size* $(l \times m)$, *such that*
  - *for every* T$_{DA}[i, j]^2, 1 \le i \le n, 1 \le j \le m,$ T$_{DA}[i, j]$ *is either* 1, *representing that decision* d_i *has attributes* a_j, *or* 0, *otherwise;*
  - *for every* T$_{GA}[i, j], 1 \le i \le l, 1 \le j \le m,$ T$_{GA}[i, j]$ *is either* 1, *representing that goal* g_i *is* satisfied *by attribute* a_j, *or* 0, *otherwise.*

We assume that the column order in both T$_{DA}$ *and* T$_{GA}$ *is the same, and the* indices *of decisions, goals, and attributes in* T$_{DA}$ *and* T$_{GA}$ *are the row numbers of the decision and goals and the column number of attributes in* T$_{DA}$ *and* T$_{GA}$, *respectively. We use* $\mathcal{DEC}$ *and* $\mathcal{DF}$ *to denote the set of all possible decisions and the set of possible decision frameworks, respectively.*

The notion of Decision frameworks is illustrated as follows, adopted from [9].

Example 1. An agent needs to decide an accommodation in London. The two tables, T$_{DA}$ and T$_{GA}$, are given in Table 1.

Table 1. T$_{DA}$(left) and T$_{GA}$(right)

	£50	£70	£200	inSK	inPic
jh	0	1	0	1	0
ic	1	0	0	1	0
ritz	0	0	1	0	1

	£50	£70	£200	inSK	inPic
cheap	1	0	0	0	0
near	0	0	0	1	0

Decision (D) are: hotel (jh), Imperial College Halls (ic), Ritz (ritz). Attributes (A) are: £50, £70, £200, in South Kensington (inSK), and in Piccadilly (inPic). Goals (G) are: cheap and near. The indices are: 1-jh; 2-ic; 3-ritz; 1-cheap; 2-near; 1-£50; 2-£70; 3-£200; 4-inSK; 5-inPic. In this example, jh is £70 and is in South Kensington; ic is £50 and is in South Kensington; ritz is £200 and is in Piccadilly; £50 is cheap and accommodations in South Kensington are near.

We define a decision *meeting* a goal as the follows:

---

^{2} We use T$_X[i, j]$ to represent the cell in row i and column j in T$_X \in \{$T$_{DA}$, T$_{GA}\}$.

Definition 2. *Given* $\langle D, A, G, T_{DA}, T_{GA} \rangle$, *a decision* $d \in D$ *with row index* i *in* T_{DA} *meets a goal* $g \in G$ *with row index* j *in* T_{GA} *iff there exists an attribute* $a \in A$ *with column index* k *in both* T_{DA} *and* T_{GA}, *such that* $T_{DA}[i, k] = 1$ *and* $T_{GA}[j, k] = 1$.
We use $\gamma(d) = S$, *where* $d \in D, S \subseteq G$, *to denote the set of goals met by* d.

In Example 1, *jh* meets *near*; *ic* meets *cheap* and *near*; *ritz* meets no goal.

Decision frameworks provide information for decision making. Given a decision framework, a *decision function* returns the set of "good" decisions. Formally,

Definition 3. *A decision function is a mapping* $\psi : \mathcal{DF} \mapsto 2^{\mathcal{DEC}}$, *such that, given* $df = \langle D, A, G, T_{DA}, T_{GA} \rangle$, $\psi(df) \subseteq D$. *For any* $d, d' \in D$, *if* $\gamma(d) = \gamma(d')$ *and* $d \in \psi(df)$, *then* $d' \in \psi(df)$. *We say that* $\psi(df)$ *are selected in* $\mathcal{DF}$ *w.r.t.* ψ.
We use Ψ *to denote the set of all decision functions.*

Definition 3 defines that if two decisions meet the same set of goals and a decision function selects one of the decisions, then the decision function must select the other decision as well.

We subsequently define three decision functions, each characterising a notion of "good decision". They all fulfil the requirement in Definition 3 but also characterise additional requirements. We start with the notion of *strongly dominant decision functions* that select the decisions meeting all goals. Formally,

Definition 4. *A strongly dominant decision function* $\psi \in \Psi$ *is such that given* $df = \langle D, A, G, T_{DA}, T_{GA} \rangle$, *for all decisions* $d \in \psi(df)$, $\gamma(d) = G$. *We say that any such* d *is a* strongly dominant decision.
We refer to a generic strongly dominant decision function as ψ_s.

In Example 1, *ic* is a strongly dominant decision as it meets both *cheap* and *near*. There is no other strongly dominant decision.

Strongly dominant decisions can be relaxed to *dominant decisions* which meet all goals that are ever met by any decision in the decision framework. Formally,

Definition 5. *A dominant decision function* $\psi \in \Psi$ *is such that given* $df = \langle D, A, G, T_{DA}, T_{GA} \rangle$, *for any* $d \in \psi(df)$, *let* $S = \gamma(d)$, *then there is no* $g' \in G \setminus S$ *and* $g' \in \gamma(d')$, *where* $d' \in D \setminus \{d\}$. *We say such* d *is a* dominant decision.
We refer to a generic dominant decision function as ψ_d.

In Example 1, *ic* is a dominant decision. There is no other dominant decision. To illustrate the case when there is no strongly dominant decision, but only dominant decisions, we introduce the following example.

Example 2. We again consider an agent deciding accommodation in London. T_{DA} and T_{GA} are given in Table 2. Unlike Example 1, there is no decision *ic* that meets both goals, *cheap* and *near*. Nevertheless, *jh* is a better decision than *ritz* as it meets *near* whereas *ritz* meets no goal. Hence, in this example, there is no strongly dominant decision, but there is a dominant decision, *jh*.

By Definition 5, all dominant decisions meet the same set of goals, formally:

Table 2. T_{DA}(left) and T_{GA}(right)

	£50	£70	£200	inSK	inPic
jh	0	1	0	1	0
ritz	0	0	1	0	1

	£50	£70	£200	inSK	inPic
cheap	1	0	0	0	0
near	0	0	0	1	0

Proposition 1. *Given $df \in \mathcal{DF}$, for any $d, d' \in \psi_d(df)$, $\gamma(d) = \gamma(d')$.*

Moreover, if all decisions meet the same set of goals, then they are dominant.

Lemma 1. *Given $df = \langle D, A, G, T_{DA}, T_{GA} \rangle$, if for all $d, d' \in D$, $\gamma(d) = \gamma(d')$, then $\psi_d(df) = D$.*

Trivially, strongly dominant decisions are also dominant.

Proposition 2. *Given $df \in \mathcal{DF}$, $\psi_s(df) \subseteq \psi_d(df)$.*

Dominant decisions can be weakened to *weakly dominant*. Goals met by a weakly dominant decision is not a subset of goals met by some other decision.

Definition 6. *A weakly dominant decision function $\psi \in \Psi$ is such that given $df = \langle D, A, G, T_{DA}, T_{GA} \rangle$, for all $d \in \psi(df)$, there is no $d' \in D \setminus \{d\}$ and $\gamma(d) \subset \gamma(d')$. We refer to a generic weakly dominant decision function as ψ_w.*

In Example 1, ic is weakly dominant; there is no other weakly dominant decision. In Example 2, jh is weakly dominant; there is no other weakly dominant decision. To illustrate the case when there is no dominant decision but only weakly dominant decisions, we introduce the next example.

Example 3. (Continue Example 1). The new T_{DA} and T_{GA} shown in Table 3.

Table 3. T_{DA}(left) and T_{GA}(right)

	£50	£70	£200	inSK	inPic
jh	0	1	0	1	0
ic	1	0	0	0	0
ritz	0	0	1	0	1

	£50	£70	£200	inSK	inPic
cheap	1	0	0	0	0
near	0	0	0	1	0

Unlike Example 1, ic no longer meets *near*. Hence ic is not strongly dominant. However, ic meets *cheap*, which is not met by jh, so jh is not dominant as in Example 2. Since ic and jh both meet goals that are not met by the other, the are both weakly dominant. $ritz$ meets no goal and is not weakly dominant.

Trivially, a dominant decision is also weakly dominant.

Proposition 3. *Given $df \in \mathcal{DF}$, $\psi_d(df) \subseteq \psi_w(df)$.*

If a set of decisions S is strongly dominant, then S is also dominant and weakly dominant; there is no other dominant or weakly dominant decision.

Proposition 4. *Given $df \in \mathcal{DF}$, let $S_s = \psi_s(df)$, $S_d = \psi_d(df)$, and $S_w = \psi_w(df)$, if $S_s \neq \{\}$, then $S_s = S_d = S_w$.*

Proof. First we prove $S_s = S_d$. By Proposition 2, $S_s \subseteq S_d$. We show that there is no d such that $d \in S_d$, $d \notin S_s$. Assuming otherwise, (1) since $d \notin S_s$, $\gamma(d) \neq \mathsf{G}$, hence there is some $g \in \mathsf{G}$ and $g \notin \gamma(d)$; (2) since $S_s \neq \{\}$, there is $d' \in S_s$ such that $\gamma(d') = \mathsf{G}$, therefore $g \in \gamma(d')$. By (1) and (2), $d \notin S_d$. Contradiction.

Then we prove $S_s = S_w$. Similarly, we assume $S_s \subset S_w$. Since $S_s \subset S_w$, there exists $d \in S_w$, $d \notin S_s$. Since $S_s \neq \{\}$, there exists $d' \in S_s$ and $\gamma(d') = \mathsf{G}$. Since $d \notin S_s$, $\gamma(d) \subset \mathsf{G}$. Hence $\gamma(d) \subset \gamma(d')$. By Definition 6, $d \notin S_w$. Contradiction.

Similarly, if there exists a non-empty set of dominant decisions S, then there is no weakly dominant decisions other than S. Formally:

Proposition 5. *Given $df \in \mathcal{DF}$, let $S_d = \psi_d(df)$ and $S_w = \psi_w(df)$. If $S_d \neq \{\}$, then $S_d = S_w$.*

Proof. By Proposition 3, we know $S_d \subseteq S_w$. We show $S_w \subseteq S_d$. Assume otherwise, i.e., there exists $d \in S_w$ and $d \notin S_d$. Since $S_d \neq \{\}$, there exists $d' \in S_d$, such that $\gamma(d') \supseteq \gamma(d'')$, for all $d'' \in \mathsf{D}$. Hence $\gamma(d) \subseteq \gamma(d')$. Since $d \notin S_d$, $\gamma(d) \neq \gamma(d')$. Therefore, $\gamma(d) \subset \gamma(d')$. By Definition 6, $d \notin S_w$. Contradiction.

As illustrated by Example 3, given a decision framework df, if there is no dominant decision in df, but only weakly dominant decisions S, then S contains at least two decisions such that each meets a different set of goals.

Theorem 1. *Given $df = \langle \mathsf{D}, \mathsf{A}, \mathsf{G}, \mathsf{T_{DA}}, \mathsf{T_{GA}} \rangle$, let $S_d = \psi_d(df)$ and $S_w = \psi_w(df)$. If $S_d = \{\}$ and $S_w \neq \{\}$, then there exists $d, d' \in S_w, d \neq d'$ and $\gamma(d) \neq \gamma(d')$.*

Proof. Since $S_d = \{\}$, by Lemma 1, $|\mathsf{D}| > 1$. Assume that for all $d, d' \in S_w, d \neq d', \gamma(d) = \gamma(d')$. Then there are two cases, both of them leading to contradictions.

1. First case, if there is no $d'' \in \mathsf{D} \setminus S_w$, then $S_w = \mathsf{D}$. Since $\gamma(d) = \gamma(d')$ for all d, d', by Lemma 1, for all $d \in S_w, d \in \psi_d(df)$, but $S_d = \{\}$. Contradiction.
2. Second case, if there exists some $d'' \in \mathsf{D} \setminus S_w$. Then there are five possibilities between $\gamma(d)$ and $\gamma(d'')$, and they all give contradictions, as follows:
   (a) $\gamma(d) \supset \gamma(d'')$. Not possible, as if so there would exists $d^* \in \mathsf{D}$ such that d^* is dominant (d could be a candidate for such d^*).
   (b) $\gamma(d) \subset \gamma(d'')$. Not possible, as if so there would exists $d^* \in \mathsf{D} \setminus S_w$ such that d^* is dominant (d'' could be a candidate for such d^*).
   (c) $\gamma(d) = \gamma(d'')$. Not possible, as if so d'' would be in S_w.
   (d) None of (a)(b)(c) but $\gamma(d) \cap \gamma(d'') \neq \{\}$. Not possible, as if so there would exist $g \in \gamma(d''), g \notin \gamma(d)$, hence there would exist $d^* \in \mathsf{D} \setminus S_w$ and d^* is weakly dominant (d'' could be a candidate for such d^*), but $\psi_w(df) = S_w$ and $d^* \notin S_w$.
   (e) None of (a)(b)(c), but $\gamma(d) \cap \gamma(d'') = \{\}$. Same as case 2(d).

Both case 1 and 2 give contradictions, this theorem holds.

Theorem 1 gives an important result. Comparing with Definition 4 ($\gamma(d) = \mathsf{G}$ for all $d \in \psi_s$) and Proposition 1 ($\gamma(d) = \gamma(d')$ for all $d, d' \in \psi_d$), showing that (strongly) dominant decisions meet the same goals, Theorem 1 shows that weakly dominant decisions meet different goals. Hence, selecting different decisions from a (strongly) dominant set makes no difference w.r.t. the decision maker, whereas selecting different decisions from a weakly dominant decision set would.

4   Computing and Explaining Decisions with ABA

As seen in [9], ABA can be used to compute and explain decisions. Given a decision framework and a decision function, we can construct an ABA framework, AF, in a way such that admissible arguments in AF are selected decisions.

We introduce *strongly dominant ABA frameworks* to compute strongly dominant decisions in a decision framework. Formally,

Definition 7. *Given a decision framework* $df = \langle \mathsf{D}, \mathsf{A}, \mathsf{G}, \mathsf{T_{DA}}, \mathsf{T_{GA}} \rangle$, *in which* $|\mathsf{D}| = n$, $|\mathsf{A}| = m$ *and* $|\mathsf{G}| = l$, *the* strongly dominant ABA framework *corresponding to* $\langle \mathsf{D}, \mathsf{A}, \mathsf{G}, \mathsf{T_{DA}}, \mathsf{T_{GA}} \rangle$ *is* $df_S = \langle \mathcal{L}, \mathcal{R}, \mathcal{A}, \mathcal{C} \rangle$, *where*

- $\mathcal{R}$ *is such that: for all* $k = 1, .., n; j = 1, .., m$ *and* $i = 1, .., l$:
  - *if* $\mathsf{T_{DA}}[\mathsf{k}, \mathsf{i}] = 1$ *then* $d_k a_i \leftarrow$;
  - *if* $\mathsf{T_{GA}}[\mathsf{j}, \mathsf{i}] = 1$ *then* $g_j a_i \leftarrow$;
  - $d_k g_j \leftarrow d_k a_i, g_j a_i$;
- $\mathcal{A}$ *is such that:* d_k, *for* $k = 1, .., n$; $N d_k g_j$, *for* $k = 1, .., n$ *and* $j = 1, .., m$;
- $\mathcal{C}$ *is such that:* $\mathcal{C}(d_k) = \{N d_k g_1, \dots, N d_k g_n\}$, *for* $k = 1, .., n$;
  $\mathcal{C}(N d_k g_j) = \{d_k g_j\}$, *for* $k = 1, .., n$ *and* $j = 1, .., m$.

The intuition behind Definition 7 is as follows: given a decision d_k, we let d_k be an assumption. We check if d_k meets all goals by defining the contrary of d_k to be $\{N d_k g_1, \dots, N d_k g_m\}$ (standing for d_k does not meet g_1, ..., d_k does not meet g_m). Each of these "negative" assumption is then attacked by a "proof" that d_k meets g_j, i.e., a "proof" for $d_k g_j$. From Definition 2, we know that d_k meets g_j iff there is an attribute a_i such that d_k has a_i and g_j is satisfied by a_i. Hence, we check in both $\mathsf{T_{DA}}$ and $\mathsf{T_{GA}}$ to see if such a_i exists.

We illustrate the notion of strongly dominant ABA framework corresponding to a decision framework in the following example.

Example 4. (Continue Example 1.) Given the decision framework df in Example 1, $df_S = \langle \mathcal{L}, \mathcal{R}, \mathcal{A}, \mathcal{C} \rangle$ has

$\mathcal{R}$ (rules):

$jh70 \leftarrow$	$jhSK \leftarrow$	$ic50 \leftarrow$	$icSK \leftarrow$
$ritz200 \leftarrow$	$ritzPic \leftarrow$	$cheap50 \leftarrow$	$nearSK \leftarrow$

$jhCheap \leftarrow jh50, cheap50$ $jhNear \leftarrow jh50, near50$
$jhCheap \leftarrow jh70, cheap70$ $jhNear \leftarrow jh70, near70$
$jhCheap \leftarrow jh200, cheap200$ $jhNear \leftarrow jh200, near200$
$jhCheap \leftarrow jhSK, cheapSK$ $jhNear \leftarrow jhSK, nearSK$
$jhCheap \leftarrow jhPic, cheapPic$ $jhNear \leftarrow jhPic, nearPic$
$icCheap \leftarrow ic50, cheap50$ $icNear \leftarrow ic50, near50$
$icCheap \leftarrow ic70, cheap70$ $icNear \leftarrow ic70, near70$
$icCheap \leftarrow ic200, cheap200$ $icNear \leftarrow ic200, near200$
$icCheap \leftarrow icSK, cheapSK$ $icNear \leftarrow icSK, nearSK$
$icCheap \leftarrow icPic, cheapPic$ $icNear \leftarrow icPic, nearPic$
$ritzCheap \leftarrow ritz50, cheap50$ $ritzNear \leftarrow ritz50, near50$
$ritzCheap \leftarrow ritz70, cheap70$ $ritzNear \leftarrow ritz70, near70$
$ritzCheap \leftarrow ritz200, cheap200$ $ritzNear \leftarrow ritz200, near200$
$ritzCheap \leftarrow ritzSK, cheapSK$ $ritzNear \leftarrow ritzSK, nearSK$
$ritzCheap \leftarrow ritzPic, cheapPic$ $ritzNear \leftarrow ritzPic, nearPic$

$$\begin{array}{llll} & jh & ic & ritz \\ \mathcal{A} \text{ (assumptions):} & NjhCheap & NicCheap & NritzCheap \\ & NjhNear & NicNear & NritzNear \end{array}$$

$$\mathcal{C} \text{ (contraries):} \quad \begin{array}{l} \mathcal{C}(jh) = \{NjhCheap, NjhNear\} \\ \mathcal{C}(ic) = \{NicCheap, NicNear\} \\ \mathcal{C}(ritz) = \{NritzCheap, NritzNear\} \end{array}$$

$$\begin{array}{ll} \mathcal{C}(NjhCheap) = \{jhCheap\} & \mathcal{C}(NjhNear) = \{jhNear\} \\ \mathcal{C}(NicCheap) = \{icCheap\} & \mathcal{C}(NicNear) = \{icNear\} \\ \mathcal{C}(NritzCheap) = \{ritzCheap\} & \mathcal{C}(NritzNear) = \{ritzNear\} \end{array}$$

Formally, we show the correspondence between strongly dominant decisions and the ABA counterpart as follows.

Theorem 2. *Given $df = \langle \mathsf{D}, \mathsf{A}, \mathsf{G}, \mathsf{T}_{DA}, \mathsf{T}_{GA} \rangle$, let df_S be the strongly dominant ABA framework corresponding to df. Then for all decisions $d \in \mathsf{D}$, $d \in \psi_s(df)$ iff $\{d\} \vdash d$ is admissible in df_S.*

Proof. Let d be d_k (k is the index of d in T_{DA}). We first prove if d_k is strongly dominant, then $\{d_k\} \vdash d_k$ is admissible. Since d_k is strongly dominant, $\gamma(d_k) = \mathsf{G}$. Hence, for every $g \in \mathsf{G}$, d_k meets g. Therefore, for every $g \in \mathsf{G}$, there exists some $a \in \mathsf{A}$, such that d_k has a and g is satisfied by a. Let the indices of g and a be j and i, in both T_{DA} and T_{GA}, respectively, then $\mathsf{T}_{DA}[\mathtt{k}, \mathtt{i}] = \mathsf{T}_{GA}[\mathtt{j}, \mathtt{i}] = 1$. Hence, $d_k a_i \leftarrow$ and $g_j a_i \leftarrow$ are in $\mathcal{R}$ for all j. Therefore $\{\} \vdash d_k g_j$ exists for all j and are not attacked. Hence, $\{Nd_k g_j\} \vdash Nd_k g_j$ is attacked for all j; and since $\{d_k\}$ is conflict-free, $\{d_k\} \vdash d_k$ is admissible.

We then show if $\{d_k\} \vdash d_k$ is admissible then d_k is strongly dominant. Let $\{Nd_k g_j\} \vdash Nd_k g_j$ be attackers of $\{d_k\} \vdash d_k$. Since $\{d_k\} \vdash d_k$ is admissible, it withstands all of its attacks. Hence, $\{Nd_k g_j\} \vdash Nd_k g_j$ must be attacked for all j. Since $\mathcal{C}(Nd_k g_j) = \{d_k g_j\}$, $\{\} \vdash d_k g_j$ must exist for all j. Because the only rule with head $d_k g_j$ is $d_k g_j \leftarrow d_k a_i, g_j a_i$, for each j there exists some i such that $d_k a_i \leftarrow$ and $g_j a_i \leftarrow$. Then, for each j there must exist some i such that $\mathsf{T}_{DA}[\mathtt{k}, \mathtt{i}] = \mathsf{T}_{GA}[\mathtt{j}, \mathtt{i}] = 1$ for all j. Therefore d meets all goals g in G and d is strongly dominant.

The relation between strongly dominant decisions and admissible arguments in strongly dominant ABA framework is shown in the following example.

Example 5. (Continue Example 4.) Given the decision framework df in Example 1, and the strongly dominant ABA framework $df_S = \langle \mathcal{L}, \mathcal{R}, \mathcal{A}, \mathcal{C} \rangle$ in Example 4, we see that $\{ic\} \vdash ic$ is admissible, as its attackers $\{NicCheap\} \vdash NicCheap$ and $\{NicNear\} \vdash NicNear$ are both attacked by $\{\} \vdash icCheap$ and $\{\} \vdash icNear$, respectively. The argument $\{\} \vdash icNear$ is admissible as $icNear \leftarrow icSK, nearSK; icSK \leftarrow$ and $nearSK \leftarrow$ are in $\mathcal{R}$. Similarly, $\{\} \vdash icCheap$ is admissible as $icCheap \leftarrow ic50, cheap50; ic50 \leftarrow$ and $cheap50 \leftarrow$ are in $\mathcal{R}$ and there is no argument attacks $\{\} \vdash icNear$ or $\{\} \vdash icCheap$. The graphical illustration is shown in Figure 1.

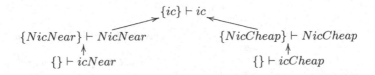

Fig. 1. Graphical illustration of Example 5. Here, $\{ic\} \vdash ic$ is admissible as it is an argument and its attackers $\{NicNear\} \vdash NicNear$ and $\{NicCheap\} \vdash NicCheap$ are both counterattacked.

Given a decision framework, dominant decisions can also be computed with ABA in its corresponding *dominant ABA framework*. Formally,

Definition 8. *Given* $df = \langle D, A, G, T_{DA}, T_{GA} \rangle$, $|D| = n$, *and* $|A| = m$, *let the corresponding strongly dominant ABA framework be* $df_S = \langle \mathcal{L}, \mathcal{R}, \mathcal{A}, \mathcal{C} \rangle$, *then the dominant ABA framework corresponding to* df *is* $df_D = \langle \mathcal{L}, \mathcal{R}_D, \mathcal{A}_D, \mathcal{C}_D \rangle$, *where:*

- $\mathcal{R}_D = \mathcal{R} \cup \{Ng_j^{\overline{k}} \leftarrow Nd_1 g_j, \ldots, Nd_{k-1} g_j, Nd_{k+1} g_j, \ldots, Nd_N g_j\}$ *for* $k = 1, .., n$ *and* $j = 1, .., m;$
- $\mathcal{A}_D = \mathcal{A};$
- $\mathcal{C}_D$ *is* $\mathcal{C}$ *with* $\mathcal{C}(Nd_k g_j) = \{d_k g_j\}$ *replaced by* $\mathcal{C}(Nd_k g_j) = \{d_k g_j, Ng_j^{\overline{k}}\}$, *for* $k = 1, .., n$ *and* $j = 1, .., m$.

The intuition behind Definition 8 is as follows: a decision d_k is selected either if it meets all goals, or for goals that d_k does not meet, there is no other d' meeting them. Hence the contrary of $Nd_k g_j$ (reads d_k does not meet g_j) is either $d_k g_j$ (d_k meets g_j) or $Ng_j^{\overline{k}}$ (all decisions other than d_k do not meet g_j). The following theorem holds.

Theorem 3. *Given* $df = \langle D, A, G, T_{DA}, T_{GA} \rangle$, *let* df_D *be the dominant ABA framework corresponding to* df, *then for all decisions* $d \in D$, $d \in \psi_d(df)$ *iff* $\{d\} \vdash d$ *is admissible in* df_D.

Proof. (Sketch.) We first prove dominance implies admissibility for $d_k \in D$. Since d_k is dominant, d_k meets all goals that is met by a decision in D. Hence, for each goal g_j, either (1) there is $a_i \in A$, such that $T_{DA}[k, i] = T_{GA}[j, i] = 1$ and $d_k a_i \leftarrow$ and $g_j a_i \leftarrow$ are in $\mathcal{R}$, therefore $\{\} \vdash d_k g_j$ exists and is not attacked; or (2) there is no argument $\{\} \vdash d_r g_j$ for all $d_r \in D$ (g_j is not met by any d_r); therefore $\{Nd_1 g_j, \ldots, Nd_{k-1} g_j, Nd_{k+1} g_j, Nd_N g_j\} \vdash Ng_j^{\overline{k}}$ is admissible. Whichever the case, $\{d_k\} \vdash d_k$ withstands attacks from $\{Nd_k g_j\} \vdash Nd_k g_j$, i.e. $Nd_k g_j$ is always attacked. Moreover, since $\{Nd_1 g_j, \ldots, Nd_{k-1} g_j, Nd_{k+1} y_j, Nd_N y_j\} \cup \{d_k\}$ is also conflict-free, $\{d_k\} \vdash d_k$ is admissible.

We then show that admissibility implies dominance. Since $\{d_k\} \vdash d_k$ is admissible, all of its attackers must be counter attacked, i.e., $\{Nd_k g_j\} \vdash Nd_k g_j$ are attacked for all j. Each $Nd_k g_j$ is attacked either because there is $\{d_k g_j\} \vdash d_k g_j$, or there is $\{Nd_1 g_j, \ldots, Nd_{k-1} g_j, Nd_{k+1} g_j, Nd_N g_j\} \vdash Ng_j^{\overline{k}}$, i.e., either g_j is met by d_k or there is no $d' \in D$ meeting g_j. Therefore d_k is dominant.

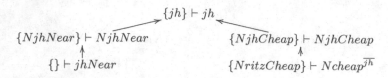

Fig. 2. Graphical illustration of ABA computation for dominant decisions

We illustrate the ABA computation of dominant decisions in Figure 2. The dominant ABA framework corresponding to the decision framework shown in Example 2 is omitted due to the lack of space. It can be seen that $\{jh\} \vdash jh$ is admissible because (1) jh is *near*, hence $\{\} \vdash jhNear$ exists and not attacked; and (2) though jh is not *cheap*, hence there is no $\{\} \vdash jhCheap$ to attack $\{NjhCheap\} \vdash NjhCheap$, but and *ritz* is not *cheap* either, so $\{NritzCheap\} \vdash Ncheap^{\overline{jh}}$ exists and attacks $\{NjhCheap\} \vdash NjhCheap$.

Similarly, we can define *weakly dominant ABA framework* to compute weakly dominant decisions, as follows.

Definition 9. *Given* $df = \langle D, A, G, T_{DA}, T_{GA}\rangle$, $|D| = n$ *and* $|A| = m$, *the* weakly dominant ABA framework *corresponding to* df *is* $df_W = \langle \mathcal{L}, \mathcal{R}, \mathcal{A}, \mathcal{C}\rangle$, *where*

- $\mathcal{R}$ *is such that: for all* $k = 1,..,n; j = 1,..,m$ *and* $i = 1,..,l$:
  - *if* $T_{DA}[k, i] = 1$ *then* $d_k a_i \leftarrow$;
  - *if* $T_{GA}[j, i] = 1$ *then* $g_j a_i \leftarrow$;
  - $d_k g_j \leftarrow d_k a_i, g_j a_i$;
  for all $r, k = 1,..,n, r \neq k$; *and* $j = 1,..,m$:
  - $Sd_r d_k \leftarrow d_r g_j, Nd_k g_j, NSd_k d_r$;
  - $\overline{S}d_k d_r \leftarrow d_k g_j, Nd_r g_j$;
- $\mathcal{A}$ *is such that:* d_k, *for* $k = 1,..,n$;
  $NSd_k d_r$, *for* $r, k = 1,..,n, r \neq k$;
  $Nd_k g_j$, *for* $k = 1,..,n$ *and* $j = 1,..,m$;
- $\mathcal{C}$ *is such that:* $\mathcal{C}(d_k) = \{Sd_1 d_k, \ldots, Sd_{k-1}d_k, Sd_{k+1}d_k, \ldots, Sd_n d_k\}$, *for* $k = 1,..,n$;
  $\mathcal{C}(NSd_k d_r) = \{\overline{S}d_k d_r\}$, *for* $r, k = 1,..,n, r \neq k$;
  $\mathcal{C}(Nd_k g_j) = \{d_k g_j\}$, *for* $k = 1,..,n$ *and* $j = 1,..,m$.

The intuition behind Definition 9 is as follows: given a decision d_k in a decision framework, d_k is selected w.r.t. ψ_w iff there is no $d' \in D \setminus \psi_w(df)$ such that the goals d' meets is a super-set of goals met by d_k. We test this for all $d' \neq d_k$ by letting the contrary of d_k be $\{Sd_1 d_k, \ldots, Sd_{k-1}d_k, Sd_{k+1}d_k, \ldots, Sd_n d_k\}$, standing for $\gamma(d_1) \supset \gamma(d_k), \ldots, \gamma(d_n) \supset \gamma(d_k)$. To "prove" $Sd_r d_k$, one needs to show two conditions: (1) there exists $g_j \in G$, such that d_r meets g_j and d_k does not (hence "prove" $d_r g_j$ and $Nd_k g_j$); and (2) there does not exist $g'_j \in G$, such that d_k meets g'_j and d_r does not (hence "prove" $NSd_k d_r$). Condition (1) is represented by having the first two terms in the body of the rule $Sd_r d_k \leftarrow d_r g_j, Nd_k g_j, NSd_k d_r$; condition (2) is represented by the last term in the body

$$\{ic\} \vdash ic \qquad\qquad \{jh\} \vdash jh$$
$$\uparrow \qquad\qquad\qquad\qquad \uparrow$$
$$\{NicNear, N\overline{S}icjh\} \vdash Sjhic \quad \{NjhCheap, N\overline{S}jhic\} \vdash Sicjh$$
$$\uparrow \qquad\qquad\qquad\qquad\qquad \uparrow$$
$$\{NjhCheap\} \vdash \overline{S}icjh \qquad\qquad \{NicNear\} \vdash \overline{S}jhic$$

Fig. 3. Graphical illustration of ABA computation for weakly dominant decisions. The figure on the left can be read as follows. (1) Claiming ic is weakly dominant (the root argument). (2) jh is better, as ic is not near but jh is (the middle argument). (3) jh is not always better than ic as jh is not cheap but ic is (the bottom argument).

of this rule. To check $NSd_k d_r$, we need to fail at proving $\overline{S}d_k d_r$, which can only be proved by using the rule: $\overline{S}d_k d_r \leftarrow d_k g_j, N d_r g_j$.

Similar to Theorem 2 and 3, the following theorem holds.

Theorem 4. *Given $df = \langle \mathsf{D}, \mathsf{A}, \mathsf{G}, \mathsf{T_{DA}}, \mathsf{T_{GA}} \rangle$, let df_W be the weakly dominant ABA framework corresponds to df. Then for all decisions $d \in \mathsf{D}$, $d \in \psi_w(df)$ iff $\{d\} \vdash d$ is admissible in df_W.*

Proof. (Sketch.) We first prove that weakly dominance implies admissibility for $d_k \in \mathsf{D}$. Since d_k is weakly dominant, then there is no $d_r \in \mathsf{D} \setminus \psi_w(df)$ such that $\gamma(d_k) \subset \gamma(d_r)$. Hence, given any $d_r \in \mathsf{D} \setminus \{d_k\}$, for each $g \in \gamma(d_r)$, either (1) $g \in \gamma(d_k)$ or (2) $g \notin \gamma(d_k)$, but there exists some $g' \in \mathsf{G}$ such that $g' \in \gamma(d_k)$ and $g' \notin \gamma(d_r)$. If it is case (1), then $N d_k g_j$ does not hold as d_k meets g_j; if it is case (2), then $NSd_k d_r$ does not hold as there is some g' met by d_k but not d_r. Hence, whichever the case, arguments for $Sd_r d_k$ are either nonexistent (case 1) or are counterattacked (case 2). Since the contrary of d_k is $\{Sd_r d_k\}$ for all $r \neq k$, and to build an argument for $Sd_r d_k$ one needs to show both $N d_k g_j$ and $NSd_k d_r$, failing at constructing arguments for $Sd_r d_k$ and $\{d_k, N d_r g_t\}$ being conflict-free jointly make $\{d_k\} \vdash d_k$ admissible.

Then we show that if $\{d_k\} \vdash d_k$ is admissible, then d_k is weakly dominant. Since $\{d_k\} \vdash d_k$ is admissible, all of its attackers are counterattacked or nonexistent. Hence, arguments for $Sd_k d_r$ are either counterattacked or nonexistent for all $d_r \neq d_k$. Since $Sd_r d_k \leftarrow d_r g_j, N d_k g_j, NSd_k d_r$, if an argument for $Sd_k d_r$ does not exist, it means there is no $d_r g_j$, hence d_r does not meet g_j. If an argument for $Sd_k d_r$ exists but counterattacked, it means either (1) $N d_k g_j$ is attacked by $d_k g_j$ or (2) $NSd_k d_r$ is attacked by $\overline{S}d_k d_r$. In case (1), either both d_k and d_r meet g_j or d_r does not meet it. In case (2), there is some g' such that g' is met by d_k but not d_r. Whichever the case, $\gamma(d_k)$ is not a subset of $\gamma(d_r)$. Therefore d_k is weakly dominant.

We illustrate the ABA computation of weakly dominant decisions in Figure 3. The weakly dominant ABA framework corresponding to the decision framework is omitted. It can be seen that both $\{ic\} \vdash ic$ and $\{jh\} \vdash jh$ are admissible because jh is *near* but not *cheap* and ic is *cheap* but not *near*. Hence each of the two meets some goal that is not met by the other. *ritz* is not weakly dominant, as it is neither *cheap* nor *near*.

5   Decisions with Preferences

Thus far, we present a decision framework characterised by two tables, T_{DA} and T_{GA}, describing the relations between decisions, attributes and goals. However, in cases where not all goals are considered equal, and there are multiple decisions meeting different goals (i.e., a decision framework with only weakly dominant decisions but no dominant or strongly dominant decision) it is useful to consider *preferences* over goals upon selecting decisions. We extend our decision framework to include preferences and define *extended decision frameworks* as follows.

Definition 10. *An* extended decision framework *is a tuple* $\langle D, A, G, T_{DA}, T_{GA}, P \rangle$, *in which* $\langle D, A, G, T_{DA}, T_{GA} \rangle$ *forms a decision framework and* P *is a partial order over goals, representing the preference ranking of goals.*
We use $\mathcal{EDF}$ *to denote the set of possible extended decision frameworks.*

We represent P as a set of constraints $g_i > g_j$ for $g_i, g_j \in G$. Extended decision frameworks are generalisation of decision frameworks as any decision framework can be considered as an extended decision framework with a uniformly equal preference order.

Example 6 illustrate the notion of extended decision framework as follows.

Example 6. We reuse Example 3 but remove *ritz* in this example. We let T_{DA} be the first two rows and T_{GA} remain the same. We also add the preference ranking: $\{near > cheap\}$.

We do not redefine Definition 2 for extended decision frameworks as this definition remains the same in extended decision frameworks.
We need to redefine *extended decision functions* over extended decision frameworks to select decisions. Formally,

Definition 11. *An* extended decision function *is a mapping* $\psi^E : \mathcal{EDF} \mapsto 2^{\mathcal{DEC}}$, *such that, given* $edf = \langle D, A, G, T_{DA}, T_{GA}, P \rangle$, $\psi^E(edf) \subseteq D$. *For any* $d, d' \in D$, *if* $\gamma(d) = \gamma(d')$ *and* $d \in \psi^E(df)$, *then* $d' \in \psi^E(df)$. *We say that* $\psi^E(edf)$ *are selected w.r.t.* ψ^E.
We use Ψ^E *to denote the set of all extended decision functions.*

More specifically, we define *best possible extended decision function* to select the decision that meets the most preferred goal that is ever met by any decision.

Definition 12. *A* best possible decision function $\psi^E \in \Psi^E$ *is that given* $edf = \langle D, A, G, T_{DA}, T_{GA}, P \rangle$, *for all* $d \in D$, *if* $d \in \psi^E(edf)$, *then (1) there is some* $g \in \gamma(d)$, *and (2) there is no* $g' \in \gamma(d')$ *for all* $d' \in D \setminus \{d\}$, *such that* $g' > g$ *in* P. *We say* d *is a* best possible decision.
We refer to a generic best possible decision function as ψ_b^E.

Given the extended decision framework *edf* shown in Example 6, since *jh* meets the top preference goal, *near*, *jh* is a best possible decision in *edf*. Neither *ic* nor *ritz* meets *near*, so neither of the two is a best possible decision.
We can use ABA to compute best possible decisions in an extended decision framework as well, as follows:

Definition 13. *Given edf* $= \langle \mathsf{D}, \mathsf{A}, \mathsf{G}, \mathsf{T_{DA}}, \mathsf{T_{GA}}, \mathsf{P} \rangle$, *the best possible ABA framework corresponding to edf is* $\langle \mathcal{L}, \mathcal{R}, \mathcal{A}, \mathcal{C} \rangle$, *where*

- $\mathcal{R}$ *is such that:*
  for all $k = 1, .., n; j = 1, .., m$ *and* $i = 1, .., l$:
  - *if* $\mathsf{T_{DA}}[\mathtt{k}, \mathtt{i}] = 1$ *then* $d_k a_i \leftarrow$;
  - *if* $\mathsf{T_{GA}}[\mathtt{j}, \mathtt{i}] = 1$ *then* $g_j a_i \leftarrow$;
  - $d_k g_j \leftarrow d_k a_i, g_j a_i$;
  for all g_1, g_2 *in* G, *if* $g_1 > g_2 \in \mathsf{P}$, *then* $P g_1 g_2 \leftarrow$;
  for all $k = 1, .., n; j = 1, .., m$: $d_k \leftarrow d_k g_j, Nsmp_j^k$;
  for all $k, r = 1, .., n, k \neq r; j, t = 1, .., m, j \neq t$: $smp_j^k \leftarrow d_r g_t, P g_t g_j$.
- $\mathcal{A}$ *is such that:* $Nsmp_j^k$, *for all* $k = 1, .., n; j = 1, .., m$;
- $\mathcal{C}$ *is such that:* $\mathcal{C}(Nsmp_j^k) = \{smp_j^k\}$, *for all* $k = 1, .., n; j = 1, .., m$.

The intuition behind Definition 13 is as follows: in order to let d_k be the best possible decision, d_k needs to meet $g_j \in \mathsf{G}$, such that there is no other $d' \in \mathsf{D}$ meeting $g' \in \mathsf{G}$ and $g' > g$ in P. Hence we have the rule $d_k \leftarrow d_k g_j, Nsmp_j^k$, standing for d_k meets g_j ($d_k g_j$) and "there is no other decision meeting goals more preferred than d_k meeting g_j" ($Nsmp_j^k$).

We illustrate best possible ABA framework in the following example.

Example 7. The best possible ABA framework corresponds to the extended decision framework shown in Example 6 is follows.
$\mathcal{R}$:

$$jhCheap \leftarrow jh50, cheap50 \qquad\qquad jhNear \leftarrow jh50, near50$$
$$jhCheap \leftarrow jh70, cheap70 \qquad\qquad jhNear \leftarrow jh70, near70$$
$$jhCheap \leftarrow jh200, cheap200 \qquad\quad jhNear \leftarrow jh200, near200$$
$$jhCheap \leftarrow jhSK, cheapSK \qquad\quad jhNcar \leftarrow jhSK, nearSK$$
$$jhCheap \leftarrow jhPic, cheapPic \qquad\quad jhNear \leftarrow jhPic, nearPic$$
$$icCheap \leftarrow ic50, cheap50 \qquad\qquad icNear \leftarrow ic50, near50$$
$$icCheap \leftarrow ic70, cheap70 \qquad\qquad icNear \leftarrow ic70, near70$$
$$icCheap \leftarrow ic200, cheap200 \qquad\quad icNear \leftarrow ic200, near200$$
$$icCheap \leftarrow icSK, cheapSK \qquad\quad icNear \leftarrow icSK, nearSK$$
$$icCheap \leftarrow icPic, cheapPic \qquad\quad icNear \leftarrow icPic, nearPic$$
$$jh \leftarrow jhCheap, Nsmp_{cheap}^{jh} \qquad\quad jh \leftarrow jhNear, Nsmp_{near}^{jh}$$
$$ic \leftarrow icCheap, Nsmp_{cheap}^{ic} \qquad\quad ic \leftarrow icNear, Nsmp_{near}^{ic}$$

$$smp_{cheap}^{jh} \leftarrow icNear, PNearCheap \qquad\quad smp_{near}^{jh} \leftarrow icCheap, PCheapNear$$
$$smp_{cheap}^{ic} \leftarrow jhNear, PNearCheap \qquad\quad smp_{near}^{ic} \leftarrow jhCheap, PCheapNear$$

$$PNearCheap \leftarrow \quad jh70 \leftarrow \quad jhSK \leftarrow \quad ic50 \leftarrow \quad cheap50 \leftarrow \quad nearSK \leftarrow$$

$\mathcal{A}$:

$$Nsmp_{cheap}^{jh} \qquad Nsmp_{near}^{jh} \qquad Nsmp_{cheap}^{ic} \qquad Nsmp_{near}^{ic}$$

$\mathcal{C}$:

$$\mathcal{C}(Nsmp_{cheap}^{jh}) = \{smp_{cheap}^{jh}\} \qquad \mathcal{C}(Nsmp_{near}^{jh}) = \{smp_{near}^{jh}\}$$
$$\mathcal{C}(Nsmp_{cheap}^{ic}) = \{smp_{cheap}^{ic}\} \qquad \mathcal{C}(Nsmp_{near}^{ic}) = \{smp_{near}^{ic}\}$$

Theorem 5. *Given an extended decision framework* $edf = \langle D, A, G, T_{DA}, T_{GA}, P \rangle$, *let* edf_b *be the best possible ABA framework corresponding to* edf. *Then, for all* $d \in D$, $d \in \psi_b^E(edf)$ *iff* d *is the claim of an admissible argument in* edf_b.

Proof. (Sketch.) We first show that if $d_k \in D$ is a best possible decision, then there is an admissible argument $\{Nsmp_j^k\} \vdash d_k$. Since d_k is a best possible decision, it meets $g_j \in G$ (we hence have $d_k g_j$), and there is no other $g_t \in G$, such that $g_t > g_j \in P$ and $g_t \in \gamma(d_r)$ for some $d_r \in D \setminus \{d_k\}$. Hence, there is no argument for smp_j^k and since $\{Nsmp_j^k\}$ is conflict-free, $\{Nsmp_j^k\} \vdash d_k$ is not attacked hence is admissible.

To show that d_k is a best possible decision given $\{Nsmp_j^k\} \vdash d_k$ being admissible, we need to show there is no $d' \in D \setminus \{d_k\}$ such that d' meets a more preferred goal than d_k meeting $g_j \in G$. Since $\{Nsmp_j^k\} \vdash d_k$ is admissible, it withstands its attacks. Since $\mathcal{C}(Nsmp_j^k) = \{smp_j^k\}$ and arguments for smp_j^k are not supported by any assumptions (no assumptions in rules: $smp_j^k \leftarrow d_r g_t, P g_t g_j$; $d_k g_j \leftarrow d_k a_i, g_j a_i$; $d_k a_i \leftarrow$; $g_j a_i \leftarrow$ and $P g_1 g_2 \leftarrow$), $\{Nsmp_j^k\} \vdash d_k$ withstanding its attacks means there is no argument for smp_j^k. Therefore it is not the case that there exists $g' \in G$ and $d' \in D \setminus \{d\}$, such that $g' > g_j$ and $g' \in \gamma(d')$. Hence d_k is a best possible decision.

In Example 7, we "prove" jh using the rule $jh \leftarrow jhNear, Nsmp_{near}^{jh}$. We "prove" $jhNear$ with rules $jhNear \leftarrow jhSK, nearSK$; $jhSK \leftarrow$ and $nearSK \leftarrow$. Since $Nsmp_{near}^{jh}$ is an assumption, we need to show it withstands all attacks. The contrary of $Nsmp_{near}^{jh}$ is $\{smp_{near}^{jh}\}$, which can only be "proved" using the rule $smp_{near}^{jh} \leftarrow icCheap, PCheapNear$. However, since there is no rule for $PCheapNear$, there is no argument for smp_{near}^{jh}. Therefore $Nsmp_{near}^{jh}$ is not attacked and $\{Nsmp_{near}^{jh}\} \vdash jh$ is admissible.

6   Related Work

Amgoud and Prade [1] present a formal model for making decisions using abstract argumentation. Our work differs from theirs as: (1) they use abstract argumentation whereas we use ABA; (2) they use a pair-wise comparison between decisions to select the "winning" decision whereas we use an unified process to map decision frameworks into ABA and then compute admissible arguments.

Matt et.al. [9] present an ABA based decision making model. Our work differs from theirs as: (1) we have studied three different notions of dominant decisions whereas they have studied one; (2) we have studied decision making with preference whereas they have not.

Black and Atkinson [2] present a multi-agent dialogue model for agent to decide actions jointly. Our work differs from theirs as: (1) we have focused on ABA based decision making whereas they have studied a dialogue model; (2) we have studied several different decision criteria where they have not.

Dung et.al. [4] present an argumentation-based approach to contract negotiation. Part of that work can also be viewed as argumentation-based decision-making taking preferences into account. The main differences between that work and ours are: (1) we give formal definition of decision making frameworks whereas they do not; (3) we make explicit connections between "good" decisions and "acceptable" arguments whereas they do not.

Fan et.al. [6] present an ABA-based model for decision making. That work is an extension of this work focused on modelling agent preferences over goals whereas this work lays the foundations by formally defining the decision making problem and identifying key components thereof, e.g., decision frameworks and functions.

7   Conclusion

We present a formal model for decision making with ABA. In this model, we represent agents' knowledge in decision frameworks, which capture relations between decisions, goals, and attributes, e.g., decisions meeting goals, goals being satisfied by attributes. We then define decision functions to model different decision criteria. We define decision functions that select decisions meeting all goals, most goals, goals no others met, and most preferred achievable goals. We then map both decision frameworks and decision functions into ABA frameworks. In this way, computing selected decisions becomes computing admissible arguments. We obtain sound and complete results such as selected decisions are claims of admissible arguments and vice versa. The main advantage of our approach is that it gives an argumentation-based justification of selected decisions, while finding them.

Future directions include (1) further studying of decision criteria / functions for decision making with preference; (2) studying decision making with other form of knowledge representation (not limited to tables), (3) linking to existed decision theoretic work, and (4) studying decision making in the context of multiple agents, in which agents sharing potentially conflicting knowledge and preferences.

Acknowledgements. This research was supported by the EPSRC project *Transparent Rational Decisions by Argumentation* : EP/J020915/1.

References

1. Amgoud, L., Prade, H.: Using arguments for making and explaining decisions. Art. Int. 173(3-4) (2009)
2. Dlack, D., Atkinson, K.: Choosing persuasive arguments for action. In: The 10th International Conference on Autonomous Agents and Multiagent Systems (2011)
3. Dung, P.M., Kowalski, R.A., Toni, F.: Assumption-based argumentation. In: Argumentation in AI, pp. 25–44. Springer (2009)
4. Dung, P.M., Thang, P.M., Toni, F.: Towards argumentation-based contract negotiation. In: Proc. COMMA (2008)
5. Dung, P.M., Kowalski, R.A., Toni, F.: Dialectic proof procedures for assumption-based, admissible argumentation. AIJ 170, 114–159 (2006)

6. Fan, X., Craven, R., Singer, R., Toni, F., Williams, M.: Assumption-based argumentation for decision-making with preferences: A medical case study. In: Leite, J., Son, T.C., Torroni, P., van der Torre, L., Woltran, S. (eds.) CLIMA XIV 2013. LNCS (LNAI), vol. 8143, pp. 374–390. Springer, Heidelberg (2013)
7. Fox, J., Glasspool, D., Patkar, V., Austin, M., Black, L., South, M., Robertson, D., Vincent, C.: Delivering clinical dec. support services: There is nothing as practical as a good theory. J. of Biom. Inf. 43(5) (2010)
8. Fox, J., Krause, P., Elvang-Gøransson, M.: Argumentation as a general framework for uncertain reasoning. In: Proc. UAI, pp. 428–434 (1993)
9. Matt, P.-A., Toni, F., Vaccari, J.R.: Dominant decisions by argumentation agents. In: McBurney, P., Rahwan, I., Parsons, S., Maudet, N. (eds.) ArgMAS 2009. LNCS (LNAI), vol. 6057, pp. 42–59. Springer, Heidelberg (2010)
10. Nawwab, F.S., Bench-Capon, T.J.M., Dunne, P.E.: A methodology for action-selection using value-based argumentation. In: Proc. COMMA, pp. 264–275 (2008)

Justifying Underlying Desires
for Argument-Based Reconciliation

Hiroyuki Kido and Yukio Ohsawa

The University of Tokyo
7-3-1 Hongo, Bunkyo-ku, Tokyo 113-8656, Japan
{kido,ohsawa}@sys.t.u-tokyo.ac.jp

Abstract. Not focusing on stakeholders' original desires, but on their underlying desires helps agents to reconcile practical conflicts. This paper proposes a logical formalization of an argument-based reasoning for justifying both underlying desires and means for realizing them. Based on the idea that an underlying desire can be obtained by abstracting an original desire, we give a problem setting for desire abstraction in terms of sufficiency and consistency using practical syllogisms. We introduce two kinds of defeasible inference rules, called positive and negative practical abductive syllogisms, as counterparts of the practical syllogisms and show their correctness in terms of sufficiency and consistency. We give three kinds of argumentation systems structured with practical abductive syllogisms or/and practical syllogisms and show that the argumentation systems can simply handle Kowalski and Toni's reconciliatory scenario for committee member selection and our reconciliatory scenario for business transfer.

Keywords: Argument-based reasoning, Practical reasoning, Deliberation, Reconciliation, Defeasible inference rules.

Introduction

Practical reasoning comprises two parts; deliberation and means-ends reasoning. Deliberation decides what state of affairs we want to achieve, and the means-ends reasoning decides how we want to achieve these states of affairs [1]. In actual practical reasoning, stakeholders often confront with the situations in which the means for realizing one's desires prevent those of the other. One possible way to resolve the conflict is to choose one of them by argument or preferences. On the other hand, a more attractive way is to reconcile the conflict by not only determining means for realizing either all or parts of the given desires but also determining means for realizing their underlying desires behind the given ones.

However, little attention has been paid to how to find underlying desires behind given desires, how to realize the underlying desires and how to handle both in a unified way as argument-based reasoning. Much work has been done for argument-based formalizations of persuasion, negotiation, practical reasoning, and so on. From the viewpoint of reconciliation, in [2,3,4,5], the authors give

E. Black, S. Modgil, and N. Oren (Eds.): TAFA 2013, LNAI 8306, pp. 143–157, 2014.
© Springer-Verlag Berlin Heidelberg 2014

mechanisms to select or combine a part of given goals or proposals using Dung's acceptability semantics [6] or dialogical status assignment [7] in order to address their individual problems on negotiation. However, determining agent's underlying desires behind the given goals or proposals, or revising them is outside the scope of these literatures. In [8,9,10], the authors give mechanisms for generating knowledge-dependent and context-dependent desires in practical reasoning. The mechanisms use deductive reasoning or default reasoning for deriving desires from given knowledge and desires. They, however, do not address the situations in which there are no means for realizing the given desires nor desires derived from the sum of the desires and knowledge using these reasoning. In [11], the authors give defeasible inference rules transferring a modal operator representing desires from the given desires to the means for realizing those desires. The argumentation framework structured with these inference rules determines the best way to achieve the given desires. It, however, also do not focus on inferences about underlying desires behind the given desires. In [12], the authors maintain the importance of the mechanisms for generating some abstract goals for reconciliation. Although they show guidelines for reconciliatory solutions to their thoughtful story, however, they do not give a formal and general method for finding underlying desires in accordance with well known scheme of practical reasoning [15].

In this paper, we provide an argument-based formalization of justifying means for underlying desires of given desires. Aiming to define underlying desires, we give a problem setting for desire abstraction in terms of sufficiency and consistency and introduce two defeasible inference rules, called positive and negative practical abductive syllogisms, as counterparts of positive and negative practical syllogisms given in [11]. The sufficiency ensures that a hypothesis derived by the rules is an explanation of why a given desire is desirable. The consistency ensures that the hypothesis is not an explanation of why a given desire is undesirable. These two rules intuitively states that it would be desirable to an agent if it is caused by realizing what the agent wants, and it would be undesirable to the agent if it is caused by not realizing what the agent wants. We give three kinds of argumentation systems, called practical abductive argumentation systems, practical argumentation systems and reconciliatory argumentation systems. We show that practical abductive argumentation systems can justify arguments whose conclusions satisfy sufficiency and consistency and the latter two are useful for handling reconciliatory solutions shown in two realistic scenarios: one is of committee member selection shown by Kowalski and Toni [12] and the other is of business transfer posed in this paper.

The paper is organized as follows. After showing logical preliminaries in Section 1, we give sufficiency and consistency conditions as a problem setting of desire abstraction and introduce two kinds of defeasible inference rules for practical reasoning. In Section 3, we give practical abductive argumentation systems and show their correctness in terms of sufficiency and consistency. In Section 4, we give practical argumentation systems and reconciliatory argumentation systems. In Section 5, we show the ability of our proposal by applying to committee member selection posed by Kowalski and Toni and business transfer posed by this paper. Section 6 describes related work and discussions and Section 7 shows conclusions and future work.

1   Logical Preliminaries

We assume a modal propositional language with a single desire operator D that cannot be nesting. An assumed logic is type KD satisfying that if $D\varphi$ is true then $\neg D\neg\varphi$ is true. A knowledge representing language $\mathcal{L}$ is a union of the modal propositional language, denoted by $\mathcal{L}_0$, and the set, denoted by $\mathcal{L}_1$, of defaults constructed on $\mathcal{L}_0$. Defaults have the form "$\varphi \Rightarrow \psi$" where φ is a conjunction of atomic propositions in $\mathcal{L}_0$ and ψ is an atomic proposition in $\mathcal{L}_0$. Informally, "$\varphi \Rightarrow \psi$" has the meaning that "If φ is the case then ψ is typically the case." $\mathcal{L}_0$ is decided into two subsets; one is a set of controllable formulae and the other is a set of uncontrollable formulae. Intuitively, a controllable formula represents a state, including an action, agents can realize, e.g., "The book is on the desk" or "I read the book," while an uncontrollable formula represents a states agents cannot change, e.g., "He is thirty years old." Note that strict distinction is beyond the scope of this paper. We assume that D operates only on controllable formulae. Agent's knowledge is a default theory $T = (F, \mathcal{D})$ where $\mathcal{F} \subseteq \mathcal{L}_0$ is a consistent set without modal operator D and $\mathcal{D} \subseteq \mathcal{L}_1$ is a set of the defaults, and agent's desire is a set $\mathcal{G} \subseteq \mathcal{L}_0$ where each element of $\mathcal{G}$ is an atomic propositions with operator D.

An inference rule without an exception is called a strict inference rule, while an inference rule with an exception is called a defeasible inference rule. We use symbol "$\leadsto$" to represent any defeasible inference rules. Defeasible modus ponens is a defeasible inference rule defined as follows.

- $DMP : \phi, \phi \Rightarrow \psi \leadsto \psi$

In [11], the authors introduce two defeasible inference rules for practical reasoning called positive practical syllogism, PPS, and negative practical syllogism, NPS. Let a and p be controllable formulae and r be uncontrollable formula. The rules have the following forms.

- $PPS : a \wedge r \Rightarrow p, Dp, r \leadsto Da$
- $NPS : a \wedge r \Rightarrow \neg p, Dp, r \leadsto \neg Da$

Informally, if an agent who desires p and believes r also believes that realizing a in a circumstance r realizes p, then this is a reason for desiring a, while if the agent believes that realizing a in a circumstance r instead realizes $\neg p$, then this is a reason not to desire a [11]. PPS transfers modal operator D from a certain formula to its possible means, while NPS negatively transfers the operator to its possible means. In this paper, we make a minor revision to NPS without losing intuition and use the following defeasible inference rule NPS' instead of NPS.

$-\ NPS' : a \wedge r \Rightarrow \neg p, Dp, r \rightsquigarrow D\neg a$

NPS' is more aggressive than NPS in the sense that it derives more than $\neg Da$ because if $D\neg a$ is true then $\neg Da$ is true. Moreover, we often use simplifications "$a \Rightarrow p, Dp \rightsquigarrow Da$" and "$a \Rightarrow \neg p, Dp \rightsquigarrow \neg Da$" of PPS and NPS', respectively. We use the following notation for representing that proposition x is derived from a set B of formulae using only PPS or NPS' only once, where PS is an abbreviation of "practical syllogisms."

$$B \vdash_{PS} x$$

Dung's acceptability semantics is defined on an abstract argumentation framework. An abstract argumentation framework is defined as a tuple of a set of arguments without any internal structures and a binary relation, called attack relation, on the set of arguments. The following is the summary of definitions of Dung's grounded semantics [6].

- An *argumentation framework* is a pair $AF = <AR, Attacks>$, where AR is a set of arguments, and $Attacks$ is a binary relation on AR, i.e., $Attacks \subseteq AR \times AR$.
- A set $S \subseteq AR$ of arguments is *conflict-free* if there are no arguments $A, B \in S$ such that A attacks B, i.e. $(A, B) \in Attacks$.
- An argument $A \in AR$ is *acceptable* with respect to a set $S \subseteq AR$ of arguments iff, for all arguments in $B \in AR$, if B attacks A then there is an argument $C \in S$ such that C attacks B.
- A characteristic function $F_{AF} : Pow(AR) \to Pow(AR)$ is defined as follows.

$$F_{AF}(S) = \{A \mid A \text{ is acceptable with respect to } S\}$$

- The *grounded extension* of an argumentation framework AF is the least fixed point of F_{AF}

An argument A is *justified* in abstract argumentation framework AF, denoted by $A \in Jargs(AF)$, iff it is in the grounded extension of AF and is *overruled* in AF, denoted by $A \in Oargs(AF)$, iff it is not in the grounded extension of AF.

2   Defeasible Inference Rules for Desires Abstraction

2.1   Problem Settings for Desire Abstraction

This subsection aims to give a formal problem setting of desire abstraction. Our idea behind desire abstraction is that as is the case that rational actions or proposals have their objects, original desires also have their objects, i.e., underlying desires, and the underlying desires are within effects caused by realizing the original desires. What we want is to hypothetically identify underlying desires from possible effects of original desires.

Formally, what we want is a set $\mathcal{H} \subseteq \mathcal{L}_0$ of atomic propositions with modal operator D, called hypotheses, that explains why a given desire is desirable in terms of its effects, but does not explain why a given desire is undesirable in terms of its effects. The prior conditions for desire abstraction consists of prior insufficiency and prior consistency.

Prior insufficiency: $\forall Dx \in \mathcal{G}(\mathcal{F} \cup \mathcal{D} \nvdash_{PS} Dx)$
Prior consistency: $\forall Dx \in \mathcal{G}(\mathcal{F} \cup \mathcal{D} \nvdash_{PS} D\neg x)$

Prior insufficiency states that no given desire can be explained by present knowledge $\mathcal{F} \cup \mathcal{D}$ using PPS nor NPS'. Prior consistency states that no given desire can be negated by the present knowledge in terms of PPS nor NPS'.

The posterior conditions for desire abstraction consists of posterior sufficiency and posterior consistency.

Posterior sufficiency: $\forall Dx \in \mathcal{G}(\mathcal{F} \cup \mathcal{D} \cup \mathcal{H} \vdash_{PS} Dx)$
Posterior consistency: $\forall Dx \in \mathcal{G}(\mathcal{F} \cup \mathcal{D} \cup \mathcal{H} \nvdash_{PS} D\neg x)$

Posterior sufficiency states that once we assume $\mathcal{H}$, every given desire can be explained in terms of PPS or NPS'. In other words, $\mathcal{H}$ is an explanation of why a given desire is desirable. This is similar to a hypothesis of abduction that gives an explanation of why a fact is the case. Posterior consistency states that even if we assume $\mathcal{H}$, no given desire can be negated in terms of PPS nor NPS'. In other words, $\mathcal{H}$ gives no explanation of why a give desire is undesirable. Now, we can summarize the problem setting of desire abstraction as follows.

Given: A knowledge $T = (\mathcal{F}, \mathcal{D})$ and a desire $\mathcal{G} \subseteq \mathcal{L}_0$ satisfying prior insufficiency and prior consistency.
Find: Hypotheses $\mathcal{H} \subseteq \mathcal{L}_0$ satisfying posterior sufficiency and posterior consistency.

2.2   Practical Abductive Syllogisms

In this subsection, we introduce two defeasible inference rules for deriving abstract desires that satisfy posterior sufficiency and posterior consistency. An inference rule approach is motivated by our observation that introducing defeasible inference rules allows us to instantiate Dung's abstract argumentation frameworks that provides fundamental principles for conflict resolution. As shown in Section 4, we will extend desire abstraction from complete knowledge to incomplete knowledge defined by a default theory, where desire abstraction should go hand-in-hand with conflict resolutions. Dung's abstract argumentation frameworks give us a unified way to handle desire abstraction within conflict resolutions.

The two defeasible inference rules, called a positive practical abductive inference rule $PPAS$ and a negative practical abductive inference rule $NPAS$, are defined as follows.

Definition 1 (Practical abductive syllogisms). *Let $a, p \in \mathcal{L}_0$ be controllable formulae and $r \in \mathcal{L}_0$ be an uncontrollable formula. A positive practical abductive syllogism, denoted by $PPAS$, and a negative practical abductive syllogism, denoted by $NPAS$, have the following forms, respectively.*

- $PPAS : a \wedge r \Rightarrow p, Da, r \rightsquigarrow Dp$
- $NPAS : \neg a \wedge r \Rightarrow p, Da, r \rightsquigarrow D\neg p$

$PPAS$ intuitively states that p would be desirable if a is desirable in circumstance r and if a is realized in circumstance r then generally p is realized. On the other hand, $NPAS$ intuitively states that p would be undesirable, or precisely it is desirable that p is not realized, if a is desirable in circumstance r and if a is not realized in circumstance r then generally p is realized. For simplicity, we abbreviate $PPAS$ and $NPAS$ as PAS, practical abductive syllogism, when we do not need to distinguish them. We say that p is an *abstraction* of a when an application of PAS derives Dp using Da.

Proposition 1. *Let $T = (\mathcal{F}, \mathcal{D})$ be a knowledge and $\mathcal{G}$ be a desire that satisfy prior insufficiency. A set $\mathcal{H} \subseteq \mathcal{L}_0$ satisfies posterior sufficiency iff, for all $Dg \in \mathcal{G}$, there is $Dh \in \mathcal{H}$ such that $\mathcal{F} \cup \mathcal{D} \cup \{Dg\} \vdash_{PAS} Dh$.*

Proof. $\mathcal{H}$ satisfies posterior sufficiency iff, for all $Dg \in \mathcal{G}$, there is $Dh \in \mathcal{H}$ such that $\mathcal{F} \cup \mathcal{D} \cup \{Dh\} \vdash_{PS} Dg$. This is true iff, for all $Dg \in \mathcal{G}$, there is $Dh \in \mathcal{H}$ such that $\mathcal{F} \cup \mathcal{D} \cup \{Dg\} \vdash_{PAS} Dh$. $\square$

Proposition 1 allows us to translate the problem of finding candidates satisfying posterior sufficiency into the problem of abstracting g using PAS, for all $Dg \in \mathcal{G}$.

Proposition 2. *Let $T = (\mathcal{F}, \mathcal{D})$ be a knowledge and $\mathcal{G}$ be a desire that satisfy prior insufficiency. A set $\mathcal{H} \subseteq \mathcal{L}_0$ satisfies posterior consistency iff, for all $Dg \in \mathcal{G}$ and $Dh \in \mathcal{H}$, $\mathcal{F} \cup \mathcal{D} \cup \{Dg\} \nvdash_{PAS} D\neg h$.*

Proof. $\mathcal{H}$ satisfies posterior consistency iff, for all $Dg \in \mathcal{G}$ and $Dh \in \mathcal{H}$, $\mathcal{F} \cup \mathcal{D} \cup \{Dh\} \nvdash_{PS} D\neg g$. This is true iff, for all $Dg \in \mathcal{G}$ and $Dh \in \mathcal{H}$, $\mathcal{F} \cup \mathcal{D} \cup \{D\neg h\} \nvdash_{PS} Dg$. This is true iff, for all $Dg \in \mathcal{G}$ and $Dh \in \mathcal{H}$, $\mathcal{F} \cup \mathcal{D} \cup \{Dg\} \nvdash_{PAS} D\neg h$. $\square$

Proposition 2 allows us to translate the problem of finding candidates not satisfying posterior consistency into the problem of abstracting g using PAS, for all $Dg \in \mathcal{G}$.

3   Justifying Underlying Desire

3.1   Successful Desire Abstraction by an Argument Interaction

The previous section introduced two defeasible inference rules, $PPAS$ and $NPAS$. This section aims to give the mechanism to justify the hypotheses by argument-based reasoning. The following examples show how arguments structured with PAS interact each other to justify hypotheses satisfying posterior sufficiency and posterior consistency.

Example 1 (Posterior sufficiency of $\{D\beta_1\}$). An officer A of a product manufacturer desires to employ a certain staff ($D\alpha_1$). A believes that all members of the staff are capable (γ_1) and also that if the employment is realized in the situation where the members are capable, then A's company promotes techno-logical advancement ($\alpha_1 \land \gamma_1 \Rightarrow \beta_1$). $PPAS$ defeasibly concludes that A desires to promote technological advancement ($D\beta_1$).

Example 2 (Posterior sufficiency of $\{D\beta_2\}$). An officer A of a product manufac-turer desires to employ a certain staff ($D\alpha_1$). A believes that all members of the staff are capable (γ_1), and also that if the employment is realized in the situation where the members are capable, then A's company increases total expenditure ($\alpha_1 \land \gamma_1 \Rightarrow \beta_2$). $PPAS$ defeasibly concludes that A desires to increase total expenditure ($D\beta_2$).

The argument in Example 1 shows posterior sufficiency of $\{D\beta_1\}$ and the ar-gument in Example 2 shows posterior sufficiency of $\{D\beta_2\}$. Obviously, we can notice that β_1 is a desirable main effect and β_2 is an undesirable side effect caused by employing the staff. Namely, $PPAS$ is defeasible in the sense that it derives false conclusions even when the premises are true. $NPAS$, however, has a role of preventing such unintentional side effects to be justified, in the following way.

Example 3 (Posterior inconsistency of $\{D\beta_2\}$). A desires to reduce the cost ($D\alpha_2$). A believes that a resource price is as-is (γ_2) and also that if A fails to reduce a cost in the situation that a resource price is as-is, then A's company increases total expenditure ($\neg\alpha_2 \land \gamma_2 \Rightarrow \beta_2$). $NPAS$ defeasibly concludes that A desires not to increase total expenditure ($D\neg\beta_2$).

The argument in Example 3 shows posterior inconsistency of $\{D\beta_2\}$. Although no argument attacks the argument in Example 1, the argument in Example 3 attacks the argument in Example 2. In other words, arguments concluding posterior inconsistency prevents arguments concluding posterior sufficiency from justified.

3.2   Argumentation System for Desire Abstraction

These intuitive analysis in the previous subsection is formally handled in argu-mentation systems defined in this subsection. Arguments are constructed from knowledge $T = (\mathcal{F}, \mathcal{D})$ and desire $\mathcal{G}$. Each argument is assumed to have a tree structures where each leaf is in $\mathcal{F} \cup \mathcal{D} \cup \mathcal{G}$ and a set of edges connecting some node and its all children is an inference rule deriving the node from its all chil-dren. A conclusion, denoted by $conc(A)$ of an argument A is the root of A. An argument A is defeasible if it has a defeasible inference rule and strict if it has only strict inference rules. An argument A is a sub-argument of an argument B iff it is a subtree of B. A notion of attacks is defined as a binary relation on a set of arguments.

Definition 2 (Attacks). *Let A and B be arguments. A attacks B iff there is a sub-argument B' of B such that B' is defeasible and $\{conc(A), conc(B')\} \vdash \bot$.*

A *practical abductive argument* is defined as follows.

Definition 3 (Practical abductive arguments). *Let A be an argument and $Dg \in \mathcal{L}_0$. A is a practical abductive argument for Dg iff*

- *Every node, except the root and leaves, is derived from its all children by a valid inference on first order logic.*
- *A's root is derived from its all children using PAS.*
- *A child of the root is Dg.*

A practical abductive argument is defeasible since PAS is defeasible.

Definition 4 (Practical abductive argumentation systems). *A practical abductive argumentation system is a tuple $< AR, Attacks >$ where AR be a set of practical abductive arguments and Attacks be a binary relation on AR such that $(A, B) \in Attacks$ iff A attacks B.*

We show correctness of the argumentation systems in terms of sufficiency and consistency.

Theorem 1. *Let AS be a practical abductive argumentation system. A set of conclusions of justified arguments in AS satisfies posterior sufficiency and posterior consistency iff, for all $Dg \in \mathcal{G}$, there is an argument a in AS such that a is a practical abductive argument for Dg and a is justified in AS.*

Proof. Both prior insufficiency and prior consistency are the cases because $\mathcal{F}$ does not include modal operator D. Obviously, posterior sufficiency is the case iff there are practical abductive arguments for all $Dg \in \mathcal{G}$ and posterior consistency is the case iff all of the arguments are justified, i.e., no argument can show inconsistency. □

Theorem 1 gives us the way to find hypotheses satisfying posterior sufficiency and posterior consistency by instantiations of Dung's abstract argumentation frameworks evaluated by Dung's semantics.

4   Justifying Means for Abstracted Desires

This section gives argumentation systems combining desire abstraction and means-ends reasoning. Moreover, we extend the assumed language from first-order theory to default theory, which allows us to desire abstraction and means-ends reasoning in incomplete information.

Definition 5 (Practical arguments). *Let A be an argument and $Dg \in \mathcal{L}_0$. A is a practical argument for Dg iff it is Dg or it satisfies all the following conditions.*

- *A's root is derived from its all children using PS.*
- *The subtree with root $D\varphi$ is a practical argument for Dg where $D\varphi$ is a child of A's root.*

– *The subtrees with roots $\psi \wedge r \Rightarrow \varphi$ and r are both valid arguments with respect to default logic where they are both children of A's root.*

Definition 6 (Reconciliatory arguments). *Let A be an argument and $Dg \in \mathcal{L}_0$. A is a reconciliatory argument for Dg iff it is a practical abductive argument for Dg or it satisfies all the following conditions.*

– *A's root is derived from its all children using PS.*
– *The subtree with root $D\varphi$ is a reconciliatory argument for Dg where $D\varphi$ is a child of A's root.*
– *The subtrees with roots $\psi \wedge r \Rightarrow \varphi$ and r are both valid arguments with respect to default logic where they are both children of A's root.*

Example 4 (A reconciliatory argument). Figure 1 is a reconciliatory argument for Da represented as a style of proof-tree. The argument is structured using positive practical syllogism on top and positive practical abductive syllogism on bottom. Db can be seen as a possible candidate for an abstracted desire of Da and Dc can be seen as a possible solution for the abstracted desire.

$$A: \quad \cfrac{c \wedge s \Rightarrow b \qquad \cfrac{a \wedge r \Rightarrow b \quad Da \quad r}{Db} \quad s}{Dc}$$

Fig. 1. A reconciliatory argument represented by a proof-tree

Definition 7 (Practical argumentation systems). *A practical argumentation system is a tuple $< AR, Attacks >$ where AR be a set of arguments except reconciliatory arguments and $Attacks \subseteq AR^2$ be a binary relation on AR such that $(A, B) \in Attacks$ iff A attacks B.*

Definition 8 (Reconciliatory argumentation systems). *A reconciliatory argumentation system is a tuple $< AR, Attacks >$ where AR be a set of arguments except practical arguments and $Attacks \subseteq AR^2$ be a binary relation on AR such that $(A, B) \in Attacks$ iff A attacks B.*

5   Two Persuasive Applications

We show usefulness of our argumentation systems by showing their ability to handle two realistic reconciliatory scenarios. Note that this section aims to show the ability of our argumentation systems to reconcile conflict independently from argumentation or dialogue protocols nor arguing agent's strategies. This section assumes that agents aim to reach an agreement even if they concede their original desires. Moreover, they are assumed to prefer to solutions obtained by abstracting desires rather than just choose compatible parts of their original ones.

We assume a default theory $T = (\mathcal{F}_1 \cup \mathcal{F}_2, \mathcal{D}_1 \cup \mathcal{D}_2)$ and desires $\mathcal{G}_1, \mathcal{G}_2$ where $(\mathcal{F}_i, \mathcal{D}_i)$ represents i's default theory, i.e., knowledge, and $\mathcal{G}_i$ represents i's desire, for $i = 1, 2$.

5.1   A Solution for Committee Member Selection

Kowalski and Toni give a thoughtful scenario indicating the importance of desire abstraction in reconciliation. Although a solution using argument-based reasoning is expected, a simple but sufficient formal solution has not yet been found. This section gives a solution for the problem by showing how our argument-based reasoning handles the problem. The following is the scenario described in [12]:

> In a recent head-of-sections committee meeting in our Department, we discussed the composition of a new resources committee. Two conflicting arguments were put forward. The Director of Administration argued that, in the interests of efficiency, the members of the new committee should consist of himself and the other principal administrative officers of the Department. The Director of Research argued, in opposition to him, that, in the interests of democracy, the committee should also contain members elected by the Department. During the course of the discussion it became clear that the two sides were focussing on different assumptions about the purpose of the new committee: the Director of Administration on its purely administrative function, and the Director of Research on its presumed policy making nature. These two assumptions could be viewed as conflicting solutions to the more general goals of deciding, on the one hand, which group should make policy about resources. By focussing on the more general goals, it was possible to identify a new solution which was acceptable to both parties: the resources committee will administer resources, whereas the head-of-sections committee will make policy about resources. In the interests of efficiency, the members of the resources committee will consist of administrative officers only. In the interests of democracy, the head-of-sections committee will represent the views and interests of the various Department sections on matters concerning policy about the allocation of resources.

We assume the following default theory and desires where "$R\text{-}cmte$" denotes the resource committee, "$H\text{-}cmte$" denotes the head-of-sections committee, "R" denotes resources and "P" denotes policies.

$$\mathcal{F} = \{administers(R\text{-}cmte, R), makes(R\text{-}cmte, P), democratic(H\text{-}cmte)\}$$
$$\mathcal{D} = \{election(X) \Rightarrow \neg efficient(X)(= r_1), election(X) \Rightarrow democratic(X)(= r_2),$$
$$administers(X, Y) \wedge efficient(X) \Rightarrow lean(Y)(= r_3),$$
$$makes(X, Y) \wedge democratic(X) \Rightarrow fair(Y)(= r_4)\}$$
$$\mathcal{G}_1 = \{D(efficient(R\text{-}cmte))\}$$
$$\mathcal{G}_2 = \{D(democratic(R\text{-}cmte))\}$$

Figure 2 represents practical arguments constructed from the above default theory and desires where defaults are substantiated with appropriate constants.

$$A_1: \quad \frac{D(\mathit{efficient}(R\text{-}cmte)) \qquad \mathit{election}(R\text{-}cmte) \Rightarrow \neg\mathit{efficient}(R\text{-}cmte)}{D(\neg\mathit{election}(R\text{-}cmte))}$$

$$A_2: \quad \frac{D(\mathit{democratic}(R\text{-}cmte)) \qquad \mathit{election}(R\text{-}cmte) \Rightarrow \mathit{democratic}(R\text{-}cmte)}{D(\mathit{election}(R\text{-}cmte))}$$

Fig. 2. Practical arguments

We can see that no argument is justified in the following practical argumentation system.

$$< \{A_1, A_2\}, \{(A_1, A_2), (A_2, A_1)\} >$$

Figure 3 represents practical abductive arguments constructed from the same default theory and desires, where r_1^*, r_3^*, r_4^* and r_4^+ are defined as follows.

$$r_1^* = \mathit{election}(R\text{-}cmte) \Rightarrow \neg\mathit{efficient}(R\text{-}cmte)$$
$$r_3^* = \mathit{administers}(R\text{-}cmte, R) \wedge \mathit{efficient}(R\text{-}cmte) \Rightarrow \mathit{lean}(R)$$
$$r_4^* = \mathit{makes}(R\text{-}cmte, P) \wedge \mathit{democratic}(R\text{-}cmte) \Rightarrow \mathit{fair}(P)$$
$$r_4^+ = \mathit{makes}(H\text{-}cmte, P) \wedge \mathit{democratic}(H\text{-}cmte) \Rightarrow \mathit{fair}(P)$$

We can see that A_3 and A_4 can both be justified in the following reconciliatory argumentation system.

$$< \{A_3, A_4\}, \emptyset >$$

$$A_3: \quad \frac{\dfrac{D(\mathit{efficient}(R\text{-}cmte)) \quad \mathit{administers}(R\text{-}cmte, R) \quad r_3^*}{D(\mathit{lean}(R))} \qquad \mathit{administers}(R\text{-}cmte, R) \quad r_3^*}{\dfrac{D(\mathit{efficient}(R\text{-}cmte))}{D(\neg\mathit{election}(R\text{-}cmte))} \qquad\qquad r_1^*}$$

$$A_4: \quad \frac{\dfrac{D(\mathit{democratic}(R\text{-}cmte)) \quad \mathit{makes}(R\text{-}cmte, P) \quad r_4^*}{D(\mathit{fair}(P))} \qquad \mathit{democratic}(H\text{-}cmte) \quad r_4^+}{D(\mathit{makes}(H\text{-}cmte, P))}$$

Fig. 3. Reconciliatory arguments

5.2   A Solution for Business Transfer

Consider the following scenario of a solution for a problem of business transfer. An officer A of product manufacturer deliberates with an officer B of parts manufacturer about the acquisition of some department X of the parts manufacturer. They argue about solutions realizing their original desires. A wants B to transfer all members of X as a means to realize her desire to employ the staff. By contrast, B does not want to transfer all members because it prevents his desire to reallocate the staff. There is no another means to realize both A's and B's desires. So, B starts to look for reconciliatory solutions. After some consideration, B conceives that A actually wants to promote technological advancement by the transition. B seeks the possible means to promote technological advancement and finds a solution that B devolves an intellectual property right to A. A does not complain about his solution and the deliberation successfully arrives at the contract signing stage.

We assume the following default theory and desires where uncontrollable formulae of practical syllogisms and practical abductive syllogisms are abbreviated for simplicity: $T = (\emptyset, \{e \Rightarrow b, g \Rightarrow a, g \Rightarrow \neg d, \neg b \Rightarrow h, a \Rightarrow h, a \Rightarrow j, k \Rightarrow j\})$, $G_1 = \{Da, Db\}$ and $G_2 = \{Dd\}$. Each formula has the following meaning: "A employs the staff from B. $(= a)$," "A reduces the cost. $(= b)$," "B reallocates the staff. $(= d)$," "B accepts the warranty against defects. $(= e)$," "B transfers all members of the department to A. $(= g)$," "A's company increases the total expenditure. $(= h)$," "A's company promotes the technological advancement. $(= j)$," and "B devolves an intellectual property right to A. $(= k)$."

$$A_1 : \frac{Da \quad g \Rightarrow a}{Dg} \qquad A_2 : \frac{Db \quad e \Rightarrow b}{De} \qquad A_3 : \frac{Dd \quad g \Rightarrow \neg d}{D\neg g}$$

Fig. 4. Practical arguments

Only A_2 is justified in the following practical argumentation system.

$$< \{A_1, A_2, A_3\}, \{(A_1, A_3), (A_3, A_1)\} >$$

Figure 4 represents all practical arguments, i.e., A_1, A_2 and A_3, constructed from T, G_1 and G_2. On the other hand, only A_6 and A_8 are justified in the following reconciliatory argumentation system.

$$< \{A_i \mid 4 \leq i \leq 9\}, \{(A_8, A_4), (A_7, A_5), (A_7, A_9), (A_9, A_7)\} >$$

where A_9 is a sub-argument of A_5 whose conclusion is Dh. Figure 5 represents practical arguments, i.e., A_1, A_2 and A_3, constructed from T, G_1 and G_2.

6   Related Work and Discussions

In [11], the authors addressed the question: what is the best way to achieve given desires? They proposed a logical formalization of an argument-based justification for actions. In contrast, we addressed the question: what is an abstract desire of given desires and what is a way to achieve the abstract desire? We proposed a logical formalization of an argument-based justification for desire abstraction. We think that practical abductive syllogisms are counterparts of practical syllogisms

$$A_4: \dfrac{\dfrac{\dfrac{\dfrac{Da \quad a \Rightarrow h}{Dh} \quad a \Rightarrow h}{Da} \quad g \Rightarrow a}{Dg} \quad d \Rightarrow \neg g}{D\neg d} \qquad A_5: \dfrac{\dfrac{\dfrac{Da \quad a \Rightarrow h}{Dh} \quad \neg b \Rightarrow h}{D\neg b} \quad e \Rightarrow b}{D\neg e}$$

$$A_6: \dfrac{\dfrac{Da \quad a \Rightarrow j}{Dj} \quad k \Rightarrow j}{Dk} \qquad A_7: \dfrac{Db \quad \neg b \Rightarrow h}{D\neg h} \qquad A_8: \ Dd$$

Fig. 5. Reconciliatory arguments and arguments attacking them

in practical reasoning as the relationships between abduction and deduction in epistemic reasoning, and that they are essential in reconciliation by showing two persuasive examples.

In [15], the authors organized various sorts of cogent reasoning in our daily life as argumentation schemes where each scheme consists of premises, conclusions, and critical questions written in natural language. Practical syllogisms are kinds of practical inference according to Walton's classification. On the other hand, on classification is given for practical abductive syllogisms in Walton's theory although they are essential to find reconciliatory solutions.

From a standpoint of negotiation, Fisher and Ury urge that determining the stakeholders' interests helps to achieve reconciliatory solutions in negotiation [17]. Negotiation theory shows that positions are what negotiators say they want and interests are the needs of concerns that underlie positions [18]. Although argument-based negotiation is outside of scope of this paper, we think that our proposal is useful for identifying latent interests by effectively using original positions. In fact, although many of argument-based negotiation handle reasoning to identify desires or goals that depend on context [2,3,4,5,8,9,10,19], no one attempt to seek latent desires behind original positions. In our opinion, not only agent's knowledge, but agent's desire can be incomplete.

The technical contribution of this paper is to propose practical abductive syllogisms, $PPAA$ and $NPAS$ as a counterpart of abduction and deduction in epistemic reasoning, and argumentation systems structured with these inference rules. Moreover, another contribution is to show usefulness of the argumentation systems by showing two persuasive examples. The argumentation systems justify means for abstracted desires of given desires as an interaction of arguments, i.e., argument-based reasoning.

7 Conclusions and Future Work

This paper proposed a logical formalization of an argument-based justification for abstract desires of given desires. We gave a problem setting for desire abstraction in terms of sufficiency and consistency and introduced two defeasible inference rules, called positive and negative practical abductive syllogisms. Practical abductive arguments hypothetically derive possible desirable effects caused by realizing the given desires and possible undesirable effects caused by not realizing the given desires. We showed that these two rules and practical abductive argumentation systems structured with the rules are correct with respect to sufficiency and consistency. We gave practical argumentation systems and reconciliatory argumentation systems and showed that the argumentation systems can simply handle reconciliatory scenarios of committee member selection posed by Kowalski and Toni, and of business transfer posed in this paper.

It is arguable that propotional modal language is the best choice for this formalization. For example, BDI logic might be more appropriate language to distinguish various notions introduced in this paper and formalize our ideas in more detail. We will apply the practical abductive syllogisms not only to practical reasoning or deliberation, but also negotiation because they are useful for promoting goals of negotiation, i.e., finding reasonable settlement through, e.g., compromise. Moreover, we will address the problems of agent's strategies showing how to an agent strategically abstracts another agent's desires, and argument protocols showing when to an agent puts forward reconciliatory solutions.

References

1. Wooldridge, M.J.: Reasoning about rational agents. MIT Press (2000)
2. Amgoud, L., Dimopoulos, Y., Moraitis, P.: A General Framework for Argumentation-Based Negotiation. In: Proc. of the Fourth International Workshop on Argumentation in Multi-Agent Systems, pp. 1–17 (2008)
3. Amgoud, L., Prade, H.: Formal Handling of Threats and Rewards in a Negotiation Dialogue. In: Parsons, S., Maudet, N., Moraitis, P., Rahwan, I. (eds.) ArgMAS 2005. LNCS (LNAI), vol. 4049, pp. 88–103. Springer, Heidelberg (2006)
4. Wells, S., Reed, C.: Knowing When To Bargain. In: Proc. of the Second International Conference on Computational Models of Argument, pp. 235–246 (2008)
5. van Veenen, J., Prakken, H.: A Protocol for Arguing About Rejections in Negotiation. In: Parsons, S., Maudet, N., Moraitis, P., Rahwan, I. (eds.) ArgMAS 2005. LNCS (LNAI), vol. 4049, pp. 138–153. Springer, Heidelberg (2006)
6. Dung, P.M.: On the acceptability of arguments and its fundamental role in non-monotonic reasoning, logic programming, and n-person games. Artificial Intelligence 90, 225–279 (1997)
7. Prakken, H.: Coherence and Flexibility in Dialogue Games for Argumentation, Institute of information and computing sciences, utrecht university technical report UU-CS-2005-021 (2005)
8. Modgil, S., Luck, M.: Argumentation Based Resolution of Conflicts between Desires and Normative Goals. In: Rahwan, I., Moraitis, P. (eds.) ArgMAS 2008. LNCS (LNAI), vol. 5384, pp. 19–36. Springer, Heidelberg (2009)
9. Amgoud, L., Devred, C., Lagasquie-Schiex, M.-C.: A Constrained Argumentation System for Practical Reasoning. In: Rahwan, I., Moraitis, P. (eds.) ArgMAS 2008. LNCS (LNAI), vol. 5384, pp. 37–56. Springer, Heidelberg (2009)
10. Hulstijn, J., van der Torre, L.: Combining Goal Generation and Planning in an Argumentation Framework. In: Proc. of the 10th International Workshop on Non-Monotonic Reasoning, pp. 212–218 (2004)
11. Bench-Capon, T.J.M., Prakken, H.: Justifying Actions by Accruing Arguments. In: Proc. of the First International Conference on Computational Models of Argument, pp. 247–258 (2006)

12. Kowalski, R.A., Toni, F.: Argument and Reconciliation. In: Proc. of the Fifth Generation Computer Systems Workshop on Application of Logic Programming to Legal Reasoning, pp. 9–16 (1994)
13. Prakken, H.: A Study of Accrual of Arguments, with Applications to Evidential Reasoning. In: Proc. of the 10th International Conference of Artificial Intelligence and Law, pp. 85–94 (2005)
14. Prakken, H., Vreeswijk, G.: Logics for Defeasible Argumentation, Handbook of Philosophical Logic, 2nd edn. Kluwer Academic Publishers (2001)
15. Walton, D.N., Reed, C., Macagno, F.: Argumentation Schemes. Cambridge University Press (2008)
16. Oliva, E., Viroli, M., Omicini, A., McBurney, P.: Argumentation and Artifact for Dialogue Support. In: Rahwan, I., Moraitis, P. (eds.) ArgMAS 2008. LNCS (LNAI), vol. 5384, pp. 107–121. Springer, Heidelberg (2009)
17. Fisher, R., Ury, W., Patton, B.: Getting to yes: negotiating agreement without giving in, Houghton Mifflin Harcourt (1991)
18. Brett, J.M.: Negotiating globally: how to negotiate deals, resolve disputes, and make decisions across cultural boundaries. The Jossey-Bass business and management series. Safari Books Online. John Wiley and Sons (2007)
19. Rahwan, I., Sonenberg, L., Dignum, F.: Towards Interest-Based Negotiation. In: Proc. of the Second International Conference on Autonomous Agents and Multiagent Systems, pp. 773–780 (2003)
20. Walton, D., Reed, C., Macagno, F.: Argumentation Schemes, 1st edn. Cambridge University Press (2008)

The Complexity of Repairing, Adjusting, and Aggregating of Extensions in Abstract Argumentation

Eun Jung Kim[1], Sebastian Ordyniak[2,*], and Stefan Szeider[3,**]

[1] LAMSADE, CNRS, Paris, France
[2] Faculty of Informatics, Masaryk University, Brno, Czech Republic
[3] Institute of Information Systems, Vienna University of Technology, Vienna, Austria

Abstract. We study the computational complexity of problems that arise in abstract argumentation in the context of dynamic argumentation, minimal change, and aggregation. In particular, we consider the following problems where always an argumentation framework F and a small positive integer k are given.

- The REPAIR problem asks whether a given set of arguments can be modified into an extension by at most k elementary changes (i.e., the extension is of distance k from the given set).
- The ADJUST problem asks whether a given extension can be modified by at most k elementary changes into an extension that contains a specified argument.
- The CENTER problem asks whether, given two extensions of distance k, whether there is a "center" extension that is of distance at most $k - 1$ from both given extensions.

We study these problems in the framework of parameterized complexity, and take the distance k as the parameter. Our results cover several different semantics, including admissible, complete, preferred, semi-stable and stable semantics.

1 Introduction

Starting with the seminal work by Dung [11] the area of argumentation has evolved to one of the most active research branches within Artificial Intelligence [4,28]. Dung's abstract argumentation frameworks, where arguments are seen as abstract entities which are just investigated with respect to how they relate to each other, in terms of "attacks," are nowadays well understood and different semantics (i.e., the selection of sets of arguments which are jointly acceptable) have been proposed. Such sets of arguments are called extensions of the underlying argumentation framework.

Argumentation is an inherently dynamic process, and there has been increasingly interest in the dynamic behavior of abstract argumentation. A first study in this direction was carried out by Cayrol et al. [6] and was concerned with the impact of additional arguments on extensions. Baumann and Brewka [3] investigated whether it is possible to modify a given argumentation framework in such a way that a desired set of arguments

* Research supported by Employment of Newly Graduated Doctors of Science for Scientific Excellence (CZ.1.07/2.3.00/30.0009).
** Research supported by the European Research Council, grant reference 239962 (COMPLEX REASON).

E. Black, S. Modgil, and N. Oren (Eds.): TAFA 2013, LNAI 8306, pp. 158–175, 2014.
© Springer-Verlag Berlin Heidelberg 2014

becomes an extension or a subset of an extension. Baumann [2] further extended this line of research by considering the minimal exchange necessary to enforce a desired set of arguments. In this context, it is interesting to consider notions of *distance* between extensions. Booth et al. [5] suggested a general framework for defining and studying distance measures.

A natural question that arises in the context of abstract argumentation is how computationally difficult it is to decide whether an argumentation framework admits an extension at all, or whether a given argument belongs to at least one extension or to all extensions of the framework. Indeed the complexity of these problems have been investigated in a series of papers, and the exact worst-case complexities have been determined for all popular semantics [7,8,11,13,14,15,19]. Abstract argumentation has also been studied in the framework of *parameterized complexity* [9] which admits a more fine-grained complexity analysis that can take structural aspects of the argumentation framework into account [12,16,24,20,17].

Surprisingly, very little is known on the computational complexity of problems in abstract argumentation that arise in the context of dynamic behavior of argumentation, such as finding an extension by minimal change. However, as the distance in these problems is assumed to be small, it seems very natural to consider the distance as the parameter for a parameterized analysis.

New Contribution. In this paper we provide a detailed complexity map of various problems that arise in in the context of dynamic behavior of argumentation. In particular, we consider the following problems where always an argumentation framework F and a small positive integer k (the parameter) are given, and σ denotes a semantics.

- The σ-REPAIR problem asks whether a given set of arguments can be modified into a σ-extension by at most k elementary changes (i.e., the extension is of distance k from the given set).

  This problem is of relevance, for instance, when a σ-extension E of an argumentation framework is given, and dynamically the argumentation framework changes (i.e., attacks are added or removed, new arguments are added). Now the set E may not any more be a σ-extension of the new framework, and we want to repair it with minimal change to obtain a σ-extension.

- The σ-ADJUST problem asks whether a given σ-extension can be modified by at most k elementary changes into a σ-extension that contains a specified argument.

  This problem is a variant of the previous problem, however, the argumentation framework does not change, but dynamically the necessity occurs to include a certain argument into the extension. This should be accomplished by a small change of the given extension.

- The σ-CENTER problem asks whether, given two σ-extensions of distance k, whether there is a "center" σ-extension that is a distance at most $k - 1$ from both given extensions.

  This problem arises in scenarios of judgment aggregations, when, for instance, two extensions that reflect the opinion of two different agents are presented, and one tries to find a compromise extension that minimizes the distance to both extensions.

We study these problems in the framework of parameterized complexity, and take the distance k as the parameter. Our results cover several different semantics, including

σ	general	bounded degree
adm	W[1]-hard	FPT
com	W[1]-hard	FPT
prf	para-coNP-hard	para-coNP-hard
sem	para-coNP-hard	para-coNP-hard
stb	W[1]-hard	FPT

Fig. 1. Parameterized Complexity of the problems σ-REPAIR, σ-ADJUST, and σ-CENTER for general argumentation frameworks and argumentation frameworks of bounded degree, depending on the considered semantics.

admissible, complete, preferred, semi-stable and stable semantics. The parameterized complexity of the above problems are summarized in Figure 1.

2 Preliminaries

An *abstract argumentation system* or *argumentation framework* (*AF*, for short) is a pair (X, A) where X is a (possible infinite) set of elements called *arguments* and $A \subseteq X \times X$ is a binary relation called *attack relation*. In this paper we will restrict ourselves to finite AFs, i.e., to AFs for which X is a finite set. If $(x, y) \in A$ we say that x *attacks* y and that x is an *attacker* of y.

An AF $F = (X, A)$ can be considered as a directed graph, and therefore it is convenient to borrow notions and notation from graph theory. For a set of arguments $Y \subseteq X$ we denote by $F[Y]$ the AF $(Y, \{ (x, y) \in A \mid x, y \in Y \})$ and by $F - Y$ the AF $F[X \setminus Y]$.

We define the *degree* of an argument $x \in X$ to be the number of arguments $y \in X \setminus \{x\}$ such that $(x, y) \in A$ or $(y, x) \in A$. The maximum degree of an AF $F = (X, A)$ is the maximum degree over all its arguments. We say that a class $\mathcal{C}$ of AFs has bounded maximum degree, or bounded degree for short, if there exists a constant c such that for every $F \in \mathcal{C}$ the maximum degree of F is at most c.

For sets E and E' of arguments we write $E \triangle E'$ to denote their symmetric difference, i.e., $E \triangle E' := (E \setminus E') \cup (E' \setminus E)$, and we define

$$\mathrm{dist}(E, E') := |E \triangle E'|.$$

Let $F = (X, A)$ be an AF, $S \subseteq X$ and $x \in X$. We say that x is *defended* (in F) by S if for each $x' \in X$ such that $(x', x) \in A$ there is an $x'' \in S$ such that $(x'', x') \in A$. We denote by S_F^+ the set of arguments $x \in X$ such that either $x \in S$ or there is an $x' \in S$ with $(x', x) \in A$, and we omit the subscript if F is clear from the context. Note that in our setting the set S is contained in S_F^+. We say S is *conflict-free* if there are no arguments $x, x' \in S$ with $(x, x') \in A$.

Next we define commonly used semantics of AFs, see the survey of Baroni and Giacomin [1]. We consider a semantics σ as a mapping that assigns to each AF $F = (X, A)$ a family $\sigma(F) \subseteq 2^X$ of sets of arguments, called *extensions*. We denote by adm, com, prf, sem and stb the *admissible, complete, preferred, semi-stable* and *stable* semantics, respectively. These five semantics are characterized by the following conditions which hold for each AF $F = (X, A)$ and each conflict-free set $S \subseteq X$.

- $S \in \mathrm{adm}(F)$ if each $s \in S$ is defended by S.
- $S \in \mathrm{com}(F)$ if $S \in \mathrm{adm}(F)$ and every argument that is defended by S is contained in S.
- $S \in \mathrm{prf}(F)$ if $S \in \mathrm{adm}(F)$ and there is no $T \in \mathrm{adm}(F)$ with $S \subsetneq T$.
- $S \in \mathrm{sem}(F)$ if $S \in \mathrm{adm}(F)$ and there is no $T \in \mathrm{adm}(F)$ with $S^+ \subsetneq T^+$.
- $S \in \mathrm{stb}(F)$ if $S^+ = X$.

Parameterized Complexity. For our investigation we need to take two measurements into account: the input size n of the given AF F and the parameter k given as the input to σ-REPAIR, σ-ADJUST, and σ-CENTER. The theory of *parameterized complexity*, introduced and pioneered by Downey and Fellows [9], provides the adequate concepts and tools for such an investigation. We outline the basic notions of parameterized complexity that are relevant for this paper, for an in-depth treatment we refer to other sources [21,26].

An instance of a parameterized (decision) problem is a pair (I, k) where I is the *main part* and k is the *parameter*; the latter is usually a non-negative integer. A parameterized problem is *fixed-parameter tractable* (FPT) if there exists a computable function f such that instances (I, k) of size n can be solved in time $f(k) \cdot n^{O(1)}$, or equivalently, in *fpt-time*. Fixed-parameter tractable problems are also called *uniform polynomial-time tractable* because if k is considered constant, then instances with parameter k can be solved in polynomial time where the order of the polynomial is independent of k, in contrast to *non-uniform polynomial-time* running times such as $n^{O(k)}$. Thus we have three complexity categories for parameterized problems: (1) problems that are fixed-parameter tractable (uniform polynomial-time tractable), (2) problems that are non-uniform polynomial-time tractable, and (3) problems that are NP-hard or coNP-hard even when the parameter is fixed to some constant (such as k-SAT which is NP-hard for $k = 3$). The fundamental complexity assumption in parameterized complexity is FPT $\subsetneq$ W[1]. Hence, W[1]-hard problems are not fixed-parameter tractable under this assumption. Such problems can still be non-uniform polynomial-time tractable. Problems that fall into category (3) are said to be para-NP-hard or para-coNP-hard. The classes in parameterized complexity are defined as the closure of certain canonical parameterized problems under *fpt-reductions*, which are many-one reductions that can be computed in fpt-time, and where the parameter of the target instance is bounded by a function of the parameter of the source instance.

We will establish our W[1]-hardness results by fpt-reductions form the following W[1]-complete problem [27].

MULTICOLORED CLIQUE
Instance: A positive integer k, and a k-partite graph $G = (V, E)$ with partition $\{V_1, \ldots, V_k\}$.
Parameter: k.
Question: Does G contain a clique of size k?

W.l.o.g. we may assume that the parameter k of MULTICOLORED CLIQUE is even. To see this, we reduce from MULTICOLORED CLIQUE to itself as follows. Given an instance (G, k) we construct an equivalent instance $(G', 2k)$ where G' is obtained from the vertex-disjoint union of two copies of G by adding all edges between the two copies.

3 Problems for Dynamic Argumentation

In this section we present the problems that we consider for dynamic argumentation. Let $\sigma \in \{\mathrm{adm}, \mathrm{com}, \mathrm{prf}, \mathrm{sem}, \mathrm{stb}\}$. Recall that for sets E and E' of arguments, $E \triangle E'$ denotes their symmetric difference and $\mathrm{dist}(E, E')$ denotes the size of $E \triangle E'$.

σ-SMALL
Instance: An AF $F = (X, A)$, a nonnegative integer k.
Parameter: k.
Question: Is there a nonempty extension $E \in \sigma(F)$ of size at most k?

σ-REPAIR
Instance: An AF $F = (X, A)$, a set of arguments $S \subseteq X$, a nonnegative integer k.
Parameter: k.
Question: Is there a nonempty extension $E \in \sigma(F)$ s.t. $\mathrm{dist}(E, S) \leq k$?

σ-ADJUST
Instance: An AF $F = (X, A)$, an extension $E_0 \in \sigma(F)$, an argument $t \in X$, a nonnegative integer k.
Parameter: k.
Question: Is there an extension $E \in \sigma(F)$ s.t. $\mathrm{dist}(E, E_0) \leq k$ and $t \in E_0 \triangle E$?

σ-CENTER
Instance: An AF $F = (X, A)$, two extensions $E_1, E_2 \in \sigma(F)$.
Parameter: $\mathrm{dist}(E_1, E_2)$.
Question: Is there an extension $E \in \sigma(F)$ s.t. $\mathrm{dist}(E, E_i) < \mathrm{dist}(E_1, E_2)$ for every $i \in \{1, 2\}$?

4 Hardness Results

This section is devoted to our hardness results. We start by showing that all the problems that we consider are W[1]-hard on general unrestricted AFs and hence unlikely to be fixed-parameter tractable.

Theorem 1. *Let $\sigma \in \{\mathrm{adm}, \mathrm{com}, \mathrm{prf}, \mathrm{sem}, \mathrm{stb}\}$. Then the problems σ-SMALL, σ-REPAIR, σ-ADJUST, σ-CENTER are W[1]-hard.*

Since the fpt-reductions used in the proof of Theorem 1 can be computed in polynomial time, and since the unparameterized version of MULTICOLORED CLIQUE is NP-hard, it follows that the unparameterized versions of the four problems mentioned in Theorem 1 are also NP-hard. We will have shown Theorem 1 after showing the following three lemmas.

Lemma 1. *Let* $\sigma \in \{\text{adm}, \text{com}, \text{prf}, \text{sem}, \text{stb}\}$. *Then the problems* σ-SMALL *and* σ-REPAIR *are* W[1]-*hard.*

Proof. We start by showing the lemma for the problem σ-SMALL by giving an fpt-reduction from the MULTICOLORED CLIQUE problem to the σ-SMALL problem, when σ is one of the listed semantics. Let (G, k) be an instance of MULTICOLORED CLIQUE with partition $V_1, \ldots, V_k$. We construct in fpt-time an AF F such that there is an $E \in \sigma(F)$ with $|E| = k$ if and only if G has a k-clique. The AF F contains the following arguments: (1) one argument y_v for every $v \in V(G)$ and (2) for every $1 \leq i \leq k$, for every $v \in V_i$, and for every $1 \leq j \leq k$ with $j \neq i$, one argument z_v^j.

For every $1 \leq i < j \leq k$, we denote by $Y[i]$ the set of arguments $\{ y_v \mid v \in V_i \}$ and by $Z[i, j]$ the set of arguments $\{ z_v^j \mid v \in V_i \}$. Furthermore, we set $Y := \bigcup_{1 \leq i \leq k} Y[i]$ and $Z := \bigcup_{1 \leq i < j \leq k} Z[i, j]$. For every $1 \leq i \leq k$, the AF F contains the following attacks:

- one attack from y_v to y_u for every $u, v \in Y[i]$ with $u \neq v$;
- one self-attack for all arguments in Z;
- for every $v \in V_i$, one attack from z_v^j to y_v for every $1 \leq j \leq k$ with $j \neq i$;
- for every $v \in V_i$, one attack from y_v to z_u^j for every $u \in V_i \setminus \{v\}$ and $1 \leq j \leq k$ with $j \neq i$.
- for every $\{u, v\} \in E(G)$ with $u \in V_i$ and $v \in V_j$, one attack from y_u to z_v^i and one attack from y_v to z_u^j.

This completes the construction of F. It remains to show that G has a k-clique if and only if there is an $E \in \sigma(F)$ with $|E| = k$. If $Q \subseteq V(G)$ we denote by Y_Q the set of arguments $\{ y_q \mid q \in Q \}$. We need the following claim.

Claim 1. *A set* $Q \subseteq V(G)$ *is a k-clique in G if and only if* $Y_Q \in \text{adm}(F)$ *and* $Y_Q \neq \emptyset$.

Suppose that $Q \subseteq V(G)$ is a k-clique in G. Then Y_Q contains exactly one argument from $Y[i]$ for every $1 \leq i \leq k$. Because there are no attacks between arguments in $Y[i]$ and $Y[j]$ for every $1 \leq i < j \leq k$ it follows that Y_Q is conflict-free. To see that Y_Q is also admissible let $y_v \in Y_Q \cap V_i$ and suppose that y_v is attacked by an argument x of F. It follows from the construction of F that either $x \in Y[i]$ or $x \in \{ z_v^j \mid 1 \leq j \leq k$ and $j \neq i\}$. In the first case x is attacked by y_v. In the second case z_v^j is attacked by the argument in $Y[j] \cap Y_Q$ because Q is a k-clique of G. Hence, $Y_Q \in \text{adm}(F)$ and $Y_Q \neq \emptyset$, as required.

For the opposite direction, suppose that $E \in \text{adm}(F)$ and $E \neq \emptyset$. Because E conflict-free it follows that $E \subseteq Y$ and E contains at most one argument from the set $Y[i]$ for every $1 \leq i \leq k$. Because $E \neq \emptyset$ there is an argument $y_v \in Y[i] \cap E$. Because of the construction of F, y_v is attacked by the arguments $\{ z_v^j \mid 1 \leq j \leq k$ and $j \neq i \}$. Hence, the arguments $\{ z_v^j \mid 1 \leq j \leq k$ and $j \neq i \}$ need to be attacked by arguments in E. However, the only arguments of F that attack an argument z_v^j with $j \neq i$ are the arguments $y_u \in Y[j]$ such that $\{u, v\} \in E(G)$. Hence, for every argument $y_v \in E \cap Y[i]$ and every $1 \leq j \leq k$ with $j \neq i$ there is an argument $y_u \in E \cap Y[j]$ such that $\{u, v\} \in E(G)$. It follows that the set $\{ v \mid y_v \in E \}$ is a k-clique in G. This shows the claim.

The previous claim shows that every non-empty admissible extension of F corresponds to a k-clique of G. It is now straightforward to check that every such extension is not only admissible but also complete, preferred, semi-stable, and stable. This shows the lemma for σ-SMALL. To show the lemma for the σ-REPAIR problem we note that $(F, \emptyset, k)$ is a YES-instance for σ-REPAIR if and only if (F, k) is a YES-instance for σ-SMALL.   □

Lemma 2. *Let* $\sigma \in \{\text{adm}, \text{com}, \text{prf}, \text{sem}, \text{stb}\}$. *Then the problem* σ-ADJUST *is* W[1]-*hard*.

Proof. We give an fpt-reduction from the σ-SMALL problem. Let (F, k) be an instance of the σ-SMALL problem where $F = (X, A)$. We construct an equivalent instance (F', E_1, E_2) of the σ-ADJUST problem as follows. $F' = (X', A')$ is obtained from F by adding one argument t and two attacks (t, x) and (x, t) for every $x \in X$ to F. Because the argument t attacks is attacked by all arguments in X it follows that $\{t\}$ is a σ-extension of F'. In is now straightforward to show that $(F', \{t\}, t, k+1)$ is a YES-instance of σ-ADJUST if and only if (F, k) is a YES-instance of σ-SMALL. This shows the lemma.   □

Lemma 3. *Let* $\sigma \in \{\text{adm}, \text{com}, \text{prf}, \text{sem}, \text{stb}\}$. *Then the problem* σ-Center *is* W[1]-*hard*.

Proof. We give an fpt-reduction from the σ-SMALL problem. Let (F, k) be an instance of the σ-SMALL problem where $F = (X, A)$. W.l.o.g. we can assume that k is even, this follows from the remark in Section 2 that MULTICOLORED CLIQUE is W[1]-hard if k is even and the parameter preserving reduction from MULTICOLORED CLIQUE to σ-SMALL given in Lemma 1. We will construct an equivalent instance (F', E_1, E_2) of the σ-CENTER problem as follows. $F' = (X', A')$ is obtained from F by adding the following arguments and attacks to F.

- two arguments t and t';
- the arguments in $W := \{w_1, \ldots, w_k\}$ and $W' := \{w'_1, \ldots, w'_k\}$;
- the arguments in $Z := \{z_1, \ldots, z_k\}$ and $Z' := \{z'_1, \ldots, z'_k\}$;
- attacks from t to all arguments in $X \cup \{t'\} \cup Z \cup Z'$ and attacks from t' to all arguments in $X \cup \{t\} \cup Z \cup Z'$;
- attacks from w_i to $\{t, w'_i\}$ and attacks from w'_i to $\{t', w_i\}$ for every $1 \le i \le k$;
- self-attacks for the arguments $z_1, \ldots, z_k$ and $z'_1, \ldots, z'_k$;
- attacks from z_i to $\{w_i, w'_i\}$ and from X to z_i for every $1 \le i \le k$;
- attacks from $\{w_i, w'_i\}$ to z'_i and from z'_i to X for every $1 \le i \le k$;

We set $E_0 := \{w_1, \ldots, w_{k/2}, w'_{k/2+1}, \ldots, w'_k\}$, $E_1 := \{t\} \cup W'$, $E_2 := \{t'\} \cup W$, and $k' := \text{dist}(E_1, E_2) - 1 = 2(k+1) - 1 = 2k + 1$. Then E_1 and E_2 are σ-extensions and hence (F', E_1, E_2) is a valid instance of the σ-CENTER problem. It remains to show that (F, k) is a YES instance of σ-SMALL if and only if (F', E_1, E_2) is a YES instance of σ-CENTER.

Suppose that (F, k) is a YES instance of σ-SMALL and let E be a non-empty σ-extension of cardinality at most k witnessing this. Then $E' := E \cup E_0$ is a σ-extension of F' and $\text{dist}(E', E_i) = k + k + 1 = 2k + 1 \le k'$ for $i \in \{1, 2\}$, as required.

For the reverse direction suppose that E' is a σ-extension of F' with $\text{dist}(E', E_i) \le k'$ for $i \in \{1, 2\}$. We need the following claim.

Claim 2. E' *does not contain t or t'.*

Suppose for a contradiction that E' contains one of t and t'. Because t and t' attack each other, E' cannot contain both t and t'. W.l.o.g. we can assume that $t \in E'$. Because E' is a σ-extension E' is also admissible. Since, the arguments $w_1, \ldots, w_k$ attack t, there need to be arguments in E' that attack these arguments. It follows that E' contains the arguments $w_1', \ldots, w_k'$. But then $\mathrm{dist}(E', E_2) \geq \mathrm{dist}(E_1, E_2)$ a contradiction.

Claim 3. $E' \cap X$ *is a non-empty σ-extension of F and E' contains exactly one of the arguments w_i and w_i' for every $1 \leq i \leq k$.*

It follows from the previous claim that E' does not contain t or t'. Furthermore, because of the self-loops of the arguments in $Z \cup Z'$, E' contains only arguments from $X \cup W \cup W'$. Since the arguments in X do not attack or are attacked by arguments in $W \cup W'$ it follows that $E' \cap X$ is a σ-extension of F. To see that $E' \cap X$ is also not empty, suppose for a contradiction that this is not the case. Then because E' is non-empty, E' has to contain at least one argument from $W \cup W'$. However, any argument in $W \cup W'$ is attacked by an argument in Z and the only arguments that attack arguments in Z are the arguments in $X \cup \{t, t'\}$. Again using the previous claim and the fact that E' is admissible, it follows that E' has to contain at least one argument from X, as required. It remains to show that E' contains exactly one of w_i and w_i' for every $1 \leq i \leq k$. Because E' contains at least one argument from X and all arguments in X are attacked by all arguments in Z', E' needs to contain arguments that attack all arguments in Z'. However, the only arguments that attack arguments in Z' are the arguments in $\{t, t'\} \cup W \cup W'$. Using the previous claim it follows that the only way for E' to attack all arguments in Z' is to contain at least one of w_i and w_i' for every $1 \leq i \leq k$. The claim now follows by observing that because E' is conflict-free, it cannot contain both arguments w_i and w_i' for any $1 \leq i \leq k$. This proves the claim.

Since E' contains exactly one of w_i and w_i' for every $1 \leq i \leq k$ we obtain that either $|W \setminus E'| \geq k/2$ or $|W' \setminus E'| \geq k/2$. W.l.o.g. we can assume that $|W \setminus E'| \geq k/2$. But then $\mathrm{dist}(E', E_2) = |E' \cap X| + 1 + 2|W \setminus E'| = |E' \cap X| + k + 1$ and because $\mathrm{dist}(E', E_2) \leq k' = 2k + 1$ it follows that $|E' \cap X| \leq k$. This concludes the proof of the lemma. $\qquad\square$

Lemmas 1, 2, and 3 together imply Theorem 1.

In the next section we will show that, when considering AFs of bounded maximum degree, then fixed-parameter tractability can be obtained for the admissible, complete, and stable semantics. Unfortunately, this positive result does not hold for the preferred and semi-stable semantics as the following result shows.

Theorem 2. *Let $\sigma \in \{\mathrm{prf}, \mathrm{sem}\}$. Then the problems σ-SMALL, σ-REPAIR, σ-ADJUST, σ-CENTER are para-coNP hard, even for AFs of maximum degree 5.*

The remainder of this section is devoted to the proof of Theorem 2.

Lemma 4. *Let $\sigma \in \{\mathrm{prf}, \mathrm{sem}\}$. Then the problems σ-SMALL and σ-REPAIR are para-coNP-hard (for parameter equal to 1), even for AFs of maximum degree at most 5.*

Proof. We will show the theorem by providing a polynomial reduction from the 3-CNF-2-UNSATISFIABLILY problem which is well-known to be coNP-hard [22]. This problem asks whether a given 3-CNF-2 formula Φ, i.e., Φ is a CNF formula where every clause contains at most 3 literals and every literal occurs in at most 2 clauses, is not satisfiable. Let Φ be a such a 3-CNF-2 formula with clauses $C_1, \ldots, C_m$ and variables $x_1, \ldots, x_n$. We will (in polynomial time) construct an AF $F = (X, A)$ such that (1) F has degree at most 5 and (2) Φ is not satisfiable if and only if there is an $E \in \sigma(F)$ with $|E| = 1$. This implies the theorem.

F contains the following arguments: (1) two arguments Φ and $\overline{\Phi}$, (2) one argument C_j for every $1 \leq j \leq m$, (3) two arguments x_i and $\overline{x_i}$ for every $1 \leq i \leq n$, and (4) one argument e. Furthermore, F contains the following attacks: (1) one self-attack for the arguments $\overline{\Phi}$ and $C_1, \ldots, C_m$, (2) one attack from Φ to $\overline{\Phi}$, (3) one attack from C_j to Φ for every $1 \leq j \leq m$, (4) one attack from x_i to C_j for every $1 \leq i \leq n$ and $1 \leq j \leq m$ such that $x_i \in C_j$, (5) one attack from $\overline{x_i}$ to C_j for every $1 \leq i \leq n$ and $1 \leq j \leq m$ such that $\overline{x_i} \in C_j$, (6) two attacks from x_i to $\overline{x_i}$ and from $\overline{x_i}$ to x_i for every $1 \leq i \leq n$, and (7) two attacks from $\overline{\Phi}$ to x_i and to $\overline{x_i}$ for every $1 \leq i \leq n$.

Note that the constructed AF F does not have bounded degree. Whereas all arguments in $X \setminus \{\Phi, \overline{\Phi}\}$ have degree at most 5, the degree of the arguments Φ and $\overline{\Phi}$ can be unbounded. However, the following simple trick can be used to transform F into an AF with bounded degree.

Let $B(i)$ be an undirected rooted binary tree with root r and i leaves $l_1, \ldots, l_i$ and let $B'(i)$ be obtained from $B(i)$ after subdividing every edge of $B(i)$ once, i.e., every edge $\{u, v\}$ is replaced with two edges $\{u, n_{uv}\}$ and $\{n_{uv}, v\}$ where n_{uv} is a new vertex for every such edge. We denote by $B(\Phi)$ the rooted directed tree obtained from $B'(m)$ after directing every edge of $B'(m)$ towards the root r and introducing a self-attack for every vertex in $V(B'(m)) \setminus V(B(m))$, i.e., all vertices introduced for subdividing edges of $B(m)$ are self-attacking in $B(\Phi)$. Then to ensure that the argument Φ has bounded degree in F we first delete the attacks from the arguments $C_1, \ldots, C_m$ to Φ in F. We then add a copy of $B(\Phi)$ to F and identify Φ with the root r. Finally, we add one attack from C_j to l_j for every $1 \leq j \leq m$. Observe that this construction maintains the property of F that if a σ-extension of F contains Φ then it also has to contain at least one attacker of every argument $C_1, \ldots, C_m$.

Let $B(\overline{\Phi})$ be the rooted directed tree obtained from $B'(2n)$ after directing every edge of $B'(2n)$ away from the root r and introducing a self-attack for every vertex in $V(B(2n))$. To ensure that also the argument $\overline{\Phi}$ has bounded degree we first delete the attacks from the argument $\overline{\Phi}$ to $x_1, \overline{x_1}, \ldots, x_n, \overline{x_n}$ in F. We then add a copy of $B(\overline{\Phi})$ to F and identify $\overline{\Phi}$ with the root r. Finally, we add two attacks from l_i to x_i and from l_{n+i} to $\overline{x_i}$ for every $1 \leq i \leq n$. Observe that this construction maintains the property of F that if a σ-extension of F contains x_i or $\overline{x_i}$ for some $1 \leq i \leq n$ then $\overline{\Phi}$ needs to be attacked by the argument Φ in F and hence such a σ-extension has to contain the argument Φ.

Clearly, after applying the above transformations to F the resulting AF has maximum degree at most 5. However, to make the remaining part of the proof less technical we will give the proof only for the AF F. We will need the following claim.

Claim 4. *If there is an $E \in \operatorname{adm}(F)$ that contains at least one argument in $\{\Phi, x_1, \overline{x_2}, \ldots, x_n, \overline{x_n}\}$ then $\Phi \in E$.*

Let $E \in \text{adm}(F)$ with $E \cap \{\Phi, x_1, \overline{x_2}, \ldots, x_n, \overline{x_n}\} \neq \emptyset$. If $\Phi \in E$ then the claim holds. So suppose that $\Phi \notin E$. Then there is an $1 \leq i \leq n$ such that either $x_i \in E$ or $\overline{x_i} \in E$. Because both x_i and $\overline{x_i}$ are attacked by the argument $\overline{\Phi}$ and the only argument (apart from $\overline{\Phi}$) that attacks $\overline{\Phi}$ in F is Φ it follows that $\Phi \in E$. This shows the claim.

Claim 5. *There is an $E \in \text{adm}(F)$ that contains at least one argument in $\{\Phi, x_1, \overline{x_2}, \ldots, x_n, \overline{x_n}\}$ if and only if the formula Φ is satisfiable.*

Suppose there is an $E \subseteq \text{adm}(F)$ with $E \cap \{\Phi, x_1, \overline{x_2}, \ldots, x_n, \overline{x_n}\} \neq \emptyset$. Because of the previous claim we have that $\Phi \in E$. Because $\Phi \in E$ and Φ is attacked by the arguments $C_1, \ldots, C_m$ it follows that the arguments $C_1, \ldots, C_m$ must be attacked by some argument in E. Let $a(C_j)$ be an argument in E that attacks C_j. Then $a(C_j)$ is an argument that corresponds to a literal of the clause C_j. Furthermore, because E is conflict-free the set $L := \{ a(C_j) \mid 1 \leq j \leq m \}$ does not contain arguments that correspond to complementary literals. Hence, L corresponds to a satisfying assignment of Φ.

For the reverse direction suppose Φ is satisfiable and let L be a set of literals witnessing this, i.e., L is a set of literals that correspond to a satisfying assignment of Φ. It is straightforward to check that $E := \{\Phi\} \cup L$ is in $\text{adm}(F)$. This completes the proof of the claim.

Claim 6. *Let $E \in \sigma(F)$. Then $e \in E$.*

This follows directly from our assumption that $\sigma \in \{\text{prf}, \text{sem}\}$ and the fact that the argument e is isolated in F.

We are now ready to show that Φ is not satisfiable if and only if there is an $E \in \sigma(F)$ with $|E| = 1$. So suppose that Φ is not satisfiable. It follows from the previous claim that $E \cap \{\Phi, x_1, \overline{x_1}, \ldots, x_n, \overline{x_n}\} = \emptyset$ for every $E \in \text{adm}(F)$ and hence also for every $E \in \sigma(F)$. Because of the self-attacks of the arguments in $\{\overline{\Phi}, C_1, \ldots, C_m\}$, we obtain that $E \subseteq \{e\}$. Using the previous claim, we have $E = \{e\}$ as required.

For the reverse direction suppose that there is an $E \in \sigma(F)$ with $|E| = 1$. Because of the previous claim it follows that $E = \{e\}$. Furthermore, because of the maximality condition of the preferred and semi-stable semantics it follows that there is no $E \in \text{adm}(F)$ such that $E \cap \{\Phi, x_1, \overline{x_1}, \ldots, x_n, \overline{x_n}\} \neq \emptyset$ and hence (using Claim 5) the formula Φ is not satisfiable. $\qquad\square$

Lemma 5. *Let $\sigma \in \{\text{prf}, \text{sem}\}$. Then the problem σ-ADJUST is para-coNP-hard (for parameter equal to 2) even if the maximum degree of the AF is bounded by 5.*

Proof. We use a similar construction as in the proof of Theorem 4. Let F be the AF constructed from the 3-CNF-2 formulas Φ as in the proof of Lemma 4. Furthermore, let F' be the AF obtained from F after removing the argument e and adding 4 novel arguments t_1, t_1', t_2, and t_2' and the attacks (t_1, Φ), (Φ, t_1), (t_1, t_2), (t_2, t_1), (t_1, t_1'), (t_2, t_2'), (t_1', t_1'), and (t_2', t_2') to F. Because F has degree bounded by 5 (and the degree of the argument Φ in F is 3) it follows that the maximum degree of F' is 5 as required. We claim that $(F', \{t_1\}, t_1, 2)$ is a YES-instance of σ-ADJUST if and only if Φ is not satisfiable.

It is straightforward to verify that the Claims 4 and 5 also hold for the AF F'. We need the following additional claims.

Claim 7. $\{t_1\} \in \sigma(F')$.

Clearly, $\{t_1\} \in \mathrm{adm}(F')$. We first show that for every $E \in \mathrm{adm}(F')$ with $t_1 \in E$ it holds that $E = \{t_1\}$. Let $E \in \mathrm{adm}(F')$ with $t_1 \in E$. Because of the attacks between t_1 and t_2 and between t_1 and Φ it follows that $\Phi, t_2 \notin E$. Using Claim 4 it follows that also none of the arguments in $\{x_1, \overline{x_1}, \ldots, x_n, \overline{x_n}\}$ are contained in E. Furthermore, because of the self-attacks in F' it also holds that none of the arguments in $\{\overline{\Phi}, C_1, \ldots, C_m, t_1', t_2'\}$ are contained in E. Hence, $E = \{t_1\}$, as required. This implies that $\{t_1\} \in \mathrm{prf}(F')$. To show that $\{t_1\} \in \mathrm{sem}(F')$ observe that t_1 is the only argument in F (apart from t_1' itself) that attacks t_1'. Furthermore, because t_1' attacks itself it cannot be in any semi-stable extension of F'. Hence, $\{t_1\} \in \mathrm{sem}(F')$. This shows the claim.

Claim 8. $\{t_2\} \in \sigma(F')$ if and only if Φ is not satisfiable.

Suppose that $\{t_2\} \in \sigma(F')$. If $\{t_2\} \in \mathrm{prf}(F')$ then there is no $E \in \mathrm{adm}(F')$ with $\{t_2\} \subsetneq E$. It follows that there is no $E' \in \mathrm{adm}(F')$ with $E' \cap \{\Phi, x_1, \overline{x_1}, \ldots, x_n, \overline{x_n}\} \neq \emptyset$, since such an E' could be added to E. Using Claim 5 it follows that Φ is not satisfiable. If on the other hand $\{t_2\} \in \mathrm{sem}(F')$ then because t_2 is the only argument that attacks t_2' and because of the self-attack of t_2' it follows again that there is no $E \in \mathrm{adm}(F')$ with $\{t_2\} \subsetneq E$. Hence, using the same arguments as for the case $\{t_2\} \in \mathrm{prf}(F')$ we again obtain that Φ is not satisfiable.

For the reverse direction suppose that Φ is not satisfiable. Because of Claim 5 we obtain that every $E \in \mathrm{adm}(F')$ (and hence also every $E \in \sigma(F')$) contains no argument in $\{\Phi, x_1, \overline{x_1}, \ldots, x_n, \overline{x_n}\}$. Because $\{t_2\} \in \mathrm{adm}(F')$ and the argument t_2 attacks the only remaining argument t_1 with no self-attack it follows that $\{t_2\} \in \sigma(F')$.

To show the lemma it remains to show that there is an $E' \in \sigma(F')$ with $t_1 \notin E'$ and $\mathrm{dist}(E, E') \leq 2$ if and only if the formula Φ is not satisfiable. First observe that because of Claim 7, $\emptyset \notin \sigma(F')$ and hence E' must contain exactly one argument other than t_1. Consequently, it remains to show that there is an argument $x \in X \setminus \{t_1\}$ such that $\{x\} \in \sigma(F')$ if and only if Φ is not satisfiable.

Suppose that there is an $x \in X \setminus \{t_1\}$ with $\{x\} \in \sigma(F')$. If $x \in \{\Phi, x_1, \overline{x_1}, \ldots, x_n, \overline{x_n}\}$ then because of Claim 4 it holds that $x = \Phi$. However, assuming that Φ contains at least one clause it follows that $\{x\}$ is not admissible, and hence $x \neq \Phi$. Considering the self-attacks of F we obtain that $x = t_2$. Hence, the forward direction follows from Claim 8.

The reverse direction follows immediately from Claim 8. This concludes the proof of the lemma. □

Lemma 6. Let $\sigma \in \{\mathrm{prf}, \mathrm{sem}\}$. Then the problem σ-CENTER is para-coNP-hard (for parameter equal to 6) even if the maximum degree of the AF is bounded by 5.

Proof. We use a similar construction as in the proof of Lemma 4. Let F be the AF constructed from the 3-CNF-2 formulas Φ as in the proof of Lemma 4. Furthermore, let F' be the AF obtained from F after removing the argument e and adding 12 novel arguments $t, t', w_1, w_2, w_1', w_2', z, z', z_1, z_1', z_2, z_2'$ and the attacks (t, z), (z, z), (t', z'), (z', z'), (w_1, z_1), (z_1, z_1), (w_1', z_1'), (z_1', z_1'), (w_2, z_2), (z_2, z_2), (w_2', z_2'), (z_2', z_2'), (t, Φ), (Φ, t), (t', Φ), (Φ, t'), (t, t'), (t', t), (w_1, w_1'), (w_1', w_1), (w_2, w_2'),

(w'_2, w_2), (w_1, t), (w_2, t), (w'_1, t'), and (w'_2, t) to F. Because F has degree bounded by 5 (and the degree of the argument Φ of F is 3) it follows that the maximum degree of F' is 5 as required. We claim that $(F', \{t, w'_1, w'_2\}, \{t', w_1, w_2\})$ is a YES-instance of σ-CENTER if and only if Φ is not satisfiable.

It is straightforward to verify that the Claims 4 and 5 also hold for the AF F'. We need the following additional claims.

Claim 9. $\{t, w'_1, w'_2\} \in \sigma(F')$ and $\{t', w_1, w_2\} \in \sigma(F')$.

We show that $\{t, w'_1, w'_2\} \in \sigma(F')$. The case for $\{t', w_1, w_2\} \in \sigma(F')$ is analogous due to the symmetry of F'. Clearly, $\{t, w'_1, w'_2\} \in \text{adm}(F')$.

We first show that for every $E \in \text{adm}(F')$ with $t \in E$ it holds that $E = \{t, w'_1, w'_2\}$. Let $E \in \text{adm}(F')$ with $t \in E$. Clearly, E does not contain Φ, t', w_1 or w_2 (since these arguments are neighbors of t in F'). Using Claim 4 it follows that also none of the arguments in $\{x_1, \overline{x_1}, \ldots, x_n, \overline{x_n}\}$ are contained in E. Furthermore, because of the self-attacks in F' it also holds that none of the arguments in $\{\overline{\Phi}, C_1, \ldots, C_m, z, z', z_1, z'_1, z_2, z'_2\}$ are contained in E. Hence, $E \subseteq \{t_1, w'_1, w'_2\}$. However, because t is attacked by w_1 and w_2 in F and w'_1 and w'_2 are the only arguments of F' that attack w_1 and w_2 it follows that $E = \{t, w'_1, w'_2\}$. This implies that $\{t, w'_1, w'_2\} \in \text{prf}(F')$. To show that $\{t, w'_1, w'_2\} \in \text{sem}(F')$ observe that t is the only argument in F' (apart from z itself) that attacks z. Furthermore, because z attacks itself it cannot be in any semi-stable extension of F'. Hence, $\{t, w'_1, w'_2\} \in \text{sem}(F')$. This shows the claim.

The proof of the previous claim actually showed the following slightly stronger statement.

Claim 10. Let $E \in \sigma(F')$ with $t \in E$. Then $E = \{t, w'_1, w'_2\}$. Similarly, if $E \in \sigma(F')$ with $t' \in E$. Then $E = \{t', w_1, w_2\}$.

We are now ready to show that there is an $E \in \sigma(F')$ with $\text{dist}(E, E_i) < \text{dist}(E_1, E_2) = 6$ for every $i \in \{1, 2\}$ if and only if the formula Φ is not satisfiable.

Suppose that there is an $E \in \sigma(F')$ with $\text{dist}(E, E_i) < \text{dist}(E_1, E_2) = 6$ for every $i \in \{1, 2\}$. Then because of Claim 10 E does not contain t or t'. If there is an $E \in \sigma(F')$ with $\Phi \in E$ then we can assume (because of the maximality properties of the two semantics) that E contains one of x_i or $\overline{x_i}$ for every $1 \leq i \leq n$. Hence, if $\Phi \in E$ and the formula Φ contains at least 5 variables (which we can assume w.l.o.g.) then $\text{dist}(E, E_1) > 5$. Consequently, $\Phi \notin E$ and it follows from Claims 4 and 5 that Φ is not satisfiable, as required.

For the reverse direction suppose that Φ is not satisfiable. Let $E := \{w_1, w'_2\}$. Clearly, $\text{dist}(E, E_i) = 3 < 5$, as required. It remains to show that $E \in \sigma(F')$. It is easy to see that $E \in \text{adm}(F')$. Furthermore, because Φ is not satisfiable, it follows from Claim 5 that no $E' \in \sigma(F')$ can contain an argument in $\{\Phi, x_1, \overline{x_1}, \ldots, x_n, \overline{x_n}\}$ and hence $E \in \text{prf}(F')$. The maximality of E with respect to the semi-stable extension now follows from the fact that w_1 and w'_2 are the only arguments that attack the arguments z_1 and z'_2 and because of their self-attacks none of z_1 and z_2 can them-self be contained in a semi-stable extension. This completes the proof of the lemma. $\square$

Lemmas 4, 5, and 6 together imply Theorem 2.

5   Tractability Results

The results of the previous section draw a rather negative picture of the complexity of problems important to dynamic argumentation. In particular, Theorem 2 strongly suggests that at least for the preferred and semi-stable semantics these problems remain hard even when the degree of arguments is bounded by a small constant. The hardness of these problems under the preferred and semi-stable semantics seems to originate from their maximality conditions. In this section we take a closer look at the complexity of our problems for the three remaining semantics under consideration, i.e., the admissible, complete, and stable semantics. We show that in contrast to the preferred and semi-stable semantics all our problems become fixed-parameter tractable when the arguments of the given AF have small degree. In particular, we will show the following result.

Theorem 3. *Let* $\sigma \in \{\mathrm{adm}, \mathrm{com}, \mathrm{stb}\}$ *and* c *a positive integer. Then the problems* σ-SMALL, σ-REPAIR, σ-ADJUST, *and* σ-CENTER *are fixed-parameter tractable if the maximum degree of the input AF is bounded by* c.

To show the above theorem we will reduce it to a model checking problem for first-order (FO) logic. For a class $\mathcal{S}$ of finite relational structures we consider the following parameterized problem.

$\mathcal{S}$-FO MODEL CHECKING
Instance: A structure $S \in \mathcal{S}$ and a first order formula φ.
Parameter: $|\varphi|$ (i.e., the length of φ).
Question: Does S satisfy (or model) φ, i.e., does $S \models \varphi$ hold?

For a formal definition of the syntax and semantics of FO logic and associated notions we refer the reader to a standard text [21]. Central to our result is the following theorem.

Theorem 4 ([29]). *Let* $\mathcal{S}$ *be a class of structures whose maximum degree is bounded by some constant. Then the problem* $\mathcal{C}$-FO MODEL CHECKING *is fixed-parameter tractable.*

We note here that we define the maximum degree of a structure S in terms of the maximum degree of its associated Gaifman graph, which is the undirected graph whose vertex set is the universe of S, and where two vertices are joined by an edge if they appear together in a tuple of a relation of S.

Several extensions of Theorem 4 to larger classes of structures are known, e.g., to classes of structures with locally bounded treewidth. Due to the technicality of the definition of these classes we refrain from stating these results in detail and refer the interested reader to [25]. Results such as Theorem 4 are also commonly refereed to as meta-theorems since they allow us to make statements about a wide variety of algorithmic problems. Similar meta-theorems have been used before in the context of Abstract Argumentation (see, e.g., [12,24,18]).

We will now show how to reduce our problems to the $\mathcal{S}$-FO MODEL CHECKING problem. To do so we need (1) to represent the input of σ-SMALL, σ-REPAIR, σ-ADJUST, σ-CENTER in terms of finite structures (whose maximum degree is bounded in terms of the maximum degree of the input AF), and (2) to give a FO sentence that is satisfied by the structure obtained in step (1) if and only if the given instance of σ-SMALL, σ-REPAIR, σ-ADJUST, σ-CENTER is a YES instance.

We start by defining the structures that correspond to the input of our problems. For all of our problems, the structure has universe X and one binary relation A that is equal to the attack relation of the AF $F = (X, A)$, which is given in the input. Additionally, the resulting structures will contain unary relations, which represent arguments or sets of arguments, respectively, which are given in the input. For instance, the structure for an instance (F, E_0, t, k) of σ-ADJUST has universe X, one binary relation A that equals the attack relation of F, one unary relation E_0 that equals the set E_0, and one unary relation T with $T := \{t\}$. The structures for the problems σ-SMALL, σ-REPAIR, and σ-CENTER are defined analogously. It is straightforward to verify that the maximum degree of the structures obtained in this way is equal to the maximum degree of the input AF.

Towards defining the FO formulas for step (2) we start by defining the following auxiliary formulas. Due to the complicacy of the FO formulas that we need to define, we will introduce some additional notation that will allow us to reuse formulas by substituting parts of other formulas. We will provide examples how to interpret the notation when these formulas are introduced.

In the following let l be a natural number, and let $\varphi(x)$, $\varphi_1(x)$, and $\varphi_2(x)$ be FO formulas with free variable x.

The formula SET$[l](x_1, \ldots, x_l, y)$ is satisfied if and only if the argument y is equal to at least one of the arguments $x_1, \ldots, x_l$:

$$\text{SET}[l](x_1, \ldots, x_l, y) := (y = x_1 \vee \cdots \vee y = x_l).$$

We note here that the notation SET$[l]$ means that the exact definition of the formula SET$[l]$ depends on the value of l, e.g., if $l = 3$ then SET$[l]$ is the formula $y = x_1 \vee y = x_2 \vee y = x_3$.

The formula CF$[\varphi(x)]$ is satisfied if and only if the set of arguments that satisfy the formula $\varphi(x)$ is conflict-free:

$$\text{CF}[\varphi(x)] := \forall x \forall y (\varphi(x) \wedge \varphi(y)) \to \neg Axy.$$

Again we note here that the notation CF$[\varphi(x)]$ means that the exact definition of the formula CF$[\varphi(x)]$ depends on the formula $\varphi(x)$, e.g., if $\varphi(x) := \text{SET}[l](x_1, \ldots, x_l, x)$ then CF$[\varphi(x)]$ is the formula $\forall x \forall y (\text{SET}[l](x_1, \ldots, x_l, x) \wedge \text{SET}[l](x_1, \ldots, x_l, y)) \to \neg Axy$ which in turn evaluates to $\forall x \forall y (\bigvee_{1 \leq i \leq l} x = x_i \wedge \bigvee_{1 \leq i \leq l} y = x_i) \to \neg Axy$.

The formula SYM-DIFF$[\varphi_1(x), \varphi_2(x)](y)$ is satisfied if and only if the argument y is contained in the symmetric difference of the sets of arguments that satisfy the formula $\varphi_1(x)$ and the set of arguments that satisfy the formula $\varphi_2(x)$:

$$\text{SYM-DIFF}[\varphi_1(x), \varphi_2(x)](y) := (\varphi_1(y) \wedge \neg \varphi_2(y)) \vee (\neg \varphi_1(y) \wedge \varphi_2(y)).$$

The formula ATMOST$[\varphi(x), k]$ is satisfied if and only if the set of arguments that satisfy the formula $\varphi(x)$ contains at most k arguments:

$$\text{ATMOST}[\varphi(x), k] := \neg (\exists x_1, \ldots, \exists x_{k+1} (\bigwedge_{1 \leq i < j \leq k+1} x_i \neq x_j) \wedge$$
$$(\bigwedge_{1 \leq i \leq k+1} \varphi(x_i))).$$

The following formulas represent the semantics adm, com, stb. These formulas are therefore evaluated over a structure with universe X the binary relation A representing an AF $F := (X, A)$, plus possibly some unary relations.

The formula $\mathrm{adm}[\varphi(x)]$ is satisfied by the structure representing an AF F if and only if the set of arguments that satisfy the formula $\varphi(x)$ is an admissible extension of F:

$$\mathrm{adm}[\varphi(x)] := \mathrm{CF}[\varphi(x)] \wedge (\forall x \forall z (\varphi(x) \wedge (\neg\varphi(z)) \wedge Azx) \rightarrow (\exists y \varphi(y) \wedge Ayz)).$$

The formula $\mathrm{com}[\varphi(x)]$ is satisfied by the structure representing an AF F if and only if the set of arguments that satisfy the formula $\varphi(x)$ is a complete extension of F:

$$\begin{aligned}\mathrm{com}[\varphi(x)] := \mathrm{adm}[\varphi(x)] \wedge \\ (\forall z((\forall a A a z \rightarrow \exists x \varphi(x) \wedge Axa) \wedge (\forall x \varphi(x) \rightarrow \neg(Axz \vee Azx))) \rightarrow \varphi(z).\end{aligned}$$

The formula $\mathrm{stb}[\varphi(x)]$ is satisfied by the structure representing an AF F if and only if the set of arguments that satisfy the formula $\varphi(x)$ is a stable extension of F:

$$\mathrm{stb}[\varphi(x)] := \mathrm{CF}[\varphi(x)] \wedge (\forall z \varphi(z) \vee (\exists a \varphi(a) \wedge Aaz)).$$

We are now ready to define the formulas that represent the problems σ-SMALL, σ-REPAIR, σ-ADJUST, and σ-CENTER.

Let $\sigma \in \{\mathrm{adm, com, stb}\}$. The formula σ-SMALL$[\sigma, k]$ is satisfied by the structure representing an instance (F, k) of σ-SMALL if and only if the AF F has a non-empty σ-extension that contains at most k arguments, i.e., if and only if (F, k) is a YES instance of σ-SMALL:

$$\sigma\text{-SMALL}[\sigma, k] := \exists x_1, \ldots, \exists x_k \sigma[\mathrm{SET}[k](x_1, \ldots, x_k, x)].$$

The formula σ-REPAIR$[\sigma, k]$ is satisfied by the structure representing an instance (F, S, k) of σ-REPAIR if and only if F has an $E \in \sigma(F)$ with $\mathrm{dist}(E, S) \leq k$, i.e., if and only if (F, S, k) is a YES instance of σ-REPAIR:

$$\sigma\text{-REPAIR}[\sigma, k] := \exists x_1, \ldots, \exists x_k \sigma[\mathrm{SYM\text{-}DIFF}[Sx, \mathrm{SET}[k](x_1, \ldots, x_k, x)]].$$

The formula σ-ADJUST$[\sigma, k]$ is satisfied by the structure representing an instance (F, E_0, t, k) of σ-ADJUST if and only if F has an $E \in \sigma(F)$ such that $\mathrm{dist}(E_0, E) \leq k$ and $t \in E \triangle E_0$, i.e., if and only if (F, E_0, t, k) is a YES instance of σ-ADJUST:

$$\begin{aligned}\sigma\text{-ADJUST}[\sigma, k] := \exists t \exists x_1, \ldots, \exists x_{k-1} T t \wedge \\ \sigma[\mathrm{SYM\text{-}DIFF}[E_0 x, \mathrm{SET}[k](t, x_1, \ldots, x_{k-1}, x)]].\end{aligned}$$

The formula σ-CENTER$[\sigma, k]$ is satisfied by the structure representing an instance (F, E_1, E_2) of σ-CENTER if and only if F has an $E \in \sigma(F)$ with $\mathrm{dist}(E_i, E) < \mathrm{dist}(E_1, E_2)$ for every $i \in \{1, 2\}$, i.e., if and only if (F, E_1, E_2) is a YES instance of σ-CENTER:

$$\begin{aligned}\sigma\text{-CENTER}[\sigma, k] := \\ \exists x_1, \ldots, \exists x_{k-1} \sigma[\mathrm{SYM\text{-}DIFF}[E_1 x, \mathrm{SET}[k-1](x_1, \ldots, x_{k-1}, x)]] \wedge \\ \mathrm{ATMOST}[k-1, \\ \mathrm{SYM\text{-}DIFF}[\mathrm{SYM\text{-}DIFF}[E_1 x, \mathrm{SET}[k-1](x_1, \ldots, x_{k-1}, x)], E_2 x]].\end{aligned}$$

Because the length of the above FO formulas is easily seen to be bounded in terms of a function of the parameter k of the respective problem, these formulas together with Theorem 4 immediately imply Theorem 3.

6   Concluding Remarks

We studied the computational problems REPAIR, ADJUST, and CENTER which arise in the context of dynamic changes of argumentation systems. All three problems ask whether there exists an extension of small distance to some given set or sets of arguments, and an upper bound to that distance is taken as the parameter. We considered all three problems with respect to five popular semantics: the admissible, the complete, the preferred, the semi-stable, and the stable semantics, with unrestricted argumentation frameworks and for argumentation frameworks of bounded degree. We have determined whether the problems remain coNP-hard, W[1]-hard, or are fixed-parameter tractable, see Figure 1.

Parameterized complexity aspects of *incremental computation* have come into the focus of recent research [10,23]. We would like to point out that some of our results, in particular our results for the REPAIR problem, can be considered as contributions to this line of research: The argumentation framework has changed, and the existing extension is not anymore an extension with respect to the semantics under consideration. When considering the admissible, the complete, and the stable semantics, and when the degree of the argumentation framework is small, then it is more efficient to repair the existing extension than to compute a new extension from scratch. On the other hand, when considering the preferred and the semi-stable semantics, repairing is not a good option since this involves an intractable task, even when the degree of the argumentation framework is small.

We close by suggesting an "opportunistic" version of the REPAIR problem. That is, given a set of arguments together with an argumentation framework, is it possible to change the framework so that the set becomes an extension? While the allowed elementary changes in the framework can be defined in various ways, the number of such changes would be required to be small. Such a problem is a natural candidate for parameterized complexity analysis.

Acknowledgment. We would like to thank Stefan Woltran for stimulating discussions.

References

1. Baroni, P., Giacomin, M.: Semantics of abstract argument systems. In: Rahwan, I., Simari, G. (eds.) Argumentation in Artificial Intelligence, pp. 25–44. Springer (2009)
2. Baumann, R.: What does it take to enforce an argument? minimal change in abstract argumentation. In: De Raedt, L., Bessière, C., Dubois, D., Doherty, P., Frasconi, P., Heintz, F., Lucas, P.J.F. (eds.) ECAI 2012 - 20th European Conference on Artificial Intelligence. Including Prestigious Applications of Artificial Intelligence (PAIS 2012) System Demonstrations Track, Montpellier, France, August 27-31. Frontiers in Artificial Intelligence and Applications, vol. 242, pp. 127–132. IOS Press (2012)
3. Baumann, R., Brewka, G.: Expanding argumentation frameworks: Enforcing and monotonicity results. In: Baroni, P., Cerutti, F., Giacomin, M., Simari, G.R. (eds.) Computational Models of Argument: Proceedings of COMMA 2010, Desenzano del Garda, Italy, September 8-10. Frontiers in Artificial Intelligence and Applications, vol. 216, pp. 75–86. IOS Press (2010)

4. Bench-Capon, T.J.M., Dunne, P.E.: Argumentation in artificial intelligence. Artificial Intelligence 171(10-15), 619–641 (2007)
5. Booth, R., Caminada, M., Podlaszewski, M., Rahwan, I.: Quantifying disagreement in argument-based reasoning. In: van der Hoek, W., Padgham, L., Conitzer, V., Winikoff, M. (eds.) International Conference on Autonomous Agents and Multiagent Systems, AAMAS 2012, IFAAMAS, Valencia, Spain, June 4-8, 3 Volumes, pp. 493–500 (2012)
6. Cayrol, C., de Saint-Cyr, F.D., Lagasquie-Schiex, M.-C.: Revision of an argumentation system. In: Brewka, G., Lang, J. (eds.) Principles of Knowledge Representation and Reasoning: Proceedings of the Eleventh International Conference, KR 2008, Sydney, Australia, September 16-19, pp. 124–134 (2008)
7. Coste-Marquis, S., Devred, C., Marquis, P.: Symmetric argumentation frameworks. In: Godo, L. (ed.) ECSQARU 2005. LNCS (LNAI), vol. 3571, pp. 317–328. Springer, Heidelberg (2005)
8. Dimopoulos, Y., Torres, A.: Graph theoretical structures in logic programs and default theories. Theoretical Computer Science 170(1-2), 209–244 (1996)
9. Downey, R.G., Fellows, M.R.: Parameterized Complexity. Monographs in Computer Science. Springer, New York (1999)
10. Downey, R., Egan, J., Fellows, M.: Frances Rosamond, and Peter Shaw. Solving hard problems incrementally. In: Presentation at the Workshop on Parameterized Complexity and the Understanding, Design and Analysis of Heuristics, Shonan Village Center, Japan, May 6-11 (2013)
11. Dung, P.M.: On the acceptability of arguments and its fundamental role in nonmonotonic reasoning, logic programming and n-person games. Artificial Intelligence 77(2), 321–357 (1995)
12. Dunne, P.E.: Computational properties of argument systems satisfying graph-theoretic constraints. Artificial Intelligence 171(10-15), 701–729 (2007)
13. Dunne, P.E., Bench-Capon, T.J.M.: Coherence in finite argument systems. Artificial Intelligence 141(1-2), 187–203 (2002)
14. Dunne, P.E., Caminada, M.: Computational complexity of semi-stable semantics in abstract argumentation frameworks. In: Hölldobler, S., Lutz, C., Wansing, H. (eds.) JELIA 2008. LNCS (LNAI), vol. 5293, pp. 153–165. Springer, Heidelberg (2008)
15. Dunne, P.E., Wooldridge, M.: Complexity of abstract argumentation. In: Rahwan, L., Simari, G.R. (eds.) Argumentation in Artificial Intelligence, pp. 85–104. Springer (2009)
16. Dvořák, W., Ordyniak, S., Szeider, S.: Augmenting tractable fragments of abstract argumentation. Artificial Intelligence 186, 157–173 (2012)
17. Dvořák, W., Pichler, R., Woltran, S.: Towards fixed-parameter tractable algorithms for abstract argumentation. Artificial Intelligence 186, 1–37 (2012)
18. Dvořák, W., Szeider, S., Woltran, S.: Abstract argumentation via monadic second order logic. In: Hüllermeier, E., Link, S., Fober, T., Seeger, B. (eds.) SUM 2012. LNCS (LNAI), vol. 7520, pp. 85–98. Springer, Heidelberg (2012)
19. Dvořák, W., Woltran, S.: On the intertranslatability of argumentation semantics. In: Proceedings of the Conference on Thirty Years of Nonmonotonic Reasoning (NonMon@30), Lexington, KY, USA (2010)
20. Dvořák, W., Szeider, S., Woltran, S.: Reasoning in argumentation frameworks of bounded clique-width. In: Baroni, P., Cerutti, F., Giacomin, M., Simari, G.R. (eds.) Proceedings of COMMA 2010, Computational Models of Argumentation. Frontiers in Artificial Intelligence and Applications, vol. 216, pp. 219–230. IOS (2010)
21. Flum, J., Grohe, M.: Parameterized Complexity Theory. Texts in Theoretical Computer Science. An EATCS Series, vol. XIV. Springer, Berlin (2006)
22. Garey, M.R., Johnson, D.R.: Computers and Intractability. W. H. Freeman and Company, New York (1979)

23. Hartung, S., Niedermeier, R.: Incremental list coloring of graphs, parameterized by conservation. Theoretical Computer Science 494, 86–98, 213
24. Kim, E.J., Ordyniak, S., Szeider, S.: Algorithms and complexity results for persuasive argumentation. Artificial Intelligence 175, 1722–1736 (2011)
25. Kreutzer, S.: Algorithmic meta-theorems. Electronic Colloquium on Computational Complexity (ECCC) 16, 147 (2009)
26. Niedermeier, R.: Invitation to Fixed-Parameter Algorithms. Oxford Lecture Series in Mathematics and its Applications. Oxford University Press, Oxford (2006)
27. Pietrzak, K.: On the parameterized complexity of the fixed alphabet shortest common supersequence and longest common subsequence problems. J. of Computer and System Sciences 67(4), 757–771 (2003)
28. Rahwan, I., Simari, G.R. (eds.): Argumentation in Artificial Intelligence. Springer (2009)
29. Seese, D.: Linear time computable problems and first-order descriptions. Mathematical Structures in Computer Science 6(6), 505–526 (1996)

Computing Preferred Extensions in Abstract Argumentation: A SAT-Based Approach

Federico Cerutti[1], Paul E. Dunne[2], Massimiliano Giacomin[3], and Mauro Vallati[4]

[1] School of Natural and Computing Science, King's College, University of Aberdeen,
AB24 3UE, Aberdeen, United Kingdom
f.cerutti@abdn.ac.uk

[2] Department of Computer Science, Ashton Building, University of Liverpool, Liverpool
L69 7ZF, United Kingdom
ped@csc.liv.ac.uk

[3] Department of Information Engineering, University of Brescia, via Branze, 38, 25123,
Brescia, Italy
massimiliano.giacomin@ing.unibs.it

[4] School of Computing and Engineering, University of Huddersfield, Huddersfield, HD1 3DH,
United Kingdom
m.vallati@hud.ac.uk

Abstract. This paper presents a novel SAT-based approach for the computation of extensions in abstract argumentation, with focus on preferred semantics, and an empirical evaluation of its performances. The approach is based on the idea of reducing the problem of computing complete extensions to a SAT problem and then using a depth-first search method to derive preferred extensions. The proposed approach has been tested using two distinct SAT solvers and compared with three state-of-the-art systems for preferred extension computation. It turns out that the proposed approach delivers significantly better performances in the large majority of the considered cases.

1 Introduction

Dung's theory of abstract argumentation frameworks [19] provides a general model, which is widely recognized as a fundamental reference in computational argumentation in virtue of its simplicity, generality, and ability to capture a variety of more specific approaches as special cases. An abstract argumentation framework (AF) consists of a set of arguments and of an *attack* relation between them. The concept of *extension* plays a key role in this simple setting, where an *extension* is intuitively a set of arguments which can "survive the conflict together". Different notions of extensions and of the requirements they should satisfy correspond to alternative *argumentation semantics*, whose definitions and properties are an active investigation subject since two decades (see [5,6] for an introduction).

The main computational problems in abstract argumentation are naturally related to extensions and can be partitioned into two classes: *decision* problems and *construction* problems. Decision problems pose yes/no questions like "Does this argument belong

E. Black, S. Modgil, and N. Oren (Eds.): TAFA 2013, LNAI 8306, pp. 176–193, 2014.
© Springer-Verlag Berlin Heidelberg 2014

to one (all) extensions?" or "Is this set an extension?", while construction problems require to explicitly produce some of the extensions prescribed by a semantics. In particular, *extension enumeration* is the problem of constructing all the extensions prescribed by a given semantics for a given *AF*. The complexity of extension-related decision problems has been deeply investigated and, for most of the semantics proposed in the literature, they have been proven to be intractable. Intractability extends directly to construction/enumeration problems, given that their solutions provide direct answers to decision problems.

Theoretical analysis of worst-case computational issues in abstract argumentation is in a state of maturity with the available complexity results covering all Dung's traditional semantics and several subsequent prominent approaches in the literature (for a summary see [21]). On the practical side, however, the investigation on efficient algorithms for abstract argumentation and on their empirical assessment is less developed, with few results available in the literature. This paper contributes to fill this gap by proposing a novel approach and implementation for enumeration of Dung's *preferred extensions*, corresponding to one of the most significant argumentation semantics, and comparing its performances with other state-of-the-art implemented systems. We focus on extension enumeration since it can be considered the most general problem, i.e. its solution provides complete information concerning the justification status of arguments (making it possible to determine, for instance, if two arguments cannot be accepted in the same extension) and the proposed approach can be easily adapted to solve also the decision problems mentioned above.

The paper is organized as follows. Section 2 recalls the necessary basic concepts and state-of-the-art background. Section 3 introduces the proposed approach while Section 4 describes the test setting and comments the experimental results. Section 5 provides a comparison with related works and then Section 6 concludes the paper.

2   Background

An argumentation framework [19] consists of a set of arguments[1] and a binary attack relation between them.

Definition 1. *An* argumentation framework *(AF) is a pair* $\Gamma = \langle \mathcal{A}, \mathcal{R} \rangle$ *where* $\mathcal{A}$ *is a set of arguments and* $\mathcal{R} \subseteq \mathcal{A} \times \mathcal{A}$. *We say that* b attacks a *iff* $\langle b, a \rangle \in \mathcal{R}$, *also denoted as* $b \rightarrow a$. *The set of attackers of an argument* a *will be denoted as* $a^- \triangleq \{b : b \rightarrow a\}$.

The basic properties of conflict–freeness, acceptability, and admissibility of a set of arguments are fundamental for the definition of argumentation semantics.

Definition 2. *Given an AF* $\Gamma = \langle \mathcal{A}, \mathcal{R} \rangle$:

- *a set* $S \subseteq \mathcal{A}$ *is* conflict–free *if* $\nexists \, a, b \in S$ *s.t.* $a \rightarrow b$;
- *an argument* $a \in \mathcal{A}$ *is* acceptable *with respect to a set* $S \subseteq \mathcal{A}$ *if* $\forall b \in \mathcal{A}$ *s.t.* $b \rightarrow a$, $\exists \, c \in S$ *s.t.* $c \rightarrow b$;

---

[1] In this paper we consider only *finite* sets of arguments.

– a set $S \subseteq \mathcal{A}$ is admissible *if S is conflict–free and every element of S is acceptable with respect to S.*

An argumentation semantics σ prescribes for any *AF* Γ a set of *extensions*, denoted as $\mathcal{E}_\sigma(\Gamma)$, namely a set of sets of arguments satisfying some conditions dictated by σ. In [19] four "traditional" semantics were introduced, namely *complete, grounded, stable,* and *preferred* semantics. Other literature proposals include *semi-stable* [13], *ideal* [20], and *CF2* [7] semantics. Here we need to recall the definitions of complete (denoted as $\mathcal{CO}$) and preferred (denoted as $\mathcal{PR}$) semantics only, along with a well known relationship between them.

Definition 3. *Given an AF* $\Gamma = \langle \mathcal{A}, \mathcal{R} \rangle$:

– *a set $S \subseteq \mathcal{A}$ is a complete extension, i.e. $S \in \mathcal{E}_{\mathcal{CO}}(\Gamma)$, iff S is admissible and $\forall a \in \mathcal{A}$ s.t. a is acceptable w.r.t. S, $a \in S$;*
– *a set $S \subseteq \mathcal{A}$ is a preferred extension, i.e. $S \in \mathcal{E}_{\mathcal{PR}}(\Gamma)$, iff S is a maximal (w.r.t. set inclusion) admissible set.*

Proposition 1. *For any AF* $\Gamma = \langle \mathcal{A}, \mathcal{R} \rangle$, *$S$ is a preferred extension iff it is a maximal (w.r.t. set inclusion) complete extension. As a consequence $\mathcal{E}_{\mathcal{PR}}(\Gamma) \subseteq \mathcal{E}_{\mathcal{CO}}(\Gamma)$.*

It can be noted that each extension S implicitly defines a three-valued *labelling* of arguments, as follows: an argument a is labelled in iff $a \in S$, is labelled out iff $\exists\, b \in S$ s.t. $b \rightarrow a$, is labelled undec if neither of the above conditions holds. In the light of this correspondence, argumentation semantics can equivalently be defined in terms of labellings rather than of extensions (see [5,12]). In particular, the notion of *complete labelling* [5,14] provides an equivalent characterization of complete semantics, in the sense that each complete labelling corresponds to a complete extension and vice versa. Complete labellings can be (redundantly) defined as follows.

Definition 4. *Let* $\langle \mathcal{A}, \mathcal{R} \rangle$ *be an argumentation framework. A total function* $\mathcal{L}ab : \mathcal{A} \mapsto \{$in, out, undec$\}$ *is a* complete labelling *iff it satisfies the following conditions for any* $a \in \mathcal{A}$:

– $\mathcal{L}ab(a) = $ in $\Leftrightarrow \forall b \in a^- \mathcal{L}ab(b) = $ out;
– $\mathcal{L}ab(a) = $ out $\Leftrightarrow \exists b \in a^- : \mathcal{L}ab(b) = $ in;
– $\mathcal{L}ab(a) = $ undec $\Leftrightarrow \forall b \in a^- \mathcal{L}ab(b) \neq$ in $\land \exists c \in a^- : \mathcal{L}ab(c) = $ undec;

It is proved in [12] that preferred extensions are in one-to-one correspondence with those complete labellings maximizing the set of arguments labelled in.

The introduction of preferred semantics is one of the main contribution of Dung's paper. Its name, in fact, reflects a sort of preference w.r.t. other traditional semantics, as it allows multiple extensions (differently from grounded semantics), the existence of extensions is always guaranteed (differently from stable semantics), and no extension is a proper subset of another extension (differently from complete semantics). Also in view of its relevance, computational complexity of preferred semantics has been analyzed early [16,17] in the literature, with standard decision problems in argumentation semantics resulting to be intractable in the case of $\mathcal{PR}$.

As to algorithms for computing preferred extensions, two basic approaches have been considered in the literature. On one hand, one may develop a dedicated algorithm to obtain the problem solution, on the other hand, one may translate the problem instance at hand into an equivalent instance of a different class of problems for which solvers are already available. The results produced by the solver have then to be translated back to the original problem.

The three main dedicated algorithms for computing preferred extensions in the literature [18,27,28] share the same idea based on labellings: starting from an initial default labelling, a sequence of transitions (namely changes of labels) is applied leading to the labellings corresponding to preferred extensions. The three algorithms differ in the initial labelling, the transitions adopted, and the use of additional intermediate labels besides the three standard ones. The algorithm proposed in [28] has been shown to outperform the previous ones and will therefore taken as the only term of comparison for this family of approaches.

As to the translation approach, the main proposal we are aware of is the ASPARTIX system [24], which provides an encoding of AFs and the relevant computational problems in terms of Answer Set Programs which can be processed by a solver like DLV [26]. Recently an alternative encoding of ASPARTIX using metaASP has been proposed [22] and showed to outperform the previous version when used in conjunction with gringo/claspD solver. ASPARTIX is a very general system, whose capabilities include the computation of preferred extensions, and both versions will be used as reference for this family of approaches.

3 The PrefSat Approach

The approach we propose, called PrefSat, can be described as a depth-first search in the space of complete extensions to identify those that are maximal, namely the preferred extensions. Each step of the search process requires the solution of a SAT problem through invocation of a SAT solver. More precisely, the algorithm is based on the idea of encoding the constraints corresponding to complete labellings of an AF as a SAT problem and then iteratively producing and solving modified versions of the initial SAT problem according to the needs of the search process. The first step for a detailed presentation of the algorithm concerns therefore the SAT encoding of complete labellings.

3.1 SAT Encodings of Complete Labellings

A propositional formula over a set of boolean variables is satisfiable iff there exists a truth assignment of the variables such that the formula evaluates to True. Checking whether such an assignment exists is the satisfiability (SAT) problem. Given an AF $\Gamma = \langle \mathcal{A}, \mathcal{R} \rangle$ we are interested in identifying a boolean formula, called *complete labelling formula* and denoted as Π_Γ, such that each satisfying assignment of the formula corresponds to a complete labelling. While this might seem a clear-cut task, several syntactically different encodings can be devised which, while being logically equivalent, can significantly affect the performance of the overall process of searching a satisfying assignment. For instance, adding some "redundant" clauses to a formula may speed up the search process, thanks to the additional constraints. On the other hand, increasing syntactic complexity might lead to worse performances, thus a careful selection of the encoding is needed.

In order to explore alternative encodings, let us consider again the requirement of Definition 4. They can be expressed as a conjunction of 6 terms, i.e. $C_{\text{in}}^{\rightarrow} \wedge C_{\text{in}}^{\leftarrow} \wedge C_{\text{out}}^{\rightarrow} \wedge C_{\text{out}}^{\leftarrow} \wedge C_{\text{undec}}^{\rightarrow} \wedge C_{\text{undec}}^{\leftarrow}$, where

- $C_{\text{in}}^{\rightarrow} \equiv (\mathcal{L}ab(\mathbf{a}) = \text{in} \Rightarrow \forall \mathbf{b} \in \mathbf{a}^- \mathcal{L}ab(\mathbf{b}) = \text{out})$;
- $C_{\text{in}}^{\leftarrow} \equiv (\mathcal{L}ab(\mathbf{a}) = \text{in} \Leftarrow \forall \mathbf{b} \in \mathbf{a}^- \mathcal{L}ab(\mathbf{b}) = \text{out})$;
- $C_{\text{out}}^{\rightarrow} \equiv (\mathcal{L}ab(\mathbf{a}) = \text{out} \Rightarrow \exists \mathbf{b} \in \mathbf{a}^- : \mathcal{L}ab(\mathbf{b}) = \text{in})$;
- $C_{\text{out}}^{\leftarrow} \equiv (\mathcal{L}ab(\mathbf{a}) = \text{out} \Leftarrow \exists \mathbf{b} \in \mathbf{a}^- : \mathcal{L}ab(\mathbf{b}) = \text{in})$;
- $C_{\text{undec}}^{\rightarrow} \equiv (\mathcal{L}ab(\mathbf{a}) = \text{undec} \Rightarrow \forall \mathbf{b} \in \mathbf{a}^- \mathcal{L}ab(\mathbf{b}) \neq \text{in} \wedge \exists \mathbf{c} \in \mathbf{a}^- : \mathcal{L}ab(\mathbf{c}) = \text{undec})$;
- $C_{\text{undec}}^{\leftarrow} \equiv (\mathcal{L}ab(\mathbf{a}) = \text{undec} \Leftarrow \forall \mathbf{b} \in \mathbf{a}^- \mathcal{L}ab(\mathbf{b}) \neq \text{in} \wedge \exists \mathbf{c} \in \mathbf{a}^- : \mathcal{L}ab(\mathbf{c}) = \text{undec})$.

Let us also define $C_{\text{in}}^{\leftrightarrow} \equiv C_{\text{in}}^{\rightarrow} \wedge C_{\text{in}}^{\leftarrow}$, $C_{\text{out}}^{\leftrightarrow} \equiv C_{\text{out}}^{\rightarrow} \wedge C_{\text{out}}^{\leftarrow}$, $C_{\text{undec}}^{\leftrightarrow} \equiv C_{\text{undec}}^{\rightarrow} \wedge C_{\text{undec}}^{\leftarrow}$. The following proposition shows that Definition 4 is redundant, identifying 5 strict subsets of the above six terms that equivalently characterize complete extensions[2].

Proposition 2. *Let $\langle \mathcal{A}, \mathcal{R} \rangle$ be an argumentation framework. A total function $\mathcal{L}ab$: $\mathcal{A} \mapsto \{\text{in}, \text{out}, \text{undec}\}$ is a complete labelling iff it satisfies any of the following conjunctive constraints for any $\mathbf{a} \in \mathcal{A}$: (i) $C_{\text{in}}^{\leftrightarrow} \wedge C_{\text{out}}^{\leftrightarrow}$, (ii) $C_{\text{out}}^{\leftrightarrow} \wedge C_{\text{undec}}^{\leftrightarrow}$, (iii) $C_{\text{in}}^{\leftrightarrow} \wedge C_{\text{undec}}^{\leftrightarrow}$, (iv) $C_{\text{in}}^{\rightarrow} \wedge C_{\text{out}}^{\rightarrow} \wedge C_{\text{undec}}^{\rightarrow}$, (v) $C_{\text{in}}^{\leftarrow} \wedge C_{\text{out}}^{\leftarrow} \wedge C_{\text{undec}}^{\leftarrow}$.*

Proof. We prove that any conjunctive constraint is equivalent to $C_{\text{in}}^{\leftrightarrow} \wedge C_{\text{out}}^{\leftrightarrow} \wedge C_{\text{undec}}^{\leftrightarrow}$, i.e. the constraint expressed in Definition 4. As to (i), (ii) and (iii), the equivalence is immediate from the fact that $\mathcal{L}ab$ is a function.

As to (iv), the constraint does not include the terms $C_{\text{in}}^{\leftarrow}$, $C_{\text{out}}^{\leftarrow}$ and $C_{\text{undec}}^{\leftarrow}$. Here we prove that $C_{\text{in}}^{\leftarrow}$ (and, similarly, $C_{\text{out}}^{\leftarrow}$ and $C_{\text{undec}}^{\leftarrow}$) is indeed satisfied. Let us consider an argument $\mathbf{a}$ such that $\forall \mathbf{b} \in \mathbf{a}^- \mathcal{L}ab(\mathbf{b}) = \text{out}$, and let us reason by contradiction by assuming that $\mathcal{L}ab(\mathbf{a}) \neq \text{in}$. Since $\mathcal{L}ab$ is a function, if $\mathcal{L}ab(\mathbf{a}) \neq \text{in}$ then either $\mathcal{L}ab(\mathbf{a}) = \text{out}$ or $\mathcal{L}ab(\mathbf{a}) = \text{undec}$. If $\mathcal{L}ab(\mathbf{a}) = \text{out}$, from $C_{\text{out}}^{\rightarrow} \exists \mathbf{b} \in \mathbf{a}^- : \mathcal{L}ab(\mathbf{b}) = \text{in} \neq \text{out}$. If $\mathcal{L}ab(\mathbf{a}) = \text{undec}$, from $C_{\text{undec}}^{\rightarrow} \exists \mathbf{b} \in \mathbf{a}^- : \mathcal{L}ab(\mathbf{b}) = \text{undec} \neq \text{out}$. The proof for $C_{\text{out}}^{\leftarrow}$ and $C_{\text{undec}}^{\leftarrow}$ is similar.

As to (v), the proof follows the same line. We prove that $C_{\text{in}}^{\rightarrow}$ (and, similarly, $C_{\text{out}}^{\rightarrow}$ and $C_{\text{undec}}^{\rightarrow}$) is indeed satisfied. Given an argument $\mathbf{a}$ such that $\mathcal{L}ab(\mathbf{a}) = \text{in}$, assume by contradiction that $\exists \mathbf{b} \in \mathbf{a}^- : \mathcal{L}ab(\mathbf{b}) \neq \text{out}$. Since $\mathcal{L}ab$ is a function, either $\mathcal{L}ab(\mathbf{b}) = \text{in}$ or $\mathcal{L}ab(\mathbf{b}) = \text{undec}$. In the first case, $C_{\text{out}}^{\leftarrow}$ entails that $\mathcal{L}ab(\mathbf{a}) = \text{out} \neq \text{in}$. In the second case, either $C_{\text{out}}^{\leftarrow}$ or $C_{\text{undec}}^{\leftarrow}$ applies, i.e. $\mathcal{L}ab(\mathbf{a}) \in \{\text{out}, \text{undec}\}$ thus $\mathcal{L}ab(\mathbf{a}) \neq \text{in}$. Following the same reasoning line, we can prove that also $C_{\text{out}}^{\rightarrow}$ and $C_{\text{undec}}^{\rightarrow}$ hold. □

More generally, we aim at exploring all the constraints corresponding to the 64 possible subsets of the 6 terms above, characterized by a cardinality (i.e. the number of

---

[2] $C_{\text{in}}^{\leftrightarrow} \wedge C_{\text{out}}^{\leftrightarrow}$ and $C_{\text{in}}^{\rightarrow} \wedge C_{\text{out}}^{\rightarrow} \wedge C_{\text{undec}}^{\rightarrow}$ correspond to the alternative definitions of complete labellings in [14], where a proof of their equivalence is provided.

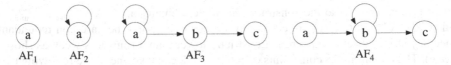

Fig. 1. Identifying some weak constraints

terms) between 0 and 6 and partially ordered according to the $\subseteq$-relation. Using basic combinatorics we get one constraint with cardinality 0 (i.e. the empty constraint), 6 constraints with cardinality 1, 15 constraints with cardinality 2, 20 constraints with cardinality 3, 15 constraints with cardinality 4, 6 constraints with cardinality 5 and one constraint with cardinality 6 (i.e. corresponding to Definition 4). The constraints can be partitioned into three classes:

1. *weak* constraints, i.e. such that there is an argumentation framework and a labelling satisfying all their terms which is not complete;
2. *correct and non redundant* constraints, i.e. able to correctly identify complete labellings and such that any strict subset of their terms is weak;
3. *redundant* constraints, i.e. able to correctly identify complete labellings and such that there is a strict subset of their terms which is correct.

The next proposition and corollary provide the complete characterization of the 64 constraints in this respect.

Proposition 3. *The following 6 constraints are weak: (i)* $C^{\leftrightarrow}_{\text{undec}} \wedge C^{\rightarrow}_{\text{in}} \wedge C^{\leftarrow}_{\text{out}}$, *(ii)* $C^{\leftrightarrow}_{\text{undec}} \wedge C^{\leftarrow}_{\text{in}} \wedge C^{\rightarrow}_{\text{out}}$, *(iii)* $C^{\leftrightarrow}_{\text{out}} \wedge C^{\rightarrow}_{\text{in}} \wedge C^{\leftarrow}_{\text{undec}}$, *(iv)* $C^{\leftrightarrow}_{\text{out}} \wedge C^{\leftarrow}_{\text{in}} \wedge C^{\rightarrow}_{\text{undec}}$, *(v)* $C^{\leftrightarrow}_{\text{in}} \wedge C^{\rightarrow}_{\text{out}} \wedge C^{\leftarrow}_{\text{undec}}$, *(vi)* $C^{\leftrightarrow}_{\text{in}} \wedge C^{\leftarrow}_{\text{out}} \wedge C^{\rightarrow}_{\text{undec}}$.

Proof. For each constraint, we identify an argumentation framework and a non complete labelling which satisfies the constraint. In particular, referring to Figure 1: for (i), see the labelling $\{(\mathbf{a}, \text{out})\}$ of AF_1; for (ii), see the labelling $\{(\mathbf{a}, \text{in})\}$ of AF_2; for (iii), see the labelling $\{(\mathbf{a}, \text{undec})\}$ of AF_1; for (iv), see the labelling $\{(\mathbf{a}, \text{undec}), (\mathbf{b}, \text{in}), (\mathbf{c}, \text{out})\}$ of AF_3; for (v), see the labelling $\{(\mathbf{a}, \text{in}), (\mathbf{b}, \text{undec}), (\mathbf{c}, \text{undec})\}$ of AF_4; for (vi), see the labelling $\{(\mathbf{a}, \text{undec}), (\mathbf{b}, \text{out}), (\mathbf{c}, \text{in})\}$ of AF_3.

Note that, in each case of the above proof, the relevant argumentation framework admits a unique complete labelling which drastically differs from the one satisfying the weak constraint, i.e. there are arguments labelled in that should be labelled undec or there are arguments labelled out or undec that should be labelled in.

Corollary 1. *All the constraints of cardinality 0, 1, and 2 are weak. Among the constraints of cardinality 3,* $(C^{\rightarrow}_{\text{in}} \wedge C^{\rightarrow}_{\text{out}} \wedge C^{\rightarrow}_{\text{undec}})$ *and* $(C^{\leftarrow}_{\text{in}} \wedge C^{\leftarrow}_{\text{out}} \wedge C^{\leftarrow}_{\text{undec}})$ *are correct and non redundant, the other 18 constraints are weak. Among the constraints of cardinality 4,* $(C^{\leftrightarrow}_{\text{in}} \wedge C^{\leftrightarrow}_{\text{out}})$, $(C^{\leftrightarrow}_{\text{out}} \wedge C^{\leftrightarrow}_{\text{undec}})$ *and* $(C^{\leftrightarrow}_{\text{in}} \wedge C^{\leftrightarrow}_{\text{undec}})$ *are correct and non redundant, 6 constraints are weak and 6 constraints are redundant. All the constraints of cardinality 5 and 6 are redundant.*

Proof. As to the first claim, it is easy to see that any constraint having cardinality 0, 1 and 2 is a strict subset of at least one (weak) constraint introduced in Proposition 3, thus it is weak too. As to the constraints having cardinality 3, $(C_{\text{in}}^{\rightarrow} \wedge C_{\text{out}}^{\rightarrow} \wedge C_{\text{undec}}^{\rightarrow})$ and $(C_{\text{in}}^{\leftarrow} \wedge C_{\text{out}}^{\leftarrow} \wedge C_{\text{undec}}^{\leftarrow})$ are correct by Proposition 2, and they are non redundant since any strict subset has a cardinality strictly lower than 3 (thus it is weak as shown above). The remaining 18 constraints of cardinality 3 can take one of the following two forms: (i) 12 constraints include $C_{\text{in}}^{\leftrightarrow}$, $C_{\text{out}}^{\leftrightarrow}$ or $C_{\text{undec}}^{\leftrightarrow}$ and another single term; (ii) 6 constraints include two "left" and a "right" terms, or vice versa. In both cases, it is easy to check that any of these constraints is a strict subset of one of the weak constraints of Proposition 3. As to the constraints of cardinality 4, $(C_{\text{in}}^{\leftrightarrow} \wedge C_{\text{out}}^{\leftrightarrow})$, $(C_{\text{out}}^{\leftrightarrow} \wedge C_{\text{undec}}^{\leftrightarrow})$ and $(C_{\text{in}}^{\leftrightarrow} \wedge C_{\text{undec}}^{\leftrightarrow})$ are correct by Proposition 2, and they are non redundant since they do not contain $(C_{\text{in}}^{\rightarrow} \wedge C_{\text{out}}^{\rightarrow} \wedge C_{\text{undec}}^{\rightarrow})$ nor $(C_{\text{in}}^{\leftarrow} \wedge C_{\text{out}}^{\leftarrow} \wedge C_{\text{undec}}^{\leftarrow})$, thus any subset is weak according to the considerations above. Moreover, 6 constraints of cardinality 4 are supersets of $(C_{\text{in}}^{\rightarrow} \wedge C_{\text{out}}^{\rightarrow} \wedge C_{\text{undec}}^{\rightarrow})$ and $(C_{\text{in}}^{\leftarrow} \wedge C_{\text{out}}^{\leftarrow} \wedge C_{\text{undec}}^{\leftarrow})$ and thus redundant, while the other 6 constraints are the weak ones identified in Proposition 3. Finally, all constraints of cardinality 5 and 6 contain at least one of the correct constraints of Proposition 2, thus they are redundant.

In this work, we consider six constraints, i.e. the 5 correct and non redundant constraints as well as $C_{\text{in}}^{\leftrightarrow} \wedge C_{\text{out}}^{\leftrightarrow} \wedge C_{\text{undec}}^{\leftrightarrow}$ as a "representative" of the 13 redundant ones, leaving the empirical analysis of the other 12 redundant constraints for future work.

The next step is to encode such constraints in conjunctive normal form (CNF), as required by the SAT solver. To this purpose, we have to introduce some notation. Letting $k = |\mathcal{A}|$ we can identify each argument with an index in $\{1, \ldots k\}$ or, more precisely, we can define a bijection $\phi : \{1, \ldots, k\} \mapsto \mathcal{A}$ (the inverse map will be denoted as ϕ^{-1}). ϕ will be called an indexing of $\mathcal{A}$ and the argument $\phi(i)$ will be sometimes referred to as argument i for brevity. For each argument i we define three boolean variables, I_i, O_i, and U_i, with the intended meaning that I_i is true when argument i is labelled in, false otherwise, and analogously O_i and U_i correspond to labels out and undec. Formally, given $\Gamma = \langle \mathcal{A}, \mathcal{R} \rangle$ we define the corresponding set of variables as $\mathcal{V}(\Gamma) \triangleq \cup_{1 \leq i \leq |\mathcal{A}|} \{I_i, O_i, U_i\}$. Now we express the constraints of Definition 4 in terms of the variables $\mathcal{V}(\Gamma)$, with the additional condition that for each argument i exactly one of the three variables has to be assigned the value True. For technical reasons we restrict to "non-empty" extensions (in the sense that at least one of the arguments is labelled in), thus we add the further condition that at least one variable I_i is assigned the value True. The detail of the resulting CNF is given in Definition 5.

Definition 5. *Given an AF* $\Gamma = \langle \mathcal{A}, \mathcal{R} \rangle$, *with* $|\mathcal{A}| = k$ *and* $\phi : \{1, \ldots, k\} \mapsto \mathcal{A}$ *an indexing of* $\mathcal{A}$, *the* C_1 *encoding defined on the variables in* $\mathcal{V}(\Gamma)$, *is given by the conjunction of the formulae listed below:*

$$\bigwedge_{i \in \{1,\ldots,k\}} \left((I_i \vee O_i \vee U_i) \wedge (\neg I_i \vee \neg O_i) \wedge (\neg I_i \vee \neg U_i) \wedge (\neg O_i \vee \neg U_i) \right) \tag{1}$$

$$\bigwedge_{\{i \mid \phi(i)^- = \emptyset\}} (I_i \wedge \neg O_i \wedge \neg U_i) \tag{2}$$

$$\bigwedge_{\{i|\phi(i)^- \neq \emptyset\}} \left(I_i \vee \left(\bigvee_{\{j|\phi(j)\to\phi(i)\}} (\neg O_j) \right) \right) \tag{3}$$

$$\bigwedge_{\{i|\phi(i)^- \neq \emptyset\}} \left(\bigwedge_{\{j|\phi(j)\to\phi(i)\}} \neg I_i \vee O_j \right) \tag{4}$$

$$\bigwedge_{\{i|\phi(i)^- \neq \emptyset\}} \left(\bigwedge_{\{j|\phi(j)\to\phi(i)\}} \neg I_j \vee O_i \right) \tag{5}$$

$$\bigwedge_{\{i|\phi(i)^- \neq \emptyset\}} \left(\neg O_i \vee \left(\bigvee_{\{j|\phi(j)\to\phi(i)\}} I_j \right) \right) \tag{6}$$

$$\bigwedge_{\{i|\phi(i)^- \neq \emptyset\}} \left(\bigwedge_{\{k|\phi(k)\to\phi(i)\}} \left(U_i \vee \neg U_k \vee \left(\bigvee_{\{j|\phi(j)\to\phi(i)\}} I_j \right) \right) \right) \tag{7}$$

$$\bigwedge_{\{i|\phi(i)^- \neq \emptyset\}} \left(\left(\bigwedge_{\{j|\phi(j)\to\phi(i)\}} (\neg U_i \vee \neg I_j) \right) \wedge \left(\neg U_i \vee \left(\bigvee_{\{j|\phi(j)\to\phi(i)\}} U_j \right) \right) \right) \tag{8}$$

$$\bigvee_{i\in\{1,\dots k\}} I_i \tag{9}$$

C_1 corresponds to the conditions of Definition 4 with the addition of the non-emptyness requirement. In particular, Formula (1) states that for each argument i one and only one label has to be assigned. Formula (2) settles the case of unattacked arguments that must be labelled in. Formulas (3), (4), (5), (6), (7) and (8) are restricted to arguments having at least an attacker, and correspond to $C_{in}^{\leftarrow}$, $C_{in}^{\rightarrow}$, $C_{out}^{\leftarrow}$, $C_{out}^{\rightarrow}$, $C_{undec}^{\leftarrow}$, $C_{undec}^{\rightarrow}$, respectively. Finally, formula (9) ensures non-emptyness, i.e. that at least one argument is labelled in.

The six encodings considered in this paper are provided in the following proposition, whose proof is immediate from Prop. 2.

Proposition 4. *Referring to the formulae listed in Definition 5, the following encodings are equivalent:*

C_1 : $(1) \wedge (2) \wedge (3) \wedge (4) \wedge (5) \wedge (6) \wedge (7) \wedge (8) \wedge (9)$

C_1^a : $(1) \wedge (2) \wedge (3) \wedge (4) \wedge (5) \wedge (6) \wedge (9)$
C_1^b : $(1) \wedge (2) \wedge (5) \wedge (6) \wedge (7) \wedge (8) \wedge (9)$
C_1^c : $(1) \wedge (2) \wedge (3) \wedge (4) \wedge (7) \wedge (8) \wedge (9)$
C_2 : $(1) \wedge (2) \wedge (4) \wedge (6) \wedge (8) \wedge (9)$
C_3 : $(1) \wedge (2) \wedge (3) \wedge (5) \wedge (7) \wedge (9)$

In particular, C_1 corresponds to $C_{in}^{\leftrightarrow} \wedge C_{out}^{\leftrightarrow} \wedge C_{undec}^{\leftrightarrow}$, C_1^a to $C_{in}^{\leftrightarrow} \wedge C_{out}^{\leftrightarrow}$, C_1^b to $C_{out}^{\leftrightarrow} \wedge C_{undec}^{\leftrightarrow}$, C_1^c to $C_{in}^{\leftrightarrow} \wedge C_{undec}^{\leftrightarrow}$, C_2 to $C_{in}^{\rightarrow} \wedge C_{out}^{\rightarrow} \wedge C_{undec}^{\rightarrow}$, C_3 to $C_{in}^{\leftarrow} \wedge C_{out}^{\leftarrow} \wedge C_{undec}^{\leftarrow}$.

In Section 4 we evaluate the performance of the overall approach for enumerating the preferred extensions given the above six encodings. In the next section we describe the core of our proposal.

Algorithm 1. Enumerating the preferred extensions of an AF

1: **Input:** $\Gamma = \langle \mathcal{A}, \mathcal{R} \rangle$
2: **Output:** $E_p \subseteq 2^{\mathcal{A}}$
3: $E_p := \emptyset$
4: $cnf := \Pi_\Gamma$
5: **repeat**
6:     $cnfdf := cnf$
7:     $prefcand := \emptyset$
8:     **repeat**
9:         $lastcompfound := SS(cnfdf)$
10:         **if** $lastcompfound \ != \ \varepsilon$ **then**
11:             $prefcand := lastcompfound$
12:             **for** $a \in INARGS(lastcompfound)$ **do**
13:                 $cnfdf := cnfdf \wedge I_{\phi^{-1}(a)}$
14:             **end for**
15:             $remaining := FALSE$
16:             **for** $a \in \mathcal{A} \setminus INARGS(lastcompfound)$ **do**
17:                 $remaining := remaining \vee I_{\phi^{-1}(a)}$
18:             **end for**
19:             $cnfdf := cnfdf \wedge remaining$
20:         **end if**
21:     **until** $(lastcompfound \ != \ \varepsilon \wedge INARGS(lastcompfound) \ != \ \mathcal{A})$
22:     **if** $prefcand \ != \ \emptyset$ **then**
23:         $E_p := E_p \cup \{INARGS(prefcand)\}$
24:         $oppsolution := FALSE$
25:         **for** $a \in \mathcal{A} \setminus INARGS(prefcand)$ **do**
26:             $oppsolution := oppsolution \vee I_{\phi^{-1}(a)}$
27:         **end for**
28:         $cnf := cnf \wedge oppsolution$
29:     **end if**
30: **until** $(prefcand \ != \ \emptyset)$
31: **if** $E_p = \emptyset$ **then**
32:     $E_p = \{\emptyset\}$
33: **end if**
34: **return** E_p

3.2 Enumerating Preferred Extensions

We are now in a position to illustrate the proposed procedure, called PrefSat and listed in Algorithm 1, to enumerate the preferred extensions of an AF $\Gamma = \langle \mathcal{A}, \mathcal{R} \rangle$.

Algorithm 1 resorts to two external functions: SS, and $INARGS$. SS is a SAT solver able to prove unsatisfiability too: it accepts as input a CNF formula and returns a variable assignment satisfying the formula if it exists, ε otherwise. $INARGS$ accepts as input a variable assignment concerning $\mathcal{V}(\Gamma)$ and returns the corresponding set of arguments labelled as in. Moreover we take for granted the computation of Π_Γ from Γ (using one of the equivalent encodings shown in Proposition 4), which is carried out in the initialization phase (line 4).

Theorem 1 proves the correctness of Algorithm 1.

Theorem 1. *Given an AF $\Gamma = \langle \mathcal{A}, \mathcal{R} \rangle$ Algorithm 1 returns $E_p = \mathcal{E}_{\mathcal{PR}}(\Gamma)$.*

The proof of the above Theorem is omitted due to space limitations, but can be found in [15]. However we provide an explanation of the algorithm.

The algorithm mainly consists of two nested **repeat-until** loops. Roughly, the inner loop (lines 8–21) corresponds to a depth-first search which, starting from a non-empty complete extension, produces a sequence of complete extensions strictly ordered by set inclusion. When the sequence can no more be extended, its last element corresponds to a maximal complete extension, namely to a preferred extension. The outer loop (lines 5–30) is in charge of driving the search: it ensures, through proper settings of the variables, that the inner loop is entered with different initial conditions, so that the space of complete extensions is explored and all preferred extensions are found.

Let us now illustrate the operation of Algorithm 1 in detail. Given the correspondence between variable assignments, labellings, and extensions, we will resort to some terminological liberty for the sake of conciseness and clarity (e.g. stating that the solver returns an extension rather than that it returns an assignment which corresponds to a labelling which in turn corresponds to an extension). In the first iteration of the outer loop, the assignment of line 6 results in $cnfdf = \Pi_\Gamma$ in virtue of the initialization of line 4. Then the inner loop is entered and, at line 9, SS is invoked on Π_Γ. Due to the non-emptyness condition in Π_Γ, SS returns ε if the only complete extension (and hence the only preferred extension) of Γ is the empty set. In this case, lines 11–19 are not executed and the loop is directly exited. As a consequence, $prefcand$ is still empty at line 22 and also the outer loop is directly exited. The condition of line 31 then holds, the assignment of line 32 is executed and the algorithm terminates returning $\{\emptyset\}$.

Let us now turn to the more interesting case where there is at least one non-empty complete extension. Then, the first solver invocation returns (non deterministically) one of the non-empty complete extensions of the framework which is assigned to $lastcompfound$ at line 9. Then the condition of line 10 is verified and $lastcompfound$ is set as the candidate preferred extension (line 11). In lines 12–19 the formula $cnfdf$ is updated in order to ensure that the next call to SS returns a complete extension which is a strict superset of $lastcompfound$ (if any exists). This is achieved by imposing that all elements of $lastcompfound$ are labelled in (lines 12–14) and that at least one further argument is labelled in (lines 15–19). In the next iteration (if any), the modified $cnfdf$ is submitted to SS. If a solution is found, the inner loop is iterated in the same way: at each successful iteration a new, strictly larger, complete extension is found. According to the conditions stated in line 21, iteration of the inner loop will then terminate when the call to SS is not successful or when $lastcompfound$ covers all arguments, since in this case no larger complete extension can be found. If a new preferred extension has been found, it is added to the output set E_p (line 23). Then, a formula is produced which ensures that any further solution includes at least an argument not included in the already found one (lines 25–27). This formula is then added to cnf (line 28). The outer loop then restarts resetting variables at lines 6–7 in preparation for a new execution of the inner loop. The inner loop is entered with $cnfdf$ updated at line 6, this ensures that the call to SS either does not find any solution (and then the algorithm terminates returning E_p as already set) or finds a new complete extension which is not a subset of any of the preferred extensions already found and is then extended to a new preferred extension in the subsequent iterations of the loop.

4   The Empirical Analysis

The algorithm described in the previous section has been implemented in C++ and integrated with two alternative SAT solvers, namely PrecoSAT and Glucose. PrecoSAT [10] is the winner of the SAT Competition[3] 2009 on the Application track. Glucose [3,4] is the winner of the SAT Competition in 2011 and of the SAT Challenge 2012 on the Application track.

This choice gave rise to the following two systems:

- PrefSat with PrecoSAT (**PS-PRE**);
- PrefSat with Glucose (**PS-GLU**).

To assess empirically the performance of the proposed approach with respect to other state-of-the-art systems and to compare the two SAT solvers on the SAT instances generated by our approach, we ran a set of tests on randomly generated AFs.

The experimental analysis has been conducted on 2816 AFs that were divided in different classes, according to two dimensions: the number of arguments, $|\mathcal{A}|$ and the criterion of random generation of the attack relation. As to $|\mathcal{A}|$ we considered 8 different values, ranging from 25 to 200 with a step of 25. As to the generation of the attack relation we used two alternative methods. The first method consists in fixing the probability p_{att} that there is an attack for each ordered pair of arguments (self-attacks are included): for each pair a pseudo-random number uniformly distributed between 0 and 1 is generated and if it is lesser or equal to p_{att} the pair is added to the attack relation. We considered three values for p_{att}, namely 0.25, 0.5, and 0.75. Combining the 8 values of $|\mathcal{A}|$ with the 3 values of p_{att} gives rise to 24 test classes, each of which has been populated with 50 AFs.

The second method consists in generating randomly, for each AF, the number n_{att} of attacks it contains (extracted with uniform probability between 0 and $|\mathcal{A}|^2$). Then the n_{att} distinct pairs of arguments constituting the attack relation are selected randomly. Applying the second method with the 8 values of $|\mathcal{A}|$ gives rise to 8 further test classes,

---

[3] http://www.satcompetition.org/

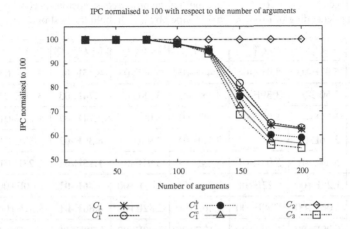

IPC normalised to 100 with respect to the number of arguments

Fig. 2. IPC w.r.t. $|\mathcal{A}|$ (all test cases), comparing **PS-GLU** using respectively encodings C_1, C_1^a, C_1^b, C_1^c, C_2, and C_3 (cf. Proposition 4)

each of which has been populated with 200 AFs. Since the experimental results show minimal changes between the sets of AFs generated with the two methods, hereafter we silently drop this detail.

Further, we also considered, for each value of $|\mathcal{A}|$, the extreme cases of empty attack relation ($p_{att} = n_{att} = 0$) and of fully connected attack relation ($p_{att} = 1, n_{att} = |\mathcal{A}|^2$), thus adding 16 "singleton" test classes.

The tests have been run on the same hardware (a Quad-core Intel(R) Xeon(TM) CPU 2.80GHz with 4 GByte RAM and Linux operating system). As in the learning track of the well-known international planning competition (IPC) [25], a limit of 15 minutes was imposed to compute the preferred extensions for each AF. No limit was imposed on the RAM usage, but a run fails at saturation of the available memory, including the swap area. The systems under evaluation have been compared with respect to the ability to produce solutions within the time limit and to the execution time (obtained as the real value of the command `time -p`). As to the latter comparison, we adopted the IPC speed score, also borrowed from the planning community, which is defined as follows:

- For each test case (in our case, each test AF) let T^* be the best execution time among the compared systems (if no system produces the solution within the time limit, the test case is not considered valid and ignored).
- For each valid case, each system gets a score of $1/(1 + \log_{10}(T/T^*))$, where T is its execution time, or a score of 0 if it fails in that case. Runtimes below 1 sec get by default the maximal score of 1.
- The (non normalised) IPC score for a system is the sum of its scores over all the valid test cases. The normalised IPC score ranges from 0 to 100 and is defined as ($IPC/\#$ of valid cases) $* 100$.

First of all, we ran an investigation on which of the alternative encodings introduced in Proposition 4 performs best. While there are cases where **PS-PRE** performs better

Table 1. Average time (in seconds) for computing the preferred extensions according to the different labellings encoding of Proposition 4 grouped by $|\mathcal{A}|$. In bold the best one.

$|\mathcal{A}|$	C_1	C_1^a	C_1^b	C_1^c	C_2	C_3
25	5.97E-03	5.91E-03	5.43E-03	5.31E-03	**6.25E-04**	3.92E-03
50	3.50E-02	3.39E-02	3.38E-02	3.38E-02	**9.74E-03**	3.10E-02
75	1.06E-01	1.02E-01	1.05E-01	1.06E-01	**2.74E-02**	1.02E-01
100	2.76E-01	2.65E-01	2.78E-01	2.91E-01	**6.39E-02**	2.89E-01
125	5.24E-01	5.03E-01	5.54E-01	5.95E-01	**1.15E-01**	6.23E-01
150	1.27E+00	1.22E+00	1.39E+00	1.43E+00	**2.46E-01**	1.60E+00
175	2.06E+00	1.98E+00	2.46E+00	2.82E+00	**4.80E-01**	3.51E+00
200	5.00E+00	4.89E+00	6.17E+00	7.90E+00	**1.38E+00**	1.00E+01

using C_1^a and others where it performs better using C_2 (with minimal differences on average), it is always outperformed by **PS-GLU** using C_2, thus we refer to **PS-GLU** to illustrate the difference of performance induced by the alternative encodings. In Figure 2, we compare the empirical results obtained by executing **PS-GLU**, and Table 1 summarises the average times. It is worth to mention that **PS-GLU** always computed the preferred extensions irrespective of the chosen encoding, therefore the differences in the IPC scores are due to different execution times only. As we can see, the overall performance is significantly dependent on the set of conditions used, where the greatest performance (considering the generated AFs) is C_2, and then in sequence, generally C_1^a, C_1, C_1^b, C_1^c and C_3, although we have empirical evidences [15] showing that on dense graphs there are situations where C_3 performs better than C_1.

In order to evaluate the overall performance of Algorithm 1 (cf. Section 3), let us compare **PS-PRE** and **PS-GLU** both using encoding C_2 with the other three notable systems at the state of the art:

- ASPARTIX with `dlv` as ASP solver (denoted as **ASP**);
- ASPARTIX-META with `gringo` as grounder and `claspD` as ASP solver (denoted as **ASP-META**) as presented in [22];
- the system presented in [28] (**NOF**).

None of five (considering also our **PS-GLU** and **PS-PRE**) systems uses parallel execution.

Concerning the ability to produce solutions, Figure 3 summarizes the results concerning all test cases grouped w.r.t. $|\mathcal{A}|$. **PS-GLU**, **PS-PRE** (both exploiting C_2 encoding), and **ASP-META** were able to produce the solution in all cases. On the other hand, the success rate of both **ASP** and **NOF** decreases significantly with the increase of $|\mathcal{A}|$. We observed that the failure reasons are quite different: **ASP** reached in all its failure cases the 15 minutes time limit, while **NOF** ran out of memory before reaching the time limit. In the light of this observation, **NOF**'s evaluation has certainly been negatively

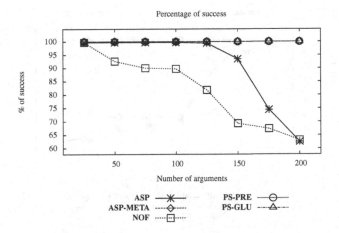

Fig. 3. Percentage of success over all test cases

affected by the relatively scarce memory availability of the test platform, but, from another perspective, the results obtained on this platform give a clear indication about the different resource needs of the compared systems.

Table 2. Average time (in seconds) for computing the preferred extensions needed by the five systems grouped by $|\mathcal{A}|$ on AF s for which all the systems computed correctly the preferred extensions. In bold the best one.

$|\mathcal{A}|$	ASP	ASP-META	NOF	PS-PRE	PS-GLU
25	7.78E-02	2.70E-01	3.24E-01	3.87E-03	**6.27E-04**
50	3.32E-01	1.00E+00	5.43E-01	2.32E-02	**1.04E-02**
75	1.03E+00	2.30E+00	1.18E+00	5.98E-02	**2.96E-02**
100	3.75E+00	4.33E+00	3.81E+00	1.36E-01	**6.84E-02**
125	1.63E+01	6.95E+00	8.50E+00	2.46E-01	**1.24E-01**
150	3.16E+01	1.16E+01	1.47E+01	4.59E-01	**2.24E-01**
175	6.65E+01	1.61E+01	2.64E+01	6.65E-01	**3.21E-01**
200	1.24E+02	2.27E+01	5.02E+01	1.02E+00	**4.79E-01**

Turning to the comparison of execution times, Figure 4 presents the values of normalised IPC considering all test cases grouped w.r.t. $|\mathcal{A}|$, while Table 2 shows the average time needed by the five systems for computing the preferred extension. Both **PS-PRE** and **PS-GLU** performed significantly better (note that the IPC score is logarithmic) than **ASP** and **NOF** for all values of $|\mathcal{A}| > 25$, and the performance gap

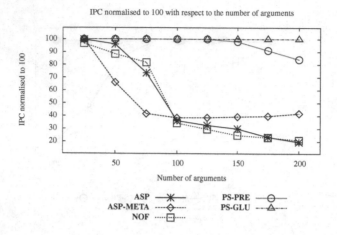

IPC normalised to 100 with respect to the number of arguments

ASP —✳—   PS-PRE ⋯◯⋯
ASP-META ⋯◇⋯   PS-GLU —△—
NOF ⋯▢⋯

Fig. 4. IPC w.r.t. $|\mathcal{A}|$ (all test cases)

increases with increasing $|\mathcal{A}|$. Moreover, **PS-GLU** is significantly faster than **PS-PRE** for $|\mathcal{A}| > 175$ (again the performance gap increases with increasing $|\mathcal{A}|$). **ASP** and **NOF** obtained quite similar IPC values with more evident differences at lower values of $|\mathcal{A}|$. Surprisingly, **ASP-META** performed worse that its older version **ASP** (and also of **NOF**) on frameworks with number of arguments up to 100 (cf. Table 2). Although this may seem in contrast with results provided in [22], it has to be remarked that the IPC measure is logarithmic w.r.t. the best execution time, while [22, Fig. 1] uses a linear scale, and this turned to be a disadvantage when analysing the overall performance. Indeed, the maximum difference of execution times between **ASP** and **ASP-META** executed on frameworks up to 100 arguments is around 1.2 seconds, while the axis of ordinate of [22, Fig. 1] ranges between 0 and 300, thus making impossible to note this difference.

5   Comparison with Related Works

The relationship between argumentation semantics and the satisfiability problem has been already considered in the literature, but less effort has been devoted to the study of a SAT-based algorithm and its empirical evaluation. For instance, in [9] three approaches determining semantics extensions are preliminary described, namely the *equational checking*, the *model checking*, and the *satisfiability cheking* of which three different formulations for, respectively, stable extension, admissible set, and complete extension are presented from a theoretical perspective, without providing any empirical evaluation.

More recently, in [11], and similarly in [1], relationships between argumentation semantics and constraint satisfaction problems are studied, with different formulation for each semantics or decision problem. In particular, [1] proposes an extensive study of CSP formulations for decision problems related to stable, preferred, complete, grounded and admissible semantics, while [11] shows an empirical evaluation of their approach through their software ConArg, but for conflict-free, admissible, complete and stable extensions only.

Probably the most relevant work is [23], where a method for computing credulous and skeptical acceptance for preferred, semi-stable, and stage semantics has been studied, implemented, and empirically evaluated using an algorithm based upon a NP-oracle, namely a SAT solver. Differently from our work, this approach is focused on acceptance problems only and does not address the problem of how to enumerate the extensions. As we do believe that the approach we showed in this paper can be easily adapted for dealing with both credulous acceptance (we have just to force the SAT solver to consider a given argument as labelled in) and skeptical acceptance (we have just to check whether a given argument is in all the extensions), we have already started a theoretical and empirical investigation on this subject. Recently, a similar approach using SAT techniques in the context of semi-stable and eager semantics has been provided in [30]. A detailed comparison with this approach is already planned and represents an important future work.

Finally, as the computation of the preferred extension using [14]'s labelling approach requires a maximisation process, at a first sight this seems to be quite close to a MaxSAT problem [2], which is a generalisation of the satisfiability problem. The idea is that sometimes some constraints of a problem can not be satisfied, and a solver should try to satisfy the maximum number of them. Although there are approaches aimed at finding the maximum w.r.t. set inclusion satisfiable constraints (i.e. nOPTSAT[4]), the MaxSAT problem is conceptually different from the problem of finding the preferred extensions. Indeed, for determining the preferred extensions we maximise the acceptability of a subset of variables, while in the MaxSAT problem it is not possible to bound such a maximisation to a subset of variables only. However, a deeper investigation that may lead to the definition of argumentation semantics as MaxSAT problems is already envisaged as a future work.

6 Conclusions

We presented a novel SAT-based approach for preferred extension enumeration in abstract argumentation and assessed its performances by an empirical comparison with other state-of-the-art systems. The proposed approach turns out to be efficient and to generally outperform the best known dedicated algorithm and the ASP-based approach implemented in the ASPARTIX system. The proposed approach appears to be applicable for extension enumeration of other semantics (in particular stable and semi-stable) and this represents an immediate direction of future work. As to performance assessment, we are not aware of other systematic comparisons concerning computation efficiency in Dung's framework apart the results presented in [28], where different test sets were used for each pairwise comparison, with a maximum argument cardinality of 45. The comparison provided in [22] is aimed just at showing the differences between the two different encoding of ASPARTIX. Java-based tools mainly conceived for

---

[4] www.star.dist.unige.it/~emanuele/nOPTSAT/

interactive use, like ConArg [11] or Dungine [29], are not suitable for a systematic efficiency comparison on large test sets and could not be considered in this work. It can be remarked however that they adopt alternative solution strategies (translation to a CSP problem in ConArg, argument games in Dungine) whose performance evaluation is an important subject of future work.

In addition, we will consider other procedures for generating random argumentation frameworks, as well as argumentation frameworks derived from knowledge bases. As pointed out by one of the reviewer, these derived argumentation frameworks can be infinite: in these case, providing a suitable algorithm using the most recent approaches for representing infinite argumentation frameworks [8] is an interesting avenue for future research.

We are also currently working to integrate the proposed approach into the SCC-recursive schema introduced in [7] to encompass several semantics (including grounded, preferred and stable semantics). More specifically, the approach proposed in this paper can be applied to the sub-frameworks involved in the base-case of the recursion: since such local application decreases the number of variables involved, we expect a dramatic performance increase.

Acknowledgement. The authors thank the anonymous reviewers for their helpful comments. In addition, they thank Samir Nofal for kindly providing the source code of his algorithm.

References

1. Amgoud, L., Devred, C.: Argumentation frameworks as constraint satisfaction problems. Annals of Mathematics and Artificial Intelligence, 1–18 (2013)
2. Ansótegui, C., Bonet, M.L., Levy, J.: SAT-based MaxSAT. Artificial Intelligence 196, 77–105 (2013)
3. Audemard, G., Simon, L.: Predicting learnt clauses quality in modern SAT solvers. In: Proceedings of IJCAI 2009, pp. 399–404 (2009)
4. Audemard, G., Simon, L.: Glucose 2.1 (2012),
   http://www.lri.fr/~simon/?page=glucose
5. Baroni, P., Caminada, M., Giacomin, M.: An introduction to argumentation semantics. Knowledge Engineering Review 26(4), 365–410 (2011)
6. Baroni, P., Giacomin, M.: Semantics of abstract argumentation systems. In: Argumentation in Artificial Intelligence, pp. 25–44. Springer (2009)
7. Baroni, P., Giacomin, M., Guida, G.: SCC-recursiveness: a general schema for argumentation semantics. Artificial Intelligence 168(1-2), 165–210 (2005)
8. Baroni, P., Cerutti, F., Dunne, P.E., Giacomin, M.: Automata for infinite argumentation structures. Artificial Intelligence 203, 104–150 (2013)
9. Besnard, P., Doutre, S.: Checking the acceptability of a set of arguments. In: Proceedings of NMR 2004, pp. 59–64 (2004)
10. Biere, A.: P{re,ic}oSAT@sc 2009. In: SAT Competition (2009)
11. Bistarelli, S., Santini, F.: Modeling and solving AFs with a constraint-based tool: Conarg. In: Modgil, S., Oren, N., Toni, F. (eds.) TAFA 2011. LNCS (LNAI), vol. 7132, pp. 99–116. Springer, Heidelberg (2012)

12. Caminada, M.: On the issue of reinstatement in argumentation. In: Fisher, M., van der Hoek, W., Konev, B., Lisitsa, A. (eds.) JELIA 2006. LNCS (LNAI), vol. 4160, pp. 111–123. Springer, Heidelberg (2006)
13. Caminada, M.: Semi-stable semantics. In: Proceedings of COMMA 2006, pp. 121–130 (2006)
14. Caminada, M., Gabbay, D.M.: A logical account of formal argumentation. Studia Logica (Special Issue: New Ideas in Argumentation Theory) 93(2-3), 109–145 (2009)
15. Cerutti, F., Dunne, P.E., Giacomin, M., Vallati, M.: Computing Preferred Extensions in Abstract Argumentation: a SAT-based Approach. Tech. rep. (2013), http://arxiv.org/abs/1310.4986
16. Dimopoulos, Y., Nebel, B., Toni, F.: Preferred arguments are harder to compute than stable extensions. In: Proceedings of IJCAI 1999, pp. 36–43 (1999)
17. Dimopoulos, Y., Torres, A.: Graph theoretical structures in logic programs and default theories. Journal Theoretical Computer Science 170, 209–244 (1996)
18. Doutre, S., Mengin, J.: Preferred extensions of argumentation frameworks: Query answering and computation. In: Goré, R., Leitsch, A., Nipkow, T. (eds.) IJCAR 2001. LNCS (LNAI), vol. 2083, pp. 272–288. Springer, Heidelberg (2001)
19. Dung, P.M.: On the acceptability of arguments and its fundamental role in nonmonotonic reasoning, logic programming, and n-person games. Artificial Intelligence 77(2), 321–357 (1995)
20. Dung, P., Mancarella, P., Toni, F.: A dialectic procedure for sceptical, assumption-based argumentation. In: Proceedings of COMMA 2006, pp. 145–156 (2006)
21. Dunne, P.E., Wooldridge, M.: Complexity of abstract argumentation. In: Argumentation in Artificial Intelligence, pp. 85–104. Springer (2009)
22. Dvořák, W., Gaggl, S.A., Wallner, J., Woltran, S.: Making use of advances in answer-set programming for abstract argumentation systems. In: Proceedings of INAP 2011 (2011)
23. Dvořák, W., Järvisalo, M., Wallner, J.P., Woltran, S.: Complexity-sensitive decision procedures for abstract argumentation. In: Proceedings of KR 2012. AAAI Press (2012)
24. Egly, U., Gaggl, S.A., Woltran, S.: Aspartix: Implementing argumentation frameworks using answer-set programming. In: de la Garcia Banda, M., Pontelli, E. (eds.) ICLP 2008. LNCS, vol. 5366, pp. 734–738. Springer, Heidelberg (2008)
25. Jiménez, S., de la Rosa, T., Fernández, S., Fernández, F., Borrajo, D.: A review of machine learning for automated planning. Knowledge Engineering Review 27(4), 433–467 (2012)
26. Leone, N., Pfeifer, G., Faber, W., Eiter, T., Gottlob, G., Perri, S., Scarcello, F.: The DLV system for knowledge representation and reasoning. ACM Transactions on Computational Logic 7(3), 499–562 (2006)
27. Modgil, S., Caminada, M.: Proof theories and algorithms for abstract argumentation frameworks. In: Argumentation in Artificial Intelligence, pp. 105–129. Springer (2009)
28. Nofal, S., Dunne, P.E., Atkinson, K.: On preferred extension enumeration in abstract argumentation. In: Proceedings of COMMA 2012, pp. 205–216 (2012)
29. South, M., Vreeswijk, G., Fox, J.: Dungine: A Java Dung reasoner. In: Proceedings of COMMA 2008, pp. 360–368 (2008)
30. Wallner, J.P., Weissenbacher, G., Woltran, S.: Advanced SAT techniques for abstract argumentation. In: Leite, J., Son, T.C., Torroni, P., van der Torre, L., Woltran, S. (eds.) CLIMA XIV 2013. LNCS (LNAI), vol. 8143, pp. 138–154. Springer, Heidelberg (2013)

Computing Preferred Labellings by Exploiting SCCs and Most Sceptically Rejected Arguments

Beishui Liao, Liyun Lei*, and Jianhua Dai

Center for the Study of Language and Cognition,
Zhejiang University, Hangzhou 310028, P.R. China
269316550@qq.com

Abstract. The computation of preferred labellings of an abstract argumentation framework (or briefly, AF) is generally intractable. The existing decomposition-based approach by exploiting strongly connected components (SCCs) of a general AF is promising to cope with this problem. However, the efficiency of this approach is highly limited by the maximal SCC of an AF. This paper presents a further solution by exploiting the most sceptically rejected arguments of an AF. Given an AF, its grounded labelling is first generated. Then, the attacks between the undecided arguments and the rejected arguments are removed. It turns out that the modified AF has the same preferred labellings as the original AF, but the maximal SCC in it could be much smaller than that of the original AF. Empirical results show that this new method dramatically reduces the computation time for some sparse AFs (for instance, when the ratio of the number of edges to the number of nodes of an AF is between 1:1 and 1.8:1).

Keywords: Argumentation, Semantics, Labellings, Computational Complexity.

1 Introduction

Argumentation is an increasingly active research area in AI. One of the most important problems of this area is that many natural problems are computationally intractable [1]. While the worst-case computational complexity of argumentation has been well formulated, how to efficiently compute the argumentation semantics is still an open problem. To the best of our knowledge, the existing work related to this problem mainly consists of the following three lines. The first line of work is on identifying tractable classes of argumentation frameworks (AFs) with special structures [1], and developing efficient algorithms for some classes of AFs with fixed parameters, such as bounded tree-width [2] and bounded clique-width [3], etc. And, in [4], Dvořák et al proposed a generic approach for solving hard problems in the area of argumentation in a "complexity-sensitive" way. The corresponding empirical results showed that their approach significantly outperforms existing systems developed for hard argumentation problems (i.e.,

---

* Corresponding author.

E. Black, S. Modgil, and N. Oren (Eds.): TAFA 2013, LNAI 8306, pp. 194–208, 2014.
© Springer-Verlag Berlin Heidelberg 2014

problems under the preferred, semi-stable, or stage semantics). The second line of work is on developing more efficient algorithms by means of some specific mechanisms. For instance, in [5], the authors proposed a more efficient algorithm for enumerating all preferred extensions, by utilizing further labels to improve labels' transitions. The third line of work is on decomposition-based computation. In [6], the authors proposed an SCC-recursive scheme for argumentation semantics, based on decomposition along the SCCs of an AF. In [7], the authors developed splitting-based algorithms for the computation of extensions. Their experimental results showed an average improvement by 50% and by 54% for preferred and stable semantics respectively, compared to Modgil and Caminada's algorithms [8]. In [9] and [10], we proposed methods to efficiently compute, respectively, the dynamic semantics and the partial semantics of argumentation, by means of decomposition and semantics combination. In [11] and [12], we formulated an approach to compute the extensions of an AF by exploiting its SCCs and acyclic fragments.

While the existing approaches have made some progress on developing tractable algorithms for some AFs with special topologies or more efficient algorithms for a general AF, it is still a challenging problem to further improve the efficiency of computing the semantics of a general AF in which the ratio of the number of attacks to the number of arguments is no less than 1:1. According to the theory formulated in [11], one possible way to cope with this problem is to decompose an AF into a set of SCCs, and compute the status of arguments in each SCC separately. However, the efficiency of this approach is highly limited by the size of the *maximal* SCC.

In this paper, we introduce a further solution by exploiting the *most sceptically rejected arguments* (or briefly, MSR arguments) and SCCs of an AF. The feasibility of this approach lies in a new discovery that after removing some attacks related to MSR arguments from an AF, the status of arguments in the AF are unaffected, while the maximal SCC of the modified AF is often much smaller than that of the original AF. Since preferred semantics is a typical semantics of argumentation, and its computation is one of the most difficult ones, in this paper, for simplicity and without loss of generality, we only consider the computation under this semantics. Furthermore, since the labelling-based approach is one of the two mainstream approaches for formulating argumentation semantics, and it is closer to algorithms, we only study the computation of the preferred semantics that is formulated by the labelling-based approach.

The remaining contents of this paper are organised as follows. In the next section, we briefly introduce some basic notions of argumentation and some typical algorithms for computing argumentation semantics. In Section 3, we introduce an approach for computing preferred labellings by exploiting the SCCs of an AF. In Sections 4 and 5, we first propose a further solution by exploiting both the SCCs and MSR arguments of an AF, and then conduct an empirical investigation. Finally, in Section 6, we conclude the paper.

2   Preliminaries

2.1   Semantics of Argumentation Frameworks

In this paper, we only deal with (abstract) argumentation frameworks [13]. An argumentation framework (or briefly, AF) is defined as a tuple (A, R), in which A is a set of arguments and $R \subseteq A \times A$ is a set of attacks. For all $\alpha, \beta \in A$, we often use $(\alpha, \beta) \in R$ to denote that α attacks β. It is obvious that an AF is in fact a directed graph (often called a *defeat graph*), where the nodes represent arguments and edges represent attacks. Figure 1 illustrates an AF (A_1, R_1).

$$1 \rightleftarrows 2 \longrightarrow 3$$

Fig. 1. (A_1, R_1)

Given an AF, a fundamental problem is to determine which arguments can be regarded as (collectively) acceptable. There are two mainstream approaches to resolve this problem: extension-based approach and labelling-based approach [14]. The former defines various criteria (called *argumentation semantics*) under which a set (sets) of arguments are regarded as acceptable, while the latter is to assign a "reasonable" label to each argument, according to some criteria.

In the extension-based approach, a set of collectively acceptable arguments is called an *extension*. A core notion of this approach is *admissible sets*. Specifically, given an AF (A, R), a set of arguments is *admissible*, if and only if it is *conflict-free* and it can *defend* each argument within the set. A set $B \subseteq A$ is *conflict-free* if and only if there exist no arguments α and β in B such that $(\alpha, \beta) \in R$. Argument $\alpha \in A$ is *defended* by a set $B \subseteq A$ if and only if for all $\beta \in A$, if $(\beta, \alpha) \in R$, then there exists $\gamma \in B$ such that $(\gamma, \beta) \in R$. An admissible set is called a *complete extension*, if and only if it contains all arguments it can defend. Given an AF, there might exist several complete extensions, in which the maximal ones (w.r.t. set inclusion) are called *preferred extensions*, while the minimal one (w.r.t. set inclusion) is called the *grounded extension* (the grounded extension of an AF is unique). The AF (A_1, R_1) has three complete extensions $\{\}$, $\{1, 3\}$ and $\{2\}$, two preferred extensions $\{1, 3\}$ and $\{2\}$, and one grounded extension $\{\}$.

On the other hand, in the labelling-based approach, there are usually three different labels: IN, OUT and UNDEC. An argument is IN if all its attackers are OUT. An argument is OUT if it is attacked by an argument that is IN. An argument is UNDEC, if it is neither IN nor OUT [15]. Given (A, R) and the three labels, a *labelling* is a total function $\mathcal{L} : A \mapsto \{\text{IN, OUT, UNDEC}\}$. The definition of labelling-based semantics is based on the notion of *legal labelling*. More specifically, an argument is legally IN if and only if it is labelled IN and each attacker is labelled OUT; an argument is legally OUT if and only if it is labelled OUT and there exists an attacker that is labelled IN; an argument is

legally UNDEC if and only if it is not the case that (1) each attacker is labelled
OUT or (2) there exists an attacker that is labelled IN. Then, a labelling $\mathcal{L}$ is
called an *admissible labelling*, if and only if each IN-labelled argument is legally
IN, and each OUT-labelled argument is legally OUT; $\mathcal{L}$ is called a *complete
labelling*, if and only if it is an admissible labelling and each UNDEC-labelled
argument is legally UNDEC; $\mathcal{L}$ is called a *preferred labelling*, if and only if it
is an admissible labelling and the set of IN-labelled arguments is maximal; $\mathcal{L}$ is
called a *grounded labelling*, if and only if it is a complete labelling and the set of
IN-labelled arguments is minimal.

Let $in(\mathcal{L}) = \{\alpha : \mathcal{L}(\alpha) = IN\}$, $out(\mathcal{L}) = \{\alpha : \mathcal{L}(\alpha) = OUT\}$ and $undec(\mathcal{L}) = \{\alpha : \mathcal{L}(\alpha) = UNDEC\}$. A labelling $\mathcal{L}$ is often represented as a triple of the
form $(in(\mathcal{L}), out(\mathcal{L}), undec(\mathcal{L}))$. Accordingly, the AF (A_1, R_1) in Figure 1 has
two preferred labellings: $\mathcal{L}_1 = (\{1,3\}, \{2\}, \{\})$ and $\mathcal{L}_2 = (\{2\}, \{1,3\}, \{\})$, as
illustrated in Figure 2.

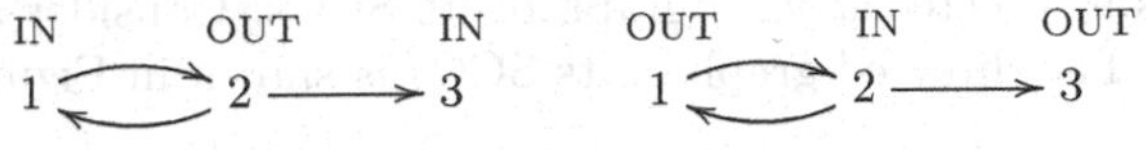

Fig. 2. Preferred labellings of (A_1, R_1)

As summarised in [14], there exists a bijective correspondence between complete (respectively, preferred and grounded) labelling(s) and complete (respectively, preferred and grounded) extension(s).

2.2 Algorithms for Computing Argument Labellings

In existing literature, there are mainly two approaches for computing labellings
(extensions): labelling-based algorithms and answer-set programming. It has
been recognised that Modgil and Caminada's labelling-based algorithms (briefly,
MC algorithms) [8] have received much attention and been compared with some
newly proposed algorithms ([7], [5], etc).

According to MC algorithms, generating the grounded labelling of an AF is
simple. It starts by assigning IN to all arguments that are not attacked, and then
iteratively: OUT is assigned to any argument that is attacked by an argument
that has just been made IN, and then IN to those arguments all of whose attackers are OUT. The iteration continues until no more new arguments are made IN
or OUT. Any arguments that remain unlabelled are then assigned UNDEC.

By comparison, the MC algorithm for computing preferred labellings is more
complex. It computes *admissible labellings* that maximise the number of arguments that are legally IN. Admissible labellings are generated by starting with
a labelling that labels all arguments IN and then iteratively, selects arguments
that are illegally IN (or *super-illegally* IN) and applies a *transition step* to obtain
a new labelling, until a lablling is reached in which no argument is illegally IN.
For the details of this algorithm, readers may refer to [8].

3   An Approach by Exploiting SCCs

In this section, based on [11,12], we introduce an approach for the computation of preferred labellings by exploiting the SCCs of an AF (called the *SCC-based approach*). The basic idea of this approach is as follows. Given an AF, it is first decomposed into a set of sub-frameworks according to the SCCs of the AF. Then, along the order of SCCs, the preferred labellings of the sub-frameworks are generated separately, and combined incrementally to form the labellings of the original AF.

Decomposing a general AF according to its SCCs Since an AF can be viewed as a directed graph and the set of SCCs of a directed graph can be obtained by a polynomial time algorithm [16], it is intuitively feasible to decompose an AF along its SCCs [6].

According to graph theory, an important property of SCCs is that every directed graph is a directed *acyclic* graph of its SCCs. Consider an AF (A_2, R_2) in Figure 3(a). The directed graph of its SCCs is shown in Figure 3(b).

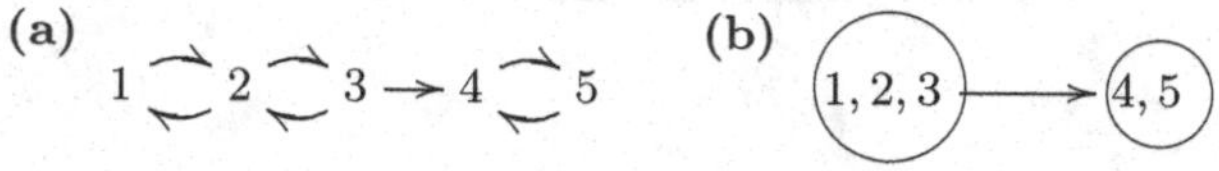

Fig. 3. (A_2, R_2) and the directed acyclic graph of its SCCs

Since there exists a partial order over all SCCs, it is possible to compute separately the preferred labellings of each *sub-framework* induced by an SCC. Now, let us define the notion of a sub-framework induced by an SCC.

Let $\{C_1, \ldots, C_n\}$ be the set of SCCs of an AF (A, R). It holds that $C_1, \ldots,$ and C_n are a partition of A. Let $R_{C_i} = R \cap (C_i \times C_i)$ be the set of attacks between the arguments in C_i, $C_i^- = \{\alpha \in A \backslash C_i : \exists \beta \in C_i,$ such that $(\alpha, \beta) \in R\}$ be the set of arguments outside C_i that attack the arguments in C_i, and $I_{C_i} = R \cap (C_i^- \times C_i)$ be the set of interactions from the arguments in C_i^- to the arguments in C_i, in which $1 \le i \le n$. In terms of [9], C_i^- is called the set of *conditioning arguments*. A sub-framework of (A, R) induced by C_i is then defined as a tuple:

$$(C_i \cup C_i^-, R_{C_i} \cup I_{C_i}) \tag{1}$$

Computing the preferred labellings of each sub-framework In Formula (1) , when $C_i^- = \emptyset$ (and thus $I_{C_i} = \emptyset$), $(C_i \cup C_i^-, R_{C_i} \cup I_{C_i}) = (C_i, R_{C_i})$. In this case, the sub-framework is not related to any external arguments. Hence, its preferred labellings can be computed independently. On the contrary, when $C_i^- \neq \emptyset$, the labels of arguments in C_i^- are not assigned within $(C_i \cup C_i^-, R_{C_i} \cup I_{C_i})$, but assigned in an external sub-framework.

Consider the example in Figure 3. According to Formula (1), we get two sub-frameworks as shown in Figures 4(a) and 4(b). The sub-framework in Figure 4(a) has two preferred labellings: $\mathcal{L}_1 = (\{1,3\},\{2\},\{\})$ (Figure 4(c)) and $\mathcal{L}_2 = (\{2\}, \{1,3\},\{\})$ (Figure 4(e)). With respect to $\mathcal{L}_k$ ($k \in \{1,2\}$), we get a *partially labelled sub-framework* of $(\{3,4,5\},\{(3,4),(4,5),(5,4)\})$, denoted as $(\{3,4,5\},\{(3,4),(4,5),(5,4)\})^{\mathcal{L}_k}$, in which the label of the conditioning argument 3 conforms to $\mathcal{L}_k$. These two partially labelled sub-frameworks are respectively illustrated in Figures 4(d) and 4(f).

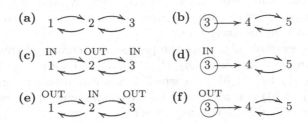

Fig. 4. Sub-frameworks and partially labelled sub-frameworks

Let $(P \cup P^-, R_P \cup I_P)^{\mathcal{L}}$ be a partially labelled sub-framework of (A, R), in which the labels of arguments in P^- conform to $\mathcal{L}$ that is a preferred labelling of an external sub-framework. Let $\mathcal{L}'$ be a labelling of $(P \cup P^-, R_P \cup I_P)^{\mathcal{L}}$, such that the labels for arguments in P^- conform to $\mathcal{L}$, while each argument in P is assigned with a new label. Then, $\mathcal{L}'$ is called an *admissible labelling*, if and only if each argument in P that is labeled IN is legally IN, and each argument in P that is labeled OUT is legally OUT. $\mathcal{L}'$ is called a *preferred labelling*, if and only if it is an admissible labelling and the set of arguments in P that are labelled IN is maximal. Let us return to the above example. It holds that $\mathcal{L}_3 = (\{3,5\},\{4\},\{\})$ is a preferred labelling of $(\{3,4,5\},\{(3,4),(4,5),(5,4)\})^{\mathcal{L}_1}$ (Figure 4(d)), in that argument 5 is legally IN, argument 4 is legally OUT, and $\{5\}$ is the maximal set of arguments in $\{4,5\}$ that are legally IN. Similarly, $\mathcal{L}_4 = (\{4\},\{3,5\},\{\})$ and $\mathcal{L}_5 = (\{5\},\{3,4\},\{\})$ are preferred labellings of $(\{3,4,5\},\{(3,4),(4,5),(5,4)\})^{\mathcal{L}_2}$ (Figure 4(f)).

Labelling combination When an AF has only two SCCs, in which one is restricted by another, the labelling combination is simple. Formally, let (A, R) be an AF, and P and Q be a partition of A, such that $P^- \subseteq Q$ and $Q^- = \{\}$. For every preferred labelling $\mathcal{L}$ of (Q, R_Q), $(P \cup P^-, R_P \cup I_P)^{\mathcal{L}}$ is a partially labelled sub-framework. Then, for every preferred labelling $\mathcal{L}'$ of $(P \cup P^-, R_P \cup I_P)^{\mathcal{L}}$, the combination of $\mathcal{L}$ and $\mathcal{L}'$ is defined as $\mathcal{L} + \mathcal{L}' = (in(\mathcal{L}) \cup in(\mathcal{L}'), out(\mathcal{L}) \cup out(\mathcal{L}'), undec(\mathcal{L}) \cup undec(\mathcal{L}'))$, which is a combined labelling of (A, R).

For instance, the preferred labellings of (A_2, R_2) in Figure 3(a) can be obtained by the following way. We combine $\mathcal{L}_1$ with $\mathcal{L}_3$, $\mathcal{L}_2$ with $\mathcal{L}_4$, and $\mathcal{L}_2$

with $\mathcal{L}_5$, obtaining three combined labellings as follows: $(\{1,3,5\}, \{2,4\}, \{\})$, $(\{2,4\}, \{1,3,5\}, \{\})$ and $(\{2,5\}, \{1,3,4\}, \{\})$. In [9], we have proved the soundness and completeness of this kind of semantics combination under the context of extension-based approach. Since there is a one-to-one correspondence between sets of preferred labellings and sets of preferred extensions, the above labelling combination is correct.

When an AF has more than two SCCs, its sub-frameworks are organised into several layers conforming to the partial order of the SCCs of the AF. Then, the labellings of the AF are computed and combined incrementally, from the lowest layer in which each sub-framework is not restricted by other sub-frameworks, to the highest layer in which each sub-framework is most restricted by the sub-frameworks located in the lower layers.

The following example illustrates the process of incremental combination of preferred labellings. Compared to (A_2, R_2), (A'_2, R'_2) in Figure 5(a) has two more sub-frameworks $(\{1,6\}, \{(1,6)\})$ (in which 1 is a conditioning argument) and $(\{3,4,7\}, \{(3,7),(4,7)\})$ (in which 3 and 4 are conditioning arguments), located in the second and the third layer, respectively.

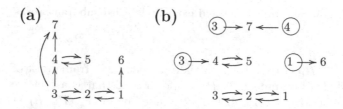

Fig. 5. (A'_2, R'_2) and a layered decomposition of it

With respect to $\mathcal{L}_1$ and $\mathcal{L}_2$ mentioned above (Figures 4(c) and 4(e)), there are two partially labelled sub-frameworks of $(\{1,6\}, \{(1,6)\})$, i.e., $(\{1,6\}, \{(1,6)\})^{\mathcal{L}_1}$ and $(\{1,6\}, \{(1,6)\})^{\mathcal{L}_2}$. The former has a preferred labelling $\mathcal{L}_6 = (\{1\}, \{6\}, \{\})$, while the later has a preferred labelling $\mathcal{L}_7 = (\{6\}, \{1\}, \{\})$.

Before the labellings of the second layer are combined with those of the first layer, the labellings of the sub-frameworks in the second layer are first combined. After combination, $\mathcal{L}_3 + \mathcal{L}_6$ is a preferred labelling of $(\{1,3,4,5,6\}, \{(3,4),(4,5),$ $(5,4),(1,6)\})^{\mathcal{L}_1}$, and $\mathcal{L}_4 + \mathcal{L}_7$ and $\mathcal{L}_5 + \mathcal{L}_7$ are preferred labellings of $(\{1,3,4,5,6\},$ $\{(3,4),(4,5),(5,4),(1,6)\})^{\mathcal{L}_2}$.

Then, the labellings of the first and the second layers are combined, resulting $\mathcal{L}_1 + \mathcal{L}_3 + \mathcal{L}_6 = (\{1,3,5\}, \{2,4,6\}, \{\})$, $\mathcal{L}_2 + \mathcal{L}_4 + \mathcal{L}_7 = (\{2,4,6\}, \{1,3,5\}, \{\})$ and $\mathcal{L}_2 + \mathcal{L}_5 + \mathcal{L}_7 = (\{2,5,6\}, \{1,3,4\}, \{\})$, which are prefered labellings of the sub-framework $(\{1,2,3,4,5,6\}, \{(1,2),(2,1),(2,3),(3,2),(3,4),(4,5),(5,4),(1,6)\})$.

And then, let $\mathcal{L}_8 = \mathcal{L}_1 + \mathcal{L}_3 + \mathcal{L}_6$, $\mathcal{L}_9 = \mathcal{L}_2 + \mathcal{L}_4 + \mathcal{L}_7$ and $\mathcal{L}_{10} = \mathcal{L}_2 + \mathcal{L}_5 + \mathcal{L}_7$. With respect to $\mathcal{L}_8$, $\mathcal{L}_9$ and $\mathcal{L}_{10}$, in the third layer, there are three partially labelled sub-frameworks of $(\{3,4,7\}, \{(3,7),(4,7)\})$, i.e., $(\{3,4,7\}, \{(3,7),(4,7)\})^{\mathcal{L}_8}$,

$(\{3,4,7\},\{(3,7),(4,7)\})^{\mathcal{L}_9}$ and $(\{3,4,7\},\{(3,7),(4,7)\})^{\mathcal{L}_{10}}$. Sets of preferred labellings of them are respectively $\{\mathcal{L}_{11}\}$, $\{\mathcal{L}_{12}\}$ and $\{\mathcal{L}_{13}\}$, in which $\mathcal{L}_{11} = (\{3\}, \{4,7\},\{\})$, $\mathcal{L}_{12} = (\{4\},\{3,7\},\{\})$ and $\mathcal{L}_{13} = (\{7\},\{3,4\},\{\})$.

Finally, the preferred labellings of the third layer and the labellings of the previous two layers are combined, resulting $\mathcal{L}_8 + \mathcal{L}_{11} = (\{1,3,5\},\{2,4,6,7\},\{\})$, $\mathcal{L}_9 + \mathcal{L}_{12} = (\{2,4,6\},\{1,3,5,7\},\{\})$ and $\mathcal{L}_{10} + \mathcal{L}_{13} = (\{2,5,6,7\},\{1,3,4\},\{\})$, which are the preferred labellings of (A_2', R_2').

4 A Further Solution by Exploiting Both SCCs and Most Sceptically Rejected Arguments

As mentioned in Section 1, the efficiency of the above SCC-based approach is highly limited by the size of the maximal SCC. Let us consider the AF (A_3, R_3) as shown in Figure 6. It has only two SCCs: $\{1,\ldots,6\}$ and $\{7\}$. The size of the maximal SCC is six. Hence, in this case, little execution time could be saved by using the SCC-based approach. In order to make the SCC-based approach more efficient, a natural idea is *to modify an AF such that the status of arguments in the original AF remains unchanged, while the size of the maximal SCC of the modified AF becomes smaller.*

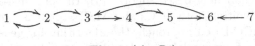

Fig. 6. (A_3, R_3)

In order to realise this idea, we resort to the *most sceptically rejected arguments* (briefly, MSR arguments) of an AF. We say an argument is most sceptically rejected, if it is labelled OUT in the grounded labelling of an AF.

Proposition 1. *Let $\mathcal{L}_g = (in(\mathcal{L}_g), out(\mathcal{L}_g), undec(\mathcal{L}_g))$ be the grounded labelling of an AF (A, R). The interactions between $out(\mathcal{L}_g)$ and $undec(\mathcal{L}_g)$ do not influence the preferred labellings of (A, R).*

Proof. Let $\mathcal{L}_p = (in(\mathcal{L}_p), out(\mathcal{L}_p), undec(\mathcal{L}_p))$ be a preferred labelling of (A, R). Since the grounded extension is contained in every preferred extension [14], the arguments labelled OUT in $\mathcal{L}_g$ are also labelled OUT in $\mathcal{L}_p$. Let (α, β) be an interaction from $out(\mathcal{L}_g)$ to $undec(\mathcal{L}_g)$. It follows that β is attacked by an argument α that is itself OUT in $\mathcal{L}_p$. Hence, whether β belongs to $in(\mathcal{L}_p)$, $out(\mathcal{L}_p)$ or $undec(\mathcal{L}_p)$, (α, β) does not influence $\mathcal{L}_p$. On the other hand, let (α, β) be an interaction from $undec(\mathcal{L}_g)$ to $out(\mathcal{L}_g)$. Since $\beta \in out(\mathcal{L}_g)$, it is attacked by a third argument $\gamma \in in(\mathcal{L}_g) \subseteq in(\mathcal{L}_p)$. Since attacking an argument that is already OUT has no effect, (α, β) does not affect $\mathcal{L}_p$.

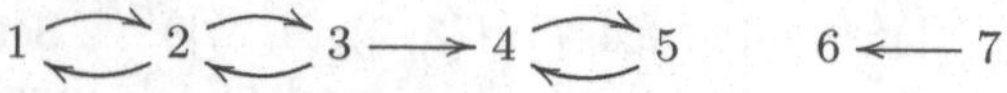

$$1 \rightleftarrows 2 \rightleftarrows 3 \longrightarrow 4 \rightleftarrows 5 \qquad 6 \longleftarrow 7$$

Fig. 7. (A_3, R_3')

Let us consider (A_3, R_3) again. Since argument 6 is an MSR argument, after we remove the attacks $(5, 6)$ and $(6, 3)$ from the framework, we get a modified framework (A_3, R_3') (Figure 7), which has the same preferred labellings as the original one. Now, the size of the maximal SCC $\{1, 2, 3\}$ is three.

Let (A, R') be the remaining part of (A, R) after removing the interactions between $out(\mathcal{L}_g)$ and $undec(\mathcal{L}_g)$. According to Proposition 1, (A, R') and (A, R) have the same preferred labellings.

Since the computation of the grounded labelling of (A, R) is polynomial time tractable, (A, R') can be obtained easily. The preferred labellings of (A, R') are then computed by the SCC-based approach described above.

5   Empirical Investigation

In previous sections, we have introduced three approaches for computing the preferred labellings of a general AF, including the MC algorithm (i.e., Modgil and Caminada's labelling-based algorithm), the SCC-based approach and the approach by exploiting both SCCs and MSR arguments (called *SCC-MSR approach*). In the SCC-based approach, the algorithm for generating preferred labellings of each sub-framework is based on MC algorithm with a slight modification such that the preferred labellings of a partially labelled sub-framework can be generated. Meanwhile, the SCC-MSR approach is in turn directly established on top of the SCC-based approach.

The above approaches were implemented in Java, and tested on a machine with an Intel CPU running at 1.86 GHz and 1.98 GB RAM.

First, we tested the average sizes of the maximal SCCs of AFs in the SCC-based approach and the SCC-MSR approach, respectively. Given an assignment of edge density (#edges/#nodes = 1, 1.2, ..., 4) and the size of AFs (#nodes =50, 500, 5000), the programs (in which the components for generating preferred labellings were disabled) of the two approaches were executed **100** times. In each time, an AF with the given edge density and size is generated at random, and the size of the maximal SCC produced by each approach was recorded. The average results are illustrated in Figure 8, where S[n] (SM[n]) ($n = 50, 500$, or 5000) denotes that the results were produced by the SCC-based approach (respectively, the SCC-MSR approach) and the size of every AF is n. From this figure, we may observe that when the edge density of AFs is sparse (#edges/#nodes ≤ 2), for a given AF, the percentage of arguments in the maximal SCC (denoted as "maxscc/#nodes" where "maxscc" represents the size of the maximal SCC) produced by the SCC-MSR approach is much smaller than the one produced by the SCC-based approach. For instance, when #edges/#nodes =1.8 and #nodes

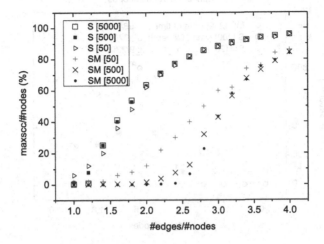

Fig. 8. Average results of the sizes of maximal SCCs generated by the SCC-based approach and the SCC-MSR approach

=500, the average number of arguments in the maximal SCCs produced by the SCC-based approach is 264, but only 2 by the SCC-MSR approach.

Second, we tested the performance of the SCC-MSR approach by comparing it with other two approaches. Given an assignment of edge density (#edges/ #nodes = 1, 1.1, ..., 2) and the size of AFs (#nodes =200,1000), the programs of the three approaches were executed **20** times. In each time, an AF with the given edge density and size is generated at random, and then its preferred labellings were generated by the three approaches respectively. The overall execution time of each approach was recorded. In the SCC-based approach, the overall execution time is mainly used for generating a set of SCCs, constructing a set of layered sub-frameworks, and generating and combining the preferred labellings of all sub-frameworks. In the SCC-SMR approach, the overall execution time is mainly used for generating the grounded labelling of a given AF, and computing the preferred labellings of the modified AF by using the SCC-based approach. Since in many cases, the overall execution time may last very long, to make the test easier, when the time for computing the preferred labellings of an AF is over **30** minutes, we stopped the execution by setting a break in the program. The average results of this test are illustrated in Figure 9, where MC[n] (n = 200, or 1000) denotes that the results were produced by the MC algorithm and the size of every AF is n, similar to the meanings of S[n] and SM[n] mentioned above. Each number near a symbol in the graph indicates the number of timeouts among the 20 times of execution (the overall rate of timeout is indicated in the legend of the plots). For instance, when #nodes = 200 and #edges/#nodes = 1.5 (in Figure 9(a)), there were 7 timeouts in the MC algorithm, 3 timeouts in the SCC-based

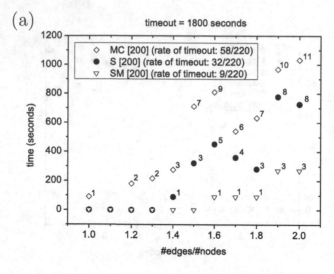

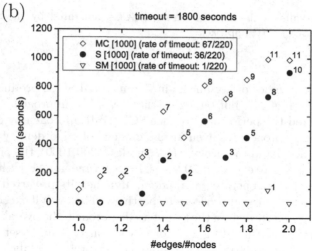

Fig. 9. Average results of the overall execution time of the three approaches

approach and 0 timeout in the SCC-MSR approach. Table 1 shows the detailed records of this case.

When an execution is timeout, we use 30 minutes (1800 seconds) in computing the average execution time. From this table we found that the execution of the SCC-MSR approach under this configuration is very low (less than 0.016 seconds in all cases), while the execution time of other two approaches fluctuates from 0.015 seconds to more than 30 minutes. In addition, from Table 1, we also observed that in the SCC-based approach and the SCC-MSR approach, the

Table 1. The overall execution time of the three approaches when #nodes = 200 and #edges/#nodes = 1.5

No.	MC [200]<1.5> (seconds)	S [200]<1.5> (seconds)	SM [200]<1.5> (seconds)
01	0.031	0.016	0.016
02	0.016	0.015	0.016
03	timeout	0.031	0.015
04	timeout	0.015	0
05	0.391	0.062	0.015
06	0.016	0.015	0.015
07	1613.016	2.141	0.015
08	timeout	timeout	0
09	0.015	0.016	0.016
10	0.015	0.016	0.016
11	0.016	0.031	0.015
12	timeout	timeout	0
13	0.046	0.016	0
14	timeout	1030.188	0
15	0.047	0.015	0.016
16	0.031	0.016	0.015
17	0.031	0.016	0
18	timeout	0.032	0
19	0.016	0.015	0.016
20	timeout	timeout	0.015
Avg.	**710.684 (7)**	**321.633 (3)**	**0.010**

time for generating SCCs, constructing sub-frameworks, combining preferred labellings and computing the grounded labelling is negligible when we compare it to the time for generating preferred labellings.

According to the results shown in Figure 9, when the ratio of the number of edges to the number of nodes of an AF is between 1:1 and 1.8:1, the execution of the SCC-MSR approach is much more smaller than other two approaches. In order to make this point more clear, we conducted a further test on the SCC-MSR approach. In this test, given an edge density (#edges/#nodes = 1.3, 1.5, 1.7) and the size of AFs (#nodes =100, 200, ..., 1000), the program of the SCC-MSR approach was executed **200** times. Meanwhile, the timeout was set to **2** seconds. The results in Figure 10 show that when #edges/#nodes = 1.3 (respectively, 1.5 and 1.7), there were only 6 (respectively, 15 and 56) timeouts among the 2000 (= 200 × 10) times of execution.

The above results show that after exploiting MSR arguments, the SCC-based approach becomes much more efficient. Now, a natural question arise: Whether the effect the MSR preprocessing is only suitable in connection with the SCC-based approach? With respect to this question, we conduct an additional test, in which we consider the following two approaches: the MC algorithm and the approach by combining the MC algorithm and the MSR preprocessing (called *MC-*

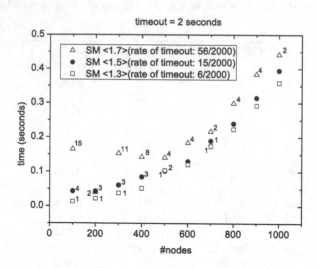

Fig. 10. Average results of the overall execution time of the SCC-MSR approach

MSR approach, or briefly MM). Similar to the above test, given an assignment of edge density (#edges/ #nodes = 1, 1.1, ..., 2) and the size of AFs (#nodes =200,1000), the programs of the two approaches were executed **20** times. The timeout was set to 600 seconds. The average results of this test are illustrated in Figure 11. It is obvious that for the MC algorithm, the MSR preprocessing has little effect.

6   Conclusions

In this paper, we have proposed an efficient method to compute the preferred labellings of a general AF by exploiting both its SCCs and most sceptically rejected arguments. The empirical results show that the computation time decreases *dramatically* when the defeat graphs are sparse. As illustrated in Figure 9, when the ratio between the number of edges (attacks) to the number of nodes (arguments) is less than 1.8:1, the SCC-MSR approach is obviously more efficient than other two approaches. Meanwhile, when the edge density keeps the same, the average computation time tends to decrease when the number of nodes becomes bigger. As shown in Figure 9, when #edges/#nodes is equal to 1,6, 1.7 and 1.8, there is 1 timeout when #nodes = 200, while there is no timeout when #nodes = 1000; when #edges/#nodes = 1.9, there are 3 timeouts when #nodes = 200, while there is only one timeout when #nodes = 1000; when #edges/#nodes = 2.0, there are 3 timeouts when #nodes = 200, while there is no timeout when #nodes = 1000. The fundamental reason behind these phenomena is that after removing the most sceptically rejected arguments, the maximal SCC of the modified AF is smaller or much smaller than that of the original AF (as shown in Figure 8).

(a)

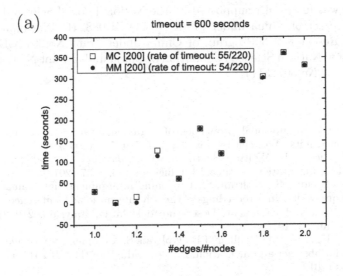

(b)

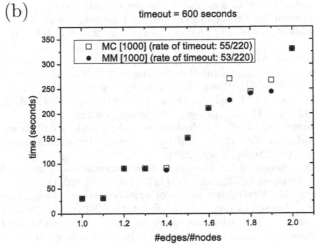

Fig. 11. Average results of the overall execution time of the MC algorithm and the MC-SMR approach

Although this paper only focused on the computation of preferred labellings, the computational mechanism of the SCC-MSR approach is not restricted to the preferred semantics. The application of this approach under other argumentation semantics will be our future work.

Acknowledgement. We are grateful to the anonymous reviewers of TAFA'13, whose constructive comments helped to improve our work. The research reported in this article was financially supported by the National Social Science Foundation Major Project of China under grant No.11&ZD088, the National Grand Fundamental Research 973 Program of China under grant No.2012CB316400 and the National Natural Science Foundation of China under grant No.61175058, No.61203324 and No.60773177.

References

1. Dunne, P.E.: Computational properties of argument systems satisfying graph-theoretic constraints. Artificial Intelligence 171, 701–729 (2007)
2. Dvořák, W., Pichler, R., Woltran, S.: Towards fixed-parameter tractable algorithms for abstract argumentation. Artificial Intelligence 186, 1–37 (2012)
3. Dvořák, W., Szeider, S., Woltran, S.: Reasoning in argumentation frameworks of bounded clique-width. In: Proceedings of the 3th International Conference on Computational Models of Argument, Desenzano del Garda, Italy, pp. 219–230. IOS Press (September 2010)
4. Dvořák, W., Järvisalo, M., Wallner, J.P., Woltran, S.: Complexity-sensitive decision procedures for abstract argumentation. In: Proceedings of the KR 2012, pp. 54–64. AAAI Press (2012)
5. Nofal, S., Dunne, P.E., Atkinson, K.: On preferred extension enumeration in abstract argumentation. In: Proceedings of the 4th International Conference on Computational Models of Argument, Vienna, Austria, pp. 205–216. IOS Press (September 2012)
6. Baroni, P., Giacomin, M., Guida, G.: Scc-recursiveness: a general schema for argumentation semantics. Artificial Intelligence 168, 162–210 (2005)
7. Baumann, R., Brewka, G., Wong, R.: Splitting argumentation frameworks: An empirical evaluation. In: Modgil, S., Oren, N., Toni, F. (eds.) TAFA 2011. LNCS (LNAI), vol. 7132, pp. 17–31. Springer, Heidelberg (2012)
8. Modgil, S., Caminada, M.: Proof theories and algorithms for abstract argumentation frameworks. In: Simari, G., Rahwan, I. (eds.) Argumentation in Artificial Intelligence, pp. 105–129. Springer (2009)
9. Liao, B., Jin, L., Koons, R.C.: Dynamics of argumentation systems: A division-based method. Artificial Intelligence 175(11), 1790–1814 (2011)
10. Liao, B., Huang, H.: Partial semantics of argumentation: Basic properties and empirical results. Journal of Logic and Computation 23(3), 541–562 (2013)
11. Liao, B., Huang, H.: Computing the extensions of an argumentation framework based on its strongly connected components. In: Proceedings of the 24th IEEE International Conference on Tools with Artificial Intelligence, Athens, Greece (September 2012)
12. Liao, B.: Toward incremental computation of argumentation semantics: A decomposition-based approach. Annals of Mathematics and Artificial Intelligence 67, 319–358 (2013)
13. Dung, P.M.: On the acceptability of arguments and its fundamental role in nonmonotonic reasoning, logic programming and n-person games. Artificial Intelligence 77, 321–357 (1995)
14. Baroni, P., Caminada, M., Giacomin, M.: An introduction to argumentation semantics. The Knowledge Engineering Review 26(4), 365–410 (2011)
15. Caminada, M.: On the issue of reinstatement in argumentation. In: Fisher, M., van der Hoek, W., Konev, B., Lisitsa, A. (eds.) JELIA 2006. LNCS (LNAI), vol. 4160, pp. 111–123. Springer, Heidelberg (2006)
16. Tarjan, R.E.: Depth-first search and linear graph algorithms. SIAM Journal on Computing 1, 146–160 (1972)

Author Index